LIFE AND LABOR IN THE OLD SOUTH

Paul Holsinger

1964

LIFE AND LABOR
IN THE OLD SOUTH

Ulrich Bonnell Phillips

LITTLE, BROWN AND COMPANY
Boston   *Toronto*

First Paperback Printing

TO

ULRIC, MABEL AND WORTHINGTON
THREE CHILDREN OF THE NORTH
WHO THEIR FATHER HOPES
MAY LEARN TO LOVE
THE SOUTH

INTRODUCTION

Ulrich Bonnell Phillips's *Life and Labor in the Old South,* first published in 1929, was announced as the first of three volumes on the history of the South that were to sum up a lifetime of work on the subject. It proved to be the only one of the projected series that the historian lived to complete, however, for he died in 1934 at the age of fifty-seven, three years after he moved from the University of Michigan to Yale. The completed volume nevertheless covered those aspects of his field of study — slavery, the plantation, agricultural history — to which Phillips had devoted most of his time since he began to publish in 1902.* It may therefore be regarded as the ripest and fullest expression of his thought and scholarship.

Until recent years the work of Phillips was looked upon as the most authoritative treatment of one of the most controversial subjects in American history. Lately, however, much of his writing — particularly that on slavery — has been called into question and subjected to criticism. There are special reasons for this criticism, as we shall see. But it should be noted that it is only part of a general wave of criticism directed at the previous generation of historians, the so-called Progressive generation, of which Phillips was a younger member. They included Frederick Jackson Turner, Charles A. Beard, Carl Becker, and Vernon Louis Parrington, each of whom has been likewise subjected to critical reassessment and fallen into disfavor.

The reasons for Phillips's fall in current favor are clear enough. Born in Georgia in 1877, he grew up in a South dedicated to reviving in a new form the tradition of dependency and subordination the ante-bellum regime had shaped for the Negro. Defense of the the new regime was built on a defense of the old, and both rested on the assumption of an inherent inferiority of the Negro race. Phillips fully cherished the

---

*Everett E. Edwards, "A Bibliography of the Writings of Professor Ulrich Bonnell Phillips," *Agricultural History,* VIII (1934), pp. 199-218; also David M. Potter, "A Bibliography of the Printed Writings of Ulrich Bonnell Phillips," *Georgia Historical Quarterly,* XVIII (1934), pp. 270-282.

values of both the new and the old regimes and shared their racial assumptions without imbibing the racial bitterness and malice growing up around him. His attitude was a paternalistic and indulgent affection toward what he regarded as a childlike and irresponsible people with many endearing traits. These attitudes and values were implicit — and often explicit — in what he wrote on the Old South.

Phillips brought a prodigious and unprecedented amount of research in plantation records to the writing of his big monograph *American Negro Slavery* (1918) and more still to his *Life and Labor in the Old South*. Only thus, he declared, could one "get away from the stereotypes." The "stereotypes" he attacked were those that pictured the old regime as one of unmitigated cruelty, baseness, and inhumanity. He could not accept that picture. In fact, he wrote, those who had "known the considerate and cordial, courteous and charming men and women, white and black, which that picturesque life in its best phases produced" would find it "impossible to agree that its basis and its operation were wholly evil." Admitting that there had been "injustice, oppression, brutality and heartburning" in this as in all systems, he emphasized evidence of kindliness, contentment, and "mutual loyalty." Slavery was, on the whole, "a curious blend . . . of tyranny and benevolence, of antipathy and affection." And plantations were "the best schools yet invented for the mass training . . . of backward people."

It was no paradox that Northern Progressives took Phillips to their heart and found his picture of the South acceptable and congenial. Racism was an ingredient of Progressivism and wholly compatible with its brand of reform. That was the generation that took up the white man's burden, acquired an overseas empire of colored people, disfranchised the Negro, preached Nordic supremacy, and deplored and despised the immigrant. Under these circumstances and moods it was easy to conciliate the South, and opposition to its views virtually disappeared.

The contrast between circumstance and mood of that generation and the present one is too striking to require comment. Criticism of Phillips since World War II reflects many of these changes. The most obvious target was the historian's racial assumptions, now no longer tenable. The mainspring of criticism was moral rather than scientific, however, and originated in the new equalitarian demand for Negro rights. On the side of scholarship Phillips was critized for drawing his evidence too much from large plantations and neglecting smaller slaveholders; for underestimating the profit of slaveholders; for overlooking evidence unfavorable to slaveholders; for blindness to miscegenation, slave breeding, mistreatment, abuse, and cruelty; for mistaking the slave's mask of contentment or happiness for real sentiments; and for playing down evidence of slave discontent and rebelliousness.

The re-evaluation of the work of the previous generation is inevitable and essential to the health of each successive generation of historians. American historians, like American politicians, however, are addicted to a tradition of rather savage abruptness and finality in their treatment of outmoded members of their respective guilds. Once he falls into disfavor the rejected member tends to be cast out of the club completely, unread, unattended, unmourned. His opinion is unsought and his experience and wisdom are disregarded. No comfortable back bench or seat in the House of Lords receives the politician and no comparable office awaits the historian. The books of the latter, worn with constant use, suddenly begin to collect dust on their shelves and disappear from required reading lists. Professors refer to them only to introduce their critics and successors, and students grow up unacquainted with the books that nourished their masters. The result for politics and scholarship alike is an uncivil lack of continuity and a rather halting and jerky flow of ideas.

Granting the validity of much of the criticism of Phillips and the seriousness of it all, what remains to be said for reading him today? As much at least, one might say, as there is to be said for reading a friendly account of the Old Regime in France or the Old Regime in Russia — assuming one of equivalent learning, grace, and elegance could be found. And this quite irrespective of one's hostility or friendliness to the particular old regime involved. Such histories as *Life and Labor* are worth reading, even at the level of polemics, and even its severest critics would concede that the book sustains a higher level than that. For another thing, much of what Phillips wrote has not been superseded or seriously challenged and remains indispensable.

In the Preface that follows this Introduction, Phillips mentions "sundry changes of emphasis and revisions of judgment" that had occurred in his thinking over the previous decade. One clear evidence of change is the degree to which the theme of racial inferiority had been subdued or eliminated. Had Phillips lived out his productive years he might well have revised his views further. "More years of research and reflection would no doubt bring further modification," he wrote. Every line he wrote, he said, was "written with a consciousness that his impressions are imperfect and his conclusions open to challenge." The modern reader

would do well to keep in mind that the gulf between him and Phillips
is not necessarily one of intelligence or charity or sophistication, but one
of time. And if one cannot bridge that gulf he is cut off from a great
many worthies who are not his contemporaries.

C. VANN WOODWARD

New Haven, Connecticut

PREFACE

If intelligence is to be gauged in political programmes, the conditions of life which gave them origin must first be known. Hence the priority of the present volume in a group which is planned as a history of the South. The second will trace the course of public policy to 1861, and a third may bring the consolidated social and political themes onward from that epochal year.

Some of the chapters here printed run parallel to those in my "American Negro Slavery." The decade since that publication has not only brought much material to light but has wrought sundry changes of emphasis and revisions of judgment. More years of research and reflection would no doubt bring further modification; but a century of continuous effort would not relieve all uncertainties nor solve the riddle of human nature, individual and collective, Caucasian and African. Every line which a qualified student writes is written with a consciousness that his impressions are imperfect and his conclusions open to challenge. If he put upon paper all that is in his mind, every third or fourth sentence would contain a saving clause — "it seems to me", "the weight of evidence tends to show", or "as others have said and I accept." If the pages do not bristle with such phrases it is not a mark of duplicity or of cocksureness. In history, science and philosophy the tentative is implicit.

When I read of Howard Odum's Black Ulysses, of DuBose Heyward's Porgy, of Stephen Benét's plantation mammy and her mistress, esteem for their creations is mingled with chagrin that my fancy is restricted by records. The characters portrayed by these writers are as true as the men and women who figure in my pages, though the breath in their nostrils is the ether in which the stars hold their courses while mine breathed mundane atmosphere and have long since found rest in earth's bosom. But only when the wind is in a rare quarter would I give rein to Pegasus if I could. In the main I am content to delve rather than try to soar.

A cartographer "generalizes" a river course if its meanders are not known in detail or if they are too small to be shown in his reduction. A merchant generalizes his customers when he prints an advertisement, and a physician, when classing his patients as cases of pneumonia, measles or smallpox. The practice is not merely convenient but necessary. On the other hand a lover may generalize his lady, to be startled by her individualization after marriage. If one thinks of posterity at all it must be by generalization, since people to come cannot make personal impressions before attaining life and acquiring character. The past, however, may remind us on occasion that its people were not lay figures but men, women and children of flesh and blood, thought and feeling, habits and eccentricities, in the grip of circumstance and struggling more or less to break it. Traditions are simple, conditions were complex;[1] and to get into the records is to get away from the stereotypes. It is from the records and with a sense of the personal equation that I have sought to speak.

Others have delved before me, and still others, as librarians, collectors and custodians, have conspired to make the labor pleasant. The Library of Congress, the Virginia State Library, the North Carolina Historical Commission, the Archive Departments of Alabama and Mississippi, the libraries of the University of North Carolina, Duke University and the University of Texas, the Charleston Library, and sundry other libraries and State and city bureaus in the region, as well as various institutions in the North, have accumulated richly in the Southern field, and with one accord their staffs give eager aid to those who seek their treasures. Private possessors have proved no less generous.

The competition announced by Little, Brown, and Company a year ago may have sped my pen unduly in the writing of the later chapters, but this does not diminish my thanks. Their judges made useful comments upon the manuscript; and Professor Gilbert H. Barnes of Ohio Wesleyan University has criticized the phrasing here and there with a most improving effect. My wife impelled the beginning of the book, and has kept a faithful eye upon its progress, though troubled often that when once at the task I could never be diverted. If acknowledgments of specific aid were here begun there could hardly be an end. Instead let me say that only the faults of the product are mine, while to its virtues the contributors have been a legion.

Ulrich B. Phillips

---

[1]For the departure of tradition from reality see Francis P. Gaines, *The Southern Plantation: a Study in the Development and the Accuracy of a Tradition* (New York, 1925).

CONTENTS

CHAPTER I

THE LAND OF DIXIE

LET us begin by discussing the weather, for that has been the chief agency in making the South distinctive. It fostered the cultivation of the staple crops, which promoted the plantation system, which brought the importation of negroes, which not only gave rise to chattel slavery but created a lasting race problem. These led to controversy and regional rivalry for power, which produced apprehensive reactions and culminated in a stroke for independence. Thus we have the house that Jack built, otherwise known for some years as the Confederate States of America.

The South is nowhere tropical except at the tip of Florida, for it has winters with killing frosts. The characteristic feature is merely the length of the summers. The growing season lasts on an average six months at Baltimore, Louisville and St. Louis; seven at Norfolk, Atlanta and Memphis; eight at Columbia, Montgomery and Dallas; and nine at Charleston, New Orleans and Galveston. The climate has fostered the cultivation of tobacco in the first zone, cotton in the second and third, and rice and sugar cane in the fourth.

The summers are not merely long, but bakingly hot, with temperatures ranging rather steadily in the eighties and nineties of the Fahrenheit scale. In the droughts which occur at some time nearly every summer, when " the sky is like brass and the ground is like iron", all shallow-rooted vegetation is parched. Thus the country in general is not well adapted to grass or to the small grains except rice, to which water is artificially supplied. The deficit of grass curtails cattle-raising, and this restricts the supply of barnyard manure and makes it hard to maintain the fertility of the fields.   So were it not for its own particular staples, the South would hardly prosper from agriculture in competition with the great grasslands of the world.

Men must eat in the main what their land will yield.   Rice is heavily consumed in its own district in sundry appetizing forms.   Elsewhere Indian corn is the chief cereal, always in its white varieties, for Southerners consider yellow corn unfit for human consumption.   The green ear is roasted or boiled, or its grains cut off and fried or made into pudding.   The ripe grain is soaked in lye to make "big hominy", or ground coarse into grits or fine into meal which is cooked in pone, hoecake, spoonbread, muffins, and other toothsome preparations.   "Potatoes" in Southern parlance are not the Irish variety which ripen in weather too hot for storage, but the sweet ones which mature in autumn and, roasted, fried, candied, or made into custard, rank second only to corn in Dixie diet.   "Peas" likewise are not the English or garden variety but the varicolored sorts, often called cowpeas, which are planted in the cornfield when the corn is "laid by", and when served on the table, suggest the beans which Boston has made famous.   Apples do not prosper except on the mountain flanks, but peaches reach perfection in the hills and figs in the lowlands.   Watermelons if left on the vine till a thumping finger brings mellow response in the dew of the morning or a straight-arm pressure gives a crunch of sugary flesh, are just ready to melt in the mouth.   Swine tended to be razor-backs, for they rooted for their living in the woods, and on occasion saved their lives by their speed.   "Keep your hogs lean or the rogues will be fat" and "A poor hog is better than no hog" were proverbs with point in the black belt;[1] but this leanness gave an epicurean result, as the Smithfield folk discovered. A slab-sided porker, quickly fattened and promptly slaughtered, yields hams beyond compare.   A little invention converted a fault into high virtue.[2]

[1] *Farmers' Register*, III, 495 (December, 1835).
[2] *Ibid.*, III, 554 (January, 1836), describes the Smithfield process and gives barely adequate praise to the product.

Gastronomic resource is fostered by the climate, to stimulate appetites which the hot weather makes languid. Indeed most of the habits of life are affected. In the tedious heat work is hard, indolence easy; speech is likely to be slow and somewhat slurred; manners are soft; and except when tempers are hot, the trend is toward easy-going practices even among healthy people. But the climate has operated through the hookworm to make many half-invalid.

Still further, whether in the very distant past or in more recent times, the climate has been responsible not only for the original forest covering of the land but in a measure also for the quality of the soil. In even the coldest of the glacial ages the sheet of ice which blanketed the northerly regions and, slowly moving, pulverized, transported and intermixed their soils, encountered rays too strong and winds too warm to cross Mason and Dixon's line. The soil virtually everywhere is accordingly the product of rocks disintegrated on the very spot or somewhere directly uphill or upstream. Most of the soils are thus mere sand and clay in varying proportions, with little or no lime and no humus except perhaps on the surface. The lack of deep frost in winter and the consequent lack of mellowing thaw in spring leaves the ground hard-packed the year round. This diminishes the absorbent capacity of the clay, and by the same token shortens the beneficial influence of rains and heightens their deleterious effects. The Southern rain seldom sifts but commonly pelts from a great height, and by its pelting packs any plowed surface. Most of the rain in the characteristic downpours must accordingly run off. Great floods on the Southern streams are on record from times when but little of the forest had been felled in their drainage basins. A sojourner in the Virginia lowlands remarked in 1686, "Never do these rivers become angry or leave their beds"; but in June of 1771 a flood from the mountains destroyed the James River crops as far down as "Westover", sweeping away houses, people, cattle and some four thousand hogsheads of tobacco from the landings. As an incident: "At Farrar's Island, which the highest freshet never before affected, above eighty acres of fine land are rendered forever incapable of cultivation, the soil being gone, and in its stead ten or twelve feet deep of sand, upon which is a layer of stones as if paved." The news report continues: "Daily accounts are received of the loss of whole families; and houses come down with people floating on them, calling for help, though none can be afforded. On the whole it is believed that history scarce affords an instance of equal damage being done to any country, if the destruction of land, loss of property, etc. be included." [1] Such havoc was happily seldom; but the mere heavy rains of commonplace occurrence impaired the soils by leaching the flat lands and eroding the hills.

❋   ❋   ❋   ❋   ❋

Extending all the length of the seaboard lies a coastal plain, broadening to two hundred miles in North Carolina, thrusting outward to form the whole Floridian peninsula, and reaching inward in a great embayment up the Mississippi River. With an elevation everywhere less than three hundred feet, its gentle slopes are often imperceptible. With very little rock exposed, the main expanses are of deep sand. In some tracts the seepage of rain-water has carried fine particles a few inches downward to fill the crevices between the grains and packed a hardpan to check percolation and make ponds. These are exemplified in the Dismal Swamp and the Okefinokee. Here and there in other quarters the clogging of a stream with driftwood, strikingly illustrated by the Red River "raft", heightened the water level, broadened the floodplain and enlarged the swamps. The ponds, marshes and swamps breed mosquitoes which plague most of the good lands in the warm seasons.

But most of the coastal plain suffers from excess rather of sand than of water. Great areas, particularly in the hinterlands of Wilmington, St. Augustine and Pensacola, were in their natural state too sandy to support any vegetation except what was extremely frugal in its food requirements. Pine trees

[1] *Virginia Gazette*, June 6, 1771, reprinted in the *Scots Magazine*, XXXIII, 380, 381 (Edinburgh, 1771).

could prosper because their habit is to hold their needles for several years instead of requiring new foliage annually. But the frugality of pines makes them very slow builders of soil; and on these excessively porous lands their falling needles gave food only for pines again or for tough wire grass. Pine forestation was accordingly an indication of poor soil, to be shunned as a rule by such settlers as could afford to discriminate in their locations. A persisting disesteem of these regions was embodied in their common designation as "pine barrens."

In sharp contrast to these are the alluvial strips and pockets which border the larger streams from the Potomac to the Rio Grande. On the Atlantic seaboard the swirl of the tides has scattered the silt and mingled it with sand in some degree; but on the Gulf coast the lack of tide has promoted concentration in deep alluvial deltas. Of these by far the greatest is that of the Mississippi, which having filled a former estuary from the mouth of the Ohio southward, now stretches its fingers of mud into the waters of the Gulf itself. The deltas have soils of high quality; but they are water-logged in many portions, they are subject to annual overflow where not leveed, and they are malarial where not drained.

Not all the silt has remained where the water laid it. Some has been caught up by the winds and carried from the dried mud-flats to settle again as dust on the adjacent hills and cover them with rich loess. Some of this occurs on the slopes of Arkansas and Louisiana; but the prevalence of westerly winds has laid it thickest on the eastward bluffs which border the flood plains from Memphis to Natchez and fade into the lowlands at Baton Rouge. The richness of the loess and likewise its distressing liability to erode were noted by many observers. Stephen F. Austin wrote of the Natchez neighborhood in 1812: "The soil . . . is very good and produces well for a few years until wash'd away by the rain." [1] Twenty years afterward J. H. Ingraham described the process in more detail: "Every plough-furrow becomes the bed of a rivulet after heavy rains — these uniting are increased into torrents before which the impal-

[1] *American Historical Association Report* for 1919, II, 208.

pable soil dissolves like ice under a summer's sun. By degrees acre after acre of what was a few years previous beautifully undulating ground, . . . presents a wild scene of frightful precipices and yawning chasms." [1]

Apart from the tracts which have received enrichment whether by water or by wind, the coastal plain contains a few districts of marked fertility, the best of which lie upon limestone and are indebted to the peculiarity of this rock's weathering. The effect of rain upon it is rather to dissolve than to disintegrate. The seepage and run-off carry away most of the limestone proper, leaving its varied impurities behind; and it is these impurities, commonly rich in phosphates, which mainly constitute the resulting soil. But a residue of lime gives a cement promoting the retention of moisture against times of drought. Most notable of these favored areas are the so-called Alabama prairies or black belt, lying in a tilted crescent from east of Montgomery to northwest of Tuscaloosa, and the "black waxy" zone of Texas, extending from north of Dallas to south of Austin. Less pronounced in fertility, yet with enough clay to make sandy loam, are several other districts, among them the plain at large about Delaware and Chesapeake bays; a broad wedge on the Flint and Chattahoochee rivers extending south to Tallahassee; and the present rice-growing district about Crowley in the center of southern Louisiana.

In all of these richer tracts the forests which the pioneers found were mainly deciduous. Bays and gums, magnolias and live oaks, along with cypress, prevailed in the moister belts of the lower South. Spanish moss draped the trees, and reeds and palmettos studded the ground below, all of which, despite their unsucculent appearance, gave browse for deer and cattle. On higher lands there were sundry sorts of oaks, along with hickories, chestnuts, walnuts, beeches and poplars, and toward Texas, pecans.

The present-day prevalence of pines on the coastal plain of

[1] *The South-West* (New York, 1835), II, 86. Solon Robinson wrote in 1845: "It is a most singular soil, and when a gulley once begins it seems to melt down, down, down into a deep ditch whose sides are as straight and perpendicular as though cut by a spade and line." — *The Cultivator* (Albany, N. Y.), n. s., III, 32.

Virginia, and also in the Piedmont region far and wide, has come as an unintended sequel of tillage; for the forests which the settlers cleared were mostly of hard wood. The clearing and cropping exhausted the shallow humus, and the land when abandoned was too lean for any trees but pines to gain footing. If left undisturbed by man these would perhaps yield eventually to oak and hickory again, their seedlings drawing sustenance from the pine-needle humus until their taproots reach depth and their laterals gain length, and the decay of their own falling leaves enriches the surface to feed a massive growth.

Except for the tracts in Texas and western Louisiana which were entered too late for full colonization by migrating slaveholders, all the more fertile portions of the coastal plain appear as districts of Negro majority in the population maps of 1860 and after, as an effect of the slave-plantation system. The same is the case with such of the Piedmont zone as proved suitable for the production and marketing of staples in the period.

*   *   *   *   *

The Piedmont and the Blue Ridge together comprise a region which anciently stood as a great island when adjacent land in all directions lay under the sea. The Piedmont soil is the fruit of crystalline rocks, largely granite, and is therefore mainly of clay and sand in varying proportions. Much of the clay has a bright red hue and it is occasionally threaded with seams of quartz crystals. Rock crops out here and there, conspicuously in the granite dome of Stone Mountain in Georgia, and occasional fields are cumbered with loose fragments; but in the main the surface is free for tilth. The ground, though lean, contains enough plant-feeding minerals nearly everywhere to support a hardwood forest.

But no white man ever saw the land in utterly virgin state, for here, as in many other quarters, the Indians before them had wrought considerable changes in the vegetation. Not only had they made petty clearings for tillage, leaving weedy "old fields", but by fire they had modified the forest far and wide.

Some of the flames no doubt spread unawares from camp fires. Others were purposely set, whether to concentrate game in a narrowing circle for slaughter or to remove undergrowth and promote fresh herbage to attract game in future seasons. The effects were diverse. In some places, perhaps where fires occurred in time of drought, all the trees were killed and the land was converted into prairie, covered with grass, wild pea vines or canebrake, all of these furnishing pasturage. But more generally the result was a mere thinning of the forest by the killing of young growth, giving the greater trees more room in which to attain yet greater size.[1]

The litter beneath the hard woods rotted into forest mold, but the long summers made this decompose into thin ashy stuff more speedily than in cooler climes.[2] Thin as they were, the mold and the litter were good as gold to the pioneers, who let in the sun by "deadening" the trees, seeded their crops and reaped with comparative abundance. But except for seldom level spaces the surface of the Piedmont is rolling, gently along its lower edge, heavily in its middle zone, and ruggedly near the mountains. With the ground kept bare by cultivation, every sloping field suffered erosion, and the rich top soil was first to go. The rivers ever since have been clouded, even in dry weather, and bright brick-red in time of flood. A Texan telling of his neighbors' troubles in 1855 said they had the same defect of title which had been complained of by a Georgian many years before, "which defect consisted in his title not being sufficient to hold his soil, as every hard rain carried much of it into the branches, creeks and rivers, entirely out of reach of recovery."[3]

[1] Hu Maxwell, "The Use and Abuse of Forests by the Virginia Indians", in the *William and Mary College Quarterly*, XIX, 75–103; John H. Logan, *History of the Upper Country of South Carolina* (Columbia, S. C., 1859), I (all published), 7 *et passim*.

[2] This is not a novel discovery. A Georgian wrote in 1848: "Manuring the lands of Middle Georgia and South Carolina . . . is almost as bad as pouring water in a sieve. . . . Why is it that our woodlands which have been manured for ages by decayed leaves and limbs are yet so poor, while those in Kentucky are so rich? . . . Notwithstanding this heavy manuring, which exceeds all that the industry and patience of man can accomplish, most of our woodlands are poor." — *Southern Cultivator*, VI, 83.

[3] *American Cotton Planter*, III, 149.

Much of the Piedmont, in fact, erodes with a facility comparable to that of the Natchez loess. As an example Sir Charles Lyell described in 1846 a gully near Milledgeville in central Georgia, which from an origin less than twenty years before had then attained a depth exceeding fifty feet, a length of near a thousand, and a breadth approaching two hundred.[1] When I last visited this chasm, fourscore years after Lyell, its length and breadth had perhaps doubled. But great pines had fallen with the caving banks, taken root afresh with trunks aslant at strange angles, and were holding the floor at a fairly permanent slope. The gully's head is now so near the hill crest that its advance is slackened; and its threat of engulfing the lonely grave of a revolutionary veteran and the slab placed thereon by the State may not be accomplished for several score years to come.

Above the Piedmont looms the Blue Ridge, so named from the look of its deep green forests when seen through the hazy distance. This range festoons the map from Pennsylvania to Georgia, with its main mass filling the western part of North Carolina. Its ancient crystalline rocks appear at some places in towering cliffs, as at Caesar's Head which looks out upon South Carolina; but commonly the stone is covered with earth or at least hidden by the trees which have gained prosperous footing. The valleys along the winding streams were proved by settlers to have soil as good as the Piedmont but quite as prone to lose it by erosion.

Throughout the great length of its northwest face the Blue Ridge drops abruptly along a great fault in the crust of the earth. All the great region beyond was once and for long the bed of the sea; but through geologic ages the surface was lifted into a plateau and its hither edge crumpled so slowly that the cross-flowing rivers were able to cut through the rising stone and hold their courses. Frost and flowing water have long since disintegrated and carried away the crust of shale and sandstone from the parallel ridges and cut into the limestone

---

[1] Sir Charles Lyell, *A Second Visit to the United States*, 2d ed. (London, 1850), II, 23-25. The picture of the gully which Lyell prints shows no trees on the brink.

beds beneath. Thereby the zone has become a continuous corrugated valley, some forty miles wide and so long that it has no single name. For a space it is called the Shenandoah and for another distant space the valley of East Tennessee; but in the intervening stretches where it is drained by the James, the Kanawha and the New rivers it is merely known as "The Valley", for in that region no other name is thought to be needed. Its hill-studded floor lies too high to have a climate suited to the Southern staples; but for grass and grain it excels every other Southern region except the Kentucky and Nashville basins.

Facing the Blue Ridge across the span of the Valley is the slightly curving wall of the Allegheny or Cumberland escarpment, beyond which the plateau, deeply scored by winding streams, slopes downward to the northwest. The lean soil and rugged contour have made it wretched for tillage except in isolated coves and on remaining bits of level upland. It took sturdy philosophizing for a settler to write in 1798: "I here hazard a conjecture that has often occurred to me since I inhabited this place, that nature has designed this part of the world [as] a peaceable retreat for some of her favorite children, where pure morals will be preserved by separating them from other societys at so respectful a distance by ridges of mountains, and I sincerely wish time may prove my conjecture rational and true." [1]   Beyond the Mississippi the Ozarks repeat in large degree the features and influences of the Alleghenies. In both of these dissected plateaus the primitive régime persisted until the latter-day invasion of logging and mining corporations.

Long spurs of the Cumberland plateau carry the lean hills far westward in southern Kentucky and southern Tennessee to set apart from one another three limestone basins — the Kentucky "Bluegrass", the Nashville district and the Tennessee River valley of northern Alabama. The praise of these must await a later singing except for a single phrase. A full century ago they were saying in the Bluegrass that heaven

[1] John Stuart, in the *William and Mary College Quarterly*, XXII, 234.

could only be another Kentucky;[1] and they are saying it yet.

But not even the Bluegrass was at first glance manifestly destined to the rearing of thoroughbred horses and thoroughbred folk. The capabilities of every part of the far-flung Southern land, plains and hills, mountains and valleys, had to be learned through the painful process of trial and error.

[1] Timothy Flint, *Recollections* (Boston, 1826), 64.

CHAPTER II

THE OLD DOMINION

WHERE Jamestown stood there are now the ruins of a church, a huddle of gravestones and a tracery of house foundations. Having served its conscious purpose as the beginning of Virginia and English America, and unexpectedly as the seed plot of the South and the United States, it yielded long ago to happier sites for towns and homes. That great results and many would flow from its founding was the confident hope of those who crossed the wilderness of water to the wilderness of land, and of those who made the plans and met the costs. The time was ripe, ambition high, and by slender margin hearts proved strong enough to withstand a terrific strain and minds fertile to win a permanent footing.

When Great Elizabeth died the claim of Spain to all America except Brazil was without effective dispute. The Dons had seized and subjugated all the regions of readiest exploitation, and the riches of Mexico had enabled Charles and Philip to conquer much of Europe and to threaten England's independence. But that nation of stay-at-homes was now going down to the sea in ships — vessels of new design with poop and stern structures diminished, sail-spread enlarged and facility of maneuver greatly improved. The sailors matched the ships in seaworth, as Drake and Hawkins, Grenville and Frobisher took pains to prove. They sought exploits on every ocean; they clustered at home to rob the Invincible Armada of its title; and then they scattered once more to profit by Britannia's rule of the waves. But could the tight little island maintain supremacy, and would it yield returns to make the great effort worth while?

Small by any modern comparison, England's population was already pressing upon her resources, particularly as concerns timber. The use of coal or coke for smelting being unknown, the forests must furnish charcoal for the tin and iron furnaces as well as framing and plank for houses and ships. Yearly the woods were dwindling under the ax, and the pinch of shortage was felt in the shipyards. Northern Europe was commonly a plentiful source, but occasional restraints of trade made the supply precarious, and the means of payment were not easily found when exports must also compensate for tar and hemp, oil and wine, silks and spices. Northern America was known to be heavily wooded in all the length of its coast. It could surely furnish boards, joists, masts and tar; it would with little doubt yield ores for smelting with its charcoal; perhaps dyes also, and glass and wine and silver and gold; and any day might open a strait or a portage to the Pacific, to give the possessor a short line to the trade of the Orient. And there were heathen to be converted to Protestant Christianity, markets to be made for English goods, lands to be snatched from Spanish expansion, traffic to employ more ships and breed more sailors.

Richard Hakluyt, who spent a lifetime collecting accounts of distant regions, expounded these matters as early as 1585, and others echoed him. Sir Humphrey Gilbert in response made a gallant failure on the shores of Newfoundland; and Sir Walter Raleigh in two efforts at Roanoke Island succeeded only in spreading the name Virginia broadly upon the American map. These failures showed that more than one man's wealth was likely to be required, and that profits might come slowly or never. But now the conception of corporations had arisen for large, distant and risky enterprise. Men of experience in Muscovy, Levant and East India companies were at hand to manage colonizing business; and King James continued the friendliness of Elizabeth toward the granting of charters, along with her frugality of purse.

In 1602 Bartholomew Gosnold returned from a voyage to the North American coast with a firm purpose of trying his fortunes there with an English colony. His enthusiasm fired the Reverend Robert Hunt, Edward-Maria Wingfield, and the doughty John Smith who now came home from incredible exploits in Turkey. These enlisted the financial interest of "certaine of the Nobilitie, Gentrie and Marchants, so that his Maiestie by his letters patent gaue commission for establishing councels, to direct here and to governe and to execute there." [1] At the end of 1606 a hundred and twenty men, including the four prime movers, took passage with Captain Christopher Newport, with arms, implements and seed, and such meager stock of stores and trading goods as three little ships could carry. After a voyage troubled by storm and quarrels, the Chesapeake was reached, its southern arm ascended, and in the middle of May permanent camp was made at a spot reasonably safe against all human enemies.

Many tasks were pressing, to build shelters and fortify, to fell trees and plant crops, to spy out the land and ingratiate the natives, to find gold or a South Sea strait, and to load the ships with some cargo as a token to those at home. While hopes remained high, provisions plenty and the weather moderate, energy was not greatly lacking, though excursions were preferred to commonplace work by the "gentlemen" who comprised most of the shore personnel. But Newport stayed on the river two months, vainly seeking minerals and a western outlet, his sailors consuming food for the want of which the settlers were destined to suffer. Upon his departure faction became rife in the governing council, heat debilitated and malaria prostrated nearly every one, the Indians turned hostile, and grave-digging became a major industry. Then the coming of autumn ended the havoc. Migrating ducks and geese yielded meat, the passing of Powhatan's enmity opened a trade in corn,

---

[1] Edward Arber, ed., *Capt. John Smith, Works* (Birmingham, 1884), 90. Many of the documents concerning Virginia's first two decades are conveniently assembled in Alexander Brown, ed., *The Genesis of the United States* (Boston, 1890); Susan M. Kingsbury, ed., *The Records of the Virginia Company of London* (Washington, 1906); and Lyon G. Tyler, ed., *Narratives of Early Virginia* (New York, 1907). The modern writings of Brown, Bruce, Eggleston, Osgood and Wertenbaker give copious accounts of the seventeenth century.

disease diminished; and the forty survivors were in good heart when Newport came again in January with a hundred recruits and some replenishment of supplies.

But a second summer and a third brought decimations like the first; and reports of continued disaster made it manifest at London that the whole enterprise must die if something heroic were not done by way of succor, enlargement and reorganization. The promoters appealed with great vigor to the spirit of the nation; and in view of the fading of early hopes for quick riches their appeals met remarkable success. By a new charter of 1609 the crown bestowed upon the company a greatly increased expanse of land and full power, which it had by no means possessed before, to control its own policy and govern the settlers. Individuals by the hundred and trade guilds by the dozen subscribed to the capital stock; and the management set itself to employ its powers and resources with all the shrewdness it could muster. The new régime came none too soon, for Lord de la Warr, arriving in Chesapeake Bay with five hundred recruits and a commission as governor for life, met the desperate survivors of the "starving time" under sail to escape another Jamestown summer. His Lordship turned them about and reoccupied the abandoned camp, only himself to be beset by "a hot and violent ague" and then in succession by dysentery, cramps, gout and scurvy. At the end of a year he sought a better clime and ruled thereafter by deputy. Men of lesser privilege must endure if they might, or die if they must.

The company was in a battle with disorder and a race with the death rate. To suppress turbulence and sloth it resolved no more "to suffer Parents to disburden themselves of lascivious sonnes, masters of bad servants and wives of ill husbands, and so to clogge the businesse with such an idle crue as did thrust themselves in the last voiage, that will rather starve for hunger than lay their hands to labor", but to accept only "sufficient, honest and good artificers."[1] The glamour of

---

[1] A *Publication by the Counsell of Virginea, touching the Plantation there* (London, 1610), reprinted in Alexander Brown, *Genesis of the United States*, I, 354–356.

high adventure gone with John Smith, prosperity, or permanence at least, was to be compelled by plain men's labor in
humdrum work. As a taskmaster Sir Thomas Dale was borrowed from the army of the Prince of Orange and furnished with
a set of "Lawes and Orders, Divine, Politique and Martiall"
by which he ruled for five years, a despot capable and complete.

Following a plan begun just before his coming, Dale distributed the colonists in groups on palisaded peninsulas along
the course of the James, for better effect in farming.   Coercion
failing to bring full effort, he found it a better stimulus to assign
three-acre plots which settlers of good behavior might cultivate
on private account in time spared them from gang work.   This
plan brought the colony to feed itself; and acclimatization
diminished mortality except among newcomers.   It was under
this régime that John Rolfe, husband of Pocahontas, learned
tobacco culture from Indians and improved upon their
method of curing so as to make a product acceptable to English
taste.   The completion of this exploit by 1616 gave Virginia
what had been sought in vain, a commodity which could bear
the high costs of labor and transportation and yield a profit.
So prompt and eager was the recourse that soon the very streets
of Jamestown were planted in "the weed."

❋   ❋   ❋   ❋   ❋

Thus far the colony was in effect a plantation owned by the
London Company and operated for its account by indentured
labor.   But the company had promised in 1609 that at the end
of seven years it would issue dividends of land and profits to
the stockholders, including the settlers as being entitled each
to a share by virtue of their emigration.   Net earnings there
were none.   Of land there was plenty; but now that fields
were yielding revenue, the management was tempted to pro-
long monopoly to replenish the coffers.   But the thievishness
of Samuel Argall, who succeeded Dale, thwarted for a time the
hope of gain; and clamor among the stockholders forced a
new régime.   Sir Thomas Smythe's administration, which had
long supported arbitrary control, was replaced by a strikingly

liberal management under Sir Edwin Sandys and the Earl of Southampton.

These men undertook to redeem all previous pledges, including the declaration in the charter of 1606 that the colonists should enjoy liberties, franchises and immunities of all sorts as if they had abided in the realm of England. This empty gesture, long since become a mockery, was made a most welcome reality when in 1619 an assembly met upon summons to initiate representative government. While granting lands liberally, the company continued to send servants to cultivate reserved lands on public account; it procured shiploads of young women to marry the bachelors and stop their longing for England as home; and it sent groups of tar makers, vine dressers and other specialists in the hope of developing some other industry to supplement or even replace tobacco.

In everything but the search for more staples the new management succeeded. The maidens found eager embrace by the bachelors and widowers alike who had wearied of womanless life. The members elected to the House of Burgesses wrought with the governor and his council amicably and sagaciously in legislation and judicature; rich men brought or sent servants to clear and till their grants; "ancient planters", as the veteran settlers were styled, were peacefully busy on their own steadings which dotted the two shores of the James throughout its tidal course, and spread to the "Eastern Shore"; tobacco exports were mounting till they gave promise of supplying the whole English demand.

But catastrophe was coming from the woods. Powhatan in friendly mood, saying there was plenty for all, had bidden the palefaces use what land they would. So long as they were but a few tenderfeet, giving trinkets, tools and weapons for surplus corn, meat and peltries, these English were welcome neighbors. Now they were gaining in woodcraft, slaying the deer, clearing broad fields, breeding cattle and swine to devour the browse, and swarming from the sea at a rate which transformed the prospect. Adding insult to injury, they were bringing preachers to convert "these naked slaves of the divell", disturbing tribal faith and wrecking the prestige of medicine men. These things were a grievance not to be borne, a menace to be destroyed ere its power became overwhelming. Opechancanough, successor of Powhatan, combined other tribes with his own for a stroke in the spring of 1622 so secret and so general that it narrowly failed to destroy the whole white population. Of the twelve hundred inhabitants nearly one third were massacred in their homes; and of those who escaped to the half-dozen stockades many died of pestilence or famine while the redskins laid waste outside.

The survivors, while waging retributive war on their own score, begged for wholesale succor which the company's funds could not furnish. The Smythe faction and others hostile to Sandys and Southampton charged them now with having invited the disaster by promoting expansion helter-skelter, without regard to safety. This played into the hands of the king, who was already adverse to the London Company as a seed bed of liberalism endangering his cherished prerogatives at large. The result was a commission of inquiry and legal proceedings which in 1624 canceled the charter and converted Virginia into a possession of the king to be ruled at his discretion.

That grave consequences did not befall the colony was due to the death of James I, the unconcern of Charles, the confusion of English public affairs and the value of the tobacco trade. The governor and council at Jamestown held over from the company régime for several years, unchanged and uninstructed. At length a new House of Burgesses was ordered to be elected on the old model in order that a contract might be considered by which the king proposed to buy the future tobacco crops at a fixed price and in restricted amount. The bargain failed, but a royal hope of eventual success induced complaisance to the people's wish for the continuance of their existing scheme of government.

The Virginians murmured at the charter of Maryland as a poaching on their own preserves; they expelled their governor, Sir John Harvey, for friendliness to Lord Baltimore and for petty tyrannies of his own; they groaned at the fall of tobacco prices; and in 1644 they suffered from a second onslaught of Opechancanough. But on the whole they were little disturbed from within or without, and under Governor Berkeley in his mild early phase and under improvised authority during the Commonwealth and Protectorate, they were consciously happy in escaping the strife so sorely besetting the mother land. Profiting by default of distant authority, they were developing an order of their own.

The Sandys régime had paved the way, notably by the device of "particular plantations." The word *plantation* is one of diverse meanings. In modern England it applies mainly to a tract of young woods; in Maine and New Hampshire it is an official designation of an unorganized township. In Tudor and Stuart England it meant a colony great or small, as for example the Plantation of Ulster, and Providence Plantations on Narragansett Bay. In this sense Virginia was from the beginning a plantation of the London Company. But in the hands of Dale the colony became a plantation of a special sort, with the settlers regimented for labor under central authority; and this began to give a new meaning to the word.

When the Sandys management issued land in dividends and offered more on "headrights" to enlist private capital in furthering emigration, it announced a policy of granting patents to such individuals, partnerships or corporations as might undertake settlements of considerable scale, empowering them to make laws for the control of their tenants and servants, pending the establishment of a general system of local government. In the case of John Martin's establishment at "Brandon" the grant of privilege broadly empowered him "to enjoye his landes in as lardge & ample a manner, to all intentes and purposes, as any Lord of any manours in England dothe holde his grounde." This prompted a question in the first House of Burgesses. On demand, the clause was read from the patent, "whereof it appeared that when the general Assembly had made some kinde of lawes requisite for the whole Colony he and his Burgesses & People might deride the whole company

& chuse whether they would obey the same or no." The house ordered the two burgesses to withdraw until Captain Martin should say whether he would yield the clause and accept the normal subordination of local units to general laws.[1] The offer of patents, whether with special or standard powers, proved widely attractive. The Leyden Separatists negotiated for one before it was decided to send the *Mayflower* to a more northerly region where the resource of the cod fishery would be more accessible. Captain William Newce, who had prospered from "planting" Scots in Ulster, procured a patent in 1621 contemplating his carriage of a thousand persons to Newport News within four years;[2] and several score others made undertakings on smaller scales. Here then were many sub-colonies actual or prospective, "particular plantations" in distinction from Virginia as a whole, which remained in the older sense the general plantation of the London Company.

Whether in the general or the "particular" thus far, the vesting of jurisdiction was a feature; and this may explain the extension of the word *plantation*. But upon the creation of parishes and counties the possession of public authority by landholders proved superfluous. Land was so plenty and cheap that a freeman would hardly become for long a tenant or a hireling, particularly if his landlord or employer should assume authoritative airs. On the other hand, the labor available being mainly in bondage temporary or permanent, a master had little need to be a magistrate for the sake of that industrial control which was his essential concern. Thus when settlement slowly expanded after the massacre which had wrecked most of the early steadings, the form it took was that of farms and private plantations. Meanwhile the London Company in the first instance and the particular planters in the second had proved the production of tobacco to be feasible in fairly large units under supervision; and incidentally their experience attached

---

[1] H. R. McIlwaine, ed., *Journals of the House of Burgesses of Virginia, 1619–1658/9,* p. 5.

[2] Susan Kingsbury, ed., *Records of the Virginia Company of London,* I, 446.

an industrial meaning to the word *plantation* in permanent American usage.

※　　　　※　　　　※　　　　※　　　　※

Meanwhile, also, the same agencies had introduced indentured labor as a main reliance and had begun to systematize a supply. This was an easy development from the device of apprenticeship then widely prevalent; and it solved a double problem of moneyless transport of would-be emigrants to a virgin land, and of procuring labor for would-be employers who must else have had no employees. Ship captains and other contractors or speculators continued the function which the Company had begun, of recruiting men, women and children in England and selling their indentures, with the persons delivered, to purchasers in the colony. At the middle of the century the procurement of a servant in England was reckoned to cost about three pounds sterling, and the transport about five pounds ten shillings more.[1] The term of service came to be somewhat standardized at five years, or until the age of twenty-four for boys and girls. It also became conventional for the master to furnish the servant at the end of his term with an outfit of tools and clothing and a barrel of corn.

For many years indentured servants comprised the main bulk of immigration to Virginia, and to Maryland and Pennsylvania as well. The personnel of course was mostly of the lower class in society, though the middle class had many representatives, and occasionally gentlefolk would indenture themselves or their children, whether from impoverishment or to gain apprenticeship in colonial industry. Some convicted felons with sentences commuted were transported and sold in later decades, despite objection by colonial governments; and on the other hand many persons, mostly of tender age, were kidnaped and sold fraudulently. The system thus had abuses which legislation could not wholly prevent. And from the planter's point of view unfree labor of any sort had essential

---

[1] William Bullock, *Virginia Impartially Examined* (London, 1649), 47. "Head Money to the Chyrurgion" increased the reckoning to a total of £8, 12*s*., 6*d*.

disadvantages in that, having been paid for in advance, it had little inducement to vigorous or careful work but was commonly prone to shirk.   As newcomers, the servants were liable to the "seasoning fever" which carried thousands to early graves; and when in health many were not averse to seeking their own fortunes promptly by running away. Not a few, on the other hand, shortened service by marrying a master or mistress or some neighbor who would buy and cancel the indenture.   For example, William Bullock wrote as to maid-servants:

"If they come of an honest stock and have a good repute they may pick and chuse their Husbands out of the better sort of people.   I have sent over many, but never could keepe one at my Plantation three moneths, except a poore silly Wench, made for a Foile to set off beautie, and yet a proper young Fellow must needs have her, and being but new come out of his time and not strong enough to pay the charges I was at in cloathing and transporting her, was content to serve me a twelve Moneth for a Wife." [1]

These matrimonial episodes aside, every planter buying indentures and instructing servants in their work automatically induced immigration and educated future freemen in the farmer's craft as competitors eventually with himself.   In due course these became free to sow and reap, to marry and multiply the free population.   As concerns the whites, therefore, unless the death rate were utterly overwhelming, which it never was, the number of the free must increasingly exceed that of the servants.   Again, the larger the scale of the plantations the greater was the excess of servants over masters, and the greater the subsequent excess of small farmers over proprietors of plantation scale.   In consequence, any community depending upon indentured labor must needs create as a by-product a mass of plain folk with little or no pretension of polish to form the bulk of the population.   Meanwhile the relative wealth of the planters would maintain them as an upper stratum, though ill fortune or extravagance might elimi-

[1] William Bullock, *Virginia Impartially Examined* (London, 1649), 53, 54.

nate some persons from the ranks of the well-to-do while others rose by talent, thrift or good luck from low to high estate. And be the individual origin exalted or humble, wealth would bring in the course of time social ambition and attainment.

Now the devotee of genealogy likes to find an English nobleman or an Indian princess in his family tree, but he is not prone to boast of an indentured immigrant. Any citizen today of "good old American stock" must have had, with a small allowance for inbreeding, some six hundred ancestors in the generation of Pocahontas. A few can trace their descent to such remove in perhaps a dozen lines; but the forty-nine dozen others are lost even to the professionals, though these may manufacture pedigrees and furnish quarterings to order. The question remains, where are the descendants of the redemptioners, some of whom, like other sires, had grandchildren by the gross? The traditional answer is, in the mountains and the pine barrens. If we add to these every other district into which Virginians, Marylanders and Pennsylvanians have spread, the reply will be nearer truth. Inevitably the high and low of early times have become very largely and quite inextricably blended in the course of three more or less democratic centuries.

The Negroes are another story, parallel as to the blending of tribal stocks among them, but sharply contrasting as regards the growth of a freely competing population. But Negroes figured little in Virginia's early generations. Twenty were imported in 1619; three hundred were reckoned to dwell among fifteen thousand whites at the middle of the century; and in 1671 Governor Berkeley reported some two thousand Negro slaves and six thousand white servants in a total of forty thousand souls. He continued: "yearly, we suppose, there comes in of servants about fifteen hundred, of which most are English, few Scotch and fewer Irish; and not above two or three ships of negroes in seven years."[1] As to significant numbers the Africans were late comers fitted into a system already de-

[1] W. W. Hening, *Statutes at Large*, II, 515.

veloped. What changes their presence wrought will be better told in another place. And so also the tale of Indian relations.

❋   ❋   ❋   ❋   ❋

But what of F. F. V's? Did the Carters, Burwells and Randolphs, the Pages, Nelsons and Braxtons, the Fitzhughs, Wythes, Washingtons and Lees derive from noble English houses through gentlefolk always living in elegance and maintaining lofty standards? If so, the records of the seventeenth century are at fault.

The founders of Jamestown are almost eliminated as ancestors. John Smith left no progeny, though he would seem to be not without namesakes. Pocahontas [1] is amply represented through a single son, if all that is told be true; but another of the very few wives was killed by her husband in the "starving time", part of her body eaten and the rest salted against future need. When the Sandys management sent young women to put the colony upon a perpetuating basis, nearly all the Argonauts were dead; and malaria germs along with Opechancanough sent most of the newcomers to untimely graves. Some of the "particular plantation" gentry survived, however, and a thin recruiting of the genteel class came from England until Cromwell's time, when fairly numerous opponents of the Roundheads sought asylum in the colony. While these were styled Cavaliers mainly as a political designation, the proportion of well-born among them was doubtless large. All this is reflected in a fairly constant recognition of social rank in public as well as private proceedings. And yet, in some sense, gentility suffered an eclipse, as it must do in a wilderness where rugged virtues are at a premium.

Until the middle of the century Virginia comprised in the main a mere series of clearings on either bank of the James, a ribbon of civilization thrown into a continent of barbarism.

---

[1] That this "princess" was not so ill-favored as an oft-printed engraving would have us believe is fairly proved by Fairfax Harrison in the *Virginia Magazine*, XXXV, 431–436.

Every steading must for years be a camp under primitive shelter; and when permanent housing was built, the need of defense was likely to give it more the look of a stockade than of a mansion. The price of tobacco fell before the end of the 'twenties from several shillings a pound to a penny; and though it rose again it never maintained bonanza levels. There was a surplus of grain for sale to the Massachusetts colonists in the 'thirties; but Indian disorders and bad seasons brought something of a new starving time soon afterward. Prosperity, in short, and even livelihood, came not with ease but with effort; and life was marked by lonely isolation, savage contacts, crude makeshifts and recurrent emergencies. Furniture and clothing were esteemed rather for service than for show; and "persons of quality" were likely to be surpassed in wealth and eventually in social rating by such men as Captain Samuel Matthews whose thrifty prowess raised him from lowly beginnings until in 1648 he was perhaps the richest man in the colony. He then had many indentured artisans and the quite unusual number of forty Negroes, producing hemp and flax, wheat, pork and beef, and making cloth, leather and shoes. The visitor who described his establishment concluded: "He married the daughter of Sir Tho. Hinton, and in a word, keeps a good house, lives bravely, and [is] a true lover of Virginia; he is worthy of much honour." [1] Others prospered in part from the private conversion of public funds, as Edward Hill and his son of the same name were charged in 1677 with having done for many years.[2] Thus one who was a gentleman in the then technical sense of a man entitled to use a coat of arms might thrive by methods not inviting scrutiny. The standards of official honor, in fact, were not exalted in that century. Reciprocally, deference to rank or office was by no means universal. As an instance of literal contempt of court, William Hatton was charged in York County in 1662 with "abusing severall Justices of this County, calling them Coopers, Hogg trough

[1] *A Perfect Description of Virginia* (London, 1649), 15.
[2] Remonstrance of the inhabitants of Charles City County, in the *Virginia Magazine*, III, 142-147.

makers, Pedlars, Cobblers, tailors, weavers, and saying they are not fitting to sit where they doe sit." [1]

✻   ✻   ✻   ✻   ✻

From the settlements on the James the course of empire seemed to lie northward, where the York, the Rappahannock and the Potomac gave additional vents from new tobacco fields. Slowly through the second half of the century migration entered these channels in succession until Virginia touched Maryland. This made the settled area roughly a square with the bay, or perhaps rather the ocean, on its front and the fall-line of the rivers as its rear, with the redskins almost completely expelled from the tide-water district into the still neglected Piedmont. This brought a new phase, a differentiation between the vicinity of the Chesapeake and the westerly zone which must be a buffer in case of war. The contrast brought armed conflict in 1676 when Governor Berkeley and his council, reflecting eastward inertia, sought to impose passive defense upon the turbulent frontier and thereby precipitated Bacon's Rebellion. Its leader's death prevented any fight to a finish; but he lived long enough to show, by placing captured women of the Berkeley faction upon his rampart in time of threatened attack, that it was possible in Virginia then to do barbarous things. Berkeley, in his crusty closing years, had little enough chivalry; Bacon, though technically a gentleman, had none.

The northward expansion, supplemented by the growth of Maryland, rapidly increased the Chesapeake output of tobacco. In 1663 the export amounted to 7,367,140 pounds, and at the end of the century it approached fifty million. Overproduction, together with the Navigation Laws and heavy taxation upon the import into England, reduced the price to levels which for two decades brought great distress. Projects of relief through legislation were thwarted by the crown and by the conflict of interest between the two colonies concerned. At length, in 1682, rioters in several Virginia counties took the law into their own hands by destroying crops in the fields.

[1] *William and Mary College Quarterly*, XXVI, 30.

Though this ungentle stroke was not repeated, many individuals persistently sought gain or comfort through tricks characteristic of middle-class laxity and shrewdness, fraudulently procuring lands, dodging taxes, evading trade restrictions, and shirking militia duty. The governors, though some were English barons, were mostly self-seeking corruptionists; the councilors combined pride of place with greed for pelf; and the House of Burgesses was inclined to be both timid and stingy, as when in 1699 it resolved that the arming and drilling of white servants would be unsafe as well as expensive because they "for the most part consists of the Worser Sort of the people of *Europe*, And since the Peace hath been concluded Such Numbers of *Irish* and other Nations have been bro^t in of which a great many have been Soldiers in the late Warrs That according to our present Circumstances we can hardly governe them, and if they were fitted with Armes and had the Opertunity of meeting together by Musters We have just reason to feare they may rise vpon us." [1] In short, Virginia was not yet the home of gallantry or serenity, though she was developing patterns which erelong were to make her so.

Immigrants, impelled almost wholly by an economic motive to transplant themselves, had sought to transfer English practices in full; and they handed on the purpose to the next generation and the next, with a notable continuity resulting as to law, religion, sports and social conventions. But a divergence in many things was a fruit of isolation and geographical contrasts. Immigrants themselves often met new predicaments by novel devices; and their native-bred children had only a diluted and modified tradition as partial guides to their own sagacity. England herself was different under William of Orange from what she had been under James I; and Virginia was now different from either, as a survey at the turn of the century will show. [2]

---

[1] H. R. McIlwaine, ed., *Journals of the House of Burgesses of Virginia, 1695–1702,* p. 188. A fear of disorders from Catholic Irish and from Negroes prompted in the same year a resolution to tax the importation of Negro slaves and such white servants as were not natives of England or Wales. — *Ibid.,* 148.

[2] This task is greatly facilitated by Hartwell, Blair and Chilton, *The Present State*

The Church was that of the motherland; maintained by taxation. In default of a bishop, the chief of the cloth was James Blair, commissary of the Bishop of London, who by serving on occasion as judge at horse races indicated what rectors might do without losing countenance. These were not strait-laced or more authoritative than suited their parishioners.[1] Fixity of pay, set by law in 1696 at sixteen thousand pounds of tobacco, forbade hopes of advancement except such as might come by shift from an Oronoco parish to another which produced and paid the more valuable "sweet-scented" leaf. Inertia was accordingly a prevailing clerical trait. The laity in the fifty parishes were moderately pious in placid undogmatic fashion, attending service quite regularly, whether from religious impulse or because it was "good form" and gave occasion for social commingling. The church door was an official bulletin board, and the churchyard before and after service a place of exchange for news, opinions and invitations. The churches themselves, like the courthouses and some residences, were coming to be built of well-made brick, mostly laid in Flemish bond, which with its alternating medium-burnt stretchers and overburnt headers gave attractive diagonal patterns on the walls. Despite the Bacchic lives of some of the clergy, the Anglican Church was a dignifying influence. Dissent had gained tolerance after a repressive period in the mid-century; and there were now four Quaker meetings and a Presbyterian congregation functioning undisturbed, and sundry Catholic families of high and low degree, though these had no place of worship short of Maryland.

The civil authority was considerably centralized by reason

of *Virginia and the College* (London, 1727). Their excellent account, which was written about 1697, is also printed from the manuscript in the Massachusetts Historical Society *Collections*, series I, vol. V, pp. 124–166 of the reprinted edition, and with slight abbreviation in the *Calendar of State Papers, America and West Indies*, 1696–1697, pp. 641–666.

[1] "We got to Church in decent time, and Mr. Betty, the Parson of the Parish, entertain'd us with a good honest Sermon, but whether he bought it or borrowed it would have been uncivil in us to inquire. Be that as it will, he is a decent Man, with a double chin that fits gracefully over his Band, and his Parish, especially the Female part of it, like him well." — J. S. Bassett, ed., *The Writings of "Colonel William Byrd of Westover in Virginia Esqr"* (New York, 1901), 323.

of the governor's growing power. Holding a royal commission, he combined executive, judicial and military functions in his own person, and he had now acquired in effect the power of appointing the members of his council as well as various other functionaries. This made his favor sought to such degree that men of wealth tended to become courtiers in his train. The council served as upper house of assembly and as the General Court, hearing appeals as well as giving administrative advice. Its nine or ten members were ex-officio colonels of militia in their several counties, while the commanders in other counties must be content with the lesser title of major. More important than military titles, councilors usually held administrative offices and often plural appointments yielding fees and salaries. Some of them waxed so great in their own esteem and so domineering in demeanor as to rouse lasting resentment among those whom they treated as underlings. The persistence of traditional unpopularity was noted by Jefferson, who remarked in 1813 that "a Randolph, a Carter or a Burwell must have great personal superiority over a common competitor to be elected by the people even at this day." [1]

The House of Burgesses endeavored to maintain a legislative predominance like that of the Commons in England, but without full success. Its bills were liable to rejection by the Council, and often met veto by the governor or the crown. Its members were as a rule unlearned in the law, and their proceedings had a confused and amateurish quality. Ambition for seats in the Council or for other office, furthermore, inclined many to curry favor with the executive rather than to stand firm for the wishes or interests of their constituents. In the chamber and among the people parties were emerging along Whig and Tory lines.

Each of the counties, which numbered twenty-four in 1700, was entitled to two burgesses in the assembly; and the borough of Jamestown elected one member. Williamsburg as the new seat of government soon replaced the old capital in representation; and afterward the towns of Norfolk and Richmond and

[1] P. L. Ford, ed., *Writings of Thomas Jefferson*, IX, 427.

the College of William and Mary were put upon the same basis. The counties were already quite uneven in size and population, but the assembly created additional ones with reluctance. Sometimes a newly settled area was given parish organization as a makeshift, to postpone the increase of backwoods burgesses.

In each county there were about a dozen justices of the peace to constitute a county court, which usually dispensed with a jury except for criminal cases. The sheriff, appointed like the justices by the governor, was also collector of poll taxes, which were the main source of public revenue. Like the governor and other executive officers, he might farm out his functions to a deputy for a share of the fees or stipend. Court days once a month excelled church service as gatherings of men for miscellaneous business, festivities and sports. Annual militia musters alone surpassed them for these purposes.

Aside from government, all affairs were extraordinarily decentralized. This came from the human practice of following the line of least resistance and readiest exploitation. The bay and the four great rivers penetrated the whole breadth of the coastal plain and put thousands of home sites upon equal footing as to access of settlers and freighting of produce. Fertile tracts with water front were sought here, there and yonder, in full confidence that ships would come in season to take tobacco directly to London, Bristol or Glasgow. Every immigrant and every importer of a servant or slave was entitled under the law to take in reward as "headright" fifty acres, to be selected at will and held permanently upon payment each year of a shilling or twelve pounds of tobacco as "quitrent." Aside from this very light burden there was no tax laid upon the land. The surveys were more generous than accurate; and their lines might meander at will, to include a maximum of good soil within the patent and leave barren ground in public possession. On the other hand, tobacco required so much labor that hardly more than three acres could well be tended per hand, and a similar space would furnish foodstuffs. But the ready exhaustion of the shallow soil by careless culture and the wish for weight and quality in every leaf, intensified now and then by restrictive legislation, made forest reserves desirable to furnish virgin fields to replace those which after a few years were to be abandoned. The copiousness and cheapness of accessible tracts[1] thus fostered a dispersion so complete as to give the colony a lasting appearance of almost unbroken wilderness. Not only was every farm likely to be separated from its neighbor by woodland, but the variation of soil within short distances led to a prevalence of small units of operation, even when large tracts were consolidated in ownership.

Thus far the rich had slight advantage of the poor. The tale of commerce is a little different. A ship would anchor off a planter's landing to take a hundred hogsheads more willingly than at a farm to load half a dozen; and the supercargo would be more eager to display his wares to purchasers of the larger scale. Many planters, indeed, served as middlemen to collect tobacco from the farmers on the creeks behind them and to sell petty supplies in seasons when ships were not peddling the rivers.

The rich felt inconvenience, and the poor still more, from the complete absence of towns, for an independent artisan had slight opportunity to ply his trade except as a journeyman in the literal sense, rowing or sailing from job to job; and in the consequent dearth of tradesmen a farmer must usually turn his hand to all tasks of construction and repair, while a planter might buy a blacksmith or carpenter under indenture. As to schooling, all were in bad case except the few whose wealth permitted the purchase of indentured tutors or the sending of sons for instruction in England. The colonial stock tended for a time to be less educated than their immigrant parents had been. The college of William and Mary was now hopefully launched as a cure; but more than a century afterward a cultured Virginian sagely said that his learning had come rather from conversation than from books.[2]

By far the most of the landowners were men who must earn

---

[1] By act of 1705 public land might be bought at a shilling for ten acres in quantities not exceeding five hundred acres. — Hening, *Statutes*, III, 305.

[2] Letter of Francis W. Gilmer to William Wirt, December 20, 1816, Manuscript in Virginia State Library.

their bread by the sweat of their brows. A quitrent roll of 1704, covering twenty counties and listing some fifty-five hundred names, returned only about one in fifteen as owning more than a thousand acres when land was yet extremely cheap; [1] and poll-tax returns in the same period show that perhaps ninety per cent of the landowners must have had no more than one or two helpers, including their own sons.[2] Amid this numerous yeomanry dwelt a few score well-to-do families, most of them so little distinguished in talent and fortune that successive governors found the range of choice quite restricted when filling vacancies in the council. The trend of policy even among the rich was not to perpetuate prestige through primogeniture but rather to bequeath estates in equal partition, for the dearth of military and professional opportunity gave a forlorn prospect for landless and slaveless younger sons.

The chief money in use was tobacco itself, and the prevailing unit was a hogshead of about five hundred pounds! [3] In this currency taxes, fines and wagers were paid and most reckonings were kept. A little Spanish coinage came in from the sale of lumber, staves, meat and grain to the West Indies; but the purchase of all sorts of imports, and especially servants and slaves, kept the purse flat and the tobacco crop often pledged in advance. The dearth of specie and the bulkiness of tobacco fostered the running of accounts instead of paying in cash. Large local transactions might be settled by bills of exchange, but the nearest bank was a merchant's counting room in London, the price and proceeds of a shipment drawn against were uncertain, and tobacco ships, which were the only letter carriers,[4] were generally at hand only in the winter season, to bring a reply next year.

[1] The roll is printed in T. J. Wertenbaker, *The Planters of Colonial Virginia* (Princeton, 1922), 183–247.

[2] *Ibid.*, 58. Their wives and daughters were ignored in the statistics of the time.

[3] The standard hogshead's capacity was increased two or threefold in later times.

[4] *E.g.* letter of Mary Washington to her brother in England, 1760: "You seem to blame me for no writing to you I do a shaur it is Not for wante of a very great Regard for you & the family but as I dont ship tobacco the Captains never call on me soe that I Never know when tha come or when tha goe." — Horace E. Hayden, *Virginia Genealogies* (Wilkes-Barre, Pa., 1891), 81.

Virginia was thus a paradise to those only, rich or poor, who took these inconveniences and uncertainties as a matter of course and made the most of the offsets at hand. The London merchants often complained of the slowness of colonial pay, but they seldom rejected planters' accounts. The planters complained of miscarriages and misfits, of poor quality and high charges, but they got a habit of homespun recourse only when hard times impelled it. The shipowners complained of months lost in sailing back and forth in the rivers, accumulating cargo in driblets before setting out for home; but they conspired with the merchants to induce royal vetoes of colonial acts for promoting towns. These mutual protests were concerned with details, or else they were not very serious. The colony was on the whole finding its lines to lie in pleasant places, and those with whom it traded esteemed the traffic. Francis Makemie, Alexander Spotswood [1] and a few other agitators for towns and a general transformation were voices crying in the wilderness. Virginia as she was seemed good enough for those to the manner born, and was getting better. Her bacon, hams and hot breads were already gaining fame, along with her leisured sociability.

❊   ❊   ❊   ❊   ❊

Here, then, was the Old Dominion at the end of her first century. Her second was to bring much further expansion and many changes. There came a great increase of slave imports and a dwindling influx of servants; a multiplication of white and black through fecundity and salubrity; a shift of tobacco culture to the Piedmont, whither thousands of lowlanders migrated; a meeting and a bit of mingling with other thousands with contrasting traditions from Pennsylvania; a rise of towns at the limits of ocean shipping on the rivers; and a most remarkable growth of gentle breeding and public spirit.

[1] [Francis Makemie] *A Plain & Friendly Perswasive to the Inhabitants of Virginia and Maryland for Promoting Towns & Cohabitation* (London, 1705), reprinted in the *Virginia Magazine*, IV, 255–271; "The official Letters of Alexander Spotswood, Lieutenant-Governor of Virginia, 1710–1722", in the Virginia Historical Society *Collections*, n. s., I, II.

Francis Makemie's remark in 1705 that "the best, richest and most healthy part of your country is yet to be inhabited above the falls of every river to the mountains" was doubtless corroborated by hunters and traders of the time; but an Indian treaty of 1684 still debarred white settlement, and a squad of rangers at the falls of each river patrolled the existing frontier. The thrust beyond this line was initiated by Governor Spotswood who settled a group of indentured Germans at Germanna on the Rapidan in 1714, to mine and smelt iron. Thence, in 1716, he led the festive "Knights of the Golden Horseshoe" on an official exploration across the Blue Ridge; and by treaty six years afterward he extinguished the Indian claim to the region in general. Several new counties were now created by the assembly; lands were offered gratis to settlers; and influential citizens, by one means or another, procured large tracts for speculative purposes. The most fortunate of these was William Byrd II as the proprietor of the sites of Richmond and Petersburg. "The Truth of it is," he wrote in 1733, "these two places being the uppermost Landing of James and Appamattux Rivers, are naturally intended for Marts, where the traffick of the Outer Inhabitants must Center. Thus we did not build Castles only, but also Citys in the Air." [1] Four years afterward he advertised lots in "a Town called Richmond, with Streets 65 Feet wide, in a pleasant and healthy Situation, and well supply'd with Springs of good Water. It lies near the Publick Warehouse at Shoccoe's, and in the midst of great Quantities of Grain and all kinds of Provisions. The Lots will be granted in Fee-Simple, on Condition only of building a House in Three Years Time, of 24 by 16 Feet, fronting within 5 Feet of the street. The Lots to be rated according to the Convenience of their Situation, and to be sold by me." [2]

The Piedmont movement was no stampede, for virgin land was yet fairly copious on tidewater. Men of small fortunes and crude steadings made the readiest response to the fresh

---

[1] Bassett, ed., *Writings of William Byrd*, 292.
[2] *Virginia Gazette*, May 6–13, 1737.

opportunity, for established families were loath to leave their homes, their neighbors, their oyster beds and their duck shooting, to settle again where all would be new and crops must needs be hauled or barged to fall-line points where merchants would intervene between the planter and the accustomed ship captain. But here and there occurred something of a community migration of gentry, as from the vicinity of Chotank Creek on the lower Potomac to the Brent Town tract near Manassas.[1]

Some of the participants in this were children of William Fitzhugh, an immigrant of 1670, who married and soon became well settled on "Bedford" near the Chotank. Indulging a homesickness in 1686, he described his property with a view to a possible exchange for an English estate. His plantation, comprising a thousand acres, was operated in three units by twenty-nine slaves, "most of them this country born, the remainder as likely as most in Virginia." His dwelling and appurtenant houses were within a palisade of locust puncheons, "which is as good as if it were walled in and more lasting than any of our bricks." He had much livestock, an orchard of twenty-five hundred apple trees, a grist mill, and more than twenty-five thousand acres at some distance, acquired as a speculation.[2] At Christmas of that year he was visited by a pleasure-seeking party of twenty horsemen, among whom was a Frenchman who wrote:

"The Colonel's accommodations were . . . so ample that this company gave him no trouble at all; we were all supplied with beds, though we had indeed to double up. Col. Fitzhugh showed us the largest hospitality. He had store of good wine and other things to drink, and a frolic ensued. He called in three fiddlers, a clown, a tight rope dancer and an acrobatic tumbler, and gave us all the divertisement one would wish. It was very cold but no one thought of going near the fire because they never put less than the trunk of a tree upon it and

[1] [Fairfax Harrison] *Landmarks of Old Prince William* (Richmond, 1924), I, 177–201.

[2] *Virginia Magazine*, I, 395. The apple trees were set with a view partly to cider and brandy. Peaches and other fruits were also copious on the better estates of the period; and as the writer next cited below said: "In the gardens they have the same vegetables we use in Europe."

so the entire room was kept warm." [1] Fitzhugh had prospered from plantation industry, the practice of law, the holding of public office and the plying of commerce; and an overture of his to a Yankee skipper [2] suggests that he may have bought slaves for sale. He died in the colony rich but not widely loved, for, being a true Tory son of the Restoration, he combined a fondness for wit and gayety with a scorn of what he freely styled the rabble of the province. His descendants were Virginians full fledged. One wrote of them in 1860, with some vainglory concerning his own generation : "Like their Chotank ancestors, their hearts were bigger than their purses. They generally broke or became embarrassed, and moved South and West to mend their fortunes. Being men of energy and education, they generally succeeded, and are now doing better than either their Brent Town or their more remote Chotank ancestors ever did." [3]

❈   ❈   ❈   ❈   ❈

The migrants to the Piedmont retained their manners and ambitions, and after surviving or escaping the frontier phase, refined them, as the lowlanders also were doing. Exalted precepts were already at hand, like that which Colonel Daniel Parke gave his daughter at the beginning of the century :

"Do not learn to romp, but behave yourself soberly and like a gentlewoman. . . . Be calm and obliging to all the Servants, and when you speak doe it mildly, even to the poorest slave; if any of the Servants commit small faults y^t are of no consequence, doe you hide them. If you understand of any great faults they commit, acquaint y^r mother, but do not exaggerate the fault." [4]

Good examples were also present as in the person of Colonel Mumford, of whom William Byrd wrote in 1733 : "An honester

---

[1] [Fairfax Harrison, tr.] *A Frenchman in Virginia, being the Memoirs of a Huguenot Refugee in 1686* ([Richmond, Va.] 1925), 67, 68.

[2] *Virginia Magazine*, I, 108.

[3] George Fitzhugh, in *DeBow's Review*, XXX, 78.

[4] Mary N. Stanard, *Colonial Virginia, its People and Customs* (Philadelphia, 1917), 111.

Man, a fairer Trader or a kinder Friend this Country never produced: God send any of his Sons may have the Grace to take after him." [1] Colonel Byrd was himself a pattern of sprightly elegance, whether in life or literature. Son of a prosperous father, educated in England, lodged in princely fashion at "Westover", accumulating a great library [2] and employing a private librarian, rambling through the wilderness and recording his observations in sparkling phrase, yet never missing an opportunity to enlarge his fortune, he was the complete notable.

Byrd's pace was too fast, his flight too high for the community to follow him; and his own son, by proving a wastrel, showed that flashing patterns were not altogether wholesome. Not only did Eton and Oxford come to be contemned as producing prigs and fops, [3] but a Potomac citizen even forbade his sons during their youth to mingle in James River society "lest they should imbibe more exalted notions of their own importance than I could wish any child of mine to possess." [4] Daughters and sons were equally liable to false pride. A former Virginia girl wrote after many years as an English matron: "There was a time when I should not have been well pleased to hear of the union between a daughter of yours and Mr.——; but, thank God, I have outlived those prejudices of education, and know now that the worthy man is to be preferred to the high-born who has not merit to recommend him." [5] Happy were those, and they were many, who had not such lessons to unlearn.

The native culture was eventually shaped by the lesser squires in their predominant numbers, compromising between plainness and pretension, rooted in the soil but not of the earth

---

[1] Bassett, ed., *Writings of William Byrd*, 326.

[2] A catalogue of its 3438 volumes is given by Bassett, 413–443.

[3] Landon Carter II wrote in 1770: "I believe everybody begins to laugh at English education; the general importers of it nowadays bring back only a stiff priggishness with as little good manners as possible." — *William and Mary College Quarterly*, XIII, 47.

[4] Will of Thompson Mason, 1785. — Kate M. Rowland, *Life of George Mason* (New York, 1892), II, 77.

[5] Letter of Sarah Cary Fairfax to her sister-in-law, 1788. W. M. Cary, *Sally Cary: a Long Hidden Romance of Washington's Life* (New York, 1916), 45.

earthy. The possession of large wealth, if accompanied by pomp, "injured a man's social standing," as a Virginian curiously said, "because it placed him on unequal terms with his neighbors, and somewhat excluded him from society." [1]

The lowlands gradually decayed, from the exhaustion of their lands for tobacco and from the cult of magnificence. Mann Page built a house on "Rosewell" so great that it fell into ruin because neither his descendants nor any one else thereabout could maintain it; [2] and Burgess Ball of "Travellers' Rest" (fittingly named) was impoverished by mere chronic excess of hospitality. [3]   Moderation, whether in the use of wealth or in the seeking of it, was the note of a soberer generation. John Dandridge of "Brandon" wrote in 1797: "The man who sets no bounds to the quantity of wealth he aims at will be very apt to overlook propriety in the means. . . . In order to avoid temptation I mean hereafter to stay at home & work, not with the hope or desire of becoming rich, but to be barely independent enough to do & say what I conscientiously think right & honest." [4]

The Tidewater at length became an appendage to the Piedmont, where touch with England was broken and where ten thousand sturdy folk in scattered homesteads were exploiting the land and polishing their manners to form an aristocratic democracy. Tobacco culture demands energetic work on special occasions and invites a steady routine for several months, but it gives release at other times to those who do not seek a profit from every passing day.   And agriculture in general, if prosperous at all, permits a sense of security against loss of capital.   If a merchant lose his market, his business may face ruin, but if a farmer lose his crop his land remains and another crop will grow.   The merchant is full aware that he needs to save his earnings for diverse investment against

[1] George Fitzhugh, in *DeBow's Review*, XXX, 78.

[2] Bishop [William] Meade, *Old Churches, Ministers and Families of Virginia* (Philadelphia, 1857), I, 331.

[3] H. E. Hayden, *Virginia Genealogies*, 113.   The handsome dwelling still stands on the southern bank of the Rappahannock, five miles below Fredericksburg.

[4] *William and Mary College Quarterly*, XX, 164, 165.

a day of crisis; the farmer, and more especially the planter, feels more free to spend his income and to take a holiday now and then, and even to engage help and reduce his own exertion. At least, so these Virginians found it.

Planter and gentleman had long since become interchangeable terms, and the planters included by courtesy many who might equally well have been termed farmers. In the sprawling, tolerant commonwealth there was variation among localities, of course, and still more among individuals. But somehow a fairly standard pattern of life became prevalent through all the region into which folk from Tidewater had flowed. This element, called "Tuckahoes" [1] in distinction from the "Cohees" of the Shenandoah, were lovers of leisure, of sports, of horses, of making and receiving visits, of conversation, politics, good cheer and chivalry. The source and process of spread were the same as those which gave and spread the pattern of speech with broadened *a's*, diminished *r's*, and the *y*-sounds in *girl* and *garden* which every one uses in *cure* and *care*. Somehow, though rurality remained almost complete, urbanity prevailed against rusticity. And somehow the Old Dominion formed a crucible in which men and women were refined until, in the times that tried men's souls, a galaxy on each occasion stood forth.

[1] Tuckahoes and Cohees will be discussed further in our concluding chapter.

CHAPTER III

THE YOUNGER COLONIES

VIRGINIA'S prosperity, slow as it was in coming, inspired Stuart courtiers, whether singly or in partnerships, to seek profit from royal favor in American promotions. Palatine powers, quitrents in perpetuity and unearned increments from reserved lands were inducements enough to the heads of ambitious houses. A religious prompting was added in the cases of Maryland and Pennsylvania, though not in Carolina or New York; but it was accident of latitude, not difference of design, which incorporated some of these eventually into the South and left others outside. Notably the rulers of Georgia sought with perfect zeal to make that province unlike its neighbors, only to be thwarted by the dictates of geography.

Like others of his kind, George Calvert, first Baron Baltimore, was ready to exploit any zone. He was concerned in the London Company from an early time; he shared in speculation as to New England grants; and he spent a disillusioning winter as chief in a Newfoundland project before he hit upon the Maryland venture. Official sanction for this last undertaking, indeed, came after his death, and the charter was issued in 1632 to his heir in his stead. The document was ambiguous throughout. The boundaries were vague by reason of topographical ignorance; the stipulations as to government contradicted one another; and the religious provisions were most ambiguous of all, since a firm purpose with father and son was to create a Catholic haven under the laws of England, which in themselves forbade it. Having gotten this charter, meaning much or little as events might prove, the second Lord Baltimore promptly sent forth a varied parcel of colonists, including three Jesuit priests. The nucleus of the colony was planted at St. Mary's, where the Potomac joins the Chesapeake.

Instructions at the outset enjoined upon the Catholics privacy of worship and avoidance of disputation, that offense be not given to their Protestant companions. When the priests violated these commands the Proprietor put a curb upon their ambitions and made it clear that Maryland was to be no Catholic preserve. Whatever may have been their own predilections, the Calverts were impelled by political necessity to be champions of religious freedom. Economic expediency pointed the same course, for in the competition of colonies for settlers no proprietor could well afford to debar or deter any important variety of religionists. Popular participation in government was fostered by the same need of numbers for the sake of strength and revenue.

Virginia had led the way to tobacco, which Maryland followed as a matter of course. But her climate was not quite so good for the crop, and the prices for her staple ranged lower than those on the James. There was, in fact, little reason for people to settle upon these upper reaches of the bay unless they were uncomfortable elsewhere. The chief increment in the second decade was of Puritans who had been expelled from Virginia and took lands about the Severn where Annapolis was to rise.

The proprietor had sought from the beginning to attract men of means by offering manorial powers to such as would bring in people enough at their expense to accumulate one or two thousand acres on headrights. First and last some threescore patents were issued on this basis; and in a few cases the manors were maintained in true medieval form for several decades. But experience put this panoply to scorn. Such records as are extant [1] show the manorial courts handling trivial business in amateurish fashion, demonstrating the futility of the scheme. How there could have been any leaseholders is not easy to see. Surely the cheap abundance of land must have reduced the manors into plantations and converted the lords of tenants into

[1] Some are printed in the *Johns Hopkins University Studies*, I, no. 7.

masters of servants or slaves. The Lord Proprietor of the province was himself eventually shorn of most of his powers.

Though the two colonies were quarrelsome neighbors for long, Maryland's development followed the Virginia pattern in all main features. She was younger, smaller, less prosperous, and later in attaining social integration. The governor expressed regret in 1664 that a projected contract with the Royal African Company for slaves by the shipload could not be financed. "I find," said he, "wee are nott men of estates good enough to undertake such a buisnesse, but could wish we were, for we are naturally inclin'd to love neigros if our purses would endure it." [1]   In later times the import of slaves reached fairly large dimensions; but the considerations of a lesser first cost per capita and a smaller risk of loss in acclimatization in that latitude made indentured servants a more general recourse than to the southward. This yielded in turn a large proportion of yeoman farmers even in the lowlands where tobacco continued to prevail. Nevertheless a plantation aristocracy held considerable sway, with Catholics numerous in its personnel and the Dulany and Carroll [2] families particularly prominent. The growth of Annapolis and then of Baltimore made the scheme of life somewhat less rural than in Virginia. The Piedmont and the Valley in Maryland were settled mainly by farmers from Pennsylvania, thriving sturdily upon grain and live stock.

In the legislature, where the various types commingled, a confused informality seems to have been chronic. Thomas Jefferson, when visiting Annapolis in 1766, described the session as a hubbub of chattering groups, with several members addressing the speaker simultaneously without rising from their seats and with no control from the chair:

"When a motion was made, the speaker instead of putting

---

[1] Maryland Historical Society, *Fund Publications*, XXVIII, 249.

[2] In quitrent accounts of 1770 (manuscripts in the Library of Congress), Charles Carroll is listed as owning "Doorhegan Manor", "Grey's Increase", "Norman's Fancy", "Widower's Cost", "Providence", "Half Pone", "Trusty Friend", "Came by Chance", "Ensign's Grove", "Carrollton" and many other tracts aggregating perhaps a hundred thousand acres.

the question in the usual form only asked the gentlemen whether they chose that such or such a thing should be done, and was answered by a yes sir or no sir: and tho' the voices appeared frequently to be divided, they never would go to the trouble of dividing the house, but the clerk entered the resolutions, I supposed, as he thought proper." [1]

❈ ❈ ❈ ❈ ❈

In the present commonwealth of North Carolina the first permanent footing was gained by the mere expansion of Virginia into what soon became a separate jurisdiction. But if there was no fanfare in England there was a picturesque prelude in America. It happened in 1653 that a trading party from the Chesapeake encountered on Roanoke Island an Indian chief who was enamored of civilization. He followed the traders on their return to Francis Yeardley's home at Lynn Haven and there made arrangements to have himself and a number of his tribesmen baptized, to place his son in Yeardley's household for instruction in reading and writing, and to cede in behalf of the Roanoke Indians "three great rivers" and the lands thereon in exchange for the construction and furnishing of an "English" house for the chief to inhabit.[2]

The sequel of Yeardley's bargain is not of detailed record. But whatever the basis adopted for land titles, there promptly began a trek to the shores of the Chowan, the Perquimons and the Pasquotank. Some well-to-do folk were among the migrants, thinking to exploit bottom lands on these broad waters. But the prospect was in a measure delusive. The sandbars parting Albemarle Sound from the sea gave channels too shallow and too shifting to invite ships from England to ply these waters; and Albemarle tobacco must await the chance

---

[1] Thomas Jefferson to John Page, Annapolis, May 25, 1766, in the New York Public Library *Bulletin*, II, 176, 177.

[2] Letter of Francis Yeardley to John Farrar, May 8, 1654, in the *State Papers of John Thurloe* (London, 1742), II, 273, 274; partly reprinted in the *Colonial Records of North Carolina*, I, 18. The publication of this latter collection has antiquated all prior histories of the colony, as is indicated convincingly in the prefatory notes to the several volumes.

of coasting craft or else be hauled overland for shipment from
Norfolk. The result was that though a settler throve modestly
here and there on a plantation scale, nearly all the people were
of a lowly sort, uncouth backwoodsmen in cabins too remote
one from another to maintain churches or schools or other
apparatus of community life.

When Carolina was created under Charles II affairs were
little changed for these folk who dwelt obscurely near its
northern border. The Proprietors appointed a succession of
deputy governors for the Albemarle region and instituted a land
office, courts and a legislative assembly; but the government
had no fixed abode and little authority. Settlement slowly
extended southward to Pamlico Sound and then up the main
streams far enough to give a thin trade to the villages of Edenton, Washington and Newbern. Meanwhile George Fox and
his disciples, profiting by the lack of other missionaries, made
many converts to Quakerism. Meanwhile also the Tuscaroras
took the warpath in 1711 and were checked and then driven
away only with help from distant Charleston. The two parts
of Carolina were officially made completely separate when the
crown displaced the Lords Proprietors; but the division cast
the Cape Fear district into the northern province, though
the plan of life which there prevailed came from the southward.

From the lack of any focus of its own and of any highway by
land or water to link the several districts even in the tidewater
zone, North Carolina had little community consciousness and
correspondingly few public men of note.[1] Such policies as
gained wide acceptance were likely to be those originating
negatively from opposition to proposals from an outside source.
In short, the community lay fallow for two centuries, only to
belie in our own day its reputation of incapacity for enlightened
public spirit.

[1] For example, a letter of Willian Hooper to James Iredell in 1785 (New York Public
Library *Bulletin*, III, 148) lamented the lack of capable men to fill the public offices
and expressed a hope that the colleges and academies would erelong supply better
material.

The tale of South Carolina is in remarkable contrast to that of her northward sister, partly because the main impulse for her settlement came from a tropical source. An extraordinary congestion in Barbados, the most easterly of the West Indies, had made that little island a potential mother of new colonies. To it had gone thousands of English during the Cromwellian disturbances who had instituted a simple farming régime. But a recourse to sugar production had shortly brought a swarm of slaves and an engrossment of land into plantation units, which pinched out many small proprietors and impelled some larger ones to look abroad for greater spaces. Thus it came about that Sir John Colleton, returning to England from residence in Barbados, enlisted six powerful courtiers to join him and Sir William Berkeley in a Carolina proprietary venture. Procuring in 1663 the charter desired, and a second within two years enlarging their area, they published proposals to grant lands on the usual quitrent basis and to erect a popular government. Finding little response to this gesture, the Lords Proprietors within a few years bestirred themselves that others might be stirred. At considerable expense they sent an explorer along the southerly coast to learn the topography,[1] and then assembled several score colonists and sent them forth by way of Ireland and Barbados to gather recruits for a settlement. Seeds of rice and indigo, roots of ginger, and stalks of sugar cane were among the things to be taken from the tropics for an experiment farm. At the same time the governor was directed to "provide for the belly by planting store of provisions" before seeking market crops on an export scale. Repeated instructions, furthermore, insisted upon the fostering of town life.

The nucleus of South Carolina was duly planted in 1670 on Charleston Harbor, though the first site of "Charles Town" soon gave place to the sandy neck across Ashley River where the city now stands. The settlement gained permanence and expansion through slow immigration from England, Scotland, Wales and Ireland, New England and New York, Germany and Switzerland, and notably from France and the West Indies.

[1] This report is printed in the *Colonial Records of North Carolina*, I, 118-138.

Some of these elements, particularly the thrifty Huguenots on Cooper and Santee rivers, maintained cultural distinction for a time in separate clusters, but a gradual blending despite much dissension brought all the white people eventually into a single integrated community, with the West Indian element contributing perhaps the major features in law and custom.

For two or three decades the livelihood of the people was drawn from Indian trade, forest industries, and farming on a small scale without any staple of note, for there was no fruitage to the experiments ordered by the proprietors at the outset. In this phase prosperity was meager, and funds for any large importation of Negroes were lacking.   But in the closing decade of the century a new trial of rice proved so strikingly successful that it became the main reliance of industry and shaped the course of the colony's further development.

As was to be expected in such case, the new staple invited calculation of prospects by the writers of promotion pamphlets. One of these argued in 1712 that an English farmer with £100 at command above the cost of passage could count upon a net earning of £40 annually from the outset, and one with £1000 would prosper proportionately.   In either instance the advice was to buy and carry English goods, which would as a rule find a market at fifty per cent profit in the colony; then to invest these proceeds in land and live stock, tools and provisions, good Negro men at £45 each and Indian slave women at £18, or perhaps Negro women at £37.   Assuming a cultivation of only three acres per laborer, two of these in rice to yield each a thousand pounds for market at fifteen shillings per hundredweight and the third acre supplying sustenance, it was argued that thirty shillings might be allowed for clothing each slave without impairing the forty per cent return upon the investment.   It was assumed that the farmer would labor in the rice field with his Negro man, but of course not the planter with his thirty-three slaves.[1]

[1] [John Norris] *Profitable Advice for Rich and Poor in a Dialogue, or Discourse between James Freeman, a Carolina Planter, and Simon Question, a West-Country Farmer* (London, 1712), 84–95. For this item I am indebted to Professor Verner W. Crane.

Though this calculation ignored contingencies, including acclimatization, it was far less fantastic than many other feats of promotive reckoning in the period. Rice, in fact, gave the best opportunity for industrial profit which America then afforded. The extent to which it was embraced is told by the growth of the population and the changing of the racial ratio. About 1708 the number of the Negroes overtook that of the whites when each was reported at some four thousand souls. Thereafter for a lifetime or two the whites tended to double, but the blacks to treble, every twelve or fifteen years. The culture of rice was extended to favorable spots up the coast as far as the Cape Fear River, where Wilmington eventually rose as a daughter of Charleston, and down the coast as fast and as far as conditions permitted. This expansion, together with blunders in diplomacy, brought war with the Yemassee Indians in 1715, which drove the tribal remnant into Florida and on the other hand wrecked the proprietary control of the province.

Thanks partly to their own errors, the Lords Proprietors had never had an easy or a profitable task. In their vigorous early years their sagacity proved at fault in the promulgation of the "fundamental constitutions", which provided for manors and baronies, authorized provincial orders of nobility under the style of landgraves and caciques, and set forth a most cumbrous form of government. Insistence upon this régime against the constant opposition of the settlers complicated the relations, which were difficult at best. Old age brought no increase of wisdom to the proprietors who survived; inheritance or purchase of shares by younger persons failed to enlighten the policy; and recurrent confusion bred belief in English government circles as well as among the settlers that a proprietary board was a useless encumbrance. The Yemassee war, together with operations against Blackbeard, Bonnet and other pirates on the coast, raised financial problems and brought an impasse which provoked the people in 1719 to repudiate the Proprietors and petition the crown to take them under its direct authority. In response to this peaceful revolt a royal governor was promptly sent to take charge. There still remained the question of title to public lands and quitrents. As to seven of the shares this was adjusted by royal purchase in 1729. Lord Carteret, afterwards Earl Granville, who refused to join in the sale, had his one-eighth undivided interest converted after a time into a broad zone along the Virginia boundary as an individual landholding. This brought him and his heirs little profit, though it embarrassed the conduct of public affairs in North Carolina through the rest of the colonial period.

*   *   *   *   *

On the coast of South Carolina the peculiar pattern assumed by the community was determined not by the plans of authority but by the lie of the land and water and the requirements of the rice crop. This throve not upon the sandy spread which filled most of the country but upon the muck of the swamps which lay in strips and patches along the streams great and small. For nearly a hundred years the cultivation was chiefly of inland swamps on the minor streams where water, so useful in this amphibious crop, could be had in times of need from reservoirs made by damming rainfall or brook water at higher levels. It was only in the latter half of the eighteenth century that the tidal swamps bordering the greater channels were found more advantageous and the main bulk of rice production shifted to the river fronts. Meanwhile a second staple was added.

The traditional accounts giving details of the introduction of rice culture as to time, place and personnel have now been discredited; but concerning indigo the record survives in authentic documents.[1] Eliza Lucas accomplished this innovation before emerging from her teens. Her father, Colonel George Lucas, after long official service in the West Indies, carried his invalid wife to South Carolina for relief from the tropic heat and settled the family on "Wappoo" plantation close to Charleston. Outbreak of war with Spain called him back to his post as governor of Antigua and left Eliza in charge at Wappoo. Now Eliza, whether from schooling in

[1] Harriott H. Ravenel, *Eliza Pinckney* (New York, 1896), 7, 104–106. Eliza Lucas married Charles Pinckney before her service regarding indigo was completed.

England or from contacts elsewhere, or perhaps from inborn genius and energy, was not only diligent in routine but alert for beneficial service. Her father, encouraging her interest in economic botany among other things, sent indigo seed to her in 1741 ; and next year she raised some plants to maturity. This had been done in the province forty years before, without sequel. But Lucas now sent a West Indian experienced in extracting the dyestuff from the leaves of the plant, to test the feasibility of this at Wappoo. Though the grade of the product was low, the result was deemed a success and was perhaps in part responsible for an act of the provincial assembly in 1744 offering bounties to encourage the production of wine, silk, olive oil, flax, hemp, wheat, barley, cotton, indigo and ginger. Within two years afterward indigo was grown so widely, from seed distributed from Wappoo, that the frugal assembly discontinued the bounty; but the British Parliament in 1748, responding to petitions from Carolina planters and English dyers, established a bounty upon this product throughout the empire. A few years after this Moses Lindo removed from London to Charleston, as an expert in grading indigo, and taught the planters how to produce a high quality. The bounty and the market returns enabled many planters to double their capital every few years; and before the close of the colonial period indigo was rivaling rice as a source of prosperity. American independence, of course, brought the loss of the British bounty; and ravages by grasshoppers and caterpillars contributed to wreck this industry before the end of the century. Production on a small scale continued in some quarters for several decades, mainly from "wild" plants; but recourse to cotton virtually eliminated indigo from the list of American staples.

Yielding a price of three or four or five shillings per pound, indigo could bear a long haul to market in vehicles of any sort. But rice, at two or threepence per pound for the milled grain, must have cheap access. For this there was happily a network of streams and inlets along the island-fringed coast for boating produce and supplies. But in contrast with the deep channels of tidewater Virginia, these Carolina waterways would not admit ocean-going craft. There was thus no peddling by ship captains, but instead an active plying of local barges from plantation landings to ports on deep harbors. Georgetown and Beaufort handled small shares of the trade, but Charleston was by far the main point of concentration.

The lowlands of South Carolina, in fact, had their affairs focused in Charleston in such degree as to make the whole district in some sense a city-state. Not only were commerce and shipping centered there, but for a long time all activities of government. As a curious evidence of this, until the upheaval of 1719 the town constituted the only polling place. Well-to-do planters, furthermore, fell early into the practice of resorting thither for the summers to escape the curse of malaria which awaited all non-immunes in the vicinity of the rice fields; and those of pronounced wealth added a winter sojourn to patronize the balls and races and participate in the manifold private activities of an urban social season. Thus the greater planters erected town houses and occupied them for perhaps the larger half of the year, contributing a polish of manner and a conservatism in public policy which a mere commercial population would hardly have developed.

Though its people hardly exceeded fifteen thousand in 1790, and half the number were Negroes, Charleston was then perhaps the most urbane of American cities, with a notable semi-public library, thriving bookstores, excellent newspapers, mantua makers and milliners in touch with Paris fashions, a thronged race course, dancing assemblies, and easy-mannered men's clubs. No golf course appears of record in this period; but there were enough Scots merchants in the town to make it presumable that the clubs in Savannah and Augusta at the end of the century had a prototype in Charleston.[1]

[1] In the *Columbian Museum and Savannah Advertiser*, October 10, 1797, is the following notice: "*Golf Club*. The members are particularly requested to be punctual in their attendance on Wednesday next, the 11th inst., at their Marquee on the East Common, in order to transact the important business which is allotted for the first day's meeting of the club for the season. Dinner will be served at the usual hour." And in the Augusta *Herald*, April 9, 1800: "The Members of the *Golf Club* are requested to meet at Mrs. M'Laws this evening at 7 o'clock."

The city was fortunate in the detail of its location. At the point of the peninsula and for some distance on either flank, shoal water forbade the building of wharves and made the neighborhood a residential district, which it remains to the present day,[1] with handsome dwellings fronting upon the blue waters of the bay. The wharves and the mercantile streets lie in midtown. It is as if in the case of New York City the water front near the Battery were bordered by balconied dwellings in gardens, and the business district began only toward Brooklyn Bridge. But apart from their having been founded in the same seventeenth century upon similar points between parallel streams, these two cities yield contrasts, not likenesses. New York, having begun after two drowsy centuries to capture the whole continent as its hinterland, has grown with ever-accelerating speed, wrecking old buildings to crowd new ones more closely, and razing these in turn that novel structures may rise to heights unexampled. The result is a congestion of traffic and a pinnacled skyline undreamed of before this latter day of steel frames and electric elevators. Not only would a Dutch gable be lost, had one survived by some caprice, but the church spires are made naught by the sky-scrapers which convert the streets into canyons. Charleston, on the other hand, reached an apex of its importance long ago, and has changed so little since that its flavor to-day is mainly that of the eighteenth century. As a rule its buildings are not as tall as their embowering trees; and the spire of St. Michael's remains a landmark for the few sailors who seek the port. Wreckage by tornado and earthquake, fire and armed occupation has been remedied from time to time by new construction; but the town wears an air of age so pronounced that one is a little disappointed to find no substantial remnant, as in Quebec, of moated walls or crenelated gates.

Charleston is distinctive in the plan and placement of its dwellings. Quite frequently they stand with ends abutting

[1] A historical map of the city, along with Mayor William A. Courtenay's centennial address, is in the Charleston *Year Book* for 1883. The general theme of South Carolina history is told in the writings of David Ramsay, Charles J. Rivers, Edward McCrady and W. Roy Smith. For Charleston in particular see Mrs. St. Julien Ravenel, *Charleston, the Place and the People* (New York, 1906).

the streets and their fronts to be seen full-face only from their gardens.   Many rise to three high-ceiled stories above their basements, with only a single room's depth except for their double-decked piazzas.   Thus, on a street running north and south, a house will front south rather than face the thoroughfare.   A door at the street admits a visitor to the piazza, while the front door at the middle of the façade still awaits him.   The main body of the house has a length about thrice its depth; and this is prolonged by a lessened structure containing service quarters and perhaps the dining room.   At the southern limit of the tree-studded garden stands a neighbor's house, with its end likewise against the street, its rear to the north and its galleries commanding its own garden to the south.   This pattern affords windows on three sides of nearly all the rooms, to invite the breeze; it shades the lower stories from the glaring southerly sun; and it gives privacy to sitters on the gallery as against wayfarers.   The homes of such grandees as the Brewtons, Heywards and Ravenels might present broad façades to the street, behind their palms and oleanders; but mere substantial citizens had no qualms in restricting the public perspective to secure seclusion, shade and much-wanted coolness.

Charleston and the rural parishes thereabout are also distinctive in dialect.   The white children for example address their parents as "papa" and "mamma", stressing the second syllable and flattening the vowel to the value of *a* in *man* or *pan*.   And *i* sounds are uttered with partly rounded lips, giving an effect of blended *i, o* and *u*.   The speech of the Negro field hands reflects these features, of course, yet it differs from that of the master class much more than a low dialect usually contrasts with nice utterance in the same locality.   The "Gullah" spoken by these blacks has a staccato tone, a frequency of elision, a confusion of genders and occasional vocabulary peculiarities which make it almost as variant as pidgin English from the norm of Anglo-American speech.[1]

[1] The Gullah dialect is analyzed by John Bennett in the *South Atlantic Quarterly*, VII, 332–347 and VIII, 39–52; again examined and illustrated in Ambrose E. Gonzales, *The Black Border* (Columbia, S. C., 1922); and again in Reed Smith, *Gullah* (*University of South Carolina Publication*, 1927).

The Negroes on the coast of Georgia speak much the same Gullah as those of South Carolina; but the whites have little trace of Charlestonian accent. From this an inference may be drawn that the slaves for early settlement below the Savannah were largely taken from the Carolina plantations, while the whites mostly came from different sources. This inference is reinforced by the fact that Savannah dwellings are of diverse types, reflecting virtually no Charleston influence.

❊   ❊   ❊   ❊   ❊

The founding of Georgia was a Utopian project framed as the first embodiment of modern philanthropy. James Oglethorpe happened to visit a friend who was in prison for debt; and horror-struck by the foul conditions, he procured a parliamentary investigation and then a statute facilitating a debtors' jail delivery. Some ten thousand men were set free, many of them only to become vagrants for lack of employ. Learning that a considerable bequest for charity at large had been left by one King, a London hatter, Oglethorpe enlisted other men of public spirit and prominent position in support of a plan to procure this and other funds to establish a new colony for the double purpose of affording unfortunates a new start in life and at the same time extending British dominions at the expense of Spain.[1] After much running to and fro, and a deal of political maneuver, a charter was procured from the crown in 1732 vesting a zone below the Savannah River in the Georgia Board, not as proprietors but as trustees. The board then appealed to the public for donations; and though it got more prayer books, pamphlets and pills than pounds sterling, it sent forth a shipload of settlers in the fall of the same year, with Oglethorpe in personal charge.

By dint of jockeying in Parliament the board procured grants in aid from the royal treasury, year after year, generally

[1] Since Charles C. Jones published his elaborate *History of Georgia* (Boston, 1883), the *Colonial Records of Georgia* have been issued by the State, and the Historical Manuscripts Commission of Great Britain has printed the *Diary of Viscount Percival, afterward First Earl of Egmont*, which throw new light upon the founding and career of the colony.

at the rate of £8000, and a regiment of troops to guard the Florida frontier. The trustees meanwhile examined applicants for colonization and sent forward such as could show presumption of honest character and an inability for English livelihood. Recruits were also accepted from among Protestant exiles from Salzburg in Austria, and indeed from the needy at large. A few "gentlemen colonists" went at their own expense, and some of these carried servants; but the main bulk was of settlers "on the charity", each family to receive a town lot and a hut upon it, a garden plot near by and a small farm in the vicinity, a cow, a sow, tools, seed and sustenance until they should become self-supporting. The trustees provided grapevines and mulberry trees from a public nursery, and silkworms along with industrial instruction and copious regulation in the affairs of life. They granted land in restricted tenure so that habitual debtors might not mortgage their real estate; they prohibited imports of rum, to keep the people sober, and of slaves, to make them industrious. No representative assembly was authorized, for the trustees considered themselves wiser than their beneficiaries. Oglethorpe, as long as he remained in the colony, was "a father to his people"; and when he returned home the paternalism was not materially diminished. Complaints erelong became rife that silk and wine could not be produced; that slave labor was essential for any crop; that rum punch was "very wholesome in this climate" and its deprivation a cruel hardship.

When the trustees, attributing steadily the lack of prosperity to the dearth of thrift among the former ne'er-do-wells, rejected all petitions for change of régime, the colony became distraught. Even the clergy lost poise. John Wesley fell into a quarrel and shook the dust of Georgia from his feet, and George Whitefield, obsessed by his plan for a great orphanage at Bethesda, denounced the trustees for debarring slaves from its service. Only the Salzburgers at Ebenezer and the Highland Scots at Darien took things uncomplainingly. The English at Savannah were loud in protest at all things; and when convinced that memorials were of no avail, they began to forsake the colony. Whither they went no man can say, though presumably most of them simply crossed the river into South Carolina. In any case, the population of Georgia shrank from some five thousand souls in 1737 to barely five hundred by 1742. The trustees for a time still clung to their restrictions; but before the middle of the century they winked at the introduction of slaves, they permitted liquors to be imported, and they yielded full title to lands. The benevolent plans had been wrecked by human and terrestrial nature. At length Parliament stopped its subsidy and in 1751 the trustees resigned their charter. After an interval Georgia was given the standard organization of a royal province, whereupon a new growth, already begun in response to the trustees' relaxations, put the colony upon a prosperous footing. Rice crops rippled in the breeze on the right bank of the Savannah as on the left, and along the Ogeechee and the Altamaha. Indigo spread likewise from Carolina, and slave ships plowed the Georgia waters as they did those to the south and the north. The people now were mostly a new people, happy to live, as they may have put it, with no peculiar institutions. They had a legislative assembly, they might run for office; they might litigate over land; they might call themselves their own masters and be masters of slaves with no captious trustees to say them nay. So content were the Georgians, blessed as they were with a particularly good governor in Sir James Wright, who himself operated a dozen rice plantations, that they found it hard to develop new grievances. Had not a group of New England families established themselves about the middle of the coast line Georgia might not have joined in the demand for American independence.

CHAPTER IV

REDSKINS AND LATINS

ENGLISH colonial charters in the main granted land in belts across the continent. This was with no thought that Connecticut or Carolina would have need for a second front on the Pacific, but merely because intervening landmarks were unknown and there was no specific occasion to find or use them. The crown could afford to be generous without western limit in allotting mere permits of exploitation. Such obstructions as might be met were to be handled by the Proprietors or the settlers, unless and until royal authority should see fit to intervene.

America was not as empty as the charters seemed to imply. A native population was to be encountered nearly everywhere, — pagan, primitive and unprepared as to policy when confronted by Englishmen on their shores. The purposes of these palefaces were as mysterious as their ships and their guns. They roamed about seeking a yellow metal, wishing merely to make discs of it to keep in their pockets, not rings to hang in their ears. They would exchange beautiful beads, excellent iron hatchets and irresistible fire water for deerskins and beaver, corn and meat, and even for the privilege of using land. They would sometimes ingratiatingly give their delectable, befuddling beverage to chieftains as a mere token of good will. But they were bafflingly strange. One might be a weakling under torture and yet possess a strong medicine enabling him to move a boat upon the water by means of a piece of cloth instead of laboring with a paddle, or to make a horse bear his weight or a cow to yield milk. And they set great store upon boundaries on land, and upon scratches on paper which they said meant the same thing yesterday, to-day and always. And when at request a chief touched the quill to make his mark at the end of a writing, it might bring trouble for years to come, for the whites were likely to say it was a treaty of cession by which the tribe had agreed not merely to let the Virginians live beside them, as the chieftain thought, but that the village was to be moved and the English be left there alone. And these people had a passion for killing trees continually; for making more tobacco than they could smoke, and sending most of it away in their ships; for working, always working, mostly at tasks fit only for squaws, and for getting other white men and black men and even red men to work for them. They rarely moved their houses or changed their wives, and they would eat little more in harvest or after a kill than if there were no reason to gorge themselves. Their restraints and their lack of restraint were equally unaccountable; and their numbers were ever swelling and their demands continuing for more and more land. They were, in truth, not neighborly neighbors, blending the colony with the tribe; but they were firm, and on occasion impolite in living their own lives and crowding the red men out. This brought battle now and then, and a few blond scalps to dangle; but in war, too, the whites were unseasonable and unreasonable. They would not wait for Indian summer; and when once they took the path they were not content with raids, ambushes and surprise attacks, but they would persist in a campaign under stanch command long after sensibly spasmodic folk had grown weary.

Thus, we may fancy, thought the Rappahannocks and the Susquehannocks, the Tuscaroras and the Yemassees, at length concluding that their first welcome had been unwise and wrecking themselves in efforts to drive the invaders out again. Meanwhile trade had penetrated to tribes far distant, even to those on what were to be famed as the western waters. For this purpose each colony was the center of a sphere of influence. Virginia competed with Maryland and Pennsylvania, regardless of colonial boundaries. To the southwest Cadwallader Jones on the Potomac, William Byrd on the James and Abraham Wood on the Appomattox sent pack trains to the Cherokee country and beyond, to such effect that among the remoter tribesmen all the British were long styled Virginians. But upon the founding of Charleston her merchants promptly began to contest the field; and by 1725 the Carolina commissioner of Indian affairs could report from a Cherokee village: "The Virginia Traders . . . I am Certain cannot do any prejudice to Ours in the way of Trade, there not being above two or three of them and their goods no ways Sortable or Comparable to ours." [1] Georgia in turn sought to divert the trade into a new channel by promoting Augusta to eclipse the near-by Carolina posts and by requiring licenses of all traders entering the limits of the colony. South Carolina promptly made official protest, saying that a royal charter could hardly give control among tribesmen who "have never owed any Allegiance or acknowledged the Sovereignty of the Crown of Great-Britain or any Prince in Europe, but have indiscriminately visited and traded with the French, Spaniards and English as they judged it most for their advantage." [2] The controversy thus initiated was the beginning of a lasting antagonism between the two governments. Meanwhile obstructions as against all expansion from Atlantic shores were spreading from Spanish and French headquarters on the Gulf of Mexico.

❋ ❋ ❋ ❋ ❋

The Southern zone of the present United States was a land of contention among the maritime powers.[3] The English knew it as Carolina, whose chartered limits extended below St.

[1] Letter of Col. George Chicken, in N. D. Mereness, ed., *Travels in the American Colonies* (New York, 1916), 137.

[2] *Report of the Committee appointed to examine into the Proceedings of the People of Georgia with Respect to the Province of South Carolina and the Disputes subsisting between them* (Charles-Town, 1736).

[3] The theme of international rivalries is copiously told in H. E. Bolton, ed., *Arredondo's Historical Proof of Spain's Title to Georgia* (Berkeley, Cal., 1925); V. W. Crane, *The Southern Frontier, 1670–1732* (Durham, N. C., 1929); P. J. Hamilton, *Colonial Mobile* (Boston, 1896, enlarged ed., 1910); Mrs. N. M. M. Surrey, *The Commerce of Louisiana, 1699–1763* (New York, 1916); A. P. Whitaker, *The Spanish-American Frontier, 1783–1795* (Boston, 1927). Indian tribal affairs are treated encyclopedically in various reports and bulletins of the Bureau of American Ethnology.

Augustine. The Spaniards called it Florida, including with the peninsula an indefinite expanse of the mainland; the French applied the name Louisiana to the middle of the Gulf coast and sought to stretch their control north, east and west.

Spain could claim priority, for whatever that might be worth. Ponce de Leon had sought youth and wealth in the "land of flowers" in 1513, to find death instead. Projects of Ayllon, Narvaez, DeVaca and DeSoto followed, with like failure. It was only when France attempted a settlement at Port Royal in the present South Carolina that a new Spanish expedition in 1565 established St. Augustine. Under its founder Menendez, this post began a promising career after the Spanish fashion. A garrison held firm possession while priests, with soldiers at their call, brought such Indians as they could under their tutelary discipline. Missions dotted the coastal islands in a province of Guale, within the present Georgia, and a province of Santa Elena, lying beyond. But these aborigines were occasionally recalcitrant enough to kill their priestly custodians, whereupon punitive expeditions would slaughter some, enslave others for sale in the West Indies, and reduce the remainder to Christian submission again. As decades passed, this task required such frequent repetition that enterprises in Santa Elena and then Guale were discontinued, and St. Augustine itself was maintained only for the protection of the treasure fleets plying from Vera Cruz *via* Havana to Cadiz. Meanwhile missions had been founded about the Suwanee River; and when it was learned that the French were planning to plant Louisiana the Spaniards occupied and fortified Pensacola. In the soft winters and hard summers year after year there was little to chronicle in these barren lands except forays by white soldiers and Indian auxiliaries, trivial episodes in the recurring conflict of empires. Spain did not develop Florida, but merely retained it.

As to Texas, a thin series of garrisons, missions and cattle ranches was extended from Mexico. There was no wealth of ore to tempt exploitation; the Comanches and Apaches were not easily subjugable, whether by priests or soldiers; and there were few colonists available until Stephen F. Austin led "American" settlers thither in the nineteenth century. On the whole, the Spanish régime within the present United States proved singularly inept and inert. Its efforts to reduce Indians to the status of passive Christian farm laborers were thoroughly thwarted by the British and French cultivation of the peltry trade.

＊　　　＊　　　＊　　　＊　　　＊

Louisiana was initiated to secure an ice-free vent supplementing the St. Lawrence River and to strengthen French domination in the great continental interior as against the British control already in prospect through commercial penetration. After LaSalle's disastrous expedition in 1685 Iberville made a settlement on the Mississippi coast; and from this headquarters Bienville founded Mobile in 1710 and built interior forts near Natchez and Montgomery. The chief concern thus far was Indian trade, with a minor interest in missionary work. But now came the Mississippi Bubble, promoted in France by that most ingenious, engaging and plausible of Scots, John Law. The court and the country were captivated by his prescription of paper money as a financial panacea and his device of using fictitious funds for exploiting all the far corners of the earth. Banks, commercial companies and colonies quickly fell into the grasp of his "system", which was expected to bring magic success in every enterprise where failure or stagnation had prevailed before. To Louisiana all colonists were sent who could be persuaded; a deficit of decent folk was filled by transporting felons and prostitutes; and Europeans were supplemented by shiploads of slaves from Africa. Lavish grants of land were issued by Law's company to many applicants, including a huge tract to Law himself, who sent some hundreds of Germans thither in apparent expectation that precious ores would be found in every rock and bounteous crops leap from the soil. New Orleans, founded in 1718 at a spot previously judged uninhabitable, became in imagination a metropolis overnight and in fact for the time being a busy camp. The speculation in France collapsed in 1720; and in Louisiana humdrum life resumed sway. Law's Germans, decimated by hardships on the Arkansas, drifted back to the Mississippi, where they were settled again as peasant proprietors on reaches of the river which are locally known as the "German Coast" to the present day.

Having reverted to royal control, the colonials tilled small fields behind low private levees which were adequate so long as upstream the floods were free to spread across the whole alluvial expanse and thus to lose their crests. But lacking the stimulus of a staple, agriculture yielded again to Indian trade as a main source of profit. The posts of Natchitoches on the Red River, Cahokia at the mouth of the Illinois, Vincennes on the Wabash and Fort Assumption at the present site of Memphis procured their goods and sent out their peltries through New Orleans, while a fort on the Tombigbee as well as that on the Alabama fed the trade of Mobile. In short, the river channels were utilized everywhere to radiate French trade and influence.

❈ ❈ ❈ ❈ ❈

The region between the Savannah River and the Mississippi was occupied by four major groups of Indians, distinguished mainly by differences of language but organized more or less as tribal confederacies and often spoken of as "nations." The Cherokees dwelt in the mountain vales of Carolina, Tennessee and Georgia; the Creeks or Muscogees, with the Seminoles as an appendage, were spread from eastern Georgia and Florida to central Alabama; the Choctaws held sway from the Tombigbee River to the Mississippi; and the Chickasaws north of them.[1] Their villages, with almost one accord, lay clustered upon stream banks where canoes might ply and fish be trapped and

[1] The first three of these each comprised fifteen or twenty thousand souls about the middle of the eighteenth century. The Chickasaws were much less numerous. Some of the best accounts of Indian life and trade are assembled in Mereness, ed., *Travels in the American Colonies*. Other valuable writings are James Adair, *History of the American Indians* (London, 1775), which is in part a relation of his own experiences as a trader; the papers of Peter Chester, in the *Mississippi Historical Society Collections*, Cenrenary Series, V, 1–183; and the *Letters of Benjamin Hawkins* (*Georgia Historical Society Collections*, IX).

where bottom clearings would yield good crops of corn. The chase, never a sole reliance for livelihood, was more and more supplemented by tillage and animal husbandry, the traders as well as the missionaries acting as agents of civilization.

Where trade was well regulated, a representative of some house in a commercial center dwelt permanently in each Indian village. He was likely to become an adviser to the chiefs in statecraft and fortification, a creditor to the huntsmen, and a pattern of plenteous living to the tribal folk, who regarded him and his like with no stolid unconcern. His house, an arsenal as well as a store, overtopped the native huts. His cows yielded milk, his chickens eggs, his peach trees fruit, his garden pulse; his hogs furnished pork, woolen clothing warmed his body, a chimney kept his lodging free of smoke, and perhaps Negro slaves tilled his fields — all of which engaged Indian approval and gradual adoption. Feasts grew more frequent and famines less familiar. Thoughtful elderly tribesmen found themselves of two minds. They rejoiced that life was more comfortable, but they sometimes lamented the lapse of archery which made the hunters and warriors wholly dependent upon European supplies of arms and ammunition; and they were not unaware of the damage wrought by white men's diseases and liquors.

The trader's house in common practice was kept by a squaw, and sometimes more than one, who bore him children as a matter of course; and by definite understanding these children, though reared more or less by their white fathers, were to be members of the tribe. Hence a crop of half-breeds and quarter-breeds, many of whom were to be reckoned with afterward as peculiarly talented "Indian" chiefs. Other traders, where and when regulation was lax, lived more or less itinerant lives, exchanging liquors and ammunition, hatchets and hunting knives, beads and blankets for pelts, wherever a market might be found. These also begot half-breed progeny but assumed no paternal duties.

Tribesmen and chieftains reared in the wigwams found it hard to grasp the meaning of such European diplomacy as reached into their woods or to give their own governments as much authority as English or French negotiators desired them to possess. Thus when Colonel Chicken, commissioner of South Carolina, exhorted the Cherokee chiefs in 1725 to keep their young men under control, "they made Answer That is what ought to be and that they intend to come into that Method, otherwise they will never be a People." But when shortly afterward he chided King Crow for his failure to maintain discipline, "He informed me that the people would work as they pleased and go to Warr when they pleased, notwithstanding his saying all he could to them, and that they were not like White Men." [1]

But not every plan of relieving Indian instability would meet official indorsement. Not that, for example, which Albert Priber carried from his native Saxony to nurse among the Cherokees. Priber was a cultured Utopian socialist wishing to found a model republic. Conceiving the noble natural red men to be the most eligible citizens, he made himself one with the Cherokee folk, adopting their dress, learning their language and soon shaping their policy. His program was elaborate. As minor matters he made steelyards for his neighbors and taught them weights and measures as a check upon tricky dealers, and he sought arrangements for traffic down the Tennessee as an offset to the Carolina trade. But the hope of his heart was to combine the Cherokees, Creeks and others in a league of peace, equality and liberty. He would have no bondage, even in the form of marriage; but children were to be in charge of the State, and their parents were to live together no longer than they liked. Property was to be communally held, and no man's house was to be finer than another's. Thus linking Lycurgus and Lenin, Priber sought office in his inchoate commonwealth as an honor to himself and a service to mankind; and at length he sent a letter on behalf of the Cherokees to the government of South Carolina, signed by himself as prime minister. This made him in the thought of Carolinians a menace to be removed. The Cherokees warmly protected

[1] Chicken's journal, in Mereness, 130, 153.

him against arrest; but at length he was apprehended in 1743, after a dozen years of unique career, and he died a prisoner in the power of another Utopian — with a difference — James Oglethorpe.[1] Savage life resumed its wonted course. Not long after Priber's death an agent of South Carolina reported to the governor:

"With regard to my preventing the Indians here from going when and where they please, to Warr or otherwise, I don't conceive a Possibility of it. Presents and Entertainment are ye only means of bringing them to the fort, and . . . it [is] impossible for me or any others without Rum to be very useful on any such occasions." [2]

❋   ❋   ❋   ❋   ❋

Aboriginal paths, following watersheds wherever feasible in avoidance of muddy going, had long since been widened from Charleston and Augusta north and west to give passage to laden horses. Tinkling pack trains of the Scots and English wound their way for half a thousand miles to compete with the silent canoes of the French. These French were the better diplomats, for they took easily to native ways; but the British, having a cheaper supply of goods and more freedom from government control, were more effective traders, carrying their packs even to the banks of the Mississippi.

Armed conflict was latent in the situation, influenced as it was by the rivalry of Old World empires. The earlier French and Indian wars were indecisive; but the last of them transformed the political map of America. When Canada was taken by Great Britain in the treaty of 1763 Louisiana was made of so little avail that France gave the province to Spain, while Spain ceded East and West Florida to Britain. So things remained until 1783 when Britain, forced to recognize the independence of the United States, returned Florida to Spain,

[1] Verner W. Crane, "A Lost Utopia of the First American Frontier", in the *Sewanee Review*, XXVII, 48–61.

[2] Letter of George Cadogan, Fort Moore, March 27, 1751, to Governor James Glen. Official manuscript copy in "Indian Book, 1750–1752" in the South Carolina Historical Commission at Columbia.

although some thousands of Loyalists had flocked thither from the rebel colonies.

Among the refugees two Scots, Panton and Leslie, gave such timely financial aid to the new Spanish administration that their partnership was granted monopoly rights in Indian trade at St. Augustine and was permitted to ramify with branches at St. Marks, Pensacola, Mobile and New Orleans. A silent partner in this firm was Alexander McGillivray, who exploited energetically the savage and civilized opportunities of a Scottish-French-Spanish-Creek quarter-breed. Educated by his uncle, a Presbyterian minister in Charleston, he settled a prosperous plantation with Negro gangs on the Coosa River, and built separate houses for his plural wives. A warrior of some talent and a diplomat of extraordinary duplicity, he played the Spanish, British, and American governments against one another for Creek advantage and personal profit. Himself a speculator in lands, he repelled encroachments by the white borderers of Georgia and Tennessee, and in 1790 he led a delegation of chieftains in gorgeous finery to New York, where a treaty was made by which the United States guaranteed to the "Creek nation" all the lands within the United States lying south and west of the boundary then established. Thereafter until his death in 1793 he held a brigadier general's commission in the American army, perhaps without ceasing to draw secret pay as a British colonel and a Spanish general.

A rival of McGillivray was General William Augustus Bowles, a white native of Maryland and by turns or simultaneously a British army officer and an adopted chief among the Creeks, though during an interval of private life he was a painter and an actor. An election of Bowles by his fellow chiefs to be commander in chief of the Creek armies earned him McGillivray's enmity, which was perpetuated by divergence of policy. Bowles forbade petty raids upon white settlements and he stood firm against land speculation. When war seemed imminent between Britain and Spain he carried a party of Creek and Cherokee chiefs to make an alliance at London; and as a means of heightening Indian power he planned a series of ports on the Gulf coast under a Creek flag but free to the trade of all nations. To check his designs the Spaniards seized him in 1792 and sent him as a prisoner to Madrid and thence to Manila. Liberated after four years, he resumed his functions as a Creek chief and a British partisan. Captured again in 1804, his career as a diplomat, merchant and soldier of fortune was ended next year by death in a dungeon of Morro Castle in Havana harbor.

Semi-barbaric also was George Galphin, thriving as a trader, traveling much among the tribes, serving as interpreter in diplomatic negotiations, entertaining red and white lavishly at his home "Silver Bluff" on the Carolina side of the Savannah River, and exerting among the Creeks an influence rivaling that of any chieftain. Less flamboyant, and by the same token more typical of those prospering at headquarters from barbaric trade, was Macartan Campbell, who removed from Charleston to Augusta to follow slowly the advance of the frontier. He lived and died a genteel townsman with a white wife and children; and he cannily put his profits into a plantation in an adjoining county. We shall have glimpses of this in a later chapter when it was under the administration of his grandson, George Noble Jones.

Exports of deerskins [1] from Charleston in the early decades of the eighteenth century attained the number of some fifty thousand a year without reducing the great herds which browsed in the forests and savannas; but the doubling of this volume before the close of the century, while the Pensacola trade was increasing with still greater speed, began a decimation of game which impelled the red men to rely more upon tillage and less upon the chase. This tended to fix the tribesmen in permanent steadings and to make them increasingly loath to yield their lands. The nineteenth century brought an impasse which was broken only by the military strokes of Andrew Jackson and the relentless will of the Georgia people.

---

[1] A dearth of beaver in the southern latitudes made materials for leather, rather than furs, the staple of this trade. Sometimes captives reduced to slavery swelled its volume.

When Britain conquered Acadia in 1754 and renamed it New Scotland in Latin form, she deported the French inhabitants and scattered them within her own thirteen colonies. But many of them, seeking asylum where their patois might prevail and familiar French jurisdiction be recovered, found their way to where Bayous Teche and La Fourche meander amid the Louisiana swamps. Simple folk habituated to peasant life, they were ever after called Acadians until English-speaking backwoodsmen corrupted the name into 'Cajuns. By definition they were Creoles — American-born descendants of the French — but in common parlance southern Louisiana was divided into the Creole parishes on the river and the Acadian parishes to the west.

Basil the Blacksmith, Evangeline and their kin were seeking no more trouble. But after the dynastic transfer of 1763 the Creoles at New Orleans gave the Spanish governor O'Reilly no choice but to be "bloody" in repressing their attempt to expel him. The sequel was a quietude of stagnation. After the Florida retrocession of 1783 the Gulf of Mexico was once more a Spanish lake, which meant a virtual death of trade except for that of the favored Panton, Leslie and Company with the Indians. But the French Revolution set events in train which were to stir even these stagnant waters. The mulattoes and then the blacks in Santo Domingo (Haiti) rose in espousal of *liberté, égalité, fraternité* and drove their French masters into the sea. Such of these as escaped slaughter sought refuge as widely as the Acadians had been scattered. Whether by direct migration or by removal after sojourn in Cuba, Virginia or Carolina, these San Domingans continued until about 1810 to flow into Louisiana, carrying any slaves they could still command. They had called themselves Creoles in their island home; they joined the Creoles on the Mississippi, contributing substantially to the vigor and wealth of the community. It was quite possibly a San Domingan impulse which prompted the recourse to sugar culture, which we shall discuss elsewhere.

Before the close of the century Spain yielded to pressure and relaxed her commercial restraints upon Louisiana, to the effect that the populace became so reconciled to Spanish sovereignty that rumors of impending cession either to the strange Bonaparte or to Britain or the United States brought apprehension. This gave place to dismay upon the double transfer through France to the United States in 1803. As had been feared, there came a swarm of "American" merchants, planters and adventurers, along with officials who knew nothing and seemed to care less about local customs, laws or language. The Creoles were already accustomed to a polyglot life in their muddy capital; but they deplored the prospect of becoming an enclave in an Anglo-Saxon continent.

＊   ＊   ＊   ＊   ＊

Florida has long been a land of intermittent booms, though until recent decades these were of somewhat petty scale. Under the British régime Andrew Turnbull sought fortune by settling more than a thousand Greeks, Italians and Minorcans in 1767 on plantations about New Smyrna, south of the present Daytona; but poverty of soil, rebellion among the laborers and hostility from the provincial governor dispersed the colony and sent its promoter to try his fortunes more modestly in South Carolina.[1] Retrocession to Spain then forbade enterprise until the turn of the century when relaxations of Spanish rule, together with anticipations of annexation by the United States, brought speculators from the northward to procure lands.[2] Many of these withdrew when tired of awaiting the expected transfer, while the rest yielded to the languorous climate in a *dolce far niente* existence. A report in 1817 showed only about one hundred fifty small steadings between the St. Mary's and St. John's rivers, a half-dozen cotton plantations below St. Augustine, and a wilderness beset by Seminoles, thence to Key West and Pensacola.[3] When the purchase was actually completed in 1821 the population of East Florida was reckoned at

[1] Carita Doggett, *Dr. Andrew Turnbull and the New Smyrna Colony of Florida* (Jacksonville, 1921).

[2] Savannah *Republican*, January 20, 1804; *Louisiana Gazette* (New Orleans), April 28, 1818.

[3] *National Intelligencer* (Washington), November 7, 1817.

fifteen thousand and of West Florida at five thousand, all described alike as loiterers.[1]

West Florida had been reduced in length by the inclusion of the tract beyond the Pearl River in the State of Louisiana after a revolt of its Anglo-American inhabitants at Baton Rouge in 1810. Additional segments were now lopped off to give salt-water frontages to Mississippi and Alabama, and the rest was combined with the peninsula to form a "territory" of the United States. There now came small stampedes to Apalachicola for commerce,[2] to the Tallahassee district for cotton planting and to the neighborhood of St. Augustine for the production of sugar[3] and oranges.[4] But thanks partly to the troublesome Seminoles, partly to the leanness of the soil and partly to the enervating summers, Florida prospered not much more than when under Spain or Britain or Spain again. As a foreign jurisdiction it had been a barrier to needful commerce, a base for smuggling and a refuge for fugitive slaves and outlaws. Its acquisition abated these nuisances. Thereafter Florida formed in the main a southward extension of the United States rather than an integral part of the South. And such it remains, though transformed into a winter playground, to the present day.

[1] *An original Memoir on Florida, with a general Description . . . by a Gentleman of the South* (Baltimore, 1821).

[2] *Georgia Courier* (Augusta), April 28, 1828.

[3] *Charleston City Gazette*, March 7, 1823.

[4] Groves of grafted trees had been valued as high as $5000 per acre when in 1835, after sixty years of exemption from severe frost, a stroke of zero weather killed the groves. Within two years afterward local nurseries were supplying thousands of new trees. — *Farmers' Register*, VI, 709, reprinting from the *Gardener's Magazine* an article by Alexander Gordon. St. Augustine had already thriven modestly for many years as a resort for people with maladies of throat or lungs. — *Ibid.*

CHAPTER V

FROM THE BACKWOODS TO THE BLUEGRASS

IN Australia the bush, in South Africa the veldt, in America the backwoods have long been designations of the fringes of civilization with population sparse, living conditions rugged and manners uncouth. Such were to be found in Massachusetts or Maine, Maryland or Mississippi, for backwoods quite inevitably abutted all seaboard settlements. As a rule they were occupied by means of a fairly steady local expansion, though unevenly because of uneven conditions. The Catskills, almost within sight of a New York skyscraper, are still in large degree vacant, and likewise the Dismal Swamp near Norfolk. The first and most rapid thrust inland, if one may disregard the Connecticut River towns, occurred in the middle zone between Pennsylvania and North Carolina.

The pioneers sifted into the wilderness from somewhat diverse former walks of life, to follow temporarily diverse occupations. First of all were Indian traders with white employees along with tribesmen to tend their pack trains. Close on their heels came professional hunters to compete with aborigines in killing the deer and curing their skins. When tribal bounds were approached the huntsmen stayed their steps, except for occasional poaching, while the traders pursued their way to the welcoming redskin villages. These traders, of course, did a bit of hunting on their own score, and some farming on occasion. Some of the huntsmen, when game grew scarce, bethought them to bring cattle to convert the herbage into cowhides and beef in lieu of deerskins and venison; and still other adventurers came driving their herds before them to embrace this opportunity. Here and there a seaboard planter participated, whether in person or as an absentee proprietor of cattle.   Thus the few grasslands and the many pea-vine pastures and cane-brakes came to be thinly stocked with kine ; and half-wild hogs doubtless rooted where half-wild cattle browsed.   This régime had many of the features which were later to make the plains of Texas famous, though the terminology was English, not Spanish.   "Cattle pen" was the designation of the corral together with the cabin homestead near by.   Spring round-ups were held, somewhat casually perhaps, to identify calves and give them their owners' distinctive brands ; wolves were hunted in neighborhood drives ; and horse thieves were sometimes given short shrift.

But the ranchers did not long persist in that employment merely.   The humid climate invited tillage, and the forest offered abundant material for fencing.   Farm clearings began to break the woodlands and the cabins to swarm with children. And as the traders and hunters had blazed the trail for cattle-men, so these now showed the way to throngs of pioneer farmers. There were advances and retreats, for the frontiersmen were by turns bold or panicky and the redskins, equally by turns, yielding or aggressive.

Before the whole of the Virginia Piedmont was reached by this filtration, a channeled flow came from an unexpected quarter into the Shenandoah Valley.   William Penn, the most effective of all colonial proprietor-promoters, had made Phila-delphia such a famous port of entry as to excel all others in the esteem of eighteenth-century immigrants.   But the "Friends" who were first on the ground had engrossed all the near-by lands when the crowds of German sectarians and the Scotch-Irish reached the Pennsylvania shore.   These mostly moved inland to settle in congregations where they might ; and the loom of mountains directed their drift into valleys which led southwest.   An increase of land prices by the proprietor has-tened the crossing of the Maryland border and the Potomac ; and the proprietory demands of Lord Fairfax and Robert Beverley, who had titles to large tracts in the Shenandoah, sped the movement up that valley to where the Virginia government was offering lands on most attractive terms to procure a buffer population against Indians.

In the middle third of the century, in fact, the Valley became an avenue of migration from Pennsylvania to the Piedmont of Virginia and the Carolinas, where human streams from the Delaware, the James and the Carolina ports met to "live in plenty and dirt." The Moravians and the Mennonites and the Presbyterians too dwelt more or less to themselves, though the course of years intermingled them with Quakers, Anglicans, Methodists and Baptists, despite some cherishing of clannishness.[1] Prosperity from tobacco, whiskey or cotton production or from speculation in lands brought a differentiation of wealth and a social cleavage which cut across the lines of race and religion. But before the new complexity had replaced the old, when the backwoods phase had merely begun to be outgrown, so great was the hunger for good land and abounding game that this people gave origin to a thrust over the mountains to the great basin beyond.

❋   ❋   ❋   ❋   ❋

The "long hunters" followed the trails through the Blue Ridge in search of deer. As hunters they might have let the Cumberland cliffs limit their roamings; but land companies desiring to learn of attractive regions for preëmption employed some of them as scouts and surveyors to explore the land of Kentucky, already rumored to possess extraordinary charms and to be free of Indian villages. Cumberland Gap, at the present junction of Virginia, Tennessee and Kentucky, was found in 1750 with a Cherokee path leading thence for a long

---

[1] This proclivity is illustrated in a letter from a former citizen of Lexington, Va., to his son-in-law who still dwelt there: "Are the people in and about Lexington as religious as they were some time ago? . . . Those good people [the Presbyterian clique] will not associate with the wicked (as they call them) but meet only for religious worship or socially with their religious friends. Had that been the case formerly we had yet been in ignorance, but mankind mixing in assemblies for innocent amusement cultivates friendship and civilizes the world. It makes their manners more mild and friendly and removes that sourness that superstition and bigotry leaves on the mind." Samuel McDowell to Andrew Reid, July 11, 1792, in Mary Y. Ridenbaugh's *Biography of Ephraim McDowell, M.D.* (New York, 1890), 49, 50.

distance northward; and erelong the troops under Braddock and Forbes cut roads across Pennsylvania to the Ohio. When the terrors of war were long enough past, in the late 'sixties, James Harrod from Pennsylvania, George Rogers Clark from Virginia, Daniel Boone from North Carolina and other hunters and company agents of lesser fame entered upon a race for the exploitation of the new Canaan. Some tried to find or make paths direct from the Shenandoah, but the walls of the river gorges proved too steep to yield footing and the laurel thickets too dense for penetration. Such parties therefore as did not cross the Pennsylvania ridges and canoe down the Ohio made the wide southward circuit through Cumberland Gap.

The land they found was exceedingly fair. An arriving recruit put his pen to paper:

"So Rich a Soil we had never Saw before, Covered with Clover in full Bloom. the Woods alive abounding in wild Game, turkeys so numerous that it might be said there appeared but one flock Universally Scattered in the woods. . . . it appeared that Nature in the profusion of her Bounties had spread a feast for all that lives, both for the Animal & Rational World, a Sight so delightful to our View and grateful to our feelings almost Induced us, in Immitation of Columbus in Transport to Kiss the Soil of Kentucky, as he haild & Saluted the sand on his first setting his foot on the Shores of America." [1]

No land less fair lying so remote could have drawn the human tide which in the following years flowed through the Gap and along the Wilderness Road to build steadings and stockades and hold them against onslaughts of the Shawanoes and Cherokees. Not all who began the long rough journey reached their destination. A family of Davises, having lost the way, stopped one winter night in the fork of a creek. Rising water extinguished their fire, the father was drowned while swimming the stream to bring embers from another camp, and the mother and some

[1] Felix Walker, quoted in Archibald Henderson's *The Conquest of the Old Southwest* (New York, 1920), 234. This is one of the best books in its field.

of the children died from exposure.[1]   Many another group was halted by illness or other mischance, some to dwell permanently in the mountains where they had never thought to stop. Men of wealth and caution might make full arrangements before removal.   Thus the Virginian James Ware made a tour of the "Bluegrass" region in 1784 and another five years afterward, when Indian dangers had ended.   He then sent an overseer with a parcel of slaves to build a steading and raise a food crop; and in 1791 he conducted his household to the new homestead.[2]   Poorer people must needs remove, if at all, with little or no prior arrangement.

In 1796 Moses Austin made notes of the route.   Along Powell's River in East Tennessee, "a Wagon road has lately been Open'd into and Down the Valley, and Notwithstanding the great panes and Expence, the passage is so bad that at maney of the mountains the waggoners are oblig'd to lock all the wheels and make fast a Trunk of Tree Forty feet long to the back of the waggon to prevent it from Pressing on the Horses." One snowy night Austin fairly forced himself into a settler's cabin, to sleep on the floor, and again he bedded with sixteen others in a filthy hut of twelve feet square.   The only tavern encountered for several days was at the northern end of the gap, kept by Moll Davis, who described herself as a "come by chance" and said that she lived only for pleasure.   All along the way he passed rag-clad, barefoot families:

"Ask these Pilgrims what they expect when they git to Kentuckey, the Answer is Land. have you any. No, but I expect I can git it. have you anthing to pay for land, No. did you Ever see the Country. No but Every Body says its good land. . . . here is hundreds Travelling hundreds of Miles, they Know not for what Nor Whither, except its to Kentuckey, passing land almost as good and easy obtain'd, . . . but it will not do its not Kentuckey its not the Promis'd land

---

[1] An episode of 1780. — Mereness, ed., *Travels in the American Colonies*, 625, 626. At this time the migration was becoming copious.   In 1780 the population of Kentucky numbered but a few hundred; in 1790 it was nearly seventy-five thousand, including twelve thousand Negro slaves.

[2] Horace E. Hayden, *Virginia Genealogies*, 41.

its not the goodly inheratance, the Land of Milk and Honey. and when arriv'd at this Heaven in Idea what do they find? a goodly land I will allow but to them a forbidden Land. exhausted and worn down with distress and disappointment they are at last Oblig'd to become hewers of wood and Drawers of water." [1]

Since 1792 Kentucky had been a State in the Union. The deer, elk and buffalo thronging the salt licks were slain and the hunter's paradise depleted. But cattle, sheep and swine came through the mountain passes to thrive upon the blue-grass and acorns, and crops were yielding good returns to those who had luck or money to get good lands and strength to till them. Droves of horses and hogs erelong were traveling south to market,[2] and the rivers as well as the Wilderness Road were beginning to serve as a commercial outlet. The rivers indeed were essential in Kentucky's promise. Hunters, ranchers and pioneer farmers might crop small clearings and ply a trade through the defiles to meet their crude wants of market goods; but substantial citizens could grow more substantial, men of comfortable habit could attain greater comfort, only where avenues of copious transport permitted the shipment of heavy produce.

But shortly before the close of the century Spain closed the lower Mississippi to cargoes from the United States. Dismayed reaction was prompt upstream. To relieve the great scarcity of money a meeting of citizens of Bourbon County resolved in 1800 to buy no cloth or leather goods, liquors or sugar unless they could be paid for in Kentucky produce, and further: "We will encourage the raising of sheep, the cultivation of hemp, flax and cotton, and produce home manu-

---

[1] *American Historical Review*, V, 523–526. Many of those who migrated in poverty became tenants or wage-earners, diminishing the need of slave labor in the Blue-grass.

[2] In 1807, when part of this road had been improved and a tollgate established, these droves comprised 3333 horses, 8340 hogs and 868 cattle, with a value reckoned at $297,837. — *Palladium* (Frankfort, Ky.), January 28, 1808. The horses were already being peddled as far away as the South Carolina lowlands. — F. A. Michaux, *Travels* (London, 1805), 189; reprinted in R. G. Thwaites, ed., *Early Western Travels*, III, 244.

factures of every kind." [1]   And strange to say, for such is not often the case, these resolutions, if not effective, were prophetic except as to flax and cotton.   The purchase of Louisiana, resulting from Kentucky-Tennessee pressure upon the Federal authorities, removed the blockade, and the western waters bore flatboats with increasing cargoes of grain, tobacco, whiskey, rope and salt meats.   But the flats could never come upstream again ; and even the keel boats, more neatly shaped to cut the current, could be rowed or poled or cordelled on the thousand-mile course from New Orleans only with such labor and expense as to make the prices of all market supplies immensely higher than on the seaboard or in the Piedmont.   Haulage across Pennsylvania, with river freight added from Brownsville or Pittsburgh, cost little less.   This meant that Kentucky must meet her own needs more diversely than Virginia had ever done. Works had arisen as early as 1779 to boil the water of saline springs and reduce the price of salt by home production ; [2] and little factories now wrought the local hemp into bagging and the by-product tow into shirting as well as wool into cloth for outer garments.   This was not a backwoods phase like the whittling of ax helves or wagon spokes by farmers or the making of cloth or candles by their wives.   It was rather a diversifica-tion of industrial specialization, a growth of local commerce and complexity.

❋   ❋   ❋   ❋   ❋

Plans were expansive and expensive.   A planter near Versailles wrote in 1809 :

"I have been and am still much engaged in building.   My dwelling house is about half finished.   I expect to git into it this fall. . . .   It will cost me at least $6000, and then it must be furnished, and before I can meet these expenses I shall be compelled to put up a large stone distillery, say 50 by 34.

[1] Humphrey Marshall, *History of Kentucky* (2d ed., Frankfort, Ky., 1824), II, 325.

[2] Mary Verhoeff, *The Kentucky River Navigation* (Filson Club *Publications* No. 28), treats this and other economic themes to good effect.   The Kentucky saline works were eventually replaced by those in the Kanawha valley where the brine was much less dilute.

This I must do this fall, and it will cost me another $1000. I shall then want a Mill which will cost $500 and a Barn say $500 more. When this is all done, if I do not break in doing it, hope to be in a situation to make money. . . . I should be glad to see you again in Kentucky. I think a view of it now would induce you to move to it. It has since you were here made the greatest progress in manufactories of any new country I suppose in the world." [1]

In 1815 it was reported from Lexington :

"This town, which promises to be the great inland city in the western world, . . . is the seat of a great commerce and has many flourishing manufactures. . . . Mechanics of all descriptions receive nearly double the price for their labor that they get to the eastward, and the expences of living is not more than one half. They are greatly wanted to keep pace with the rapid improvement and increase of manufactories in the place. . . . The farms in the neighborhood are well cultivated, and the farmers are generally rich and opulent, and many of them have coaches and carriages, made at Lexington, that cost one thousand dollars. . . . It is with delight we notice the great prosperity and rapidly rising importance of the future metropolis of the west; where *town lots* sell nearly as high as in Boston, New-York, Philadelphia or Baltimore, which shews that it is not a place in the *wilderness* as some people suppose it to be!" [2]

The introduction of steam navigation seemed for a time to brighten the brilliant prospect. The planter near Versailles whom we quoted above wrote in 1818 : "The Steam Boats have brought N. Orleans to our doors, West India fruits are as common here now as in your [Virginia] Sea Port Towns." All produce was bringing high prices, and thanks partly to the building of turnpikes, land values were swiftly rising. But the

---

[1] Nathaniel Hart to James McDowell, June 18, 1809. Manuscript in McCormick Agricultural Library, Chicago.

[2] *Niles' Weekly Register*, VII, 339, 340. In 1817 the factory investment at Lexington was reckoned at two million dollars. — H. B. Fearson, *Sketches of America* (London, 1819), 245. This attainment was the more remarkable in that Lexington lay fifteen miles from navigable water.

steamboat was to prove a Trojan Horse, for it brought the competition of the world against the local factories, and it hastened the grain and tobacco rivalry from Illinois and Missouri. In 1825 our formerly buoyant Kentuckian wrote in plaintive tone:

"I suppose you are like myself trying to make a little in these hard times, but unless you are more successful than I am it is but little that either of us are making. What can you git for whisky, and does it pay the charges of making? I observe the American Farmer quotes it at 25 cts. [per gallon], the barrel given in, at Baltimore. This I am certain will not pay for making and transporting to market. Are you still opposed to the tariff? Would not a higher duty on Molasses have a good effect on the grain growing States? And would not the Eastern States drink our whisky as low as their N. England rum?"

Another, less favored by previous fortune, wrote in 1822:

"When I reflect upon the amazing distance that there is between the profits of a small farm tolerably managed and the requirements of a starting family even economically indulged, I feel so shrunk as hardly to occupy the space of a dwarf upon my chair."

But gloom gave place to contentment, for the Bluegrass remained the Bluegrass and the Pennyroyal was nearly as good. Food crops and pasturage permitted the handling of large acreage by small personnel;[1] and in tobacco and hemp culture there was little advantage in largeness of scale. Kentucky therefore did not develop great plantations nor import hordes of slaves to till them. Only two or three counties, in fact, ever had more Negroes than whites in the population. But earnings per hand were always greater than on the leaner lands of the seaboard States, and some thousands of proprietors became sufficiently well-to-do to cultivate amenities. A tourist in 1818 described the homes as having a "cleanliness which strongly

---

[1] The utilization of land was far more complete than anywhere else in the South, for the woods when cleared of undergrowth made good pastures without the felling of trees. — *Cultivator*, n. s., II, 372 (1845). Such a policy in Virginia or Georgia provided the cows with grounds for exercise rather than grazing.

contrasts with the dirty Ohio homes and the Indiana and Illinois pigsties in which men, women and children wallow in promiscuous filth. But the Kentuckians have servants; and whatever may be the future consequences of Slavery, the present effects are in these respects most agreeable and beneficial. A Kentucky farmer has the manners of a gentleman; he is more or less refined according to his education, but there is generally a grave, severe dignity of deportment in the men of middle age, which prepossess, and commands respect." [1]

Praising the hospitality, as did every one, a writer in 1845 was unusually specific as to homesteads:

"In point of comforts, of luxuries and even elegancies, the Kentucky farmer compares well with the English, Irish or Scotch gentleman-farmer *in every respect*. Their houses generally speaking have been built within the last 30 years; are of brick; well and tastefully planned; large and roomy; and if any fault is to be found at all they are too magnificently furnished for a 'farmer's' residence. They all stand some distance from the road and are approached by a wide avenue, shaded on either side with large forest trees, and the ground immediately surrounding the dwelling is invariably tastefully laid out in shrubbery, evergreens and flowers. Every farmer has his elegant family carriage and his one horse buggy for himself, with horses and saddles innumerable for the younger branches to use when their inclination leads them to gallop uncontrolled from one neighbor's house to the other." [2]

The tale of Kentucky horses will not here be told. In youth I was in my own esteem something of a horseman; but overhearing at New Orleans, Nashville and Lexington the chatter of breeders, jockeys and touts upon the points, pedigrees and performances of thoroughbreds, cobs, trotters and pacers, I found myself a landlubber at sea, content to leave technique

---

[1] Elias P. Fordham, *Personal Narrative* (Cleveland, 1906), 216. Timothy Flint's *Recollections*, Mellish's *Travels* and Fearon's *Sketches* are to similar effect; but Thomas Joynes in a diary of travel to western Kentucky in 1810 (*William and Mary College Quarterly*, X, 145–158, 221–232) gives notes of squalor as well as of elegance.

[2] *Cultivator*, n. s., II, 373.

to those who made it a profession. Suffice it then to say that fine horse-flesh which came with early gentry from Virginia yielded foals with yet finer points and greater speed, as their lineage lengthened in this horse-loving salubrious land.[1] Factories might fail at Lexington but the race course throve, attracting annual throngs and promoting familiar acquaintance of "everybody who was anybody" throughout the fifty-mile radius of the Bluegrass bowl.

❈   ❈   ❈   ❈   ❈

Contemporary with the founding of Kentucky was the settlement of eastern and middle Tennessee, which lay alike upon western waters but were in sharp contrast as to commercial outlet.

Colonization on the headwaters of the Tennessee was a mere continuance of the familiar thrust along the great trough amid the mountains, and the topography and climate were little different from those in the Shenandoah. Exit from Virginia jurisdiction was made unawares by these home seekers, as had been the case with pioneers on Albemarle Sound long before. There was fighting with Cherokees, and battles of words with North Carolinian authorities before land titles were fully secured and firm government established; and as an interlude a local force rode eastward and helped to turn the tide of war against the British at King's Mountain.

With the heroic phase ended for all but irrepressible John Sevier, life took the humdrum form of moderate plenty in food but dearth in all things else. Kentuckians might complain sometimes that money was scarce; East Tennesseans hardly knew the feel of it. What little they saw came north from the cotton belt in pay for horses, mules and hogs, and this promptly went in the lumbering "Knoxville wagons" on their month-long journey to Baltimore to buy powder and lead, needles and axes. The best currency left for home use was 'coon skins, though goose feathers would serve if nothing more compact were on hand. Luckily there were salt works not far away

[1] The humbler subject of the mule will be discussed in Chapter VII.

in Virginia, and eventually fulling mills and small iron works rose to meet more or less the local needs of cloth and hardware.

When the cotton belt was extended into northern Alabama flatboats from the Knoxville neighborhood rode the "spring fresh" each year to sell foodstuffs at Huntsville; but from the great market of New Orleans the rugged stretch of the Muscle Shoals excluded all but the boldest of boatmen in the highest floods. Nothing short of railroads could conquer the isolation of East Tennessee; and indeed the denizens of its remoter coves dwell in the primitive poverty of the backwoods to the present day.

＊   ＊   ＊   ＊   ＊

The Nashville basin was topographically and historically a diminished replica of Kentucky Bluegrass. Daniel Boone and his fellows discovered its charms; and Richard Henderson, who had grubstaked Boone a decade before to roam the Bluegrass, was the promoter of the new speculation. James Robertson from East Tennessee went as his agent in 1779, threading Cumberland Gap and crossing Cumberland River, then turning west and south to strike the river again at French Lick. There he planted corn against the coming of families next year, some of whom followed his trail while others, encountering still greater hardships, went by canoe, running a Cherokee gauntlet, shooting the Muscle Shoals rapids and stemming the Ohio and Cumberland currents.

Though threatened repeatedly with extinction, the settlement survived and gradually drew recruits. The land was nearly as good as the best in Kentucky, the climate conduced to the same productions while also permitting some cotton culture, and the river gave the same access to New Orleans. Younger than Lexington, and for some decades drawing trade from a smaller province, Nashville eventually gained rank as a major focus of inland commerce and industry. Memphis, much younger still, shared the fortunes of the cotton belt and the Mississippi trade.

Each of these westerly tracts continued for many years to receive migrants from eastward as roads were improved and reports of prosperity continued to flow "back home." Polly Davis in Spotsylvania County, Virginia, wrote in 1789 to her brother in the Bluegrass: "A great many people here are talking of Settling in that Country, for their Land is getting so poore here and Money hard to get hold of." And three years afterward: "God must be prospering you if you can have a Silver Teapott & Shugar Dish. I did not think Lexington was big enough to have a silversmith. . . . Are you going to have [the Fielding arms] on your Teapott? I guess the Davises never had any. . . . We made a pore Crop Tob° this year, the Crop of Corn is Pretty Good. Money seems harder to get hold of than during the War." [1] Such letters doubtless might be matched by hundreds of others if all that were written were now at hand.

Yet as each land of promise became a land of performance its charms diminished for part of its people. The Bluegrass, for example, became a token, an earnest of what might be found farther on if men sought soon and shrewdly. Some who had come too late to get space there or who lost their substance through extravagant living or misfortune trekked again across the Ohio, or boated to Missouri or Mississippi, seeking a new rainbow's end, willing to resume backwoods life in hope of getting cheap land which would grow dear in turn. And new caravans from seaboard commonwealths wound their way through the older west to the younger west and thence to the still younger west again.

Among the leapfrogs was "Major" Ebenezer Burgess Ball, born in Loudoun County, Virginia, in 1817, who first went to the near-by Washington as a dry-goods clerk. Desiring an outdoor life, he moved to Missouri, where he spent his happiest years in a primitive settlement on Osage River. Catching the gold fever, he set out for California but was diverted to Oregon where he "packed" provisions from the seaboard to the mining camps. Upon the outbreak of the Civil War he returned to

[1] *Virginia Magazine*, XII, 435, 436.

Virginia to care for his mother. With his farm at Ball's Bluff gutted and himself penniless at the close of the war, he began a butter-and-egg business at Washington. When this failed he applied to the government without success for a job as night watchman. When writing an autobiographical sketch [1] from which this account is taken, this kinsman of George Washington, who is said to have resembled him closely in appearance, was peddling chewing gum and photographs of Mrs. Cleveland.

Other stones which likewise gathered no moss rolled but a short space, paused and rolled again. Young Rutherford Hayes, when traveling with friends in Texas, made a diary jotting in 1849:

"In the course of the day passed the house of the identical man whose chickens come up in the spring and *cross their legs to be tied*, so strong is the force of habit — their owner having moved once a year a day's journey (or a week's) until he reached Texas, all the way from Kentucky!" [2]

❉   ❉   ❉   ❉   ❉

At the close of the War of 1812 exalted prices for produce of all sorts brought a new epidemic of the western fever. Currents of migration set from everywhere every whither, and in the middle latitude as usual the thrust was farthest west. The Missouri River was navigable after a fashion as far as the Great Bend which Kansas City now adorns, and the novel steamboats could breast the current and shorten the trudge of those who

---

[1] Printed in H. E. Hayden, *Virginia Genealogies*, 134, 135.

[2] C. R. Williams, ed., *Diary and Letters of Rutherford B. Hayes* ([Columbus, Ohio] 1922–1925), I, 259. Humor of exaggeration had long since become a western tradition. When the preceding century had yet a dozen years to run, a man returning east was reported to have been asked whether such things were true as that if a crowbar were planted, tenpenny nails would sprout overnight. Denying this, he said: "But this . . . I can bear witness to: . . . That just before I left the Muskingum, one day, horseback, having taken some pumpkin-seed into my hand at the door of a house, several of which I dropped, turning about to speak to a person then passing, so instantaneous was their growth — so surprisingly rapid their extension and spread, that before I turned back, the seed had taken root in the earth to such a degree that I was dangerously encompassed about with enormous serpentine vines, which threatened keeping pace with my utmost exertions to escape being tied in, as I immediately clapped spurs to my horse and with difficulty was disentangled." — Salem, Mass., *Mercury*, November 4, 1788.

could pay the fare.   Valley lands there were said to be as rich as those of the Bluegrass.   This then was a present land of promise for pioneers and for stay-at-home speculators as well who were always eager to invest anywhere ahead of a boom.

John Preston, treasurer of the State of Virginia, bethought him in 1816 to form a company, and invited his brother-in-law James McDowell to become its field agent.

"With every intelligent person I have met, and many others," he wrote, "Missouri has been the subject of conversation.   I find *all* have their minds turned that way.   I have no doubt but it will be *all the rage* in two or three years, just like the Ohio was ten years ago or less.   The time for making *great use* of our money is going by fast, we ought to be on the business now.   Last year was the most glorious time.   Every year and day will make it worse for us.   We may for a long time do well, but it will require so much capital more a year or two hence than it now will."

Again in the same autumn: "We learn that the spirit of emigration to that country [Missouri] is so great in the State of Ohio that lands have actually fallen there in price. . . . I want to be beforehand; get good choices and at low prices; and this I fear cannot be done unless we set about the work seriously this fall and winter."

He said he was ready to risk twenty thousand dollars in the project, and apparently did so.   The panic of 1819 proved that he had entered a risk indeed, for next year he was insolvent.[1]

Joseph Walker, a farmer and wagon maker on the southern edge of the Kentucky Pennyroyal, was for several years on the point of removal.   On July 4, 1819, he wrote: "I will start to the Missouri tomorrow or next day if all is well.   I have been disappointed in almost every instance in geting money and will have verry little to take with me."   Instead of posting his letter he held it for six weeks and added a plaint, August 10: "Money

[1] Manuscripts in private possession.   Preston's folly in speculation was matched by his gallantry when bankrupt.   In the summer of 1820, though disabled by gout, he was arranging to sell his "unfortunate slaves" in family groups among his kinsmen and friends to assure them good masters, "as it is perhaps the last kindness I will ever have it in my power to bestow on them."

cannot be got hier.   There is not any in Sirculation but Independent Notes and the most of them Banks is or soon will be
broke and there Notes is not in good Credit and will not doe
to take to the Missouri. . . . I know not what will B. done."

Two years later his eyes had not left the west but his feet
were still stayed: "We had a fine crop last year of Wheat Rie
and Corn   But there is no Sale for anything   we made two
hundred and seventy dollars worth of Waggon work this last
winter and did not get one dollar in money   I sold a Waggon
last faul and one this spring but got no money   I have a new
Rode wagon now that I made this winter and I have a new
dearborne wagon that we have just finished   We have Eight
horses and stock of all Kinds But Canot sell for money."[1]

A decade later he would have joined a local stampede to
Illinois had it not been for a "pore deranged daughter" who
could neither be taken along nor left behind.   In earlier years,
at least, he might have set forth with flocks and herds and laden
wagons at any time, had not the wheels been scotched by his
resolve to carry money for landed investments.

A young nephew, John K. Walker, reached St. Louis in 1816,
with a few dollars and an education procured in the Shenandoah.[2]   After a spell of ague he began to teach school, finding
his pupils hard to govern.   "Indeed," he wrote next spring,
"the people here are generally a rude, immoral set, very much
given to profanity and intemperance, pay very little respect to
the Sabbath. . . .   On the whole I like the country a great deal
better than the people."   That summer a steamboat began
to ply from the falls of the Ohio, taking twelve days for the
voyage.   Many people were exploring the country, and the
town was full of land jobbers.   In the fall of 1818 he was himself land-looking:

"I intend going to farming and expect to keep batchelor's
hall as I cannot prevail on any of these territorienes to unite

---

[1] Manuscripts in private possession. Frustration did not improve his spelling but
brought a loss of all regard for punctuation.

[2] A long series of letters to his elder brother at Brownsburg, Virginia, is in private
possession.

their destiny with mine, so that I expect to have to go to V^a for a wife." But before Christmas his distaste for a rural celibacy reconciled him to town life; while to quiet the fears of his Virginia kindred he wrote: "I trust I never shall court a girl that I would consider a disgrace to me or my relations."

He now served for several years as a deputy sheriff, at times on rural duty which enabled him to turn a few trades in land, and again in charge of the St. Louis jail where he had custody of some who had plunged more heavily. In January, 1820: "Times here are very searching, numbers of those over-high fellows are coming through the grates. . . . It is my painful duty to have to house divers of them." Times continued hard, and men donned homespun when their broadcloth wore out.

"Farmers . . . are turning their attention to tobacco, which will be our staple commodity. Wheat would be, were there mills to manufacture it into flour. There are several distilleries erecting, . . . so that instead of importing whiskey as we have done heretofore we will [be] able to export large quantities."

He was now sheriff in his own right for a decade except for a term when a Jacksonian majority put him out of office. Meanwhile he found a wife and settled a farm within convenient distance of St. Louis. His early concern with religion was renewed by a revival which swept St. Louis in 1832: "It has pleased the Lord in his merciful goodness, I trust, to lift my feet out of the miry clay and to place them on the rock of Christ Jesus."

Cholera that year and the next suspended traffic for a time, but when the epidemic was ended immigration and business became brisk again:

"The people seem to have forgotten the chastisements they have experienced. . . . We are rather in a cold state here, not much feeling on the subject of religion, that one important subject above all others." The "cold state" of his community soon chilled his own ardor, if the dearth of later allusions to religion is an index.

In the middle 'thirties, no longer sheriff, "I am busily engaged in clearing land, improving my farm, etc." At the end of 1837 he was prosperous and inclined to expand:

"Labor is still so high that it is very expensive improving. We have to give from 150$ to 200$ a year for a good hand. . . . What is the price of first rate farm hands with you [*i.e.* slaves in Virginia,] not those that would be sold to any and every one, but such as could be recommended for their good qualities and would be sold only with their own consent to humane owners? and is there any of this description that could be purchased?"

From some source he procured a corps of slaves; but his location proved uncomfortably near the border. In 1840:

"This spring, just at the commencement of the planting season, two of my negro boys were enticed away by a white man from Illinois who had been working in the neighborhood. There were in all six that started. He persuaded them that by going with him he would make them free. We succeeded in getting them back, though it has cost us about 150$ each negro, beside the loss of time. They got off about 100 miles before they were taken."

So the years passed, with notes of the trend of migration to the northern part of the State, with family news including the birth of a grandchild, with disapproval of the Mexican War, with regret at the menace to the permanence of the Union, and with continued praise of Missouri. Long ago, as these letters remarked, Texas had tempted some; but now came an utter stampede to California. In February, 1850: "The accounts from the gold country are so flattering that it threatens to depopulate the western section of our state"; and in June: "The California movement has so far had an unfavorable influence upon the prosperity of the State at large. It has taken off from sixty to eighty thousand of our producing population, and a good deal more gold than has yet been brought back. It may give us that remain better prices for what we make. All our products are now very high."

The last letter of his writing, September 13, 1853, shows him still rejoicing at good prices and looking forward to an era of railroads:

"There was an immense number of cattle driven from the State last spring to California, estimated beyond a hundred thousand head. Our State is going ahead with our railroads. The Pacific road is finished about forty miles, cars running. The Northern road is located to St. Charles, and the Iron Mountain road located the whole route."

CHAPTER VI

THE COTTON BELT

COTTON plants are of many breeds, differing in the shape of the leaves, the distribution of the bolls upon the branches, the firmness with which the fibers adhere to the seed, and the length, strength, tint and texture of the lint.[1] The genus is native to most warm regions of the world, its varieties will readily combine into hybrids, and its fruitage responds to differences of climate. The number of strains is therefore without end, though those of North American concern may be grouped into two main categories. One is the sea-island with glossy black seed and loosely adhering silky lint which may attain a length of two inches; the other is the upland, with a fuzzy greenish seed and tightly adhering lint which rarely exceeds an inch in length except on alluvial fields where "upland cotton" is in fact a misnomer. The two, long staple and short, have little in common as to habitat or history. One served to make lace or cambric, the other in more plebeian style to clothe common men, to sail ships and cover the tented field. Seldom the twain have met except upon the wharves of Charleston or Savannah. It was accidental that their commercial beginnings in the United States occurred about the same time.

The first black seeds of a fine strain appear to have been sent in 1786 by a Loyalist exile in the Bahama Islands to an old friend in Georgia as a token of a continued good will and a suggestion that this culture might replace the dying indigo industry. Success was doubtful for a time; but after a few years prosperity began, and the planting spread up and down

[1] Among useful books are E. J. Donnell, *Chronological and Statistical History of Cotton* (New York, 1872); M. B. Hammond, *The Cotton Industry* (New York, 1887); Harry B. Brown, *Cotton* (New York, 1927).

the seaboard from the Santee River to the St. John's.[1]   Trials
made at some distance inland with disappointing results proved
that high grades could be had only from fields within a few
miles of the ocean.   Here was available the specially long
season which the variety required for maturing, as well as the
salt air which, if tradition be true, was needed to carry this
crop to perfection.   Now the low-lying coast on that stretch
lay frayed by tide and storm into a fringe of islands, divided
narrowly from the mainland by salt creeks and called "sea
islands" merely to distinguish them from others which did not
front the sea.   Here were John's Island, Edisto, St. Helena
and Hilton Head, Ossabaw, St. Catherine's, Sapelo and St.
Simon's, all sandy except in unused marshes, the land of little
value for rice by default of fresh-water streams, but thriving
moderately from indigo and then from the fleeciest brands of
the fleecy staple.

On the typical island of Edisto, which had been settled for
a century, the régime was described in 1808,[2] when the white
population numbered two hundred and thirty-six and the
Negroes nearly twelve times as many.   There were two schools
for white children, each with a teacher on a salary of one
thousand dollars; and nine boys were away at college.   There
was an Episcopal church whose rector was also a planter, a
Presbyterian church, a general store, but no ferry, tavern or
smithy.   Lacking a butcher's shop the planters were grouped
in fours or eights, each to slaughter animals in turn and distribute portions among the membership.[3]   A convivial club,
the Free and Easy, had eaten semimonthly dinners for thirty-
five years, each member serving as host in turn and all using
the occasion "to transact their private and public business,
to consider and digest their schemes of planting, and to hear
and discuss the news and politics of the day."   There was little

[1] The best history and description is by Whitemarsh B. Seabrook: *Memoir on the
Origin, Cultivation and Uses of Cotton . . . with Especial Reference to the Sea-Island
Cotton Plant* (Charleston, 1844).

[2] By the Reverend Donald M'Leod in David Ramsay's *History of South Carolina*
(Charleston, 1809), II, 539–568.

[3] This device was common in plantation districts nearly everywhere.

sport except fishing; and pride ran rather to boats than to horseflesh. One of the planters had maintained since 1792 a register of births, deaths and other island events, which showed a tendency of whites and blacks to double in twenty years by natural increase; but among the whites emigration had offset the excess of births and kept the households at about forty in number. The climate was more salubrious than in the near-by rice district, and the planters, dwelling on their estates the year round, commonly dispensed with overseers. The Negroes were notably musical, but less boisterous than they had been forty years earlier, when religion had not repressed their "dancing, dissipation and irregularities." Lands were reckoned to be worth from thirty to sixty dollars per acre, and prime field hands at seven or eight hundred dollars.[1] No fertilizer was put upon the sandy fields, though marsh mud came into copious use not long afterward. Furthermore there was not a plow on the island, and virtually none until near the middle of the century. The planters explained their sole reliance upon the hoe by saying the plow would pack their soil; but critics were already attributing it rather to inert habit. The cast of crops was about four acres per hand in cotton plus an acre or two in foodstuffs — corn, sweet potatoes, peas and peanuts. The best land in the best year for cotton had yielded lint to "the enormous amount of 435 pounds to the acre", and a planter had once realized proceeds of nearly five hundred dollars per hand; but common experience ran at about 140 pounds per acre and from $170 to $260 per hand as gross earnings.

"In favorable years," this report of 1808 recited, "more than 750,000 pounds of net cotton wool are grown. This at its common price, two shillings sterling per pound, yields an annual income of $321,300; a sum which is equal to $11 for every acre on the island, and would afford $110 to every inhabitant, or $1350 for every white person, or $8683 for each married pair of its white population."

[1] From general evidence which will be charted in another chapter this estimate of slave values appears exaggerated.

The total output of sea-island cotton was already approaching ten million pounds, which it seldom exceeded before the middle of the century.[1] After the 'twenties production tended rather to contract than expand, for the market became highly discriminating if not capricious. In some years the best bags of some planters would bring a dollar or two per pound, while all others must accept from fifteen to thirty cents.

At all times "to pay as well as the short staple cotton, the long staple must sell for twice as much per pound," [2] mainly because of the higher cost of ginning; and this was due to the delicacy of the fibers and the importance of keeping them unbroken. The sea-island lint could be cleared from the seed by clutching a tuft and sharply pressing the seed away. A machine, an engine, for short a *gin*, to do this had been devised before the culture was brought to the continent. It consisted essentially of a pair of small rollers revolving almost in contact and commonly driven by a treadle. These rollers, catching and pulling the lint forward, forced the seed to fly out backward, thus freeing the fibers without cutting them. Some of the seed, however, were crushed and carried with the lint: and these and other "motes" must be removed by a careful inspection and sorting. Finally, to prevent clotting, the lint must be packed in sewn bags, rather than pressed into bales. Each treadle gin would turn out as a rule not more than twenty-five pounds of lint per day; and the gin-house processes as a whole, the whipping, ginning, moting, sorting and packing, with labor estimated at fifty cents per day, was reckoned to cost nearly ten cents per pound of market product.[3] The black-seed long staple continued as the product of a restricted locality, while the green-seed short staple culture was continually expanding over an immense region.

❖   ❖   ❖   ❖   ❖

The Carolina-Georgia Piedmont was initially peopled by the same strains and streams which thrust into the Southern

---

[1] In the 'fifties and afterward this culture was extended into Florida; but in the twentieth century the boll weevil has reduced it to the vanishing point.

[2] J. A. Turner, *The Cotton Planter's Manual* (New York, 1857), 131.

[3] Seabrook, *Memoir*, 31.

backwoods at large. Through the eighteenth century subsistance was the chief concern of husbandry, though surplus grain was floated to the seaboard and low-grade tobacco served as a make-shift staple. Here and there in a river bottom lay a unit approaching plantation scale, but by far the most of the thinly scattered settlers dwelt and wrought upon primitive small farms, for they had not wherewith to buy slaves.

Green-seed cotton was known in Jamestown's early years, and it continued thereafter familiar in the Southern colonies as a thing convenient to grow for home use. The fingers of the housewife tore the fiber from the seed, a few ounces in the spare time of a day; her wheel spun this into yarn which her needle knitted into stockings or a domestic loom wove into cloth, and any surplus lint went into the padding of quilts.[1] Laborious processes all; but life in isolation must be hard for women as for men. News came eventually here and there that machines were invented in England to spin and weave at a rapid rate, and that cotton of every sort was wanted in large quantity at good prices.

The seaboard responded as we have seen. The great interior was ready to respond if a device could be had to save labor in tearing the familiar short fiber from its woolly seed; and in the hope of such an invention it appears that considerable crops were grown in 1791 and the next year with a view to market. The remaining link in this chain of industry was quickly forged by Eli Whitney under the prompting of Catherine Littleton Greene and Phineas Miller.

General Nathanael Greene, though sprung from Rhode Island Quakers, had proved so zealous and adept in his campaign against the British in the South that the Commonwealth of Georgia gave him a plantation upon which his widow continued to dwell after his death. The sprightliness of Mrs. Greene had been something of a scandal in Providence; but in the

[1] Governor Fauquier wrote from Williamsburg in 1766: "The Planters' wives spin the cotton of this country and make a strong cloth with which they make gowns for themselves and children; and sometimes they come to this town and offer some for sale. Of this cotton they make coverlids for beds, which are in pretty general use throughout the Colony." — *William and Mary College Quarterly*, XXI, 170.

rice district it made her home a popular place of call. Returning in the fall of 1792 from a Northern visit she found a shipboard companion in Whitney, who had been a mechanic before entering Yale College and was now going to Savannah on the prospect of a tutorship in a planter's family. Upon arrival the appointment was found to have been filled; and Whitney became a guest at "Mulberry Grove", where Miller was tutor of the Greene Children and erelong became the second husband of their talented mother. While Whitney was waiting for something to turn up, a party of men from up the river stopped and stayed awhile at this hospitable house. Between soft speeches to the wealthy widow these men talked, as they must, of crops and weather, of produce and prices, of land and labor, and of problems including cotton. They spoke in particular of the need of a gin to handle the upland variety; and Miller urged Whitney to undertake the invention, offering on a partnership basis to meet all expenses.

Whitney solved the essential problem within a few weeks by setting wires in a wooden cylinder somewhat after the fashion of the quills on a porcupine, and revolving this against the slatted side of a box of cotton. The wire points upon entering the box caught bits of the fiber, and as they made exit they tore the lint from the seed which were too large to follow between the slats. The teeth becoming clogged with lint, Mrs. Greene cleaned them with a hearth broom, which suggested a second cylinder set with brushes to clear the lint as fast as it came from the hopper. Whitney had it in mind from the beginning to substitute saw-toothed discs of steel for his bristling wires, but his lack of promptitude in the matter involved him in litigation over patents; and this, together with an ill-considered attempt of the partnership to monopolize the business of ginning, brought disaster to his personal fortunes. But his troubles and his after career belong to biography rather than history.

For centuries calico from Calicut, madras from Madras and muslin of the Moslems had been products of India. Thanks to the new machines of Hargreaves and Arkwright, Crompton and Cartwright, English labor could now compete in making these cloths and add to the list osnaburgs and gingham, twills and drills, duck and denim, coarse goods and fine. And through Whitney's gin, soon improved into very cheap and efficient operation, America with labor far dearer than in India could overmatch the raw product of that ancient home of "tree wool." The world's demand has never ceased to grow, and our cotton belt has never failed in time of peace to meet the mounting need. In most periods indeed the difficulty has been rather to avoid outrunning the demand. But this phase did not begin until settlement had spread far beyond the Atlantic slope.

❋   ❋   ❋   ❋   ❋

"This part of the country is at present in a rude uncultivated state.... Land is too cheap, too easy to be acquired.... It is nothing uncommon ... for men settled on land of their own, and sufficiently cleared, inclosed and tilled ... on hearing of a better place of range," to sell or even leave without selling.[1] Thus wrote a correspondent in the South Carolina Piedmont in 1786. A decade afterward a Georgia politician wrote from the interior to a colleague at Savannah that people by thousands were swarming toward the Indian border at the Oconee River, and said: "If Congress do not take some steps, they must & will rush like a torrent over the Oconee in search of subsistence. How much more politic would it be in the United States to appropriate a hundred thousand Dollars to procure the land, than to drive a frontier to desperation which must end in bloodshed." [2] Settlers' cabins at this time were commonly not less than the backwoods measure of "two whoops and a holler" apart. To speak of the need of expansion for the sake of sustenance was absurd. Yet the demand was cogent then and thenceforward, with appetite never sated but always whetted by the potentialities ahead. The few here and

[1] Charleston *Morning Post*, July 3, 1786, quoted by D. H. Bacot in the *American Historical Review*, XXVIII, 685.

[2] James Jackson to John Milledge, January 25, 1787, in T. U. P. Charlton's *Life of James Jackson*, Atlanta reprint, 167.

there who happened upon durable soils tended to stay and become integrated into a steadfast community. The rest were logically right in thinking that better lands lay beyond the horizon and resolving to win them; right also in believing that acquiring or maintaining well-to-do status in the wilderness depended upon a quick exploitation of the best-favored localities, upon getting ahead of the crowd.

Prosperity from tobacco was at the time a prompting impulse,[1] and sundry villages throve as places for its inspection and shipment. The substitution of cotton, which erelong deprived these tobacco towns of their reason for existence, came with some hesitation.[2] A merchant in the South Carolina midlands wrote in 1796 that his neighbors were planting some cotton to test the market, and next year he sent samples to Charleston and England with an explicit purpose of trying to conquer the trade's aversion to the saw-ginned product. The response from Charleston was adverse;[3] but that from overseas, though it is not of record, must have been favorable. At any rate Wade Hampton, who had eighty-six slaves on a plantation near Columbia in 1790, made six hundred bales in 1799[4] with a value of some ninety thousand dollars. And Hampton's example was followed so copiously, whether on

[1] *South Carolina Gazette*, March 17, 1785.

[2] In a salutatory as editor of the *American Cotton Planter* (I, 21) in 1853, Dr. N. B. Cloud reminisced of his boyhood in South Carolina during the transition from tobacco to cotton. The lint was beautiful and valuable, said the tobacco growers, but the gin would require a trained mechanic at high wages to produce a bale per day: "and hundreds upon hundreds of tobacco hogsheads continued to roll on to Augusta. In the meantime, however, some public-spirited planter determined to try Sambo, and very soon his negro-ship was found to gin as successfully as Whitney himself. And from that day tobacco hogsheads and tobacco inspection migrated to the Old North State."

[3] Letters of William Murrell, quoted by Kate Furman in the *Southern History Association Publications*, VI, 237, 238.

[4] Seabrook, *Memoir*, 16, 17. Knowledge gained by military service at New Orleans prompted Hampton to transfer part of his slaves in 1811 to a sugar plantation on the Mississippi. Both establishments throve to such effect that at his death in 1835 he is said to have owned three thousand slaves and to have been the richest planter in America. The Carolina homestead, maintained by his son of the same name, was described in 1847 by R. L. Allen in the *American Agriculturist*, VI, 20, 21. His Louisiana establishment, expanded into three plantations under his son-in-law, and sold in 1857 for about $1,500,000, was described in 1861 by William H. Russell in his *Diary North and South* (Boston, 1863), 268–283.

large scales or small, that by the spring of 1807 an appeal was published urging planters in view of "the dear bought experience of the present season" to raise more corn and less cotton.[1] The price had declined within seven years from forty-four to twenty cents per pound. The descent continued through the years of troublous foreign relations; and when on July 8, 1812, an express brought the news to New Orleans that Congress had declared war upon England the price fell in one day from nine and a half cents to five or four and a half.[2] The depression, though somewhat mitigated, continued till the return of peace carried the price rapidly to thirty cents in 1815 and still higher two years afterward. The world was demanding lint at any price, but until the end of the 'teens the American producers could not exceed their previous maximum export of nearly a hundred million pounds.[3]

*   *   *   *   *

Wanted: lands like those of the Bluegrass, in the climate of middle Georgia, on rivers flowing smoothly to the sea, under laws favorable to the holding of Negroes in bondage. Such a notice might well have been signed by any of ten thousand men in the 'teens; and the 'twenties, 'thirties, 'forties and 'fifties brought no end to the demand. In Georgia the pressure for Indian cessions became irresistible, whether by the Creeks or Cherokees; in Alabama the land office did a business which became proverbial; and the farther West waited little upon the nearer. When the prices of produce were low men in the older, leaner districts cursed their niggard soils; and when cotton was high they felt the tug of richer profits to be gained from fresher lands.

About 1825 cotton was widely planted in Virginia, but a slump in the market conspired with early frosts to wreck this

---

[1] Augusta *Chronicle*, reprinted in the *Farmer's Gazette* (Sparta, Ga.), April 11, 1807.

[2] Stephen F. Austin to Moses Austin, New Orleans, July 12, 1812, in the *American Historical Association Report* for 1919, II, 216. The collapse at New York was not so great, because there was little cotton on hand in that market.

[3] As early as 1810 the volume of upland cotton exports was tenfold that of seaisland.

enterprise.[1] In North Carolina success was definite in a southerly zone, though the marketing was costly. In Tennessee there was prosperity about Columbia and young Memphis. By trial and error the northern limits of the belt were being defined. To the west not only was no limit yet in sight, but reports indicated exhilarating prospects in all the southerly fertile areas. From Louisiana came statements as early as 1817 that specified planters in the Opelousas and Attakapas districts had made six or seven bales per hand and realized as many hundred dollars.[2] And from Texas in the middle 'twenties Austin wrote: "We have most extraordinary crops this year . . . the average highth of cotton on the bottom lands is from 9 to 12 feet and yields generally 2500 to 3000 pounds to the acre."[3]

A cotton crop in western prospect became a golden fleece. From Maryland to Mississippi, from Virginia to Alabama, from Missouri to Texas, every whence every whither, people took ship or flatboat, or set forth in carryalls or covered wagons, with tinkling cattle and trudging slaves if they had them.[4] The fleece was found; but in the hands of its finders it changed to silver and at times to lead. The prodigious increase of output broke the structure of prices now and again. Many planters were bankrupted in the panic of 1819, others in that of 1825, many more in the long, drastic depression from 1837 to 1845; yet until 1861 the stream of slowly jolting wagons never ceased for long.

There was of course a deal of squatting by men who disregarded the formality of getting titles to land; and equally of

[1] Charleston *City Gazette*, October 3, December 1, 1825, February 20, 1826, quoting the Norfolk *Herald*, the Richmond *Compiler* and the Alexandria *Gazette; Farmers' Register*, I, 581, 582, V, 5, VI, 303; *American Farmer*, VII, 299. A crop of cotton was even raised on Long Island. — *Ibid.*, V, 27 (1823).

[2] *National Intelligencer* (Washington, D. C.), September 5, 1817.

[3] *American Historical Association Report* for 1919, II, 1427. The yield of lint was likely to be from a fourth to a third of the weight of the crop as harvested. The height of stalks in the Carolina-Georgia Piedmont generally ranged from one to four feet, and a crop of a thousand pounds per acre unginned was an unusual attainment.

[4] Travelers' notes and newspaper items are too numerous to cite. Some are given in U. B. Phillips, *American Negro Slavery* (New York, 1918), 168–198. T. P. Abernethy, *The Formative Period in Alabama* (Montgomery, 1922), is among the best monographs.

course an occasional stampede from soils which had proved shallow to those which it was hoped would prove deep. A Mississippian wrote in 1841 of deserted villages in the south-eastern corner of the commonwealth:

"It is dispiriting indeed to ride through one of these old counties . . . and [see] all around vestiges of the people departed and dispersed. . . . The town is literally tumbling to pieces, and one finds only the skeleton of the flourishing Winchester which existed twenty years ago. . . . The treaty of 1830 with the Choctaws, that threw open such an immense tract of productive territory in the center of our state, drew off her [Wayne County's] population by the hundreds."

Traveling into the next county northward, "my flagging horse sinking above the fetlocks in the sand, . . . the ancient village [of Perry] stood before me, an extensive parallelogram garnished round with some twelve or fifteen crumbling tenements — the wrecks of by-gone days! Not a tree stood in the gaping square for the eye to rest upon; the grass was all withered up; the burning sun fell on the white and barren sand . . . and was reflected back until the cheek scorched and the eyes filled with tears."

One log cabin, however, served as a tavern, and the landlord, being a jolly Virginian, soon concocted an ample julep "which lessened by a little the silence and solitude." [1]

To a somewhat more durable district at the northern end of the State John F. Finley migrated from the Shenandoah in 1836, with slaves, and bought a tract near Holly Springs. He expressed delight at the good soil, copious vegetables, healthful climate and pleasant society of the countryside, and he shared the community's impulse to speculate in lands, loans and slaves when his funds would permit. Two years afterward a drought cut his crop in half, and times were "somewhat awful . . . in the way of money"; but as an index of his own sense of permanence he was building a new homestead — "none of your scutchdowns, but of nicely hewed logs and nailed

[1] Letters of J. F. H. Claiborne, assembled from contemporary newspapers in the *Mississippi Historical Society Publications*, IX, 489-538.

roofs", so that when visitors came again in cold weather they would not have to do as in the old cabin, with its wide crevices and its wooden chimney, "get up to the fire and then to get away from it and warm t'other side." [1]

This item ends our knowledge of this planter's career; but a letter of E. N. Davis, who dwelt in the same locality and by his mention of Mrs. Finley suggests that perhaps he was a son-in-law, tells of a diversion of interest.

"I undertook [in October, 1854] a large Levee contract on the Mississippi river, the whole of Desoto County, for $15,000. I was prepaid in swamp scrip, say 30,000 acres of land. . . . I am now over half done the work. I shall make a crop with the hands and finish the work the ensuing fall and winter. My hands are doing a good business, averaging me some 200 Acres of Land per day. If I shall be able to pay the taxes on my Land and it comes on the Market soon it will be a small fortune. . . . I see a great feeling manifested by the planters of the hill country to go to the bottom lands, for our hill country is exhausting so fast they will be compelled to send their force to better lands. I have or shall have between fourteen and fifteen thousand Acres of Land in Arks., 10,200 Acres of which I have just purchased at 19 cts. per Acre. . . . And now I would like to purchase some 6 or 8 negro men and boys. Will you have the goodness to post me up of the price of such in your county round about you [in Virginia]. If I have sufficient inducements held out I will make a little fly round this spring. I am wanting fellows . . . to settle a bottom plantation." [2]

The broad alluvial tracts on either flank of the great river had long been accessible and known to be lastingly fertile. But their liability to flood caused them to be shunned except by a few who could operate on a scale warranting the private embankment of their fields. Now, at the middle of the century, continuous levees were being undertaken at public ex-

---

[1] Manuscript letters in private possession.

[2] E. N. Davis, Holly Springs, Miss., February 12, 1855, to J. D. Davidson, Lexington, Va. Manuscript in McCormick Agricultural Library, Chicago.

pense; and the grade of cotton produced began to bring a premium in the market because its lint often attained a length appreciably more than an inch. Here and there, as about Lake Washington in Mississippi and Concordia Parish, Louisiana,[1] rose groups of large and prosperous plantations usually possessed by men who had been friends in their former homes. The method by which one establishment led to another may be seen from a Tennessee woman's letter in 1855, saying that her brother, Jefferson Truehart, was visiting Mr. Sheppard in Arkansas who had prospered greatly there, and from a desire to have Truehart for a neighbor had offered to make a first payment on a tract of land for him. Sheppard himself, a former Virginian, had bought twelve hundred lowland acres at the beginning of 1853 and made a crop that year which sold for twice the price of the land; and in 1854, working about forty-five hands, "he made between 600 and 700 bales of cotton, besides the greatest abundance of everything else."[2]

To the northward cotton culture was thrust as far as the climate would permit the crop to mature. Of western Tennessee, settled in the 'thirties, a pioneer wrote in 1841: "The interior counties were settled first, because the river counties were supposed to be . . . luxuriant in disease and death. But the very superior advantages they possessed in proximity to market soon found adventurers who for the sake of the price were willing to encounter the risk; and it was then found out that the immediate borders of the Mississippi River were but little if any more sickly than the Mississippi Valley generally." Ten years ago, he continued, Jackson was the chief town of the region; but Memphis was now rapidly drawing a cotton trade from Arkansas and Mississippi as well as from Tennessee, and a heavy flatboat traffic in supplies from upstream. Cotton shipments from Memphis had attained sixty thousand bales in

[1] *DeBow's Review*, XXVI, 581. For a North Carolinian's account of his establishment in the lowlands of Mississippi see J. G. de R. Hamilton, ed., *Papers of Thomas Ruffin* (Raleigh, 1918), II, 549, 582.

[2] Mrs. M. E. Coleman to J. L. Truehart, January 21, 1855. Typescript in the Rosenberg Library, Galveston, Texas.

1840, and those from Randolph, sixty miles upstream, were half as many.[1]

In Texas uncertainty as to the status of slaves had hampered development so long as it remained a province of Mexico; and the wars of independence and annexation, along with Indian troubles, obstructed exploitation till near the middle of the century. But in 1853 a local newspaper could report: "The cotton crop of Texas raised last year is estimated at 120,000 bales. The crop has been doubling itself for the last twelve or fourteen years, and at the present rate of progression, in three more all the ox-teams that can be mustered will prove insufficient to haul the enormous load." [2]

On the whole, so great was the space, the freshness and fertility and so rapid the transit of a lusty population that the region draining into the Gulf of Mexico surpassed the Atlantic slope in cotton production before 1830, and in 1860 furnished three of the whole country's four million bales.[3] Cotton had now for a number of years comprised more than half the value of all exports from the United States; it had come to employ more than three fourths of all the slaves engaged in agriculture, besides nearly as many whites; and it had made New Orleans excel even New York in the volume and value of its export trade.

All this was accomplished not merely by migratory expansion but in large part by betterment of method. A South Carolina planter answered a friend's enthusiastic account of Alabama: "I have never visited your country truly because I have always feared I should either move or always after wish to do it. I

---

[1] *The Cultivator*, VIII, 99, 100 (1841). Some fourteen years earlier the Duke of Saxe-Weimar had written (*Travels*, Philadelphia, 1828, II, 90): "Upon the fourth Chickesa Bluff stood the quondam Fort Pickering. . . . A short mile above the fort stands a group of rather miserable houses: it is the town of Memphis."

[2] LaGrange, Texas, *Monument*, March 3, 1853, reprinted in the New Orleans *Picayune*, March 10, 1853.

[3] The hypothetical weight of the standard bale in 1860 had advanced to four hundred pounds, from half as much at the beginning of the century, but in general practice the western bales ranged nearer five hundred pounds while those of the east often fell short of three hundred. This difference arose mainly from the greater prevalence of baling presses or "screws" in the western country. After the 'sixties the present "standard" of five hundred pounds was established.

know of but one disadvantage . . . viz. there would be no
land to make better by manure. From that consideration I
derive nine tenths of the pleasure of cultivating the earth." [1]
Such mental reactions brought campaigns in the press and
through local societies for eastern improvement, with substantial results in many quarters. But wherever men dwelt, east
or west, the stress of competition impelled wide adoption of
such new things, at least, as became commonly discussed and
easy to procure. In the 'twenties, for example, a quickly
maturing strain of cotton was noted in Tennessee which escaped "rot" or anthracnose; and in the 'thirties a strain which
had been brought from Mexico to the vicinity of Petit Gulf,[2]
Mississippi, developed a special vigor of growth and fruitage
and the great merit of opening every ripe boll so wide that its
contents could be reaped with a single snatch. The Tennessee, the Petit Gulf and sundry other new breeds were speedily spread afar, and, though not all of these justified the claims
of their promoters, the net effect was a great increase of *per
capita* production.[3]

Incidentally not all the migration was westward, nor all of
it in pursuit of wealth. A father who had moved from the lowlands to the highlands of South Carolina narrated some family
history to enforce his precepts upon a son in Texas:

"I wish you were all here with me in this poor country and
healthy climate. You must not do as my father done to stay
in a feverish place Charleston, James Island &c, and bury 10
children, and as I have done in the same place. . . . I staid
untill I was bailed up in flannels to keep Soul and body together and had turned yellow with the climate. . . . Of what
use is all the lands in Texas or the figures on a Bank book to
a dead man. I lost a great estate by leaving of Charleston,
but I gained a hundred times as much by saving my children

---

[1] David R. Williams to Bolling Hall, March 16, 1824. Manuscript in Alabama
Department of Archives. A description of his methods and achievements was contributed by Williams to the *American Farmer* in 1825, reprinted in Harvey T. Cook, *Life
and Legacy of David Rogerson Williams* (New York, 1826), 218-228.

[2] The village has been renamed Rodney.

[3] *American Agriculturist*, II, 51 (1843); *The Plantation*, I, 131-148 (1860).

and my own life. Praises be to God that I had sence enough to leave it   we have here all that is nessasary and usefull in the world, and good health in the bargain." [1]

*   *   *   *   *

As to human equations in the new lands it is a happy chance that a keen observer dwelt in Alabama during the flush 'thirties and the flat but roaring 'forties. His clearest portrait is of the typical son of the Old Dominion: [2]

"The Virginian . . . does not crow over the poor Carolinian and Tennesseean. He does not reproach him with his misfortune of birthplace. No, he thinks the affliction is enough without the triumph. . . . He never throws up to a Yankee the fact of his birthplace. . . . I have known one of my countrymen, on the occasion of a Bostonian owning where he was born, generously protest that he had never heard of it before. . . .

"A Virginian could always get up a good dinner. . . . In *petite* manners, the little attentions of the table, the filling up of the chinks of the conversation, . . . the Virginian, like Eclipse, was first, and there was no second. . . . Every dish was a text, horticulture, hunting, poultry, fishing . . . a slight divergence in favor of fox-chasing, and a detour towards a horse-race now and then, and continual parentheses of recommendation of particular glasses or dishes. . . .

"In the fullness of time the new era had set in — the era of the second great experiment of independence; the experiment, namely, of credit without capital, and enterprise without honesty. . . . The condition of society may be imagined: — vulgarity — ignorance — fussy and arrogant pretension — unmitigated rowdyism — bullying insolence, if they did not

---

[1] Samuel Maverick to Samuel Augustus Maverick, December 12, 1841. Manuscript in the University of Texas Library. The writer had no qualms of unconformity in spelling: "I beleave you have one of my Lexicon, to inable you to desipher any words or spelling above common conception, there is many a man of common sence who cannot play on a jews harp or dance a minuet."

[2] Joseph G. Baldwin, *The Flush Times of Alabama and Mississippi* (New York, 1854), 73–99, *passim.*

rule the hour *seemed* to wield unchecked dominion. . . . Superior to many of the settlers in elegance of manners and general intelligence, it was the weakness of the Virginian to imagine he was superior too in the essential art of being able to hold his hand and make his way in a new country, and especially *such* a country and at *such* a time. What a mistake that was! The times were out of joint. . . . If he made a bad bargain, how could he expect to get rid of it? *He* knew nothing of the elaborate machinery of ingenious chicane. . . . He lived freely, for it was a liberal time, and liberal fashions were in vogue, and it was not for a Virginian to be behind others in hospitality and liberality. He required credit and security, and, of course, had to stand security in turn. When the crash came . . . they broke by neighborhoods. . . . There was one consolation — if the Virginian involved himself like a fool, he suffered himself to be sold out like a gentleman. . . . Accordingly they kept tavern and made a barter of hospitality, a business the only disagreeable part of which was receiving the money."

Or they became schoolmasters or overseers, though generally not with those undignified titles. In conclusion:

"One thing I will say for the Virginians — I never knew one of them under any pressure, extemporize a profession. The sentiment of reverence for the mysteries of medicine and law was too large for a deliberate quackery; as to the pulpit, a man might as well do his starving without hypocrisy."

❋   ❋   ❋   ❋   ❋

As a foil to these new poor there were *nouveaux riches*, styled at the time cotton snobs, who had come to their estate by thrift, successful speculation or chicane, and who sought recognition, like snobs elsewhere, through ostentation and professions of what they fancied to be social orthodoxy.[1] More sinister were the men of lawless habit, ready variously to pick a fight, cut a purse, cheat at cards, traffic with slaves

[1] "Cotton snobs" are the subject of the fourth chapter in D. R. Hundley, *Social Relations in Our Southern States* (New York, 1860).

for stolen goods, or steal a slave by kidnaping a child or decoying an adult. Tricksters and desperadoes in flight from earlier haunts were a feature of every frontier; and a new country where wealth was manifest was for them a welcome resort. From the Piedmont to the Texas cattle country and the mining camps they plied their vocations; but the flow of passengers and freight on the Mississippi gave special opportunity to smooth gamblers and heavy-handed bandits. Though Natchez-under-the-hill was the most notorious, the water front of every town was more or less noisome, and every swamp a potential rogue's harbor. A migrant's letter of 1860 describing the plight of himself and a companion at Vicksburg is perhaps typical of many that were written:

"I wrote to your son Greenlee yesterday and begged him to send me the $200 I left with him, for the simple reason that whilst coming down the river from Memphis to this place night before last we were robbed of every dollar we had. . . . We know not what to do, and can do nothing at all till we get some money somewhere. I wrote Greenlee to send it by very first mail, and now, my dear Sir, for God sake hurry him up." [1]

At various times and places the menace to property and life became so great that citizens combined to suppress lawlessness even by lawless method. Thus in 1841 regulators in Coahoma County, Mississippi, raided Islands nos. 64, 68 and 69, drowned eight of the most notorious of their captives, and whipped the rest and let them go; [2] and in 1859 in Attakapas Parish, Louisiana, those who would take the law into their own hands for the sake of public security and those who decried action except by the paralyzed courts, were virtually in battle array for months on end. [3] The main crisis, however, had long since been passed when the widespread Murrell gang of slave stealers and miscellaneous blackguards was wrecked by the

[1] Dr. Joseph F. Cross to J. D. Davidson, August 21, 1860. Manuscript in the McCormick Agricultural Library, Chicago.

[2] C. F. H. Meason, *Narrative of the Horrible Massacre of the Counterfeiters, Gamblers and Robbers in Coahoma Co., Mississippi, which occurred in August, 1841* (n. p., 1841).

[3] Alexandre Barbe, *Histoire des Comités de Vigilance aux Attakapas* (Saint-Jean-Baptiste, La., 1861).

execution of their leaders, and in the same year vigilantes at Vicksburg overcame their barricaded "gamblers" and hanged enough to intimidate the rest.[1]

No cotton-belt commonwealth even on the Mississippi seems to have attained the ratio reported from New Mexico for 1852 : "This is the fifth execution, we believe, in this Territory in less than a year under sentence of the high court of Judge Lynch, with one under the sentence of the civil court." [2] It is clear that lynch law was essentially a fruit of frontier conditions with population sparse and officials amateurish and easygoing. That it prevailed in the South to a degree comparable at all to that in the mining camps was due doubtless to the thinness of settlement and to the occasional hysteria from rapes and rumors of revolts by Negroes.[3]

The seamy side is perhaps unavoidable, whether life be simple or complex. That the cotton belt was more complex than the contemporary corn and wheat belts to the northward was due to the plantation system and its numerous Negro slaves. Pioneers here as elsewhere left most of the apparatus of law and culture behind them when they plunged into the forest. A student of the time remarked that a prospering migrant might build a fine house and embellish its grounds "in imitation of those he has seen in a more highly cultivated region. But it is not so easy to transport to that forest the intellectual society of the mother-land, and to rear there a school or a college in all the perfection of older institutions of the same kind." Children of the few cultured parents must needs talk of hounds and horses, as their crude companions were doing, rather than of Shakespeare and Milton. "Until society has been pushed far beyond this condition, you cannot expect good schools or cultivated men. Everything like polite learning will be

---

[1] H. R. Howard, compiler, *History of Virgil A. Steward and his Adventure in capturing and exposing the great "western land pirate" and his gang, . . . and the execution of five professional gamblers by the citizens of Vicksburg, on the 6th July, 1835* (New York, 1836). There promptly followed an expulsion of undesirables from Natchez and a rally of citizens to improve order at New Orleans. Charleston *Courier*, July 28, 1835.

[2] Santa Fé *Gazette*, January 1, 1853.

[3] For data concerning these matters see Phillips, *American Negro Slavery*, 454–488.

despised, and ignorance will be respectable because it will be fashionable." [1]

But another, while admitting a prevalent emphasis upon the roughly practical, found in plantation slavery a ground for optimism. "In a few years, owing to the operation of this institution upon our unparalleled natural advantages, we shall be the richest people beneath the bend of the rainbow, and then the arts and the sciences, which always follow in the train of wealth, will flourish to an extent hitherto unknown on this side of the Atlantic." [2]

And a third said: "The effect of introducing cheap compulsory labor into a new unpeopled or thinly peopled country is to anticipate both the advantages and the evils of civilization, by creating at once a wealthy class of proprietors who form the aristocracy of the country, and a laboring class who seem born for little else save the ministering to the wants and gratifications of their superiors." [3]

All of these analyses and prognostications were correct in a degree. Dogs and horses, 'coons and 'possums, crops and prices did prevail in conversation, while Caesar and Cicero were more often the names of Negroes in the yard than of authors on the shelves. Yet culture, if residual, did not approach extinction before prosperity and ambition for fine life brought renaissance. What had happened in the Virginia Piedmont was occurring again in the cotton belt. Some households were stanch enough to hold their standards in the thick of the wilderness and to radiate refinement instead of yielding to rough mediocrity; and the stratification of society facilitated the recovery of culture by those who had relinquished their grasp. It led even the "cotton snobs" to seek refinement when consciousness of their errors taught them to distinguish false patterns from true.

It was said of Troup County and its neighbors in western

---

[1] William Hooper, *Lecture on the Imperfections of Our Primary Schools* (Newbern, N. C., 1832), 7.

[2] Alexander B. Meek, in the *Southern Ladies Book* (Macon, Ga.), 1840.

[3] [Henry Middleton] *Economical Causes of Slavery in the United States, and Obstacles to Its Abolition* (London, 1857), 9.

Georgia that they were settled in controlling degree from the first by gentle folk and never knew a rough régime.[1] A similar transit of civilization unimpaired, or else a rapid recovery, was noted as to the Huntsville neighborhood in Northern Alabama [2] and the Natchez and Petit Gulf districts on the Mississippi; [3] and such may be surmised as to sundry other communities. Society in general was rapidly emerging from the pell-mell phase. Many backwoodsmen, like many urban laborers, remained uncouth from poverty, dissipation or stubborn choice; but the people of every rank and quarter were so sociable and chatty, by Southern habit, that each new settlement rapidly became integrated within itself and interlinked with its neighbors on every side. The patterns of conduct and aspiration differed in the several strata of the social order; but each group was likely to have members from such widely scattered easterly regions that its customs tended to become a blend of those from the older South at large. Thus the cotton belt differed not much from the upper South except for its comparative immaturity and the greater proportion of Negroes in its population.

[1] Absalom H. Chappell, *Miscellanies of Georgia* (Atlanta, [1874]), part II, p. 22.

[2] George A. McCall, *Letters from the Frontiers* (Philadelphia, 1868), 277.

[3] Lowry and McCardle, *History of Mississippi* (2d ed., Jackson, Miss., 1891), 503–505.

CHAPTER VII

STAPLE ECONOMY

THE several major crops had these features in common : that they were produced for market rather than for home consumption, and they were grown in hills or drills, with the ground intervening kept bare and mellow by cultivation. Thus the routine of summer had some similarity from one staple to another. But seed time, and conspicuously the harvest, brought processes quite distinct.[1]

When St. Matthew mentioned mustard seed as the least of all seeds he showed an ignorance of the tobacco plant, for ten thousand of its seed will hardly overflow a teaspoon. To strew these in a field is not to be attempted. They must be sown in a seedbed; and even for this they are usually mingled with sifted ashes or other powdery stuff to facilitate an even scattering. In plantation practice[2] a site was chosen where forest mold was virgin, and in midwinter a copious pile of logs and brush was burnt upon it for the double purpose of adding rich ashes and killing any competing seeds or sprouts. The seed were there sown before the winter's end; and the sprouting plants were protected from frost by coverings of brush or cloth, and from ravages of the "fly" by sprinklings or powderings with materials repellent to these pests.

[1] A useful assemblage of essays from various pens describing methods in the several staples as prevailing at the middle of the nineteenth century is printed in alphabetical arrangement in J. D. B. DeBow, ed., *The Industrial Resources, etc., of the Southern and Western States* (New Orleans, 1852–1853). A slenderer collection is in Francis S. Holmes, ed., *The Southern Farmer and Market Gardener* (enlarged ed., Charleston, 1852).

[2] Of tobacco methods and problems there are many discussions in the contemporary farm journals, particularly the *Farmers' Register* (1834–1843), edited by Edmund Ruffin. As to varieties of "the weed" such divergencies prevailed in local designations that I cannot undertake a discussion with any confidence.

By the end of spring, when the plants were large enough to handle, the fields, preferably of freshly cleared woodland, must be put into tilth and marked with little hills, usually three feet apart, ready for a rain to soak them. When the rain came, all available hands must work at the transplanting. Some drew the plants carefully from their bed; others carried them in baskets through the fields, dropping one at each hill; and the rest of the gang set them in the ground, making a little hole in the hill, inserting the roots of the seedling therein, and lightly packing the mud about them. The return of dry weather would suspend this work and call for a gentle scraping of the hills to break the crusts of mud. Another rain and another would bring transplanting again, including the replacement of dead plants in the previous plantings. Cultivation ensued with plow and hoe until the spread of the great leaves brought the "lay-by."

The tobacco plant, if permitted to follow its own habit, will produce a tall stalk and many leaves of moderate size and thin texture. But the market wants large leaves of full body. Therefore when the plant begins to bud at the top as a preliminary to blooming, the whole top is taken off, leaving upon the stalk such number of leaves as the plant is likely to force to full size. Thereupon shoots spring from each junction of leaf and stalk in an effort of the plant to produce branches. These "suckers" must be removed as they appear and reappear. Furthermore the crop must be guarded from consumption by the great juicy hornworms which are addicted to a diet of green tobacco leaves. Flocks of turkeys were useful in this, but many worms and eggs must be sought on the under side of the leaves and crushed by human hands. As an added task, some growers "primed" their standing crops by pulling off the bottom leaves, which if allowed to ripen would produce only "lugs" of low grade. Others refrained from this on the ground that it caused the plants to lose much of their sap by bleeding. The topping was a task for experts; but all hands joined in the worming and suckering when they could be spared from the work of cultivation. This filled the routine of summer quite full, for the heaviest "glut" of worms came after the lay-by and shortly before the cutting.

When in late summer or autumn the leaves began to yellow, the plants were cut off at the base and allowed to wilt in the field. Then whether split, pierced or pegged for the purpose, they were strung upon laths for future convenience of handling. They were now carried for drying on scaffolds, or else directly to tall barns where the laden sticks were arranged upon joists, tier under tier, not too thickly for the completion of the drying whether by the circulation of outdoor air or by the heat of fire. This curing made the leaves too brittle for further manipulation until moist weather rendered them pliable; and as a rule spring was awaited for further processing. Then, after a wet day, the laths were lifted down, the stalks taken off and "bulked" in orderly piles to keep the leaves soft [1] for the time being. The slow task of stripping ensued, with a sorting simultaneously into three grades as a rule, — bright, dark and lugs. The leaves as sorted were bound into little bundles or "hands", and these again were bulked in moist weather to await "prizing." This concluding process was a careful packing into hogsheads for market. A barefoot man inside the container would place the parcels in smooth layers until it was full. Then pressure was applied with weights and levers, more tobacco laid in and pressed again, and so on until the hogshead was tightly full with about a thousand pounds of the leaf. With its head inserted and securely hooped, the hogshead was ready to be rolled or hauled to a river landing.[2] The work in any year's crop extended from before seedtime to beyond the seedtime of the next year, with no great intervals except perhaps in late fall and winter. And the crop required such detailed attention that a laborer could hardly tend more than three or four acres. On the other hand no heavy work was involved, unless

---

[1] Any cigar smoker will be aware of the pronounced effect of atmospheric moisture upon the pliability of the cured leaf. The bulking served the same purpose as a humidor.

[2] This routine is substantially unchanged to the present day except that the packing may be dispensed with since the factories have largely moved to the vicinity of the fields.

the housing be so considered, and no exposure except for the transplanting into the wet fields of early summer.

❋   ❋   ❋   ❋   ❋

Thanks doubtless to the copiousness of water and the dearness of labor, rice culture in America never adopted the Oriental practice of planting in seed beds and transplanting the seedlings into the fields. Generally, however, the fields had the standard equipment of a source of water and an embankment to hold the flood upon the crop. In addition there were ditches great and small to drain the fields on occasion. In the Carolina-Georgia lowlands the fields, after a preliminary breaking, were laid off in broad shallow drills, twelve to fifteen inches apart, in which the seed were strewn. If these had previously been "clayed" by soaking in mud, the water was at once let on to cover the furrows and sprout the crop. But if unclayed seed were used they were covered lightly by hoeing and the "sprout flow" was omitted. Some planters followed one plan and some the other. Practice also varied as to the schedule of the later flows, though most commonly where the tide was available they included the "point flow", begun when the seedlings were visible above ground, the "long flow" in mid-season, and the still longer "lay-by flow" when the stalks were approaching full height and needed help in upholding their heavy heads against the winds. Between the flows the fields were drained and the weeds and grass pulled or chopped out.

As soon as the last flow was drained the harvest began. Each laborer grasped with his left hand a group of stalks, cut them with a sickle-stroke below his grip, laid the handful upon adjacent stubble to dry, and continued thus through the field. Next day the stalks were gathered in armfuls, bound into sheaves, and in due time carried to a stack-yard for further drying. The threshing, like that of other sorts of small grain was done with flails or by the treading of animals until machines were invented. But the final process, milling, was unique, for the occasion was merely to remove the husk from the kernel with as little breakage of the brittle grain as might be. Until recent years this was done by pounding a pestle upon the deep contents of a mortar. In early times the pounding was a manual process; but before the end of the eighteenth century mills were introduced for the purpose. The mechanical problem was met by setting a row of slotted timbers to slide vertically as pestles. The revolving of a horizontal beam near-by, pierced with spokes long enough to reach into the slots, would successively lift the pestles and let them fall into the grain-filled mortars below.[1] After the pounding there came the winnowing, sifting and polishing of the rice. The whole grains were barreled for market, the broken grains were mainly kept for home consumption, and the by-product rice flour was fed to livestock unless it could be sold to brewers.

Narrow limits were set for the locale of the rice industry by its need for copious water cheaply applied. Brook swamps, the first recourse, afforded as a rule but small scattered tracts rich enough and level enough to serve the purpose when a reservoir had been built at a higher level to catch water for flooding on occasion. The petty size and scattered location of these fields, their deficit of water for a full schedule of labor-saving flows, their poor adaptation for drainage, their shallow soils and the smallness of their yield caused most of them to be abandoned within a half-century after McKewn Johnstone led the way in 1758, by an enterprise near Winyah Bay, to the reclamation of river swamps for tideflow. For this it was necessary to use the floodplain on the tidal course of a fresh-water stream. The land surface must be low enough to be flooded at high tide and high enough to be drained when the tide was out. With such a tract selected, the proprietor would clear the timber, build a bank along the front and banks to separate the fields as expedient; dig a main ditch behind the levee,

---

[1] A picture of this apparatus is printed in John Drayton, *View of South Carolina* (Charleston, 1802), facing p. 122; and rice processes are described in the adjacent pages. Fuller discussions are in R. F. W. Allston, *Memoir on the Introduction and Planting of Rice* (Charleston, 1843); Edmund Ruffin, *Agricultural Survey of South Carolina* (Columbia, 1843); and R. F. W. Allston, *Essay on Sea Coast Crops* (Charleston, 1854), reprinted in *DeBow's Review*, XVI, 589–615. J. J. Ampère, *Promenade en Amérique* (Paris, 1855), 112, 113, marveled at the nicety of the force in the pounding, to strip the husks without crushing the grain.

sundry drains perpendicular to this at intervals of about three hundred feet, and "quarter drains", perpendicular again at intervals half as great, thereby laying off the field into plats of substantially an acre in size. Further, he would pierce the levee here and there with a culvert or "trunk", boxed in and equipped at each end with a door, pivoted above and controlled by a ratchet. Such a trunk, laid at the level of low tide and connecting the main ditch with the river outside, would keep the field flooded or drained at will, according as the doors were set. To flow the crop, the outer door was racked up and the inner one let down to close the trunk's mouth. At high tide the pressure of water from without would open the inner door, and a stream would flow through until the water levels inside and out were equalized. But when the tide fell, the beginning of any return current would promptly close the door and keep the water impounded upon the crop. When drainage was desired instead, the inner door was raised and the outer one lowered. At low tide this would expose the ground and empty the ditches, and empty them again at each recurring low tide while preventing inflow at all times.

The control thus established was automatic and complete as long as the drains, trunks and gates were kept in good order. The tide-flow system was hazardous nevertheless. Alligators might undermine a bank, or muskrats or crawfish bore through to give a channel which the water, if undetected, might enlarge into a break. More damaging, a flood from the uplands might overtop and wreck the levee, perhaps to the ruin of the crop; or, most serious of all, a hurricane might drive ocean water inshore and raise it to an overtopping height, not only breaking the bank but salting the field to such effect as to make the land useless for tillage until a leaching through several years could render the soil sweet again. These tide-flow fields, furthermore, were in many cases so narrow that upkeep of banks, trunks and drains involved heavy expense per acre; and finally in some tracts continuance of cultivation through many years brought an oxidation of the humus in their soil and a consequent lowering of the surface to a point where it was no longer above the level of low tide. This would eliminate the field from further use. With these risks and tendencies there conspired eventually the cheapening of power and improvement of both pumps and harvesting machinery to give advantage to districts in Arkansas, Louisiana, Texas and California, where the climate is equally adapted to rice, where the ground is firm enough to invite the use of reaping machines, where water can be lifted from streams or wells, and where the space available is limited perhaps only by the horizon. The costs have proved so much less in these newer districts that on the Carolina-Georgia coast rice growing is now discontinued. The fields once banked and ditched at great expense, and valued in the middle of the nineteenth century as high as two hundred dollars per acre, are now frequented only by waterfowl; and the pounding mills at Charleston stand as empty relics of a bygone day.

✻   ✻   ✻   ✻   ✻

Indigo has nothing in common with rice except climatic needs. Grown on the higher lands of the seaboard and for many miles inland, it was often cultivated on the same plantations with rice, the work in the two crops alternating in a dovetailed schedule. The plant, though it is a legume, suggests asparagus in size and in the fineness of its fronds of tiny leaves. Its valuable product, which often brought four shillings or more per pound, was a violet-blue material into which part of its leaf-substance was converted by fermentation. The distinctive task in this crop was the conversion and recovery of this dyestuff. The plants when in bloom were cut and carried, with care not to rub the leaves, and immersed in a vat of water. After a steeping the liquor was drawn into another vat where it was vigorously beaten while fermenting. Here it must be watched by day and by night until a certain stage was reached at which the ferment must be stopped by adding some such agent as limewater. The suspended matter was then allowed to settle, the water drained off, the solid stuff scooped out, strained, pressed, cut into cubes, dried and sent to market for use by dyers and laundresses.[1] The plant was delicate, and the manipulation at the vats required expert attention if a good quality was to result. Though the product seldom attained a hundred pounds per acre and a laborer could hardly tend more than four acres, the crop clearly yielded high profits for a time. But an increase in its output in the East Indies, together with an invasion of its American fields by a destructive caterpillar a decade or two before the end of the eighteenth century wrecked the industry in Carolina, Georgia and Louisiana alike.[2] In our own times a coal-tar product has driven vegetable indigo from the world of commerce.

❊   ❊   ❊   ❊   ❊

In a few very fertile tracts in the West Indies the roots of the sugar cane will sprout new crops for perhaps a dozen years without replanting. And the tropical exemption from frost permits the cane to reach full ripeness and to be harvested at leisure. On the other hand, cane will grow as far north as middle Georgia, yielding sweet enough juice for concentration into sirup. But for commercial extraction of sugar a degree of ripeness is required which is not attained in less than eight months of growth; and this is not afforded northward of southern Louisiana. The industry would not flourish there, in fact, did not the rich delta lands yield a crop great enough in gross weight per acre to offset some deficit of ripeness and a necessity of replanting after two or three crops have been harvested. For any pronounced prosperity, furthermore, the Louisiana industry depends upon tariff protection against foreign competition.

That Louisiana cane juice would yield crystalline sugar with profit was proved by Etienne de Boré in 1796 when the milled

---

[1] Accounts of the process are in *A Short Description of the Province of South Carolina* (London, 1770), reprinted in B. R. Carroll, ed., *Historical Collections of South Carolina* (New York, 1836), II, 532–535; *John Tobler's Almanac*, 1776, reprinted in A. H. Hirsch, *The Huguenots of Colonial South Carolina* (Durham, N. C., 1928), 313–315, and [J. H. Ingraham] *The South-West* (Philadelphia, 1835), I, 273, 274.

[2] This was not to be regretted on all scores, for the refuse from the vats had spread a most unpleasant stench and furnished breeding places for flies by the million.

crop of his plantation near New Orleans brought a return of some twelve thousand dollars. The pursuit of his example was slow, however, because the cost of apparatus was high and the provision of seed cane for a new plantation generally required several years of propagation on the spot. By 1822, when steam engines began to be used to drive the mills, the output was about thirty thousand hogsheads of a thousand pounds each, with some fifty gallons of molasses as a by-product from each hogshead of sugar. In 1827, when detailed statistics are first available, there were three hundred and eight sugar-producing units, with slaves to the number of some twenty-one thousand, and an output of nearly ninety thousand hogsheads. Stimulated, stricken and spurred again by tariff revisions, the number of plantations in 1844 had increased to seven hundred and sixty-two, with more than half of their mills driven by steam; the number of slaves upon them exceeded fifty thousand, the product filled more than two hundred thousand hogsheads, and upon more than three hundred plantations on the border of the district mills were being built with a view to change of staple from cotton to sugar. Further expansion carried the number of plantations by 1858 to twelve hundred and ninety-eight, producing three hundred and sixty-two thousand hogsheads and maintaining a proportionate number of slaves. The industry meanwhile had been introduced upon the Brazos and adjacent rivers in Texas, where there were now some forty plantations producing some six thousand hogsheads.[1]

In Louisiana, from the leveed front of the Mississippi and from the banks of sundry bayous, the cane fields generally stretched in solid expanse, whether for a hundred yards or for the depth of a mile, to where the surface of the land lay too low to invite reclamation from swamp or marsh. Complete freedom from stones made tillage easy to any depth a plow might reach; and the deeper the better for this luxuriant crop.

[1] E. J. Forstall, *Agricultural Productions of Louisiana* ([New Orleans] 1845); P. A. Champomier, *Statement of the Sugar Crop made in Louisiana* (New Orleans, annual, 1845–1859). Champomier gives the name, location, mill equipment and output of each proprietor.

Though the cultivation invited some use of the hoe, it differed quite sharply from tobacco and cotton in calling for the most part for sturdy men and in affording less employment for women and children. The process of seeding consisted in laying two or three rows of cane parallel in a deep furrow, and covering them with the plow. This was best done before the end of February. Shoots emerged erelong from eyes at the joints of each buried cane, and a cultivation was begun which ended only with late summer. The beginning of harvest was determined not by the state of the crop but by consultation of the calendar, for the process must be well-nigh complete by the time sharp frost was due. The cane cut during the first few days was laid, unstripped of its leaves, in great beds or "mats" for protection against frost until wanted as seed for the next year's planting. Then the true harvest began. With four slashes of a heavy knife a stalk would be ready for the cart, one stroke stripping the leaves from the right side, another from the left, a third severing the stalk at the ground, and the fourth cutting off the still-green joints at the top. The crop as cut was carted to the mill, which was a feature of every plantation.

As long as the weather continued mild the cutting, grinding and boiling operations continued simultaneously. But an occurrence of frost emptied the mill of its operatives, for all hands were sent to the field to cut the crop at top speed, piling the unstripped stalks in the furrows to diminish the damage.[1] Then the mill crew was doubled, to work night and day to get the juice past the danger of souring after thaw. Sometimes a perfect salvage was accomplished, and sometimes indeed frost held off till harvest was ended. But in other years caprice of weather spoiled much of the crop; and on rare occasions not even seed cane were saved.[2]

[1] This device of "windrowing" was initiated by John Anderson on the Houmas plantation in Ascension Parish in 1828. As a rule the canes from four rows were laid in a single furrow. — *Farmers' Register*, II, 547.

[2] The processes in field and mill were discussed by Judah P. Benjamin and others in J. D. B. DeBow, *Industrial Resources*, III, 195-321; by R. L. Allen in the *American Agriculturist*, VI, *passim*; and by numerous travelers in their respective books. The régime has been analyzed historically by V. A. Moody, *Slavery on Louisiana Sugar Plantations* ([New Orleans] 1924).

Most of the cells in the stalk are filled with a pure, dilute solution of sugar, but other cells contain the sap of the plant which when expressed adds impurities to the juice which will prevent any crystallization unless removed or diminished by clarification. This was done by an application of moderate heat, and some limewater, producing a scum which must be removed. In common plantation practice the clarified juice was boiled in a series of open caldrons, with heat increased as the liquor thickened, until the content of the small kettle at the end of the row was fully concentrated. This heavy stuff (boiling water will hold in solution five times its own weight of sugar) was then carried to a shed and allowed to cool in boxes or hogsheads. Finally as much of the mother-liquor as would obey the force of gravity was drained away. The resulting sugar was brown and moist, because each crystal, though white in itself, held a coating of the gummy molasses.

These processes were known to be crude. Extraction by pressure between iron rollers often yielded hardly more than half the juice, because the spongy crushed cane ("bagasse") reabsorbed a large proportion before the liquid could flow away. Furthermore the consumption of fuel ran to two or three cords of wood for each ton of sugar produced; the high degree of heat required in the last stage of the boiling carameled some of the material in process; and perhaps a quarter of the saccharine substance as put into the coolers was marketed in the cheap form of molasses instead of being recovered and sold as sugar. West Indian molasses was largely converted into rum, whether on the spot or in the ports of New England; but in Louisiana the competition of whiskey from Kentucky and Ohio kept rum distilling within small dimensions.

Beginning with beet-sugar enterprises in France during the Napoleonic wars a series of inventions wrought great improvements in mill apparatus, which were adopted where feasible in Louisiana. The chief of these was the vacuum pan, a great closed retort connected with a steam-condenser and an air pump. This permitted boiling at temperatures where caramelization could not occur, it economized fuel, greatly diminished molasses as a by-product, and produced a much better grade of sugar. This and the other devices, however, demanded more expert attention than could normally be expected of slaves, and added salary costs to the expenses of operation. The modern appliances were therefore not suited to plantations of small or medium scale.

Other improvements came through the introduction of ribbon cane [1] in 1817, which ripened earlier than the preceding varieties; through the application of guano and the plowing in of the cane tops and leaves as fertilizer instead of burning them as waste; through the widening of the spaces between the rows; and through the replacement of oxen with four-mule teams for deeper plowing and better drainage.

❃   ❃   ❃   ❃   ❃

Of indigo I have merely seen a few volunteer plants growing in a rice field. Tobacco, rice and sugar crops I have inspected as an occasional visitor, questioning the proprietors and the laborers upon their tasks and problems. But I was "bawn an' bred" in the cotton belt, and thought it a goodly land until riper knowledge taught me that my red hills were niggard for all pecuniary purposes. In happy childhood I played hide-and-seek among the cotton bales with sable companions; I heard the serenade of the katydids while tossing on a hot pillow, somewhat reconciled to the night's heat because it was fine for the cotton crop. I rejoiced with my elders at the sight of sheet-lightning on the northern horizon because in that part of Georgia it always brought rain within a day's time — except perhaps in dry weather. Later I followed the pointers and setters for quail in the broom-sedge, the curs for 'possums and 'coons in the woods, and the hounds on the trail of the fox; and for one season, suspending my college course for more serious affairs, I guided the plow and plied the hoe in a crop of my own, gaining more in muscle and experience than in cash.

The planting, plowing and chopping proved of interest both in theory and practice. The cotton stalks of the year before

[1] So called from the stripes of greenish yellow and purple which alternate in its rind.

were not large enough to requ re knocking down before breaking the land, but they scratched my mare so sharply that she
would not let me plow down the row. On advice from a Negro
neighbor I set my course diagonally from one curving terrace-
balk to another, and this went very well. With the soil thus
loosened, it was ridged in contour lines again and the crests
of the ridges lightly opened to receive the seed. These were
strewn thickly, and when the young plants had put forth two
or three leaves they were thinned to clusters a foot or so apart.
When the plants had grown beyond the menace of cutworms
they were chopped again to leave a single stalk where each
cluster had stood. Light plowings alternated with the hoe-
ings and were repeated after each rain, to break the crust and
kill the grass. In short, I followed the custom of the country.
In due time, amid their heavy foliage, the plants put forth buds
or "squares" and these produced blossoms, creamy in the morning, white at noon, pink at evening, and on the second day
a purplish red, deepening until the petals fell. While the
young pods or "bolls" were swelling to the size of an egg the
cultivation was ended. Some damage was done by lice, leaf-
worms and bollworms; but the boll weevil had then just
crossed the Rio Grande and was not known even by reputation
in Georgia. In mid-August the bolls, in series beginning near
the bases of the lowest branches, changing color from green to
brown, and splitting along segment lines, yawned wide to
expose their "locks" — little masses of lint and seed which had
filled the four or five compartments. In earlier life I had picked
cotton for short periods as a diversion. But the harvest of this
crop of my own brought pain of mind and body. My hands,
cramped from the plow-stock, made no speed in snatching the
fluffy stuff, and my six-foot stature imposed a stooping intolerable in its day-long continuance. The college year beginning,
a woman and her brood were engaged to finish the job and
I hied me again to the halls of academe. Here ends autobiography, with a remark that none of the work was beyond the
strength of a stripling, and the sunshine, though very hot, was
never prostrating.

Cotton processes have remained thus simple for a century past. Initially the seed were dropped in hills, but in early years this gave place to the thick strewing in furrows. The seed whose sprouts are killed in the chopping remain to fertilize the plants which are permitted to grow. The scraping with plow and hoe continues as of yore, and picking-machines, though promised often,[1] are still of the future. When these come, if ever, they will change the cast of the crop, for it is alone the contemplation of prospects in picking which limits the seeding to five or six acres per hand.

❋   ❋   ❋   ❋   ❋

As to the scale of units, the greatest advantage to large plantations was given by sugar cane because of the importance of the manufacturing process as an element in production. A small farm could hardly warrant the construction of even the crudest equipment for grinding, boiling and curing. A plantation with less than a dozen laborers producing less than a hundred hogsheads, or fifty tons, of sugar could support only a horse-power mill along with a set of open pans for evaporation. A somewhat larger crop would warrant an investment of the five or six thousand dollars required for a steam engine to drive the mill; but vacuum pans and refinery apparatus were not justified by less than a thousand-hogshead scale.[2] Economies of quantity production were so pronounced that, though the aggregate output usually increased, the number of properties diminished year by year after 1850 through the consolidation of

[1] For example, inventions were announced in the *Farmers' Register*, III, 678 (1836, with a description of the machine); the *American Cotton Planter*, I, 271 (1853); *De-Bow's Review*, XVIII, 333 (1855), a thresher in this case rather than a picker; the *World's Work*, XXI, 13748 (1910). A settler near Palestine, Texas, wrote in 1856: "I like to forgot to tell you about our great Labor saving machine, the Cotton Harvester. I saw one in Town & subscribed for one   they cost 26 dollars   I think they will answer & one hand can pick as much cotton in a day as 3   they will be delivered here in the fall   they are certainly a great advantage to the Planter & a fortune to the inventor." But in later letters of the series there is no further mention of the device. — Manuscripts in private possession.

[2] It was in 1844 that a plantation was first equipped, at a cost of $20,000, with apparatus for making white sugar direct from cane juice; four others followed the example next year (E. J. Forstall, *Agricultural Productions of Louisiana*), but the number did not advance to above ten during the rest of the *ante-bellum* period.

small estates into large ones.[1] As early as 1833, when the whole world had hardly a thousand miles of railroad in operation, Valcour Aime built a railroad on his plantation to enlarge the feasible radius for hauling cane to his refinery.[2] Engrossment has ever since proceeded remorselessly, until in our day the production of sugar, whether from cane or beets, is in the main a business proper only to great corporations.

Tobacco lay at the other extreme in the list of staples. A Virginian sagely said: "Tobacco cannot be grown profitably in large quantities. Six hands often make double as much money at tobacco as at cotton or sugar; but a crop of tobacco that employs sixty hands always brings the farmer in debt."[3] The reason lay in the complete absence of machine processes and the need of judicious care at nearly every turn — at least in the transplanting, topping, cutting, curing and sorting. Since the labor of slaves was essentially crude, care must be supplied by detailed oversight.

Rice was nearest to sugar in the matter of scale. No scrupulous care was needed; the threshing and milling gave some advantage to quantity production after the introduction of machinery; and the scheme for control of the flooding reinforced this. Economy of embankment suggested flood compartments of a score or more acres, and the need of cultivating every such field quickly between flows called for laboring corps of considerable size.

It was remarked about 1760: "They reckon thirty Slaves a proper number for a Rice Plantation, and to be tended with one Overseer."[4] The scale tended to increase thereafter, though not hugely. James L. Pettigru, when alluding in 1837

---

[1] Although as a rule many new sugar plantations were inaugurated each year, the gross number in Louisiana shrank from above fifteen hundred at the beginning of the 'fifties to about thirteen hundred at the end of the decade, because those using horses or mules to turn their cylinders diminished from 650 to 300, while those using steam power increased from 865 to 987. In addition there were perhaps a hundred farmers growing cane to be ground at some neighbor's mill.

[2] *Diary*, extracts reprinted in U. B. Phillips ed., *Plantation and Frontier Documents* (Cleveland, O., 1909), I, 218, 219.

[3] George Fitzhugh in *DeBow's Review*, XXX, 89 (January, 1861).

[4] B. R. Carroll, ed., *Historical Collections of South Carolina*, II, 202.

to his property of two hundred acres in rice and about one hundred and fifty slaves of all ages, said, "a little plantation is a sorry undertaking in the low-country,"[1] but he was perhaps indulging in a false humility; and the cause of his bankruptcy five years afterward lay less in the smallness of his scale, we may suspect, than in his own absenteeism and a visitation of cholera. An uplander practicing law in Charleston could not conduct such a property on the Savannah River with success as a side issue.

Wheat had none of tobacco's limitations, for it required less attention than any other crop in our list. It was, and is, merely seeded and harvested, with no work whatever demanded in the interim. Wherever wheat replaced tobacco in Virginia or cotton in North Carolina it promoted consolidation of units; and each improvement in harvesting apparatus increased the tendency. There are no tales told in the South to compare with the California tradition of wheat ranches so vast that plowmen, carrying their lunches, turned each a single furrow for his morning's work and plowed homeward through the afternoon; but the scales of Edward Lloyd[2] in Maryland, Philip St. George Cocke[3] in Virginia and the Burgwyns[4] in North Carolina were a challenge to the wheat growers of any region in their day. In the few cases where corn was grown as the main staple[5] the tendency was not unlike that of wheat; and indigo, so far as can be ascertained, was analogous to tobacco.

Cotton was adapted to cultivation on any scale great or small, with no peculiar disadvantage in any case. The harvested crop, imperishable and not of great weight, could be stored

[1] J. P. Carson, *Life of Pettigru* (Washington, 1920), 194.
[2] *American Farmer*, VIII, 59–61.
[3] Diary of his plantation, "Belmead", in *Plantation and Frontier Documents*, I, 208–214.
[4] Discussed in Chapter XIII herein.
[5] For an example see the discussion of Josiah Collin's plantation in Chapter XIII herein. But no Southern instances have been encountered equal to that of James Davis near the junction of the Miami with the Ohio, whose crop in 1849 from eighteen hundred acres at about fifty bushels per acre was reported to fill a corn crib ten feet high, six feet wide and three miles long! — *The Cultivator*, n. s., VII, 185, quoting the Cincinnati *Gazette*.

indefinitely or hauled for many miles if no gin were at hand; and every neighborhood was likely to have a ginnery for public patronage. One-horse farmers and hundred-slave planters competed on fairly even terms, acre for acre. The planter stood to gain or lose more heavily than the farmer, merely, for the most part, because he had more acres in the crop. In sea-island cotton the need of care in handling, which tended to restrict the scale, was offset by the need of expert seed selection, which gave some advantage to large producers, and still more by the climatic insalubrity for white laborers. The net effect of this interplay of tendencies on the sea islands appears to have been a predominance of moderately large producers.

❊   ❊   ❊   ❊   ❊

Whatever the scale maintained, the staple usually absorbed the thought of the proprietors in great degree. Basil Hall, when voyaging on the Alabama, found the name of cotton almost as constantly in his ears as the scent from the bales on board was in his nostrils: "All day and almost all night long the captain, pilot, crew and passengers were talking of nothing else; and sometimes our ears were so wearied with the sound of cotton! cotton! cotton! that we gladly hailed a fresh inundation of company in hopes of some change — but alas! Wiggin's Landing or Choctaw Creek, or the towns of Gaines or Cahawba or Canton produced us nothing but fresh importations of the raw material. 'What's cotton at?' was the first eager inquiry. 'Ten cents.' 'Oh, that will never do!' From the cotton in the market, they went to the crops in the fields — the frost which had nipped their shoots — the hard times — the overtrading — and so round to the prices and prospects again and again." [1] Many another visitor in the century since Hall's tour has found the talk of cotton relieved only by that of rice or sugar when his journey chanced to carry him into their particular provinces.

The staple's absorption of land and labor was usually less

[1] Basil Hall, *Travels in the United States* (Edinburgh, 1829), III, 310.

than might be judged from its monopoly of conversation; for while cotton, sugar or tobacco constituted a man's prospect of treasure, his food supply generally came from his own ancillary crops, and much of his equipment was made by his men and women when "out of crop." The degree of concentration was determined not so much by the characteristics of the staple as by the degree to which commercial facilities made it economical to procure needed goods through purchase. As early as 1800 some of the planters near Charleston, producing nothing but rice and sweet potatoes, depended even for corn upon distant supply; [1] and before the middle of the century sugar planters on the Mississippi were buying barge loads of coal from Pittsburgh to diminish the labor of wood cutting in their own swamps. Yankee craft, furthermore, peddled salt meat and fish, apples, cabbages and cranberries, hats and harness along the Atlantic seaboard; and Ohio flatboats performed similar functions yet more copiously on the western waters.

In the main, therefore, by-industries were either optional or imperative, according to locality. Fencing, ditching, road repair and carpentry must of course be done on the spot, and blacksmithing and grist milling were best near at hand; but the stemming of tobacco, the refining of sugar, the conversion of molasses into rum, of grain into whiskey, fruit into brandy, or flour into ship's bread, like the weaving of cloth and of baskets, the making of chairs, buckets and barrels, leather and shoes, candles and soap and many other things, were done or not done according as expediency or inclination determined. If a plantation lay remote, it were well to cultivate self-sufficiency; if markets were near and varied supplies cheap, a more thorough specialization was to be followed. But this was not without exceptions. A short haul to a city would invite the sale of melons, fruits, cordwood, cured Spanish moss, dairy products or the like; and access by fast freighting, whether by land or water, would suggest perishable produce for distant markets — early fruits, berries and vegetables for northward cities. Thus as early as 1787 a ship from South Carolina carried a thousand

[1] John Drayton, *View of South Carolina* (Charleston, 1802), 113.

watermelons to Boston,[1] and sweet potatoes followed to relieve the monotony of the New England "boiled dinner." In 1845 the orchards of Major Reybold and his four sons, containing upwards of a hundred thousand trees in Delaware and Maryland, shipped nearly a hundred thousand baskets of peaches by steamer and schooner to New York and Philadelphia;[2] and in 1858 a South Carolinian made factorage arrangements to supply several thousand bushels of early peaches by railroad to the Richmond market.[3] Meanwhile the Norfolk vicinity had put large acreage into strawberries, tomatoes and cucumbers, and a single planter near the Dismal Swamp was using twelve hundred bushels of Irish potatoes for seeding purposes, to satisfy at a profit New York's craving for fresh food in springtime.[4] One or another of these crops, not to mention peanuts which, like peaches, were good for hogs if they couldn't be sold, might become to all intents the staple of a plantation, or equally of a farm. More commonly they were supplements to a more orthodox crop.

Where a common carrier was not at hand, and this was the general case, a planter might keep a wagon plying somewhat constantly, and procure goods when wanted; but a farmer could spare himself and his "critter" only when his crops gave leisure, and he must often make what he needed or make shift without it. On the other hand, each plantation as a rule had some partially disabled slaves who could render no service unless employed in spinning or in making baskets, mule collars and the like. Furthermore, the mere scale of a plantation invited specialization by some of its personnel, whether as millers, blacksmiths, wheelwrights, carpenters, coopers, weavers or seamstresses in fairly steady pursuit of their crafts — while a self-sufficing farmer and his wife must be a Jack and a Jane of all trades, presumably good at none. Few units of any scale were utterly specialized, and none were completely

---

[1] *Gazette of the State of Georgia* (Savannah), September 6, 1787.

[2] *Southern Cultivator*, III, 165, reprinting from the *Boston Cultivator*.

[3] Letter of J. C. Hunt, September 2, 1858. — Manuscript in Massie papers, University of Texas.

[4] *Southern Planter*, XIII, 211 (Richmond, Va., July, 1853).

self-sufficing. The régime varied endlessly with locality, capabilities and predilections; but good husbandry and housewifery were apt to sustain a pride in meeting many home wants with home products.

✳ ✳ ✳ ✳ ✳

The problems of staple economy were not to be divorced from husbandry in general. Rain fell on the just and the unjust whether in the needful showers or in ruinous deluge. Drought blasted planter and farmer alike and the many who maintained a scale 'twix' an' 'tween. Men and beasts must be fed whether the main product of the farm was edible or not. Ditches and fences were wanted for one field much as for another. Gullies tended to form and soil to be lost, whether the fields were in tobacco, cotton or corn. Mere patience and routine perseverance would not meet all the needs in a changing world, particularly not those of agriculture on lean hills tending always to grow leaner. The challenge to students was manifold; and the students were, of course, mostly to be counted among the planters. These had in varying degree leisure, education, funds permitting travel, and a wide range of personal contacts. They had also much to gain individually from any improvement of seed, method or machinery on their estates. The farmers, with backs bent over the plow by day, had little energy to pore over print by night or to tabulate experimental results of their own. They stood to gain little by change of detail in method, and improved apparatus might readily be beyond their financial reach. The government in those days maintained no experiment farms or bureau demonstrators. Innovations must come from private initiative.

Aside from Cyrus McCormick, who was a Shenandoah farmer when he made his famous reaping machine, the chief contributors were planters: the Virginians, John Taylor of Caroline and Edmund Ruffin, enthusiastic and indefatigable advocates of crop rotation and fertilizing; James H. Hammond of South Carolina, a promoter of draining, terracing and fertilizing; the Georgians, Jethro V. Jones, a breeder of new cotton strains, and

David Dickson, a demonstrator in making every slave an expert operative; and Doctor N. B. Cloud of Alabama, a champion of deep plowing in winter and the shallowest cultivation in summer.[1] Among the men who went less often or not at all into print one and another added, here a little and there a little, to the body of knowledge or the betterment of device. Horizontal plowing, to raise contour ridges and check erosion, was introduced in Virginia as early as 1785, and was spread through the Piedmont by the advocacy of Thomas Mann Randolph, and thence to the south and southwest.[2] Various men waged high debate upon the relative merits of horizontal balks *versus* gently sloping ditches in supplement on hillsides where mere furrows failed to stop the scour.[3] There were sundry claimants for priority in the *morus multicaulis* craze which swept the country in the 'thirties, only to fall silent when this project of riches through the culture of silk proved an utter failure. A planter who initiated a new strain of cotton or tobacco might advertise it and profit by the sale of the seed at fancy prices. More often one took his pen to prick some bubble of this kind or to describe his own methods and experiences; and with remarkable frequency in the 'forties and 'fifties one would launch an agricultural monthly, to have it die within a year or two, quite properly, for lack of subscribers.

In rare cases an item of striking interest is encountered in these fugitive journals. The most notable perhaps is an analysis of stance and movement by H. W. Vick in 1842, savoring of the most advanced industrial study in the twentieth

[1] Each of these wrote copiously upon plantation problems at large. Taylor's *Arator* and Ruffin's *Essay on Calcareous Manures* ran through many editions; and Ruffin's *Farmers' Register* was doubtless the best agricultural journal in the world of its time (1833–1842). Hammond, Jones and Cloud may be pursued only through fugitive prints; but some of Dickson's articles have been assembled in *David Dickson's and James M. Smith's Farming* (Atlanta, 1910). Dickson said (p. 119): "I have in five minutes taught a hand [*i.e.* a slave] to pick one hundred pounds more of cotton per day than he had picked on the previous day, and from that point he will continue to improve. The greatest efficiency I have obtained in hands picking cotton was seven hundred pounds" — an amazing day's accomplishment.

[2] *E.g.*, *Farmers' Register*, II, 558, 667, 744.

[3] These ridged, grass-grown balks, which were far more common than the ditches, gradually converted many a Piedmont hillside into a series of linchets or terraces by catching the wash of soil.

century. Describing his practice in clearing canebrakes from Yazoo-Mississippi delta lands, he wrote that he instructed his gang minutely to work in pairs. The swifter slave in each couple "took a strip of four feet, say, and turning his right arm to the body of the cane, which was *kept invariably in that position*, caught with his left hand (the palm out) the reed (or two if very close) next the road or opening, and bending it a little, shivered the joint at or just above the ground. The slower hand followed, throwing with his own any cane cut and left standing by his leader entangled at the top with his. By observing the rule of keeping the right arm to the body of the cane they were compelled to move the body laterally, thus saving the time that would have been lost in changing the position frequently to a face or a half-face to the right and back again." In a dry season these reeds might have burned as they stood; but the merit of cutting them before burning lay in the thorough killing of the roots of the reeds, along with other sprouts and seeds, to such effect that no plowing would be required in the production of two years' crops.[1]

Shall we now summarize the numerous contributions and clippings on the vices of the fence laws which made every man the defender of his own fields against invasion by ranging cattle, on the virtues of the cherokee rose for hedging, on crop rotation and fertilizers, on Bermuda grass and alfalfa (then called lucerne), on cows and sheep and horses and hogs and chickens and bees? Let us rather follow the discussion of the humble mule, who was little known in this land until a parcel of asses came from Malta as "a present from the honourable the Marquis de la Fayette to his Excellency General Washington." [2]

---

[1] Letter to the editor in the *Southern Planter*, vol. I, Nos. 9, 10, 11 and 12 ("September, October, November, and December, 1842"), p. 17. This was the expiring quadruple number of this periodical, which began publication at Natchez and ended at Washington, Mississippi. The same text was printed in the *American Agriculturist*, IV, 339 (October, 1845), with an attribution to S. S. W. Vick and with no acknowledgment of its former appearance.

[2] *Massachusetts Gazette*, December 1, 1787. In Rhode Island, however, mules were bred on an export scale before the American Revolution. — Newport *Mercury*, May 9, 1774.

A farmer in the Shenandoah gave rhapsodic praise in 1834: "Of all animals subservient to agriculture the mule stands preëminent. I have no terms adequate to bespeak his merit — none that could be employed could exaggerate it; he is a long liver, a small consumer, a powerful, faithful and enduring laborer. I speak with the confidence of more than thirty years' experience of the relative qualities and capacities of the mule and the horse when I pronounce the superiority of the former to the latter in *every respect* and for *every purpose* connected with the operations of husbandry."[1] Every commonwealth wanted to rear its own mules for the purpose of keeping its money at home; but the primacy of Kentucky[2] was elucidated in 1857 by one familiar with the Bluegrass:

"The mule is fed from weaning time (which is generally at the age of five or six months) to the full of his capacity to eat, and that too on oats and corn together with hay and fodder," with summer grazing in pastures provided with shade. Thus "receiving a sort of forcing, hot-house treatment", the colts might pass from hand to hand, a farmer sometimes borrowing money from a bank to assemble perhaps a hundred head to consume his surplus provender, confident that a buyer would come when they were two years old to take them at a profit and drive them to a southward market. They were not broken to the draft before the droving because the purchasing planters preferred to see a coltish demeanor as an evidence of youth, well knowing that breaking would come easily through service as teammate to a steady companion. Mules, he continued, were more prone to kick than were horses, but less apt to run away. They were fond of company, and strong in attachments to other mules and horses. They could live and work on a diet of corn husks and wheat straw while horses must have rations of grain; they seldom fell sick or went lame; they stood neglect

---

[1] Henry S. Turner, in the *Farmers' Register*, II, 15. This indorsement was often echoed by John S. Skinner in the *American Farmer*, of which he was editor, as well as in other journals.

[2] But competition in the mule supply of the cotton belt came as early as 1826 from remote Sante Fé. — Bernhard, Duke of Saxe-Weimar-Eisenach, *Travels through North America* (Philadelphia, 1828), II, 88.

and abuse remarkably; and a blemish such as the loss of an eye did not greatly impair one's value. As a consequence of the "mania" for mule breeding, he concluded, the sport of racing is in collapse and good horses have become somewhat scarce, for pedigreed mares are now prostituted to jacks while stallions are slenderly patronized.[1]

The scale of their employment in the district of most intense demand was indicated in a communication from Louisiana:

"A sugar planter below New Orleans who has acquired much deserved notoriety for improving his estate and for large yields, Mr. Packwood, could not be induced to buy a cheap mule; he would not believe that he loses by having a number one mule to each hand and surplus team besides. What think ye, friends? Feeding fifty or sixty horses and mules, and in a press of work to change team every six hours! Do ye believe it? Visit Mr. Packwood, see his machinery, look at his returns, the condition of his teams, and then inquire of anyone how was the prior management and what the extent of former crops." [2]

❊   ❊   ❊   ❊   ❊

An English student has recently advocated a plantation system for his own country, saying: "For obvious reasons the small farm is less efficient, less economic of human labor than the large one. It is handicapped physically in that the size of its fields does not permit of the effective use of machinery or the orderly disposition of labor." In relief he recommends copious consolidation: "The unit of farming should be something between two and ten thousand acres of mixed farming, and the management should be a hierarchy of director and

---

[1] B. Munroe, in the *Tennessee Farmer and Mechanic*, II, 394, reprinted from the *Veterinary Journal*. As early as 1822 a settler in Kentucky wrote of mad competition to buy asses because mules, which would sell for fifty or sixty dollars at eight or ten months of age, furnished the one fine prospect of prosperity. — Manuscript in private possession.

[2] Letter of "Harry Bluff" to the editor, in the *Southern Cultivator*, VI, 136 (September, 1848). Theodore J. Packwood owned a thousand-hogshead plantation in Plaquemines Parish and was a partner of Judah P. Benjamin in the ownership of "Bellechasse" which faced his homestead across the river. — P. A. Champomier, *Statement of the Sugar Crop made in Louisiana in 1849-50*, p. 28.

assistants such as prevails in any great business." [1]   Such
a scale is excelled nowadays by many corporation properties
in cane and beet sugar and a few in cotton.   But in the slave
régime it was equaled seldom by individual plantations, for
every unit was limited in its feasible expansion by the factor
of distance from the steading to the peripheral fields.   When
the trudge of a gang, morning and evening, reached a half-
hour's length it would cost more in time and energy than could
be offset by economies of quantity production.   A two-mile
radius was perhaps an extreme limit, and except in sugar it is
probable that one mile was not often exceeded.   This would
have more or less meaning as to the volume of labor and of
tilled acreage, according to whether the headquarters were near
or far from the center of the estate and whether the fields were
of solid spread or broken by woods and waste land.   Alluvial
districts offered the greatest continuous fields, but the steadings
were generally at an edge rather than in the middle — on the
river front along the Mississippi, and on the high land behind
the riparian strips of the rice coast.   In the Piedmont at large
the ruggedness of surface, together with the practice of clearing
new grounds and abandoning old, often restricted the tilled
portion of a property to a small fraction of its total area.

But granting that a hundred slaves tilling a thousand acres
might constitute a unit of maximum efficiency, its attainment
could be realized only when some person acquired a sufficient
fortune or, as was fairly common in the sugar district alone,
formed a partnership or corporation for the purpose.   Such
a goal tempted men's ambitions and involved some in debts
which brought bankruptcy.   More cautious folk would fain
use only what was fully their own, to make sure that a bailiff
need never come with a creditor's lien.   As one Federal census
followed another it seems on the whole that the average size
of estates, whether measured in slaves or crops, remained fairly
constant.   A fairly matched fecundity as between the races
tended to parcel the slaves among the heirs in each generation
on a scale not unlike that which had prevailed in the same

[1] Sir A. Daniel Hall in the *Atlantic Monthly*, CXXXV, 684, 685 (May, 1925).

family a generation before. The case with land was different yet similar. A tract could not be stretched to match a family's increase; but in all the time with which we are concerned the West gave outlet, and even the East would furnish great enlargement of tilth if it were deemed worth while to reclaim abandoned fields. Reclamation, in fact, was done in Virginia and Maryland in the middle decades of the nineteenth century, with soiling crops and fertilizers, to such extent as to bring a genuine rejuvenation of those old commonwealths.[1] This proved, if proof were wanted, that slave labor need not exhaust the soil. Any slave could spread manure or could seed clover or cowpeas quite as well as a freeman. The process of restoring soils lagged somewhat in the lower South, whether because the pinch of need was not as yet so sharply felt or because the call of the cotton West was more alluring to the cotton East.

❈   ❈   ❈   ❈   ❈

The producers of any market crop were of course in full competition one with another. The several staple industries, in addition, competed for labor in a somewhat open market, and for land on the borders of their several provinces. Rice was an exception by reason of its aquatic habit; but sugar trenched upon the cotton belt when the protective tariff was high, and turn about when the tariff rate was lowered. Cotton surged north to the neighborhood of Richmond when the market boomed in 1825; but frosts nipped the prospect within a year or two and set the border of the great belt back again. Only tobacco among the major Southern staples had a greatly expansible range in latitude. Nowadays it is grown commercially from Cuba, Florida and Louisiana to Connecticut, Ontario and Wisconsin; and Connecticut was on the tobacco map of *ante-bellum* times, though the main crop came from the middle zone, Virginia to Missouri.

Wheat and corn, as we have seen, were also among the potential staples for plantation slave labor; and these had

---

[1] This is well described and buttressed in Avery O. Craven, *Soil Exhaustion in Virginia and Maryland* (*University of Illinois Studies*, XIII), 122–161.

a northern range greater than tobacco.   Does it follow that the distinctive Southern pattern of life, in which Negroes were an essential element, was capable of expanding beyond its historic bounds ?   The question was answered when the act of Congress took effect at the beginning of 1808 prohibiting the further importation of slaves.   Thereafter a swelling stream of immigrants flowed in from Europe, but only a trickle by smuggling from Africa.   The spread of the South in the face of competition by the white farmers and laborers in the Northern régime was conditioned by the natural increase of the Negroes on hand and by the limitations of special geographic opportunity. Virginians and Kentuckians removing to Missouri might cling to their old customs and grow tobacco; but they could hardly buy slaves copiously when Alabamians, Louisianians and Texans were taking all that were offered and paying prices which only the cotton or sugar prospects would warrant.   Good tobacco required so much painstaking that small farmers had the advantage unless the prices of slaves were lower than Missourians ever knew them.   The crop itself, in fact, was largely discontinued after the passing of the generations which had brought its culture from Kentucky.

Wheat gave a still poorer prospect for Southern expansion, though for the very different reason that its work season occupied but a small part of the year.   Planters on the Potomac and the James, it is true, had turned from tobacco to wheat when the device of converting scythes into cradles and the substitution of these for sickles increased their harvesting capacity and when the wars of the French Revolution sent the price of grain to great heights.   These men had slaves already and wanted to retain them and their homesteads.   And by keeping abreast of all improvements and by finding off-season work for their corps they managed to live in comfort.   Such cases were exceptional.   If we may judge from the present régime on the western plains, the normal system requires migratory harvest hands who follow the schedule of the ripening grain and supplement the force which has seeded the fields. But an essential tendency of the slave plantation system was to keep all the labor on a single place throughout the year. Provoked by political strife, Southerners might attempt a thrust into Kansas and develop a fine frenzy in their effort. But to hold a footing there was hopeless.

Counter-invasions by Northern system and personnel, though less noted, were more significant. Within five years during the 'forties upward of two hundred families from New York settled in a single Virginia county,[1] and this was but an index of a continuing movement. Other indications of the prospect were the census returns which showed the slave population of Delaware in 1860 to be but one fifth as large as it had been in 1790, the slaves in Maryland almost overtaken in 1860 by the number of the free Negroes, and the slaves in Virginia, Kentucky and Missouri shrinking in their ratio to the whites. California was taken of course by the Northern system; and it was remarked at the time by a Southern senator that a slave code was enacted in the territory of New Mexico merely through a political trick. Access to either of these was too costly and arduous for slaves in substantial numbers to be carried thither. The South could barely hope to maintain its established borders whenever the filling of the western free lands should bring the two systems to the grip of direct competition. The Northern free whites were too many, the Southern slave Negroes too few.

[1] *Cultivator*, VIII, 77, 78 (March, 1847).

CHAPTER VIII

TRAFFIC

A PLANTER'S cotton crop ranges at least "from fair to middling"; and if the harvest weather is not perfect there will be bales of inferior grade. But a factory works on orders for definite sorts and qualities of cloth which can be made only from specific lengths and grades of lint. As a rule, therefore, a factory would not buy the miscellaneous output of a plantation even if it lay within a stone's throw of the planter's gin. The product of many fields must needs be assembled and sorted in dealers' hands to await the varied calls of factories upon the stock. In tobacco the supply and demand were likewise diverse, and to some degree in rice and sugar. Furthermore the markets, if not in every case world-wide, were always distant enough to require local concentration for bulk shipment and brokers to handle the transactions. On rare occasions a planter would seek to escape some of the middlemen's charges by dealing directly with a distant purchaser, but this involved such enterprise and risk, and brought as a rule so little gain, that the more common practice was not only to submit to brokerage but to engage the services and accept the charges of factors in addition.

The larger the scale of a man's affairs the more expedient an agency became. If one's whole crop were contained in a single hogshead, it were well to sell it near home and pocket the slender proceeds without ado. But if his hogsheads were a hundred instead, good business required that they be sent to a major market and sold there by some one concerned in procuring a maximum price. Likewise if one's effective wants from market were limited by a small farmer's earnings they might be supplied in plain goods by a local merchant; but if they were amplified to a grandee's income and exalted to fashionable taste they must be met from a metropolitan market and selected there by a discriminating agent. The colonial tobacco planters accordingly fell into the practice of sending shipments and orders to London merchants who sold and bought for them as permanent factors at a fairly standard commission of two and a half per cent on all transactions.

A prospering settler in the West Indies, feeling the need of a wife, ordered from London along with his annual supplies by next ship "a young woman of the qualifications and form following: As for a portion I demand none, let her be of an honest family; between twenty and twenty-five years of age; of a middle stature and well proportioned; her face agreeable, her temper mild, her character blameless, her health good, and her constitution strong enough to bear the change of the climate. . . . If she arrives and conditioned as above said, with the present letter endorsed by you, . . . that there may be no imposition, I hereby oblige and engage myself to satisfy the said letter by marrying the bearer at fifteen days sight."

The agent promptly sent a maiden who carried the document indorsed, along with certificates of temper, character and health from neighbors, her curate and four physicians; and in due time the twain were made one.[1] Though commissions as marriage brokers were few, the factors found themselves called upon for a great variety of services, including particularly the payment of drafts, and often the honoring of overdrafts, to a degree which made them virtually bankers for their plantation clients. There were profits and losses, courtesies and quarrels in the business, enduring until the war of American independence cut the ancient connection.[2]

What London was to the colonial Tidewater, Richmond became to the tobacco Piedmont in the nineteenth century,[3]

[1] *Jamaica Courant*, January 10, 1751, reprinted in the *South Carolina Gazette*, July 15 to 22, 1751.

[2] J. S. Bassett, "The Relation between the Virginia Planter and the London Merchant," in the *American Historical Association Report* for 1901, I, 553–575; W. C. Ford, *George Washington* (Paris and New York [1900]), I, 115–123.

[3] The tobacco trade of Richmond is illuminated by the Massie manuscripts at the University of Texas.

Charleston and Savannah to the eastern cotton belt, and New Orleans to her own great hinterland. A chain of minor markets arose not only at the lesser seaports but at the heads of steamboat navigation — Fayetteville, Columbia, Augusta, Macon, Columbus, Montgomery — and at convenient points on the mighty Mississippi and its branches; and in supplement to these a miscellany of villages at county seats, mill sites, or merely where highways of some importance happened to cross.[1] Finally when railroads began to change the channels of commerce, a few junction points gave origin to incipient highland cities, the chief of which was Atlanta.

The greater among the ports and river towns developed factorage as a feature of their commerce.[2] The planters preferred urban to village dealings because, despite factors' commissions, their trades were to better effect, and particularly for the sake of copious credit which the factors could supply or assist in procuring. This régime of course restricted the growth of inland centers, for it denied them a large volume of commerce and hampered the rise of local manufactures.

The development of avenues and vehicles was in the main similar to that in the world at large. A grapevine ferry plying on a Virginia stream in 1780 might perhaps be matched in Massachusetts, though the muscadine afforded a better strand than the foxgrape. The pine barrens furnished many a "highway where the slow wheel pours the sand", though a poet of New England coined the phrase. Accumulated crops awaited the "spring fresh" on the Yadkin and the Yazoo as they did on the Delaware and the Wabash. At the same time there were distinctive features. The rivers were never icebound below

---

[1] The scheme of early village business is suggested by an advertisement in the *Georgia Republican & State Intelligencer* (Savannah), February 28, 1803: "To Merchants. A Person in the Mercantile line, settled at a small village in the country where business may be done to great advantage, is desirous of a Partner who can advance Four thousand dollars in cash or dry goods well laid in to that amount, or would have no objection to being concerned in a large importing wholesale house which would supply full assortments at cost and charges."

[2] Cotton factorage and allied matters are elaborated in N. S. Buck, *The Development of the Organization of Anglo-American Trade, 1800–1850* (New Haven, 1925). This monograph exploits among other sources the records of a factorage firm at Augusta.

the James; and by the same token the roads were never smoothed by snow, hardened by frost or softened by thaw. For most of each winter, in fact, and sometimes in other seasons, rains made them almost impassable [1] except where sandy soil gave better going in wet weather than in dry.

The land was granted in square parcels in western Georgia by the State, and by the Federal Government in the region from Alabama to Arkansas. But everywhere except in Missouri the roads curved at will, ignoring the "section lines." In Virginia the meanders are often excessive for modern purposes because the location was fixed by the needs of tobacco haulage when wagons were few. Pierced with a pole and rigged with shafts, a hogshead was converted into a vehicle. There were no bridges, and the thin-built rolling hogshead could not pass a ford without the ruin of its contents. Therefore these "rolling roads" must follow the watersheds, however devious the lines of their crests might be.

Tobacco rolling was done mainly in summer when the crop was cured and the roads were dry; cotton haulage was in fall and winter unless mudbound into spring when the diversion of teams from plowing was greatly deprecated.[2] Some of the hauls, as from North Carolina to Charleston, were more than a week in length at a rate of some twenty-five miles per day. These were shortened early in the nineteenth century by the rise of markets at river towns; but the merchants of

[1] When Louis F. Tasistro (*Random Shots and Southern Breezes*, II, 31) went from New Orleans by steamboat in February, 1841, intending to present a play at Vicksburg, the town proved to be so completely fast in mud that he departed in bafflement without even reporting at the theater. "I found the streets absolutely choked with mud. . . . Trade was at a standstill; the market place was deserted; nor was there the least likelihood of amelioration for many days to come." It was no place for an actor when an audience could not assemble.

[2] A Mississippian wrote at the end of a January: "I suppose more cotton was sold last week in Holly Springs than in any previous week of the season, partly for the reason that the roads have not been in a condition for delivering it until last week, and partly because the prices were very good and almost every one had to sell to meet bills, pay accounts, etc., as this is the time of year with us for paying up." A Georgian wrote in a February: "I am mightily behind in ginning at the Hurricane, owing to having had the old gin out of repair during my absence. There are 150 bags of cotton there yet, and the hauling off to the depot will be a job, as it will come on in ploughtime." — Manuscripts in private possession.

the interior must themselves depend upon wagons when their shelves became bare in seasons when the rivers were too low for navigation. A considerable number of teamsters arose as common carriers, analogous to stage drivers and comparable to the "half horse, half alligator" boatmen. The "Knoxville wagons" were a famous feature in the Valley traffic, plying the long, long road to Baltimore until the partial completion of the James River Canal diverted them to Lynchburg. It was doubtless this heavy freighting which prompted the construction of the Valley Pike as one of the few macadamized roads in the older South.

❋   ❋   ❋   ❋   ❋

For the primitive business of droving, primitive highways would suffice, regardless of distance. Until the railroad era this comprised the main bulk of traffic across the mountains — hogs and cattle from Kentucky to the slaughterhouses of Baltimore or from East Tennessee to the cotton belt, and mules from Kentucky, Missouri or Tennessee to the farthest confines of the plantation zone. The drovers were a dependence of the farmers along the road for the sale of their corn and hay. A passing parcel of hogs turned into a corn patch for a night or a week would pay the farmer and save him the labor of harvest, while enabling the drover to ply his trade and perhaps increase the weight of his porkers *en route*. A Virginia mountaineer wrote in the spring of 1828 : "I am not making any money at present, and cannot until I sell my corn to Hog-drovers, from which I never have failed to make every fall something like four or five hundred dollars." And a settler on the flank of Lookout Mountain, on the way from Chattanooga to the midlands of Alabama, said when reporting in September, 1850, that a drought had cut the local crops in half :

"I do not know what the poor hog drovers will do for corn this season if they drive as many as they did last. They must have drove some 80 thousand . . . last season, and it would take no inconsiderable part of the corn raised in our valley . . . to feed that number during their passage this season. The mules have commenced going already. For the last two weeks there has hardly been a day that a drove or two has not passed." [1]

In the Bluegrass the abundance of limestone, the density of settlement and the general prosperity fostered road improvement on a large scale through the device of chartered companies to build turnpikes and charge toll for their use. Kindred projects arose in other States. Gravel was used for surfacing where it was at hand, and plank roads were laid through sandy forests. But in many cases the corporations failed from dearth of patronage. The cultivated acreage nearly everywhere comprised but a very small part of the land; and tobacco and cotton alike yielded small tonnage per acre for market. Even in Kentucky frugal wayfarers used byroads, nicknamed "shun pikes", to escape the tolls except when in haste or hauling heavy loads.[2] Similar avoidance in regions of lighter freighting had the effect which all but optimists might have foreseen.

In the South at large there was no concentration of highway traffic at all comparable to that on the National Road from Cumberland on the Potomac to Wheeling and thence across Ohio. The famous Natchez Trace, which led to Nashville, served somewhat copiously for the return of the flatboatmen who had steered their arks down the Mississippi; but soon after this was widened under an act of Congress into a road for vehicles, the introduction of steamboats removed the occasion for its characteristic use.[3] The similar project of a federal road from Washington to New Orleans by way of the State capitals at the heads of navigation came to little more than a mere felling of trees on the route. Road maintenance at large was left for the most part to the local inhabitants under legal requirement of laboring for two or three days in the year or paying a proportional head tax. This resulted in little more than filling the ruts on seldom occasions.

---

[1] Manuscripts in private possession.

[2] Mary Verhoeff, *The Kentucky Mountains, Transportation and Commerce* (Filson Club No. 26), 49 *note*.

[3] R. S. Cotterill, "The Natchez Trace", in the *Tennessee Historical Magazine*, VII, 29–37.

The river improvements undertaken by the several States contemplated in the main merely the removal of snags, though in some places dams and locks were built to drown troublesome rapids; and on the Red River a special undertaking by Captain Henry Shreve removed the hundred-mile log-jam known as the "raft." The "canal mania", which loaded sundry Northwestern States with heavy debts, had echoes to the southward of Virginia in mere projects, as a rule, rather than in actual construction. Even the plan of a canal around the Muscle Shoals of the Tennessee River was happily superseded by a railroad before excessive sums were spent.[1]

❀   ❀   ❀   ❀   ❀

As long as primitive avenues prevailed, inward and outward freight followed in the main the same channels between the several seaports and their respective hinterlands. But the construction of railroads promptly resolved the traffic into its three elements: an outward flow of the staple to markets which were mainly overseas; an inward flow of manufactured goods mainly from New York; and an inward flow of foodstuffs from the Northwest. Ships, boats and wagons in combination could always meet the first and second of these after a fashion; and the third branch of traffic might be dispensed with if the freight rates made it more economical to produce full food supplies at home than to buy them from a distance. It was only by virtue of cheap and speedy service that railroads could thrive.

Nearly all the early railroads, in fact, owed their origins not to the demands of rural folk for better transit but to the desires of seaboard merchants to enlarge the trade of their respective ports. Charleston at the beginning of the 'twenties found her wagon trade severely diminished by the rise of the

---

[1] Among pertinent monographs are U. B. Phillips, *History of Transportation in the Eastern Cotton Belt to 1860* (New York, 1908), which includes a brief traffic and railroad survey of the whole South; C. C. Weaver, *Internal Improvements in North Carolina previous to 1860* (*Johns Hopkins University Studies*, XXI, Nos. 3 and 4); W. F. Dunaway, *The James River and Kanawha Canal Company* (*Columbia University Studies*, CIV, No. 2); Mary Verhoeff, *The Kentucky River Navigation* (Filson Club No. 28).

river towns, while her lack of waterways to the interior prevented the growth of wholesale business to compensate. The invention of steam railways offered the possibility of recouping, in part by encroachment upon Savannah's trade. With a charter procured in 1827, Charlestonians undertook a railroad which when it reached the river bank opposite Augusta in 1833 was the longest line in the world — one hundred and thirty-six miles. Savannah, to offset this, promoted the Central of Georgia Railroad and its extensions which made Macon and Columbus tributary and even diverted some trade from Mobile. This Alabama port in turn instituted the Mobile and Ohio to encroach upon the commerce of the Crescent City; and then New Orleans, finding the Father of Waters not invincible, launched a line through the length of Mississippi which now comprises the southern division of the Illinois Central. Meanwhile citizens of Charleston and Augusta combined with others in the Piedmont to build the Georgia Railroad to a common terminus with the main extension of the Central of Georgia where Atlanta now stands and whence the State of Georgia built a railway northward to connect with lines already thrusting from Louisville through Nashville to Chattanooga. Hoping to cancel the advantage of Louisville, citizens of Cincinnati responded, but lukewarmly, to the call of Charleston in an unsuccessful effort to pierce two mountain ranges in a line *via* Knoxville. Meanwhile also Baltimore and Richmond, like Charleston, Savannah and Mobile, were seeking to rival New York, New Orleans and Philadelphia as outlets of the Ohio valley; and Norfolk, Wilmington and other ports were trying to rise out of their subsidiary rank.

At the middle of the century the branching of the main lines here and there gave rise to projects parallel to the coast, eventually rivaling the perpendicular stems. A series of railways threaded the valleys of Virginia and East Tennessee to Chattanooga, and another was linking through the length of the Piedmont from the Potomac to the Alabama. Furthermore, while New Orleans, Memphis, St. Louis and Chicago strove against one another for the location of a projected railroad to the Pacific, many a short line was boomed in a local prospectus as bound to become a "connecting link" and thrive from heavy long-distance hauls. The hopes of the companies to handle through traffic, however, were balked here and there by the desire of towns to be termini rather than way stations. Thus the draymen, omnibus owners, innkeepers and city fathers of Augusta prevented the linking of lines through the town until 1852; and those of Petersburg maintained their obstruction until overcome by the military needs of the war-time.

In the main the railroads prospered but modestly because, for reasons we have seen, their main-haul traffic was not great and their back-hauls were very light. The development of heavy industries, such as coal mining and iron smelting in the Birmingham district, had only faint beginnings prior to the war, except for copper in East Tennessee. For the time being the railroads had as their main effect the broadening of the plantation area and the intensification of staple agriculture. In fact they brought ruin to some of the Piedmont cotton factories by putting the distant specialized mills into competition with local plants which had been meeting home needs by making diverse kinds of cloth.

*　　　*　　　*　　　*　　　*

Father Mississippi rolled on to the Gulf, bearing an increasing burden until the middle of the century when the railroads and the Great Lakes boats began to make their competition felt.[1] The first steamboat, the *New Orleans*, descended from Pittsburgh in 1811; but its draft was so deep and its engine so weak that its later career was a mere local plying about the city of its name. The *Washington*, built by Henry Shreve in 1816, had a much better engine and a vastly better hull design, for its builder, observing that river craft needed no ballast

---

[1] Increased size and draft of ocean ships tended to diminish the grain exports through New Orleans because the deepest of the "passes" at the mouth of the river had not more than seventeen feet of water until a channel was deepened by the Eads jetties after the war. So soft was the mud, however, that a sailing ship with a strong wind could plow very slowly through a two-foot depth of it.

against winds and waves, discarded the pattern of ships and planned a boat to ride upon the water instead of cutting through it. The boats, now capable of breasting the current briskly by force of their high-pressure engines, multiplied year by year. The packets, which ran on fairly definite schedules, grew steadily larger until the *Eclipse*, built in 1852, attained a length of three hundred and sixty-three feet and a beam of seventy-six. Embellishments kept pace. In 1824 the "elegant steamboat *Caledonia*" carried a library for the use of passengers, comprising history, voyages, biography, sermons, reviews and the latest novels "including St. Ronan's Well and the Pilot." [1] In 1843 St. Clair Thomasson, a Frenchman, made the dietary on his *Concordia* as luxurious as that in the finest hotels, and made "high living" a feature of passenger traffic.[2] In the next decade there are notes even of daily newspapers printed aboard, and of shower baths which were quite as remarkable at the time.

The hurricane deck of a packet was at the service of honeymooners and flirting couples; the bar was for otherwise-minded men and a lair of professional gamblers; and even the staterooms were not immune from visitation by thieves. Fine folk and plain, virtuous and depraved, patronized these craft on the muddy, sinuous artery of the continent. They did yeomen service with more than yeoman dispatch at meal times; they crowded the rails to see a race or a wreck or to chaff a flatboatman or watch the brisk labor of the roustabouts at a landing. They gathered at evening to sing of working on the levee, just to pass the time away. And they went to bed — retired for the night, in their Victorian parlance — perhaps to be wakened by the grating of the hull upon a sandbar, the ripping of the planks by a snag, the bursting of a boiler, or the dread cry of fire.[3]

The steamboats, packets included, were designed for general

---

[1] *Louisiana Gazette*, March 30, 1834.

[2] H. S. Fulkerson, *Random Recollections* (Vicksburg, 1885), 20.

[3] The career of a Mississippi steamer hardly attained four years on an average. A list of historic endings is given in *Lloyd's Steamboat Directory and Disasters on the Western Waters* (Cincinnati, 1856).

utility, passengers above and cargo below; though sometimes cotton bales would be laid on the gunwales in so many tiers that candles or sperm lamps in the cabins must replace the excluded sunlight. Every boat as a rule would stop anywhere to deposit freight or passengers on the bank, or to take traffic on signal. This practice, together with the accommodating habits of officers in executing commissions at the terminus for patrons along the route, brought a dwarfing of the villages. Donaldsonville and Plaquemine, Baton Rouge and Bayou Sara, Grand Gulf [1] and Petit Gulf could not hold their trade when the purser would buy a keg of nails or a lady's fan at New Orleans to be delivered on the return voyage. Natchez and even Vicksburg found themselves in some degree way-stations in the traffic from plantations in their rear to the great market of New Orleans.[2]

   ❋   ❋   ❋   ❋   ❋

Have you ever been in New Orleans? If not you'd better go,
It's a nation of a queer place; day and night a show!
Frenchmen, Spaniards, West Indians, Creoles, Mustees,
Yankees, Kentuckians, Tennesseeans, lawyers and trustees,
Clergymen, priests, friars, nuns, women of all stains;
Negroes in purple and fine linen, and slaves in rags and chains.
Ships, arks, steamboats, robbers, pirates, alligators,
Assassins, gamblers, drunkards, and cotton speculators;
Sailors, soldiers, pretty girls, and ugly fortune-tellers;
Pimps, imps, shrimps, and all sorts of dirty fellows;
White men with black wives, *et vice-versa* too.
A progeny of all colors — an infernal motley crew!
Yellow fever in February — muddy streets all the year;
Many things to hope for, and a dev'lish sight to fear!
Gold and silver bullion — United States' bank-notes,
Horse-racers, cock-fighters, and beggars without coats.

[1] Grand Gulf also suffered from the pranks of the river, which cut its bank to the left, carrying many houses downstream, and then shifted its channel so far to the right that the remnant of the village found itself two miles inland. Lowry and McCardle, *History of Mississippi*, 2d ed., 459.

[2] "The Race of the Cities", in the New Orleans *Daily Tropic*, October 2, 1845. Peddling boats and floating theaters added to the diversion of business from the minor towns.

Snapping turtles, sugar, sugar-houses, water-snakes,
Molasses, flour, whiskey, tobacco, corn and johnny-cakes,
Beef, cattle, hogs, pork, turkeys, Kentucky rifles,
Lumber, boards, apples, cotton, and many other trifles.
Butter, cheese, onions, wild beasts in wooden cages,
Barbers, waiters, draymen, with the highest sort of wages.
Now and then there are *Duels*, for very little cause,
The natives soon forget 'em — they care not much for laws.[1]

Walt Whitman would have done it better; but Colonel
Creecy, who burst into verse only on special provocation, did
the best he could and his catalogue contains little exaggeration.
The pirates as represented by the famous Jean Lafitte were
already of the distant past. They had been more truly priva-
teers and smugglers; and they turned patriots when Jackson
confronted Pakenham on the battle field of Chalmette.
Robbers and other disorderly persons were numerous enough
in all conscience;[2] and finely clad Negroes were impressive at
least on Sundays.[3] Slaves had veritably been found in chains,
and tortured too, when a fire at Madame Lalaurie's house

[1] Colonel James R. Creecy, *Scenes in the South* (Philadelphia, 1860), 275, 276. This
description was of 1829.

[2] At the middle of 1860 a journalist when praising the chief of police tabulated the
arrests made during his service, which embraced the preceding twenty-three months:
for murder, 62; stabbing with intent to murder, 146; assault with deadly weapon, 734;
arson and attempt, 42; burglary, 44; highway robbery, 53; larceny, 2148; swindling,
232; suspicious characters, 2110; assault and battery, threats and miscellaneous trans-
gressions, 47,403. — New Orleans *Daily Crescent*, June 18, 1860. The population then
comprised about 150,000 whites, 11,000 free Negroes, and 14,500 slaves. Within the
preceding twenty years the free colored and the slaves had each diminished by nearly
half, while the whites had trebled. This change of complexion seems not to have
lessened the task of the police.

[3] The Sunday scene can hardly have been inferior to that described in Richmond in
1856: "Dashing satin bonnets now cover wooly false curls, a handsome veil conceals
a sooty face, which is protected from being sun-burnt by a stylish parasol. A silk
dress of gaudy colors sweeps the ground. . . . The beau who struts beside this cham-
bermaid is attired in a talma or shawl, pants whose checks or stripes exceed the circum-
ference of his leg, and a vest in which every color vies for pre-eminence. He twirls his
watch-chain and his cane, and might almost put a Broadway dandy to the blush.
These gentry leave their visiting cards at each other's kitchens, and on the occasion
of a wedding Miss Dinah Drippings and Mr. Cuffie Coleman have their cards connected
by a silken tie, emblematic of that which is to connect themselves, and a third card an-
nounces, 'At home from ten to one', where those who call will find cakes, fruits and all
sorts of refreshments." — *DeBow's Review*, XXVIII, 198, 199.

admitted wayfarers and revealed her sadist practices.[1]   The inter-racial matings, while on the basis of concubinage instead of marriage, were constant enough to yield numerous progeny, some of whom in the course of generations were paler than quadroons.   Yellow fever was true enough, if not in actual February; and the mud was not to be gainsaid.

The city was at the same time French and English, Southern and Western, cosmopolitan and unique.   The rectangle within the demolished colonial ramparts was the French Quarter, from which the Creole population expanded for some distance down-stream.   The narrow streets of old were built solid with houses of Spanish or French type, with grilled balconies overhanging the sidewalks and covered ways leading to courtyards at the rear.   Among the public buildings were the French Market near the levee, thronged in early morning with chaffering vendors of all things edible, the Cathedral, the Archbishop's house, the Cabildo with prison cells in its courtyard, the huge Hotel Royal with a famous block for the auction of slaves in its ro-tunda, and the Opera House whose stage was extended for dancing at the masked balls of Mardi Gras.   This quarter had its own banks and business houses.[2]

Above the linguistic border at Canal Street lay the ever-growing "American" city, with warehouses and cotton com-presses paralleling the roofless wharves of the levee.   Behind these was a cluster of wholesale and plantation-supply houses, then a line of retail shops and theaters with the great portico of the St. Charles Hotel [3] in their midst.   Next beyond St. Charles lay Carondelet, the street of banks and counting houses, its flagged sidewalks crowded in season with bargaining brokers.

---

[1] The discovery of seven mutilated slaves in shackles and the gutting of the Lalaurie house after the villainess had fled were described by the editor in *L'Abeille*, a New Orleans newspaper in French and English, May 11 and 12, 1834, and veraciously re-counted in G. W. Cable, *Strange True Stories of Louisiana* (New York, 1889), 200–219.

[2] The latest and best account of the old city is by Lyle Saxon, *Fabulous New Orleans* (New York, 1928), well illustrated by E. H. Suydam.   The business régime, whether above or below Canal Street, still awaits a full analysis.

[3] On the scale and style of the great hotels, with a note on electric bells, see J. J. Am-père, *Promenade en Amérique* (Paris, 1855), II, 132; James Stirling, *Letters from the Slave States* (London, 1857), 150–152.

A mile or two upstream lay the formerly separate suburb of La Fayette, now in mid-century the "garden district", inhabited by such "Americans" as could afford mansions and the equipages needed for plying back and forth to business. In this tract, above the streets of the nine Muses, colonnaded L-shaped houses, so designed to invite the breezes, stood in embowered grounds behind stout if ornamental fences. Each gate was locked and equipped with a pull-knob which by means of an unobtrusive wire to the service quarters would agitate a bell on a vibrant coil and summon a maid or butler to admit the waiting caller.[1]

The Creoles were not all of one volatile, punctilious and leisure-loving sort, for they contributed their share of the city's talent and vigor in many callings. The "Americans" were far more diverse and for some decades much less integrated. The Southerners and the Yankees, the Jews, the Germans and the Irish rather mingled than blended. Pleasurable dissipation was alluring in that city of crawfish bisque and gumbo filé, Spanish mackerel and pompano, fried plantains and baked bananas, claret and Bourbon, absinthe, Sazerac and silver fizz.[2] Yet there were Puritans who resisted Creole glamour, Methodists and Presbyterians who, while acquiring a graciousness of manner, walked ever in the strait and narrow path. These even converted some Creoles, mostly by force of matrimony.

The French of the Creoles was a definite patois, rooted in the Vieux Carré and in the soil of the sugar parishes. The English of the "Americans" had no such distinctiveness as in Charleston, the Virginia lowlands, or the back country from Alabama to Texas, because the people speaking it had come somewhat recently from widely different sources and because the well-to-do flocked out of the city for each summer to White Sulphur,

---

[1] This item is from my own adolescent memory of the 'nineties. The locked gates may possibly have been an innovation of the Federal military occupation under "Spoon" Butler; but sailors, boatmen and Irish laborers, not to speak of Negroes, were sufficient to suggest precautions long before. To lock the gate was simpler than to lock the numerous outer doors of the ell.

[2] This particular gin fizz may not have been devised before the later nineteenth century.

Newport or Saratoga, where any special dialect would have its corners rubbed off.

❉   ❉   ❉   ❉   ❉

The methods of trade in plantation produce was described in 1833 by a Virginian who had gone to New Orleans for a new start in business.[1] Sugar was bought mainly by brokers who visited the plantations in the interest of Northern clients; though sometimes one, expecting the market to rise, would buy a planter's crop on personal speculation. In this case he must reckon upon a considerable loss of weight by the seepage of molasses from the very moist contents of the hogsheads. Again, a planter would send his crop to New Orleans for storage on the levee or in warehouses until competing brokers made an acceptable bid. Molasses was handled in much the same way. Bacon was either sold by the owner or agent on board the boat which brought it, or stored and sold in the warehouses. Salt pork, from far up the river, came generally in flatboats and was bought by the city "smokers" who hung it over smoldering sawdust or pine wood to give it flavor and color; but this Virginian connoisseur said: "Next year if the bulk pork is a moderate price I will smoke with a different kind of wood and try to make it good."

"Cotton is all stored," he continued, "and for foreign shipment all compressed to about 2/3 the original size, which is easily done by steam presses. . . . Brokers sell nearly all the cotton, for which they charge the man they buy for 1/2 p. ct., & the man they buy of 1/4 p. ct. When cotton is high they make a good deal. The storage & such charges is light on cotton." The trade in tobacco he found to be decentralized. Shipments might be deposited in any warehouse along the four or five miles of city frontage, where public inspectors would grade them by samples from the top and side of each hogshead. The warehouseman would get his fees for storage, weighing and cooperage, together with perhaps from twenty to

[1] S. H. Davis to Ammon Hancock of Lynchburg, June 4, 1833. — Manuscript in the Massie papers at the University of Texas.

fifty pounds of leaf left out when the hogshead was headed up again. The subsequent sale followed much the same plan as cotton, whether with or without the service of factors. The reason for official grading of tobacco lay mainly in the serious loss which every sampling involved. Cotton was sampled by merely slitting the cover and grabbing out a handful of the lint without material damage to the commercial package.

❉   ❉   ❉   ❉   ❉

As New Orleans was the main focus of sugar and cotton sale, so she was of slave purchase.[1] Planters from all quarters of the expanding Southwest, going to town to sell their crops or renew touch with factors, would visit the slave dealers on Gravier or Bienville streets to enlarge their field forces or procure artisans or domestics; and the dealers at Mobile, Natchez or Galveston, when their stocks "direct from Virginia" ran low, would replenish them by purchase at New Orleans.

A Louisiana law effective in the early 'thirties required that with each slave from another State be brought a certificate from the former vicinage concerning title and character. Such certificates, attached to the bills of sale which are filed copiously among the notarial records at New Orleans, might yield a directory of slave dealers and indicate the relative volume of their merchandise coming from the several districts of origin. In default of such analysis we may note some characteristic items of 1831.

James Huie, of Rowan County, North Carolina, sold to James R. Trimble of New Orleans for $1600 a husband, wife and three young children whom he had bought in the preceding month of A. F. Caldwell and Company, of Charlotte, North Carolina.

---

[1] The clearest account of this traffic at large is by E. A. Andrews, *Slavery and the Domestic Slave-trade* (Boston, 1836), describing particularly the well-ordered assembling house of Franklin and Armfield at Alexandria, Virginia. A place of sale at Natchez, probably belonging to the same firm, is described, with notes of nonchalance on the part of the merchandise, in [J. H. Ingraham] *The South-West*, II, 192–203, 236. Visits to slave auctions are narrated, with various reactions, by Russell L. Carpenter, *Observations on American Slavery* (London, 1852), 28; J. J. Ampère, *Promenade en Amérique*, II, 113; William Chambers, *Things as They Are in America* (2d ed., London, 1857), 273–286; E. A. Pollard, *Black Diamonds* (New York, 1859), 28, 29.

Granville Sharp Pierce of Summer County, Tennessee, sold to John Wesley Vick [1] of Warren County, Mississippi, Ned, twenty-five years old, for $550, Albert, nineteen, for $525, and Mary, fifteen, for $425, all with certificates from Davidson County, Tennessee. The same Pierce transferred to Thomas H. Maddox of Rapides Parish, Louisiana, for $3950 six young men and a girl from various Tennessee counties, except for one who had been bought at New Orleans in the preceding month. Thomas McCargo of Halifax County, Virginia, with certificates from that and a neighboring county, sold to Alfred I. Lowry of Concordia Parish, Julius, twenty-three years old, Harrison of fifteen and Moses of thirteen, all black, at $500 each, and other boys and girls at prices ranging from $275 to $550. Léon Chabert of New Orleans delivered to Julien Tournillon of Assumption Parish three young men at $625 each, a fourth at $900, a boy of seventeen at $550 and two young women at $425 each, with certificates reciting their several purchases for "L. Chabert, by his agent" from sundry citizens of Charleston and one of Orangeburgh, South Carolina.

Some of the documents exhibit special features. In the bill recording in 1831 the sale by William Bonville, attorney of John P. Cobbs of Amherst County, Virginia, to William Lake of New Orleans of two quadroons, Polly and her son Jim, twenty-five and seven years old, it is written: "And thereupon the said purchaser declared that he hereby binds himself, his heirs and assigns, to grant freedom to the said boy James or Jim, so soon as he shall have attained the age of twenty-one years, calculating his age as above specified from the date hereof." In some cases also a letter is attached. One such was from W. M. Varnell & Company of Indianola, Mississippi, in 1855, to J. T. Baldwin of New Orleans: "We this day forward you by S. S. Perseverance a negro woman of light complexion (or a mulatto) named Lawrena, aged about nineteen years (19) which we wish you to take possession of and sell at the earliest opportunity

---

[1] The Christian names of Pierce and Vick have a bit of sardonic significance. These items of 1831 are drawn from documents validated by the notary Carlile Pollock and shelved under his name in the record room of the municipal courts building.

on our %. The girl is sound, and you may give a clear bill
of sale of her. She is not very sprightly, as you will per-
ceive, but said to be a good field hand. She has been left with
us for sale, and this not being a good market we take this
method of disposal as the best for all parties. Select your own
time and put her on the Block and let her rip for what she will
bring accordon to looks with *good title*." The bill accompanying records the sale of Lawrena, at auction with guarantee
of title only and not of health or character, for $375.

A terser letter of the same year was from Oliver Anderson at
Lexington, Missouri, to Haggerty and Latting of New Orleans:
"I send by Sam Cloon to be reshipped at St. Louis a man named
John, about 23 years old, sound and well in every respect, who I
desire you to sell to the best advantage and place the proceeds
to my credit. I bought the negro about two weeks ago at about
$1000. He ran off from me twice since, and I will not be
plagued with him. I hope you will get a good price for him."
The bill of sale recited the sale of John, with no warranty other
than that of ownership, to John Farrell of New Orleans for $850.

Robert Huie, whose name we have encountered at New
Orleans, published advertisements frequently in the newspapers of the North Carolina Piedmont:

"NEGROES WANTED. The subscriber wishes to pur-
chase likely negroes, from ten to thirty years old, and will pay
the most liberal prices in cash. All who have such property to
sell would do well to call on him, or on Mr. John Jones his agent.
He can be found at Mr. Slaughter's Hotel in Salisbury, and
Mr. Jones at Dr. Boyd's Hotel in Charlotte."[1]

A Virginian wrote when reminiscing in 1835 of his boyhood
thirty years before, "I recollect a profane old gentleman who
was in the habit of selling a negro every year or two, to pay off
his scores for corn and meat, . . . swearing that his negroes
should never eat him, but one the other."[2] As if to corrobo-
rate this, except as to tone, a letter is at hand from one Virginian
to another in 1805: "I have set down to write one more to you

[1] *Western North Carolinian* (Salisbury, N. C.), July 12, 1834.
[2] *Farmers' Register*, II, 612.

on a very disagreeable affair my necesaty compells me to it. . . .
I am oblige to sell propity to pay of sum old ballons [1] which I
wish you to have   its Rachel & a child.   if you would buy her
I had rather you should than for her to go to a stranger." The
suggestion in this, of strong preference for selling to neighbors
except as regards unruly slaves, is copiously confirmed in many
other letters; and yet the dealers first and last procured many
thousands, with and without warrant of character. Sheriffs'
and executors' sales are a partial explanation; and perhaps
common field hands with whom their masters were not in close
touch were not subjects of solicitude.

A locomotive engineer on a North Carolina railroad said
that he had once carried six hundred slaves southward on a
single train.[2] While it may be doubted that an engine of that
day was likely to haul six hundred persons even in box cars, it is
clear that great numbers went south and west, whether in
company with their migrating masters or in the custody of
dealers. In this aspect the long-distance slave trade was
essentially a part of the westward movement, supplementing the
flow of people who went without involving purchase and sale.

The routes taken by the traders and their coffles were the
same as those followed by the migrants — the sea lanes, the
Ohio and Mississippi, and the long roads overland. Speed was
desired to shorten the period of sustenance and interest charges;
but health was yet more important, and sufficient good will to
prevent mutiny or flight on the road or sulkiness in the mart at
the destination. The dealers were not full of the milk of human
kindness or they would not have entered upon their calling.
On the other hand they cannot have been fiends in human form,
for such would have gone speedily bankrupt. The social
stigma laid upon them can hardly have been so stringent as
tradition tells, for many a planter and perhaps most of the
general merchants turned a trade on favorable occasion, and
sundry citizens of solid worth and esteem can be identified as
regular participants.

---

[1] *I.e.*, balances, debts.
[2] Robert Russell, *North America* (Edinburgh, 1857), 157.

A Virginian jotted in 1762: "My brother much out of order by . . . a cut in his head, which misfortune happened to him last week by one Thos. Williams about the sale of some negroes." [1] Another in 1802 wrote: "With respect to the negro business we perfectly concur, 'tis cruel and dangerous, and I am fearful subject to many accidents. I have advised with several good councilors who all oppose the plan." Those who did ply the traffic might possibly have told some tales to freeze the marrow in our bones; but the records they have left are nearly all mere bills of sale.

[1] *William and Mary College Quarterly*, XI, 230.

CHAPTER IX

THE PECULIAR INSTITUTION

FOR a man to be property may seem barbaric and outrageous. But in this twentieth century thousands of divorced husbands are legally required to pay periodic alimony to their ex-wives, and if one seeks escape from the levy upon his earnings he may be clapped into prison until he gives adequate pledges of compliance. The woman has a property right which the law maintains. This institution of alimony has developed somewhat unawares; and so, in some degree, did Negro slavery.

During the first half of the fifteenth century Portuguese navigators had found their way to the coast of Guinea and brought home natives who proved exemplary servants. Employment of Negroes in a fairly definite status of slavery soon spread to Spain, and thence to the West Indies in the time of Columbus. To the Spanish colonists in those tropic lands, who languidly developed a plantation system, occasional cargoes of Africans were sold to replace the subjugated and rapidly dying aborigines. When vigorous Englishmen seized great spaces in the new world they procured labor from every convenient source and in any convenient status. Indians captured in sporadic wars were deemed fair spoil, though prudence prompted their transfer to places beyond the reach of their kinsmen. But Negroes in America, though in the same legal category with Indian captives, were as completely broken from their tribal stems as if they had been brought from the planet Mars. If any people were to be held to involuntary service, they were perfect for the purpose.

In Guinea the Negroes as a rule were not caught by the crews of the slaving ships, but were bought from African proprietors, and they were heathen who by transportation to some Christian land might attain eternal bliss at the mere price of lifetime labor. By such thoughts were salved such few consciences as needed soothing. The slave trade, most prosperous of all traffic in its heyday, was not shunned by sinner or saint; and Negro slave labor, for some purposes cheaper even than the service of oxen or horses, was excluded nowhere in the stretch of two continents from New France to Chile. Circumstances of climate and industry, not of religion or ethics, concentrated it in certain zones to a degree which added a social problem to the initial concern of mere exploitation.

No preceding statute was requisite for the buying and holding of a Negro in bondage. In this, as in the development of most other institutions, custom preceded law and fixed its course. Negroes in fact were held as slaves in every English colony, even including Georgia and of course New England, prior to the enactment of laws to sanction it. But slaves were property, and in a civilized order property needs definition and official recognition so that writs may run for detinue, replevin or the like, and a constable be required to serve the proprietor's interest. Slaves were also persons presumably dangerous to the social order, for they were deprived of the privileges and ambitions which commonly keep freemen self-restrained. On that score, as well as because of the contrasts in race and culture, a distinctive system of police was developed.

No colony or commonwealth lived a hermit life, but as each took, somewhat selectively, the institutions of its mother land, so it borrowed from its neighbors any devices which seemed expedient in meeting local needs. In Northern jurisdictions, where Negroes were so few that they were nearly negligible as a social factor, the lawmakers could afford to concern themselves merely or mainly with slaves as property; [1] in the South, as in the West Indies, the social phase was at least equal to the economic in legislative regard, and enactments concerning

[1] There was nevertheless great ado in the town of New York in 1721 and again in 1741 over plots for insurrection, whether real or fancied.

both aspects went hand in hand.[1] As with other livestock, the proprietor of the female parent became possessed of her offspring; and as the owner of a horse might use force in breaking him to harness, so the master of a slave might coerce him into subjection, though the law forbade cruel treatment or the destruction of life or limb except when meeting resistance or by mishap in the course of "moderate correction." A runaway slave, too, was like a stray horse, to be seized, impounded, advertised, and reclaimed by his owner upon payment for services rendered and expenses incurred.

A slave could own no property unless by sanction of his master, nor make a contract without his master's approval. His mating was mere concubinage in law, though in case of subsequent emancipation it would become a binding marriage. The rape of a female slave was not a crime, but a mere trespass upon the master's property! In general for any damage done by a slave the master was not liable unless it were done by his order; but to the slave himself, or to the community, the master was responsible for maintenance throughout life and for needful medical service. Any neighbor or stranger furnishing these when in default was entitled to reimbursement. But slaves themselves could not be parties to suits at law nor give testimony against white persons.

In Santo Domingo and Louisiana the body of law applicable to the colored population was called *le code noir*. Black it was, except for mulattoes and quadroons, as to the complexions of the people to whom it applied, and black in its exclusion of liberty from their lives. Even blacker was that of Anglo-America in its deprivation of the slender immunities which

[1] The statutes in the several colonies, territories and States are summarized chronologically in J. C. Hurd, *The Law of Freedom and Bondage in the United States* (Boston, 1858). The legal régime at large is analyzed from contrasting points of view in William Goodell, *The American Slave Code in Theory and Practice* (New York, 1853), and T. R. R. Cobb, *An Inquiry into the Law of Negro Slavery in the United States* (Vol. I, which deals with slaves only as persons, was alone published, Philadelphia, 1858). Monographs of note concerning individual commonwealths are J. C. Ballagh, *A History of Slavery in Virginia* (Baltimore, 1902), and H. M. Henry, *The Police Control of the Slave in South Carolina* (Emory, Va., 1914). For further bibliography and for elaboration of the themes of the present chapter see Phillips, *American Negro Slavery*, chaps. 20-24.

the French laws afforded.[1]   The regulatory statutes everywhere were frankly repressive. They forbade slaves to possess weapons, to beat drums or blow horns which might serve to convey signals, to strike any white person even in self-defense, to be out of their quarters after curfew, to travel singly without written authorization, to travel in groups without a white escort, to assemble at night unless a white person were present; and rural citizens in their capacity as militia were embodied into squads to patrol their designated beats and chastise any slaves caught in transgression.   Laws forbade the teaching of slaves to read and write, and restricted their opportunities at every turn where a privilege might impinge upon the security or interest of the whites; and except for the discontinuance of cruel methods of inflicting death penalties, the severity of the statutes was not lessened as the decades passed.

❊   ❊   ❊   ❊   ❊

"Wisdom, justice, moderation" was adopted as an official motto by Georgia, not with ironic intent but in serious aspiration.   The stereotyped slave laws which she and her sisters maintained permit no apology; yet they invite explanation, for they were enacted and reënacted by normal representatives of normal American citizens, commonplace, acquisitive, fearful of disorder, resentful of outside criticism, and prone to cherish accustomed adjustments even if they put to scorn their own eloquence on each Fourth of July.   They might have said in Grover Cleveland's phrase, not a theory but a condition confronted them.   Fresh Africans were manifestly not to be incorporated in the body politic; and Negroes to the third and fourth generations were still in the main as distinctive in experience, habit, outlook, social discipline and civilian capacity as in the color of their skins or the contour of their faces.   'Twere better, it was thought, for them to suffer the ills they had than for all to fly to those they knew not of.

[1] For example, by the royal decrees which constituted law in the French colonies, slaves were secured in the possession of any property they might acquire; and masters were forbidden to sell young children apart from their mothers.

The peace of the plantation realm was menaced by the Stono revolt in 1739, Gabriel's uprising in 1800, Denmark Vesey's plot in 1822, Nat Turner's rebellion in 1831 and minor episodes now and then. The cataclysmic disorders in Santo Domingo in sequel to the French Revolution were a warning from abroad; and agitations in England and New England for complete equalization of the races gave prospect that an outside incitement would reach the Negroes if they were not kept *incommunicado*. Each outbreak, plot or agitation brought as a fruit of apprehension a new crop of statutes to make assurance increasingly sure that the South should continue to be "a white man's country."

As those who live under (or over) the Volstead Act are aware, a law may be so drastic that the community, though not procuring its repeal, will render it of slight avail. This was copiously the case in the slave régime. When times were quiet, as they generally were, burdensome statutes were conveniently forgotten. Patrol duty was evaded so widely, despite the complaints of grand juries, that performance was exceptional rather than the rule. Hundreds, doubtless thousands of slaves were taught their letters; and they traveled the roads in groups or assembled by night for Christian worship, voodoo ceremonies or mere pastime, with white persons conspicuously absent and none disposed to say them nay. A master or an overseer must needs accommodate himself with the slaves in his corps, to concede privileges for the sake of good will; and even a constable had a life of his own to lead, preferably not too strenuous. The legislators alone could afford to be as thorough as their whims or their fears dictated.

As a mayor of Charleston reported, slaves in town were arrested numerously for being "out after the beating of the tattoo, fighting and rioting in the streets, following military companies, walking on the battery contrary to law, bathing horses at forbidden places, theft or other violation of the city and state laws." Questioned in a petty court, some were dismissed, some had small fines imposed which their masters paid, some were sentenced to whipping or brief imprisonment, and a few were held for prosecution on serious charges. In the country trivial offenses were punished by masters, overseers or patrols without the formality of trial; and many a crime which must have brought grave retribution if carried to court was dealt with privately in the master's interest. Under the common law, for example, grand larceny was a capital crime. But as a South Carolinian said, a master who had been robbed by one of his own slaves would not usually institute judicial process, for that "would add the loss of the value of the negro to that of the article stolen." And if the theft were of a neighbor's goods, comity suggested conference and informal punishment, for this neighbor knew not how soon some slave of his own would stand in the culprit's place. As to still graver offenses: "When crimes of greater magnitude are committed, the commutation of capital punishment for transportation (that humane feature of penal law) saves many of its victims. It is applied not only to those cases which policy permits and humanity dictates, but whenever the welfare of society can be made to accord with the interest of the proprietor." [1]

To remove the pecuniary motive of masters to conceal and "compound" the felonies of their slaves, a Virginia law provided public compensation for the loss of such as were capitally convicted and sentenced to death or deportation. A file of the vouchers for such payments, nearly complete from 1780 to 1864, has permitted analysis of such convictions in that commonwealth. Of the 1418 offenders all told, including 91 women, there were 346 convictions of murder, 56 of poisoning or attempt, 73 of rape and 32 of attempts, 91 of insurrection or conspiracy, 119 of arson, 257 of burglary, 15 of highway robbery, 20 of horse-stealing, 111 of miscellaneous assault, and 301 of unspecified felonies. In the small residue there were two convictions of the fantastic offense of administering medicine to white persons.[2]

[1] C. C. Pinckney, *Address to the South Carolina Agricultural Society, August 18, 1829* (Charleston, 1829), 16, 17.

[2] These vouchers, preserved in the Virginia State archives, are discussed by U. B. Phillips in the *American Historical Review*, XX, 336–340; *American Negro Slavery*, 457–459. Incidentally they yield important data concerning slave prices.

The courts for the trial of slaves, even on capital charges, were of inferior grade, presided over by groups of justices of the peace rather than by full-fledged magistrates. But in the plantation districts these justices as a rule were men of dignity and substance, and the freeholders whom they selected to sit with them were commonly of similar traits and standing. In the diary of John A. Selden, which we shall use again, there is a characteristic item, July 23, 1859: "I was all day attending a special court. Set on the bench 9 hours. Trial of John Walker's woman, Mary, for breaking open John Slater's house. Punished her with stripes." A trial of nine hours indicates a considerable sifting of evidence.

Even on the frontier, proper form was followed if the courts had knowledge of it. From Wilkes County, Georgia, in 1787, when that upland community was very young, an available group of documents relates the history of a case. The first item, signed by a justice of the peace and twelve jurors, is in the nature of a coroner's inquest reciting that on the preceding day, as confessed by her, "Negro Jude, the property of John Mills", had caused the death of her master's son John by administering poison, "and so the aforesaid Jude him the said John Mills then and there Feloniously Killed and Willfully murdered, contrary to the Peace, Law and Good order of the said State." The second is a warrant from the justice next day, directing the sheriff of the county to keep Jude in custody until discharged by due course of law. The third, undated, is a certificate from a sworn jury of nine women [1] that in their opinion Jude was not with child. The fourth, dated January 11, is a verdict of guilty returned by a jury of six to a court of three "Esq^{rs}" or justices of the peace, together with the sentence of the court: "Negro Jude, you are to be carried to the Goal from whence you came and there to be kept till Friday Weak at which time you are to be taken to the place of Execu-

---

[1] This is validated by the forewoman "Jean + Duke." In the report of the coroner's
inquest four of the jurors have their names accompanied by the same symbols of illiteracy.

(marginal note above "Jean + Duke": hir mark)

tion or Gallows when you are to be hanged till you are dead and then your Body Burnt to ashes." [1]

✻   ✻   ✻   ✻   ✻

In the higher courts, whose decisions were currently printed in stout volumes to fill the shelves in lawyers' offices, slaves were dealt with as a rule only as property; but even these records are often threaded with personal equations. When a certain group of slaves was auctioned in settlement of an estate, so strong were the ties of affection between them and their accustomed mistress that she bought them, regardless of cost. The agent of the estate admitted that his by-bidder had run up the price excessively, and a court, while adjudging the purchase to be valid, ordered a reduction of the price to the market level.[2] On the other hand slaves might validly be sold for less than nothing. A judgment in bankruptcy directed that two who were aged and infirm "be sold to the lowest bidder — that is to the one who would provide for them and bury them plainly and decently for the least sum — to be paid out of the assets of the insolvent debtor" as a means of meeting an obligation which rested upon him in ethics and in law.[3]

The killing of a slave, though without the malice which would have made it a crime, might give ground for suit by the owner for trespass and the destruction of property;[4] and a jailor's neglect of a runaway in his custody cost him four hundred dollars in indemnification of the master for the maiming of the slave by frost.[5] A physician having administered medicine without the master's assent was adjudged liable for the

[1] Manuscripts in private possession. In that day cremation was thought to strengthen the terror of death.

[2] Helen T. Catterall, ed., *Judicial Cases concerning American Slavery and the Negro*, I (Washington, 1926), 96. This excellent compendium in which as yet only the cases adjudicated in England, Virginia, West Virginia and Kentucky are summarized, illuminates many phases of the slave régime.

[3] The two were bought by a bank, perhaps to lessen the loss which it would sustain as a creditor of the insolvent; and, in sequel, the abolition of slavery by the thirteenth amendment before these Negroes died was adjudged to terminate the obligation which the bank had assumed. — Catterall, *Judicial Cases*, 464. For the loss of a bequest to prospective freedmen by reason of the thirteenth amendment, see *ibid.*, 261, 262.

[4] *Ibid.*, 118.   [5] *Ibid.*, 145.

value when the Negro died,[1] and a citizen employing a Negro for twenty-five cents to swim his horse was held responsible as in effect an insurer against the loss of the slave during that employment.[2]   The fellow-servant rule, inertly persisting from the simple times when a man at work might effectively look out for himself, ran to the effect that an employee could not procure compensation from his master for an injury suffered through the negligence of a fellow servant.   But when a slave who was hired as a brakeman by the Louisville and Nashville Railroad had his leg crushed in a collision, the court awarded damages to his master, saying that the slave status removed the man from the normal fellow-servant category: "A slave may not, with impunity, remind and urge a free white person, who is a co-employee, to a discharge of his duties, or reprimand him for his carelessness and neglect; nor may he with impunity desert his post at discretion when danger is impending, nor quit his employment on account of the unskillfulness, bad management, inattention, or neglect of others of the crew. . . . He is fettered by the stern bonds of slavery — necessity is upon him, and he must hold on to his employment." [3]

But the tenderness of courts toward the pecuniary interests of masters was not without limits.   To prevent a repetition of robbery, a warehouseman had rigged a gun which killed an invading slave.   Upon suit of his owner for damages the claim was denied because, "though the robbery attempted in this case would only have been a misdemeanor in a slave, yet in a white person it would have been a felony"; and the gun, lawfully set against a felon, put no liability upon the warehouseman when it killed a mere misdemeanant instead.[4]

Some early statutes had classed slaves with real estate for certain purposes, mainly in order to diminish their liability to dislocation; and after the legislatures had made them chattels again the courts adopted a rule that slaves must not be seized

---

[1] Catterall, *Judicial Cases*, 404.
[2] This was on the ground that the bargain had been made without the master's knowledge or approval. — *Ibid.*, 402.
[3] *Ibid.*, 427.
[4] *Ibid.*, 322, 323.

for debt when other movables were sufficient to satisfy general creditors. This increased the degree to which slave property was a peculiar institution. But as a rule the hardest of all questions to decide were those as to whether certain persons were bond or free. A Kentucky slave was inherited by five heirs jointly, three of whom relinquished to him "their right and interest in him as a slave, and executed a partial deed of emancipation and licensed him to go abroad as a free man"; but the remaining part-proprietors had not released their claims when a suit was entered to determine the question of status and privilege. The law, sanctioning slavery and freedom in sharp distinction, contemplated no fractional combination of the two conditions. The court, saying in plaintive understatement "the case is one of rare occurrence and by no means free from difficulty," could only express a pious hope that the remaining part-owners would complete the manumission.[1]

Suits for freedom were handled in a manner specially prescribed. For example, under a South Carolina statute of 1740, borrowed by Georgia in 1770, when a judge received complaint, whether in session or in recess, that a person was illegally held as a slave, he must appoint a guardian for the claimant and expedite the trial before a jury. "Upon general or special verdict found," to quote the Georgia text, "judgment shall be given according to the very right of the cause, without having any regard to any defect in the proceedings, either in form or substance, and if judgment shall be given for the plaintiff a special entry shall be made declaring that the ward of the plaintiff is free, and the jury shall assess damages which the plaintiff's ward hath sustained . . .; but in case judgment shall be given for the defendant, the said court is hereby fully empowered to inflict such corporeal punishment, not extending to life or limb, on the ward of the plaintiff as they in their discretion shall think fit." [2]

How many claimants were flogged for having troubled the

<hr />

[1] Catterall, *Judicial Cases*, 364, 365. In a similar case the court found an extraneous technicality upon which it declared the Negro free. — *Ibid.*, 385-387.

[2] Marbury and Crawford, *Digest of the Laws of Georgia* (Savannah, 1802), 426, 427.

courts with flimsy pretenses cannot be known; but it is of record that a great number of suits for freedom were tried and that the judges, maintaining the Roman maxim, *In obscura voluntate manumittentis, favendum est libertati*,[1] gave to numerous petitioners the benefit of doubts.

❋　　　❋　　　❋　　　❋　　　❋

"Free persons of color" were an unintended but inevitable by-product of the recourse to Negro labor.[2]　Brethren to the slaves, and some of them unacknowledged half-brethren of the whites, they were an increasing complication.　A few Negroes attained freedom in early Virginia because the first comers, imported before definite slavery was established, were dealt with as if they had been indentured servants.　Others here and there were manumitted by benevolent masters for meritorious service or in compliance with scruples of conscience; and a small number of mulattoes born of white mothers were free by birth.　As long as Negroes and mulattoes of every status were but a small part of the population and constituted no public social problem, the free group gave little concern.　But no sooner did the number of slaves evoke a special system of police than the free Negroes began to be considered a menace. The closing decades of the seventeenth century brought the first laws to check manumission and miscegenation, and the eighteenth began their definite exclusion from the voting suffrage and the militia.

The libertarian fervor of the Revolution swept away some of these laws and prompted a multitude of private manumissions at the South as well as the legal disestablishment of slavery in all the States north of Delaware.　But problems of order came in quick sequel to independence.　The free Negroes, who numbered some sixty thousand in 1790, were nearly doubled in 1800 and, thanks to Louisiana's addition, were more

---

[1] Catterall, I, 158.　See her index, under manumission, for a long series of cases.

[2] The best monographs are J. H. Russell, *The Free Negro in Virginia* (*Johns Hopkins University Studies*, XXXI, No. 3); and J. M. Wright, *The Free Negro in Maryland* (*Columbia University Studies*, XCVII, No. 3).　C. G. Woodson, *Free Negro Heads of Families in the United States in 1830* (Washington [1925]), comprises not only a list of names from the census returns but an introductory sketch of legislation and status.

than thrice as many in 1810. By 1830, when Garrison's agitation intensified the reaction, they exceeded three hundred thousand, the larger half distributed as neighbors to the two million slaves in the South. As these and later decades passed, the restraints of aforetime were imposed afresh and variously supplemented. Influx from abroad and from sister States was forbidden; manumission if permitted at all was conditioned upon removal; and the free Negroes on hand were required to register, pay fees, and procure guardians and licenses. With plans for promoting their emigration to such distant havens as Liberia bearing little fruit, and projects for general expulsion coming to naught, the laws more and more bracketed free Negroes with the slaves in restricting education, testimony, peregrination and employment.

The grounds for these drastic restraints were official apprehensions of several sorts: that through vagrancy, vice and mere indolence the free Negroes must be an economic burden; that social exclusion from white circles must needs make them discontented; that their sense of grievance would ally them with the slaves in plots for upheaval; and if educated and free to travel they would be most effective conspirators. As methods were revealed or imagined by which these people might injure the whites whether as mere business competitors, as receivers of stolen goods and sellers of liquor to slaves, or as teachers and preachers of incendiary notions, one restrictive statute followed another to make them the more surely passive.

In unofficial opinion severity of legislation was often deprecated. For example, a Charleston editor said of the local free colored people, their conduct "has been for the most part so correct, evincing so much civility, subordination, industry and propriety, that unless their conduct should change for the worse, or some stern necessity demand it, we are unwilling to see them deprived of those immunities which they have enjoyed for centuries without the slightest detriment to the commonwealth." [1] In fact, almost with one accord, they were

[1] Charleston *Courier*, December 9, 1835, quoted in H. M. Henry, *Police Control of the Slave in South Carolina*, 182.

the most acquiescent of mankind. Aware fully that they dwelt upon sufferance and that in any embroilment disaster was assured unless a white protector were enlisted, they were obsequiously self-effacing and readily compliant with every public or private demand. Indeed their main vices, aside from idleness, were those of concubines or procurers in gratification of white men's lusts. Some prospered from these employments, and others, as barbers, cabmen, mechanics, merchants, fishermen or farmers. A few became slaveholders of plantation scale,[1] and some were soldiers of acknowledged service in the Revolution and the War of 1812. Some had the manners of Chesterfield and the diction of Samuel Johnson. Of high degree were these in the sharply defined strata of urban colored society. Others, more numerous, were thriftless, inert underlings, content if they could find jobs which no others wanted, and accustomed to live without seeking steady means of support. These were slaves by nature or habit, "loud laughers in the hands of fate", who had been cast loose in misguided philanthropy.

Ranging as they did in complexion from a tinged white to full black, in costume from Parisian finery to many-colored patches, in culture from serene refinement to sloven superstitious uncouthness, these people showed a diverse reflection of the patterns presented by the other groups in the community. Originating nothing, they complied in all things that they might live as a third element in a system planned for two.

[1] In the main, however, the slaves owned by free Negroes were their own kindred, bought and held merely because the laws forbade manumission without exile. In the *Journal of Negro History*, IX, 41–85, is a list of the free colored owners of slaves and the numbers held by them, compiled from the Federal census returns of 1830.

CHAPTER X

THE COSTS OF LABOR

THE Reverend Jesse H. Turner, with a strong concern for treasures of earth, shifted from a Richmond pulpit to a near-by plantation and explained his prosperity by saying in part: "I keep no breeding woman nor brood mare. If I want a negro I buy him already raised to my hand, and if I want a horse or a mule I buy him also. . . . I think it cheaper to buy than to raise. At my house, therefore, there are no noisy groups of mischievous young negroes to feed, nor are there any flocks of young horses to maintain." [1]

This practice was fairly common among railroad companies, blast-furnace proprietors and urban industrialists, not because it was the cheaper but rather because their operations did not give work for women, their administrative apparatus did not facilitate a cherishing of health or a training of youth, and their limitations of capital excluded investment in persons who were not laborers. These, in short, like modern rolling mills and automobile factories, were masculine enterprises conveniently ignoring family complications. But among plantation instances Turner's policy of avoiding the encumbrance of children was without parallel, so far as my knowledge extends.

Whether it were cheaper to "breed" or to buy slaves depended upon the market price as compared with food and clothing costs

[1] *Farmers' Register*, X, 129 (March, 1842). Another device which he described had not the same uniqueness. It was to give each slave at Christmas the value of a barrel of corn less the value of any tools lost and double the value of anything stolen. If the thief had not been identified the deduction was distributed through the whole corps. "By this means I also secure my property from the depredations of the neighboring negroes. Thus a few barrels of corn are made the means of saving my property to perhaps ten times the amount, the whole year; and I am also spared the painful necessity of frequent chastisements."

during a decade or two, together with the rate of juvenile mortality and other hazards. In any case the choice could hardly be of the moment, for purchase meant a prompt employment while rearing involved a continuous outlay with a view to deferred returns.

Slave children were a by-product whose volume could hardly be controlled and whose costs had no relation to market price. Oftentimes a woman when offered for sale was described as "a good breeder", but she brought little more than a barren sister and not so much as a man of her age.[1] This was for the same reason that a mare commonly sells for no more than a gelding. Her service was worth far more than her future progeny, and her fruitfulness as a mother must automatically diminish her performance of work during pregnancy and the nursing period.[2]

A new-born pickaninny had a value purely because at some day his labor would presumably yield more than the cost of his keep. If he died early his owner was out of purse to an amount somewhat greater than his maintenance had cost. If he proved an idiot, or blind or crippled, the case would be worse, for he must prove a "dead" expense until in fact he died. But if he throve his value would commonly rise faster than his costs accumulated, and would reach a maximum before the end of his teens,[3] when he had barely begun to cover his costs. This value would be maintained so long as he continued to be classed as a "prime field hand", say until about the age of thirty years. For two decades longer, if things went well, he would continue to do the work of a "full hand"; but year by year his value would decline because the time was shortening in which the net proceeds of his labor would serve as a sinking fund to reimburse

---

[1] Prices for women ranged as a rule about one fourth lower than for men, and the average for slaves of all ages at any time and place was about half the price for male prime field hands.

[2] E.g.: "Negroes for hire. Two men, good farm hands. Also a negro woman with several children. Said woman is a good house servant, cook &c., and will be hired at a good home for board and clothing." — Union and American (Nashville, Tenn.), January 23, 1861, advertisement.

[3] Unless he were an apprentice artisan, when his maximum value would come at the end of his training.

his owner for the investment which must be extinguished by his death or disability. If our one-time pickaninny should live to three score and ten, he would be worth substantially less than nothing, for he could render no service of worth and his master must maintain him indefinitely on a pensioner's dole.

Masters were fully conscious of this liability, and the market faithfully reflected the negative value of superannuates. A Virginian in France wrote in 1860 to a kinsman: "Please let me know the condition of the old negroes at Cherry Grove, and whether there is the remotest likelihood of their closing this life during the present century. They must be very helpless; and will soon, if not now, require the personal attention of a young negro. Suggest some mode of making them comfortable the balance of their lives, and at the present or a less expense." And a broker at Savannah reported to a client in 1856 that when a local plantation gang was offered as a unit, "the purchaser gave $2000 more than the asking price for 85 with the privilege of rejecting 10 old people." In other words he paid the proprietor two thousand dollars to retain the ten superannuates on his own hands.[1]

The prospect that life would outlast labor had a perceptibly depressing effect upon slave prices after prime age was past; and the possibilities of untimely death, disability or flight put some restraint upon price at every age. For example, when the newspapers reported in 1833 that the deaths of slaves from cholera in Louisiana had brought losses estimated at four million dollars,[2] would-be purchasers everywhere might well take it as a warning that precarious property should not be bought too dearly.

❋   ❋   ❋   ❋   ❋

Slave prices bore a definite relation to wages but by no means a fixed ratio, for the one was determined by the value of work immediately to be done while the other was affected by much the same influences which play upon the market for corporation

---

[1] Manuscripts in private possession. In another the remark occurs: "I cannot get Flora a home without paying 80 dollars a year. No person will take her for less money."

[2] *Niles' Register*, XLV, 84.

stocks — optimism and pessimism as to conditions in coming years, and conjectures as to the prospect of selling the purchase at a profit. Wages, as is well known, follow the rise and fall of commodity prices laggingly, and wages in one area are affected slowly by changes in a distant quarter. But in sundry times after the stoppage of imports from Africa slave prices changed with stock-market speed in response to changes in prosperity near or far and in response also to fluctuations in the supply of credit and the rate of interest.

On the accompanying chart [1] the price-curves for prime field hands are plotted from records of the nineteenth century in four communities which represent as nearly as may be the seats of tobacco, rice, cotton and sugar. Tobacco and rice were old staples which, having brought the slaves from Africa, could now yield some of their increase to new employments. Cotton and sugar were young, short of labor and restricted mainly in slave supply to those who might be procured from within the United States. The cotton belt and the sugar bowl accordingly made a market to attract labor by offering prices higher than rice or tobacco earnings would warrant. The younger staples thus, on different schedules of buoyancy, were the main factors determining slave prices in every corner of the South. Cotton, by reason of its immense area and volume of production, reduced even sugar to a secondary rôle; and the fluctuations of its price are accordingly plotted on the same chart.[2]

---

[1] Reprinted, by permission of D. Appleton and Company, from U. B. Phillips, *American Negro Slavery*, with modifications. The sources and methods used in the charting are described *ibid.*, 368–370. At all points the curves are mere approximations, for the correlation of individual prices with the market grade and range was continually disturbed by intrusions of the personal equations — and for various years in the several markets a deficit of records has been met by conjecture. The curves as they stand are the fruit of scanning thousands of bills of sale and similar documents.

[2] For convenience, the annual averages for middling uplands in the New York market are used; but it should be noted that in the period of the Embargo and the War of 1812 this market did not move quite parallel to those which directly served the cotton-producing localities. The semi-weekly range of cotton prices at New York and Liverpool from 1816 to 1872 is tabulated in E. J. Donnell, *Chronological and Statistical History of Cotton* (New York, 1872). The curve here used is from the U. S. Department of Agriculture, *Atlas of American Agriculture*, part V, "The Crops", section A, "Cotton" (Washington, 1918), p. 20. This publication contains many maps, tables and charts of interest and value concerning the cotton industry.

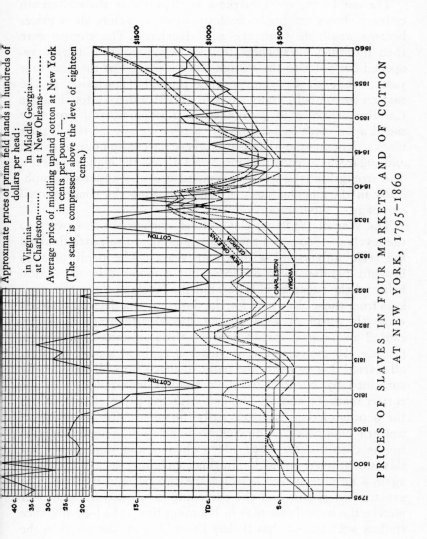

Approximate prices of prime field hands in hundreds of dollars per head:

in Virginia——— in Middle Georgia:———
at Charleston········· at New Orleans-·-·-·-·

Average price of middling upland cotton at New York in cents per pound —;

(The scale is compressed above the level of eighteen cents.)

PRICES OF SLAVES IN FOUR MARKETS AND OF COTTON AT NEW YORK, 1795–1860

The rise in the older markets at the close of the eighteenth century shows the tug of fresh opportunity before slave prices became available from the new districts. The curves were then flattened everywhere in 1803 when South Carolina reopened her ports to the foreign slave trade. For the next four years, while slaves were pouring through Charleston to the eastern cotton belt, many ships from Africa merely touched the Carolina wharves to legitimate their imports, and promptly sailed upon what was technically a coasting voyage to sell their black cargoes on the Mississippi, where the conjunction of cotton and sugar was already making New Orleans the highest market. The strength of the western demand becomes apparent graphically in the singular peak of price following the congressional stoppage of slave imports.

The War of 1812 sent slave prices everywhere downward to the levels of 1800; and the flush times after the peace doubled the scale universally within four years. The panic of 1819 brought parallel steep declines; but a rebound in the cotton belt and the sugar bowl separated the levels in these two markets from those elsewhere for the duration of a decade. Meanwhile the tariff of 1828, giving special advantage to sugar, caused an unusual spread between the Louisiana and Georgia prices. All the curves were clustered again at a peak in 1837; all started downward in the panic of that year; all were briefly sustained by Nicholas Biddle's reckless manipulation of the cotton market; and all plunged with the price of cotton into the depths of the disastrous early 'forties. After five years of western bankruptcy a new climb was begun, roughly parallel to the cotton curve until 1857, when cotton went down but slaves continued upward. In this concluding decade there was again a notable spread between the two pairs of markets. In explanation of this and the preceding divergencies I can offer merely the hypothesis that in booming times the long-distance traders were fearful that if they should bid up the prices in the districts of supply the market might collapse before their merchandise could reach the districts of demand. Some, indeed, were caught by one panic or another with coffles on the march or stocks on hand which could not be sold without loss or kept without ruinous costs of sustenance.

The peaks in the price curves are pointed, while as a rule the troughs are rounded if not flat; slave prices, in other words, tended to remain on the lower levels and to return precipitately in sequel to each ascent. This reflects a disposition in the community to concern itself in the main only with routine earnings and to realize that even prime hands were worth only six or eight times the rates at which they could be hired for a year. But when the market was thought to be going up, sundry speculative buyers would purchase greedily with a view to profit by resale. In doing this they would incur debts; and when uneasy creditors demanded liquidation the structure of prices would fall faster than it had risen.

That the floor of each trough was as a rule higher than that of its predecessor was due mainly to the mere decline in the value of money, which as the decades passed raised the price of all property. But in still greater degree the crests of the peaks reached higher and higher altitudes; and this probably means that the spirit of speculation grew more intense and the volume greater as the century lengthened its tale of years. This was in line with stock-market history wherein "bull movements" have tended each to excel all which have gone before. The slaves themselves were "securities" — investments made with a view to future income. They were, however, not analogous to bonds, for there was no repayment of the par value in prospect; nor to preferred stocks, for the slave's own sustenance was a first charge upon his earnings; nor to the shares of railroad or manufacturing companies whose operations are intended to be permanent; but rather to mining stocks as liquidating investments which lose value as the ore-beds approach exhaustion. The price of a slave was affected by the price of cotton for the same reason that copper shares are influenced by the current price of copper metal.

❈ ❈ ❈ ❈ ❈

In each period of rising quotations the question recurred as to whether inflation were in progress and how far it would go. This discussion was particularly vigorous after the middle of the century. A Georgia commentator said in 1855 that the rise must erelong bring a fall; another in 1858, puzzled that the current panic in commodities and securities had not affected the slave market, believed that a collapse was coming; a third in 1860 thought the speculators demented:

"The old rule of pricing a negro by the price of cotton by the pound — that is to say, if cotton is worth twelve cents a negro man is worth $1200.00, if at fifteen cents then $1500.00 — does not seem to be regarded. Negroes are 25 per cent higher now with cotton at ten and one half cents than they were two or three years ago when it was worth fifteen and sixteen cents. . . . A reverse will surely come." [1] A New Orleans writer undertook a rebuttal: "The theory that the price of negroes is ruled by the price of cotton is not good, for it does not account for the present aspect of the slave market. . . . Nor do we agree with our contemporaries who argue that a speculative demand is the unsubstantial basis of the advance in the price of slaves — that the rates are too high and must come down very soon. It is our impression that the great demand for slaves in the Southwest will keep up the prices as it caused their advance in the first place, and that the rates are not a cent above the real value of the laborer who is to be engaged in tilling the fertile lands of a section of the country which yields the planter nearly double the crop that the fields of the Atlantic States do. The Southwest is being opened by a great tide of emigration. The planter who puts ten hands to work on the prolific soil of Texas and Western Louisiana soon makes money enough to buy ten more, and they have to be supplied from the older States — hence the prices which rule in Virginia, the Carolinas and Georgia. A demand founded in such causes cannot fall off for a score or more years, and the prices of negroes must keep up. They will probably advance somewhat." [2] In fact, the prices

---

[1] *Southern Banner*, January 11, 1855; *Southern Watchman*, January 21, 1858; *Federal Union*, January 17, 1860, reprinted in Phillips, *American Negro Slavery*, 374, 375. *Cf.* also William Chambers, *Slavery and Colour* (London, 1857), 207, 208.

[2] *Daily Crescent* (New Orleans), January 30, 1860.

were sustained through most of the year.[1] But surely a peak was being shaped, whose farther side must have been a steep descent, whether in time of peace or war.

The great oscillations of the slave market did not help industry, but hindered it. When in time of inflation a planter unwarily enlarged his corps by purchase, he increased his investment at a cost which his future earnings were not likely to warrant; and if he used credit in the transaction he might even be bankrupted by the maturing of the debt in a time of deflation. Thousands of employers, particularly those of small scale, avoided these risks by hiring slaves instead of buying them. This was readily feasible in older districts where many proprietors had more slaves than they needed in service and were disposed to hire out rather than sell the surplus. But when a shift to a distant region was involved, hire would not serve; sale was essential unless the master himself migrated.

Slaves were hired by the day or the month, but most copiously by the year, the employer providing shelter, food, clothing and medical service in addition to paying the stipulated wage. If the slave were invalided or ran away the wage was not abated; but if he died the liability ceased. Annual contracts ran not for three hundred and sixty-five days but for fifty-one weeks, from New Year's to Christmas; for every hireling went home for his traditional holiday. In fact, an employer was lucky if he recovered control before a week in January had elapsed. Wage rates varied with the fluctuations of prosperity. In the lower South full hands commonly brought somewhat less than a hundred dollars a year in 1800, and about two hundred in 1860; but in Virginia the scale was about one third less at either period.

❈   ❈   ❈   ❈   ❈

[1] From an account book of Hector Davis, an auctioneer of slaves at Richmond (manuscript in the New York Public Library), it may be gathered that prime field hands in that market fell from about $1350 in June to $1250 in September, 1860, and to $1000 by the end of the next year. Quoted in Confederate currency, they rose in 1862 to $1400 in September and $1700 in December. When the currency was nearer its collapse, in the latter part of the war, slaves brought several thousand dollars each.

As long as African imports were unrestrained, the cost of tilling a field or building a house with slave labor might be less than if whites were employed. The closing of the ports to slaves while they remained open to freemen changed this, for if slaves were preferred on grounds of custom, sentiment, convenience or prestige, the prices or wages of a restricted market must be paid. The money wages for slaves, it is true, might continue to range lower than those of whites, and the cost of their board and lodging was less; but the schedule of performance was commonly so much greater by whites as to outweigh these differentials heavily. Olmsted made a comparison in 1856. In his home district in New York native American farm hands were hired for ten dollars a month, plus board and lodging, and immigrant Irish or Germans for somewhat less. In eastern Virginia able-bodied slaves brought $120 per year on an average, plus board, lodging, clothes and medical service. But in his opinion the work of the slaves, by reason of slackness and indifference, was hardly half as effective as that of the New York white laborers. In addition there was a cost of supervision, which with white laborers was much less.[1]

Corroboration which Olmsted took pains to quote from his contemporaries might have been reinforced from the writings of Benjamin Franklin, Alexis de Tocqueville, John Taylor, Edmund Ruffin, Daniel R. Goodloe and various others. A British visitor had written with some exaggeration: "Nothing can be conceived more inert than a slave; his unwilling labour is discovered in every step that he takes; he moves not if he can avoid it; if the eyes of the overseer be off him, he sleeps; the ox and the horse, driven by the slave, appear to sleep also; all is listless inactivity."[2]

Thomas Cooper, economist as well as chemist and philosopher, had written studiously while resident in South Carolina: "The usual work of a field hand is barely two thirds what a white day labourer at usual wages would perform; this is the

---

[1] F. L. Olmsted, *Seaboard Slave States* (New York, 1856), 185, 203, 717.

[2] W. Strickland, *Observations on the Agriculture of the United States of America* (London, 1801), 33.

outside. . . . Nothing will justify slave labour in point of
economy but the nature of the soil and climate which incapaci-
tates a white man from labouring in the summer time, as on the
rich lands in Carolina and Georgia, extending one hundred
miles from the seaboard. In places merely agricultural, as
New York, Pennsylvania, Illinois, Indiana, Missouri, slave
labour is entirely unprofitable. It is so even in Maryland and
Virginia." [1]

Reports were circulated concerning one district or another
in the lower South that slaves were systematically worked to
death in seven years.[2] These may have originated from a dis-
tortion of the fact that the price of a prime slave in the districts
of demand amounted to some seven times his annual hire,[3] and
from the practice of slaveholders to blacken the reputation of
a distant region as a device for keeping their slaves amenable
under threat of sale.[4] The nearest approach to a valid assertion of this which I have encountered was made by a North
Carolinian traveling to seek a more prosperous location.
Reporting from Alabama that he had found there a rich and
healthful district, he said of the farther west: "Well au-
thenticated accounts from the Yazoo concur in representing
that whole section of country as very sickly, though it is very
productive. . . . It is calculated that . . . the negroes die
off every few years, though it is said that in that time each hand
also makes enough to buy two more in his place. . . . These
are sufficient reasons in our view to prevent our going thither." [5]

[1] Thomas Cooper, *Lectures on the Elements of Political Economy* (Columbia, S. C.,
1826), 94, 95.

[2] For a discussion of remarks by Fanny Kemble, William Goodell and others, see
Phillips, *American Negro Slavery*, 382–387.

[3] *Slavery not forbidden by Scripture, or a Defence of the West India Planters.* By a
West Indian (Philadelphia, 1773), 8, *note.*

[4] That all Virginians were not more tender than other men appears from a letter
of 1814 from a Valley citizen, reporting that a slave of his had deserted from a distant
employment and come home, saying the work was too hard. This the writer took as
proof that his own overseer was too lenient; and he said in conclusion: "I shall make
this affair of Lewis the groundwork of new rules, & certainly work mine until they run
away or be very unwilling to come back when I send or sell." — Manuscript in private
possession. The tone of this is more stringent than I have encountered elsewhere.

[5] J. H. Ruffin, Tuscaloosa, Ala., April 30, 1833, to his father. J. G. de R. Hamilton,
ed., *The Papers of Thomas Ruffin*, II, 77.

This attributes the mortality to local diseases which had not yet been conquered. For any one accustomed to the management of slaves to say that, when of prime age at least, they could be worked to death in any space of time would have been absurd.

Interest and sentiment were clearly combined in a general sustentation of life. After an epidemic of cholera in 1849 a Savannah physician wrote: "I wish an Abolitionist could see the care & attention bestowed upon our Negroes, first to avoid the pestilence & next to cure the sick. A manufacturing Cotton Lord can easily fill the place of his dead operative & he loses nothing by his death. A planter loses so much capital by the death of every one of his operatives, & hence to save his capital is to save his negroes." [1] In 1866 he said: "The altered status of the negro has materially affected (& injuriously) the income of every Physician"; [2] for attendance upon slaves had been paid for at standard rates, while that upon freedmen usually brought no pay. To similar effect, a British voyager on an Alabama steamboat just after the war was told: "A gentleman of colour, working on one of the boats, was asked the other day whether he was best off now or before he was free. He scratched his wool and said, 'Wall, when I tumbled overboard before, the captain he stopped the ship and put back and picked me up; and they gave me a glass of hot whiskey and water; and then they gave me twenty lashes for falling overboard. But now if I tumble overboard, the captain he'd say, What's dat? Oh! only dat dam nigger — go ahead!'" [3] The slaves might be chastened but they were sure to be cherished.

The fact that every purchase of a slave involved an outlay of capital and a diversion of assets from other investment was generally understood and occasionally deplored. Governor Spotswood remarked in 1710 that the importation of slaves had run the Virginians deeply into debt; [4] and a Yorktown mer-

---

[1] Letter of Richard Arnold, M.D., in the *Johns Hopkins Hospital Bulletin*, XLII, 170.
[2] *Ibid.*, 226.
[3] Henry Latham, *Black and White: A Journal of a Three Months' Tour in the United States* (London, 1867), 144.
[4] *Virginia Historical Society Collections*, I, 52.

chant when proposing a partnership in importing slaves said in 1750: "There is not the least fear of selling here, for there is in general as many Purchasers as there is slaves imported, and the pay is always better than for any other commodity." [1]

A Charlestonian wrote in 1738: "Although a few negroes annually imported might be of advantage to most people, yet such large importations as 2600 or 2800 every year is not only a loss to many but in the end may prove the ruin of this province. . . . Negroes may be said to be the bait proper for catching a Carolina planter, as certain as beef for catching a shark. How many under the notion of 18 months' credit have been tempted to buy more negroes than they could possibly expect to pay for in 3 years?" [2]   And fifty years afterward, in a debate in the South Carolina legislature, David Ramsay said that all church-going members ought to vote for a pending bill to prohibit slave imports. "They had devoutly prayed not to be led into temptation, and negroes were a temptation too great to be resisted." [3]   To the same effect, but without either jocularity or disapproval, J. B. D. DeBow said when secession was already in process: "The universal disposition is to purchase. It is the first use for savings, and the negro purchased is the last possession to be parted with." [4]

❋   ❋   ❋   ❋   ❋

This proclivity for buying slaves was the worst feature of the régime from an economic point of view, for it drained capital out of every developing district and froze the local assets into the one form of investment. While the farmers of Ohio and Illinois were obtaining white laborers on wages to be paid from current earnings and were investing their profits in land improvements, railroads and local factories, the planters of Alabama and Louisiana were applying their cash and straining their credit to buy slaves whose lifetime labor must be paid for

[1] *William and Mary College Quarterly*, XI, 157.
[2] *South Carolina Gazette*, March 19, 1738, quoted in the Charleston *Courier*, September 28, 1855.
[3] Charleston *Morning Post*, March 23, 1787.
[4] *DeBow's Review*, XXX, 74 (January, 1861).

in advance. The greater the profits of a year, the stronger was the desire to expand operations and the higher was likely to be the capital cost of the slaves bought. Prosperity thus brought little divergence from the stereotyped investment programme. Adversity, coming from over-production and lowered prices for the staples, would impel projects for diversifying industry; but funds for factory stocks and the like were scarce at such a time, and any fresh rise in the cotton or sugar market would turn the thoughts of men again to staple expansion — to buy more slaves to make more cotton for the continued purpose of buying more slaves to make more cotton.[1] The slavery of the Negroes made it easy to shift them from place to place and it assured regularity of work by reducing turnover of employment to an almost utter minimum. But these merits were at the cost of exalting routine, the utilization of crude labor where zealous and expert service would have been advantageous, the expansion of a permanent problem of racial control, and an endless absorption of earnings in the mere enlargement of plantation corps.

When prices were high, slaves became too precious for employment in any but the safest of tasks. In 1835 a British visitor at New Orleans noted hundreds of Irishmen digging a canal through the pestilential swamp to Lake Pontchartrain. "Slave labour," he was told, "cannot be substituted to any extent, being much too expensive; a good slave costs at this time two hundred pounds sterling, and to have a thousand such swept off a line of canal in one season would call for prompt consideration." [2]

When immigration grew more copious in the next decade and the next, this utilization of Irish and Germans became common among planters throughout the seaboard and along the Mississippi for digging ditches, for building levees, for every sort of work indeed which would expose the workers to the hazards

---

[1] Factory development, nevertheless, was quite substantial, particularly during the 'fifties. Doubtless the sellers of slaves in the older districts put some of their proceeds into these diversified investments.

[2] Tyrone Power, *Impressions of America* (Philadelphia, 1836), II, 149, 150.

of sickness, injury or death.[1] Peaks of price in the slave market, reflecting a scarcity of labor in general, implied a vigorous enlargement of demand for free labor, white or black, in employments of all sorts.[2] White labor, in fact, was alone flexible in supply, for the laws of the several states forbade free Negroes to enter, and the slaves at any time available in the South at large were essentially those on hand and no more. The slaves by their very status had a complete insurance against unemployment. Every day in a decade brought them three coarse meals, whether free wage-earners were being employed or discharged as the demand for products waxed or waned in the "business cycle." Europe had replaced Africa as a source of added labor; and in spite of the precariousness of employment in competition with slaves, the proportion of the foreign-born in the Southern population was as large by 1860 as it has been at any time since. Had it not been for influx from the North and abroad, along with some smuggling of slaves, the peaks in the curves of slave prices must have reached still greater heights.

[1] Cf. *Harper's Magazine*, VII, 755; *DeBow's Review*, XI, 401; Olmsted, *Seaboard Slave States*, 90, 550; W. H. Russell, *Diary*, 272, 278; Robert Russell, *North America*, 272; A. de P. Van Buren, *Sojourn in the South*, 84, 318.

[2] In the late 'fifties, for example, there was a noteworthy substitution of white women for slaves in the tobacco factories at Petersburg and Richmond. — *Hunt's Merchant's Magazine*, XL, 522. At New Orleans, whites had already replaced Negroes extensively as cabmen, draymen and hotel waiters and chambermaids. — Lyell, *Second Visit*, 2d ed., II, 160, 161. The long-continued and accelerating substitution of white labor at New Orleans is reflected in the Federal census returns from Orleans Parish. In 1810 the percentage of slaves in its population was forty-four, and of free colored twenty-three; in 1820 they were thirty-four and seventeen respectively; in 1830 they were thirty-two and twenty-four; in 1840, twenty-three and eighteen; in 1850, sixteen and nine; in 1860, eight and six. The white percentage advanced from thirty-three to eighty-six in the half-century. During the disorders of the 'sixties, however, Negroes thronged into the city; and perhaps their percentage may never fall again to its level at the close of the slavery régime.

CHAPTER XI

LIFE IN THRALDOM

NOT all Negroes in America were at any time slaves, nor were all slaves Negroes; yet except for mere antiquarian detail slavery was Negro slavery and none other. The reason lay partly in the traits and customs of the Negroes themselves. In Africa slavery, along with polygamy, human sacrifice, cannibalism and other primitive institutions, prevailed very widely; and millions were habituated to slave status. Their masters were accustomed likewise to their own prerogatives, with power to sell or even to kill their slaves at will. Barbaric African slaveholders, indeed, conspired in a sense with civilized European sailors to introduce their institution into America; and the acquiescence of the slaves themselves made the conspiracy successful. Europeans or Americans in turn, by offering irresistible market inducements, stimulated African activity in catching more slaves, till warring, raiding and deportation reached such a scale as to constitute the rape of a continent. No coast south of the Sahara and no tribe in the interior escaped its effects, though the west coast and its hinterland were the main field of its operations.

Negro tribes were many and their people various. In stature they ranged from dwarfs well-nigh to giants, in complexion from dark brown to an almost perfect black, in facial contour from a type approaching the Caucasian to one suggesting an orang-outang. In methods of life they were equally diverse. While most had no domesticated animals, some depended for diet almost wholly upon the milk and blood of their cattle. While for the most part mere palaver was perhaps the chief business, high artistry in sculpture was attained in some communities and in others there were notable inventions such as the Zulu blowgun and the drum-telegraph of upper Guinea.[1] And as to courage, the shrinking Pygmies of the equatorial forest were offset by the Sudanese of whom Kipling sings in the language of Tommy Atkins:

> 'E rushes at the smoke when we let drive,
> > An', before we know, 'e's 'ackin' at our 'ead;
> 'E's all 'ot sand an' ginger when alive,
> > An' 'e's generally shammin' when 'e's dead.
> 'E's a daisy, 'e's a ducky, 'e's a lamb!
> 'E's a injia-rubber idiot on the spree,
> 'E's the on'y thing that doesn't care a damn
> For the Regiment o' British Infantree.

> So 'ere's *to* you, Fuzzy-Wuzzy, at
> > your 'ome in the Sowdan;
> You're a pore benighted 'eathen
> > but a first-class fightin' man;
> An' 'ere's *to* you, Fuzzy-Wuzzy, with
> > your 'ayrick 'ead of 'air —
> You big black boundin' beggar — for
> > you bruk a British square.

One tribal stock of a full Sudanese quality found representation in the slave cargoes under the name of Coromantees or Fantyns from the Gold Coast. An observer said: "A Cormantee will never brook servitude, though young, but will either destroy himself or murder his master";[2] and their prominence in insurrections gave them a reputation of being "haughty, ferocious and stubborn." Yet when handled with considera-

[1] For communication the drum preferred is a log shaped somewhat into the form of a hippopotamus and hollowed through a slot along the back. When struck on the slot and on the side this gives contrasting tones. A recent student says that the drummers merely imitate the tone-changes in spoken language and therefore use no code. (A. S. Rattray, "The Drum Language of West Africa", in the *Journal of the African Society*, XXII, 226–236.) This remark seemed to me doubtful from the first. Having heard performances in the Sudan since this book was first published, I am now the more convinced that a code is used.

[2] *Gentleman's Magazine*, XXXIV, 487 (London, 1764). The spelling of African tribal names has never become fully standardized.

tion, as experience proved, they might give the most handsome response. Of another sort were the Mandingoes, Foulahs and other stocks from the Senegambian region of the northwest, who doubtless owed to an Arabic infusion the talents which made some of them esteemed for responsible functions; but many of these had a delicate physique which unfitted them for heavy labor. From another extreme, the far south, came Congoes and Angolas, slender and sightly, mild and honest, but as a rule notoriously stupid. But from the middle zone, the Slave Coast, where the Niger threads its delta to the sea, where in the fetid ports of Bonny and Benin, Lagos and Calabar a stream of slaving ships met converging streams of slave coffles and bartered their firearms and fire water, goods and gewgaws, there came the main supply of living "ebony." Hence were brought Eboes of jaundice tinge in eyes and skin, with prognathous faces and mournful natures inclining them in duress to seek death by their special device of "swallowing their tongues." Hence also the Whydahs, Nagoes and Pawpaws, whose disposition to take floggings "as the chastisement of legal authority to which it is their duty to submit" made them ideal slaves for the generality of masters. But at the bottom of the scale were the Gaboons, from shortly southward, of whom a West Indian wrote: "From thence a good negro was scarcely ever brought. They are purchased so cheaply on the coast as to tempt many captains to freight with them; but they generally die either on the passage or soon after their arrival in the islands. The debility of their constitutions is astonishing." [1] Only to an unpractised eye could all Africans look alike.

But the processes of transferring them to America and "breaking them in" on the plantations were such as to mingle the tribesmen, eliminate the weak and willful, and blend the surviving types. Of the initial procurement in the jungle very little

---

[1] *Practical Rules for the Management and Medical Treatment of Negro Slaves in the Sugar Colonies.* By a Professional Planter (London, 1803). The passages relating to Negro tribal traits are reprinted in *Plantation and Frontier*, II, 127–133. Slaves from Calabar, a port near the Gaboon country, were strongly disesteemed in the Charleston market. — Elizabeth Donnan, "The Slave Trade into South Carolina before the Revolution", in the *American Historical Review*, XXXIII, 817.

can be learned. It is fairly clear, however, that native opera-
tors tended to seize and sell new captives rather than demoralize their own domestic staffs by selling their habituated
servants. This meant a pell-mell assemblage at the source.
When a parcel, however procured, was to be sent to market, its
members were bound by thongs into a coffle and conducted by
footpath to a seaboard stockade to await some buyer's coming.
The journey was likely to decimate the coffle whether by am-
bush, rebellion and punishment, or illness and exhaustion. On
the coast again there was debilitation from anguish, illness and
injury, and a selection by the white purchasers. Elderly or
invalid slaves were not wanted. They were commonly left
upon the hands of their black owners, who themselves had no
desire to keep and feed unsalable stock. Death quick or slow
was clearly the prospect; and it is not to be wondered that a
witness reported "the most piteous entreaties made by the
poor rejected creatures to the captain to take them." [1]

As the slaves were bought by the whites they were generally
branded for identification and shackled on shipboard for
security. When the cargo was full — and its filling often took
many weeks and a toll of death among whites and blacks on that
pestilential coast — the ship would set sail. The slaves were
crowded into 'tween-decks too low to permit standing, lodged
upon bare boards, stifled in tropic heat, sometimes afflicted with
infectious disease, and always at the mercy of brutal and lustful
men. The only mitigating features were the speed of the ship
in the trade-wind latitudes and the interest of the owners in
keeping their merchandise alive and salable. And yet in their
misery and bewilderment some of the victims had room in their
minds for great curiosity. A slaving sailor's reminiscences run:
"They were very inquisitive about their future destination,
and asked if we always lived on the water? — whether we had
no women? — if we had any, where they were?" [2] More
striking than this, a Coromantee had the bravado to say to

[1] Sir Thomas F. Buxton, *The African Slave Trade* (London, 1839), 91. This book
has many items illustrating the miseries inflicted by the trade.
[2] William Butterworth, *Three Years Adventures of a Minor* (Leeds [1831]), 124, 125.

the ship captain who had sentenced him to be hanged for the killing of a sentry, that "he desired me to consider that if I put him to death I should lose all the money I had paid for him." [1] But high spirits did not save even all who possessed them; and the voyage decimated again those who had survived the African experience and debilitated many who were not yet dead when western shores were attained.

In America some cargoes were disposed of wholesale, wherein all slaves who could go over the ship's side on their own legs brought a uniform price, except for young children. More commonly the sales were by retail whether "by scramble" of purchasers on shipboard after a beginning signal, or by the ship's peddling along river shores, or through factors who kept slaves in stock at the ports for sale to shopping planters. In any case invalid residues might be sold to speculative physicians on the chance of restoration to health, or in last resort Yankee skippers might carry such to their Northern homes for disposal on a bargain basis. In the American market again, some of these Africans were noted for their nonchalance. An English woman visiting the West Indies wrote in 1775: "I was some days ago in town, when a number for market came from on board a ship. They stood up to be looked at with perfect unconcern. . . . They were laughing and jumping, making faces at each other, and not caring a single farthing for their fate." [2]

But still another decimation awaited even the able-bodied in their induction into the plantation régime. The climate was new, the food strange, and the work at which they were driven, with lashes on occasion, was disheartening. There was in fact a seasoning period, usually reckoned at three years, during which many newcomers were likely to die. The planters were well aware of this and laid their plans accordingly. When large lots were bought they were generally distributed among the seasoned slaves somewhat as foundling orphans; or otherwise old Negroes were appointed as guardians for the concen-

[1] William Snelgrave, *Guinea and the Slave Trade* (London, 1734), 182.
[2] Evangeline W. Andrews, ed., *Journal of a Lady of Quality* (New Haven, 1921), 128. A similar item is in the "Diary of Edward Hooker", in the *American Historical Association Report* for 1896, I, 882.

trated group and special food was provided. In either case the result was likely to be such as was experienced in the only instance of which detailed records are available. In 1792 and 1793 the proprietor of Worthy Park plantation in Jamaica added one hundred and eighty-one new Congoes and Coromantees to the corps of three hundred and fifty-five slaves already on hand, and built thirty new huts to house them. Quantities of special foodstuffs were bought and special nurses detailed; but in 1794 an alarming prevalence of "the bloody flux", as dysentery was then called, prompted the construction of a large new hospital and finally led to the sending of some fifty of the survivors to a mountain haven in the hope of saving their lives. At least forty of the new Negroes died within three years;[1] and the management may well have esteemed itself happy not to have lost many more, for experienced opinion in Jamaica strongly deprecated wholesale induction by any system whatever.[2]

In North America induction was handled on a small scale nearly everywhere, not so much from policy as because the plantations themselves were comparatively small in corps. Climatically the continent imposed a greater change from Africa than did the West Indies, though to a climate eventually more salubrious even to folk accustomed to life at the equator. There were fewer disease-breeding insects and bacteria, there was better food, and surely better care by reason of the domestic tone of the régime in contrast with the absentee commercialism of the islands. But in whatever quarter the seasoning occurred, a considerable mortality was usually encountered. As a result of the transition on the whole from jungle tribesmen to seasoned plantation hands, probably not nearly half of those who had been seized in Africa were alive in America at the end of three or four years. But the survivors were enough proportionally to keep the business of getting them remunerative. Their living and learning were desired by master and mistress; and

[1] U. B. Phillips, "A Jamaica Slave Plantation", in the *American Historical Review*, XIX, 545, 546.
[2] *E.g.*, [Edward Long] *History of Jamaica* (London, 1774), II, 435.

adequate food and shelter, together perhaps with something of a sense of being cherished, brought to most of them a will to live, to mate and to multiply.

*   *   *   *   *

The simplicity of the social structure on the plantations facilitated Negro adjustment, the master taking the place of the accustomed chief.[1]   And yet these black voyagers experienced a greater change by far than befell white immigrants.   In their home lands they had lived naked, observed fetish, been bound by tribal law, and practiced primitive crafts.   In America none of these things were of service or sanction.   The Africans were thralls, wanted only for their brawn, required to take things as they found them and to do as they were told, coerced into self-obliterating humility, and encouraged to respond only to the teachings and preachings of their masters, and adapt themselves to the white men's ways.

In some cases transported talent embraced the new opportunity in extraordinary degree.   A contemporary Spanish narrative of the English conquest of Jamaica in 1655 says of a slave captured while carrying an enemy message: "Although an Angola black, this negro was clever.   He could read and write, knew the movable feasts, conjunctions, moon and tides, as well as though he had especially studied them; he was a good sugar-master, and could give an excellent account of himself when necessary." [2]   On the other hand some of the captives rebelled with violence against the new authority.   Thus in Georgia in 1774 "six new Negro fellows and four wenches" killed their overseer, murdered his wife and ran amok in the neighborhood until overpowered.[3]   But in general, as always, the common middle course was passive acquiescence.

To make adaptation the more certain, it was argued that "no Negro should be bought old; such are always sullen and un-

[1] Cf. N. S. Shaler, "The Nature of the Negro", in the *Arena*, III, 28.

[2] *Camden Miscellany*, XIII (London, 1924), no. 5, p. 11.   The captive was put to the garrotte.

[3] *Georgia Gazette* (Savannah), December 7, 1774.   Their leaders were burned at the stake.

teachable, and frequently put an end to their lives." [1] And indeed planters who could afford an unproductive period were advised to select young children from the ships, "for their juvenile minds entertain no regrets for the loss of their connections. They acquire the English language with great ease, and improve daily in size, understanding and capacity for labour." [2] The proportion of children in the cargoes was great enough to permit such a policy by those who might adopt it.[3] But the fact that prices for imported Negroes, even after seasoning, ranged lower than for those to the American manner born is an evidence that the new habituation as a rule never completely superseded the old. Thanks, however, to plantation discipline and to the necessity of learning the master's language if merely to converse with fellow slaves of different linguistic stocks, African mental furnishings faded even among adult arrivals.

To the second and later generations folklore was transmitted, but for the sake of comprehension by the children an American Brer Rabbit replaced his jungle prototype. If lullabies were crooned in African phrase their memory soon lapsed, along with nearly all other African terms except a few personal names, Quash, Cuffee, Cudjoe and the like.[4] And even these may have owed such perpetuation as they had to the persistence of the maritime slave trade which long continued to bring new Quashes and Cuffees from the mother country. In short, Foulahs and Fantyns, Eboes and Angolas begat American plantation Negroes to whom a spear would be strange but a "languid hoe" familiar, the tomtom forgotten but the banjo inviting to the fingers and the thumb. Eventually it could be said that the Negroes had no memories of Africa as a home.[5] Eventually, indeed, a Virginia freedman wrote after thirteen years

[1] *Gentleman's Magazine*, XXXIV, 487 (London, 1764).
[2] *Practical Rules*, reprinted in *Plantation and Frontier Documents*, II, 133.
[3] For example there were 102 below ten years of age among the 704 slaves brought by five ships to South Carolina between July and October, 1724. — British transcripts in the South Carolina archives, XI, 243.
[4] A table of the names most common among imported Negroes, which were derived from the days of the week, is printed in Long's *Jamaica*, II, 427.
[5] Charleston *Courier*, July 8, 1855.

of residence in Liberia, "I, being a Virginian," rejoice that "the good people of my old state are about to settle a colony on the coast of Africa"; and went on to say of himself and his compatriots, "there is some of us that would not be satisfied in no other colony while ever there was one called New Virginia."[1] His very name, William Draper, is an index of his Anglo-Americanization; and a pride which he expresses that Virginia Negroes have been the founders and the chief rulers "of almost all the settlements" in Liberia proves him a true son of the Old Dominion, "the mother of states and of statesmen." But William Draper was an exceptional specimen. In the main the American Negroes ruled not even themselves. They were more or less contentedly slaves, with grievances from time to time but not ambition. With "hazy pasts and reckless futures", they lived in each moment as it flew, and left "Old Massa" to take such thought as the morrow might need.

❊   ❊   ❊   ❊   ❊

The plantation force was a conscript army, living in barracks and on constant "fatigue." Husbands and wives were comrades in service under an authority as complete as the commanding personnel could wish. The master was captain and quartermaster combined, issuing orders and distributing rations. The overseer and the foreman, where there were such, were lieutenant and sergeant to see that orders were executed. The field hands were privates with no choice but to obey unless, like other seasoned soldiers, they could dodge the duties assigned.

But the plantation was also a homestead, isolated, permanent and peopled by a social group with a common interest in achieving and maintaining social order. Its régime was shaped by the customary human forces, interchange of ideas and coadaptation of conduct. The intermingling of white and black children in their pastimes was no more continuous or

[1] Letter of William Draper, Bassa Cove, Liberia, August 17, 1837, to William Maxwell, Norfolk, Va. — T. C. Thornton, *An Inquiry into the History of Slavery* (Washington, 1841), 272.

influential than the adult interplay of command and response, of protest and concession. In so far as harmony was attained — and in this the plantation mistress was a great if quiet factor — a common tradition was evolved embodying reciprocal patterns of conventional conduct.

The plantation was of course a factory, in which robust laborers were essential to profits. Its mere maintenance as a going concern required the proprietor to sustain the strength and safeguard the health of his operatives and of their children, who were also his, destined in time to take their parents' places. The basic food allowance came to be somewhat standardized at a quart of corn meal and half a pound of salt pork per day for each adult and proportionably for children, commuted or supplemented with sweet potatoes, field peas, sirup, rice, fruit and "garden sass" as locality and season might suggest. The clothing was coarse, and shoes were furnished only for winter. The housing was in huts of one or two rooms per family, commonly crude but weather-tight. Fuel was abundant. The sanitation of the clustered cabins was usually a matter of systematic attention; and medical service was at least commensurate with the groping science of the time and the sparse population of the country. Many of the larger plantations had central kitchens, day nurseries, infirmaries and physicians on contract for periodic visits.[1] The aged and infirm must be cared for along with the young and able-bodied, to maintain the good will of their kinsmen among the workers, if for no

---

[1] For example, James Hamilton, Jr., while Congressman from South Carolina, engaged Dr. Furth of Savannah to make visits on schedule to his plantation a few miles away. In 1828 he wrote from Washington to his factor at Savannah: "I have just received a letter from Mr Prioleau, informing me that the eyes of my old and faithful Servant Peter were in a perilous condition. I will [thank] you to request Dr Furth to attend to them promptly and effectually. . . . I will thank you to supply for my Hospital on his requisition all that may be necessary *in his opinion* to make my negroes comfortable when they are sick. I will thank you to request him to drop me a line occasionally of the health of my people and the success of the reform I propose thro him to institute in attention to the sick. . . . Be so good as to give to Peter the value of a couple of Dollars monthly for comforts to his family." — Manuscript in private possession.

On rations, quarters, work schedules and the like see [Ebenezer Starnes] *The Slaveholder Abroad* (Philadelphia, 1860), appendix; *DeBow's Review*, VII, 381, X, 621, XI, 369; *Southern Literary Messenger*, VII, 775; and travelers' accounts at large.

other reason. Morale was no less needed than muscle if performance were to be kept above a barely tolerable minimum.

❋   ❋   ❋   ❋   ❋

The plantation was a school. An intelligent master would consult his own interest by affording every talented slave special instruction and by inculcating into the commoner sort as much routine efficiency, regularity and responsibility as they would accept. Not only were many youths given training in the crafts, and many taught to read and write, even though the laws forbade it, but a goodly number of planters devised and applied plans to give their whole corps spontaneous incentive to relieve the need of detailed supervision. Thus John McDonogh near New Orleans instituted in 1825 an elaborate scheme of self-government and self-driving with a prospect of self-emancipation by his corps as a unit;[1] and a plan of trial by a jury of his peers for any slave charged with a plantation offense was followed by Joseph and Jefferson Davis on "Hurricane" and "Briarfield" in Mississippi.[2] The traveler Liancourt when visiting the Pringle plantation in the South Carolina lowlands in 1796 found its proprietor "in every respect a worthy man, amiable and communicative, and so happy that his equals are but seldom found. He is an excellent master to his Negroes, and asserts, against the opinion of many others, that the plantations of mild and indulgent masters thrive most and that the Negroes are most industrious and faithful. He is beloved by his slaves. The cultivated part of his plantation is in the best order, and the number of his slaves increases yearly by a tenth."[3] A similar achievement was described to Frederika Bremer as that of Thomas Spalding of Sapelo on the

---

[1] James T. Edwards, ed., *Some Interesting Papers of John McDonogh* (McDonogh, Md., 1898), 43–71. The self-emancipation was completed on schedule in 1842, and the freedmen went to Liberia.

[2] Walter L. Fleming, "Jefferson Davis, the Negroes and the Negro Problem", in the *Sewanee Review*, XVI, 407–427.

[3] La Rochefoucauld-Liancourt, *Travels* (London, 1799), I, 601, 602. This ten per cent rate of increase invites a discount.

Georgia coast, "a rich old gentleman who upon the beautiful island where he lives has allowed the palmettoes to grow in freedom, and the Negroes to live and work in freedom also, governed alone by the law of duty and love, and where all succeeds excellently." [1] We share Miss Bremer's regret that she could not accept an invitation to visit this Elysium. We have, however, from the pen of William Faux a description of such an establishment in the Carolina uplands, that of the venerable Mr. Mickle, who said of his slaves: "They are all, old and young, true and faithful to my interests; they need no taskmaster, no overseer; they will do all and more than I expect them to do, and I can trust them with untold gold. . . . I respect them as my children, and they look on me as their friend and father." And the traveler says: "This conversation induced me to view more attentively the faces of the adult slaves; and I was astonished at the free, easy, sober, intelligent and thoughtful impression which such an economy as Mr. Mickle's had indelibly made on their countenances." [2]

The civilizing of the Negroes was not merely a consequence of definite schooling but a fruit of plantation life itself. The white household taught perhaps less by precept than by example. It had much the effect of a "social settlement" in a modern city slum, furnishing models of speech and conduct, along with advice on occasion, which the vicinage is invited to accept. The successes of Pringle, Spalding and Mickle, if correctly reported, were quite extraordinary. Most planters did not even attempt an emulation, for not one in a hundred could hope by his own genius and magnetism to break the grip of normal slave-plantation circumstance. The bulk of the black personnel was notoriously primitive, uncouth, improvi-

---

[1] *Homes of the New World* (New York, 1854), I, 390.   Spalding was a prolific writer on the history and cultivation of sea-island cotton, but I have encountered no discussion by him of personnel management.

[2] William Faux, *Memorable Days in America* (London, 1823), 68, reprinted in Thwaites, ed., *Early Western Travels*, XI, 87.   For other examples and arguments see *Niles' Register*, XVI, 275; [Zephaniah Kingsley] *A Treatise on the Patriarchal System of Society as it exists under the name of Slavery* (4th ed., 1834).

dent and inconstant, merely because they were Negroes of the time; and by their slave status they were relieved from the pressure of want and debarred from any full-force incentive of gain.

Many planters, however, sought to promote contentment, loyalty and zeal by gifts and rewards, and by sanctioning the keeping of poultry and pigs and the cultivation of little fields in off times with the privilege of selling any produce. In the cotton belt the growing of nankeen cotton was particularly encouraged, for its brownish color would betray any surreptitious addition from the master's own fields. Some indeed had definite bonus systems. A. H. Bernard of Virginia determined at the close of 1836 to replace his overseer with a slave foreman, and announced to his Negroes that in case of good service by the corps he would thereafter distribute premiums to the amount of what had been the overseer's wages. After six months' trial he wrote: "I can say for this experiment that never certainly in my life have I had so much work so well done nor with equal cheerfulness and satisfaction, not having had occasion to utter an angry word except to a little cattle minder."[1] And in Louisiana sundry planters made it a Christmas practice to distribute among the heads of industrious families a sum amounting in aggregate to a dollar for each hogshead of sugar in the year's product.[2]

But any copious resort to profit-sharing schemes was avoided at large as being likely to cost more than it would yield in increment to the planter's own crop. The generality of planters, it would seem, considered it hopeless to make their field hands into thorough workmen or full-fledged men, and contented themselves with very moderate achievement. Tiring of endless correction and unfruitful exhortation, they relied somewhat supinely upon authority with a tone of kindly patronage and a baffled acquiescence in slack service.

For example a French traveler in South Carolina at the middle of the nineteenth century reported his observations on the

[1] *Farmers' Register*, V, 172, 173.
[2] Olmsted, *Seaboard Slave States*, 660.

plantation of a German, "certainly the least cruel and tyranni-
cal of men, . . . who does not wish to beat his slaves. The
ungrateful slaves work with great laziness and carelessness.
When he entered a hut where the Negresses were cleaning
cotton he was content to show them how badly it was done. . . .
The result of his remarks was a pout and a little grumbling."
And there was no sequel except a plea from the planter for the
visitor's commiseration.[1]

It has been said by a critic of the twentieth century South:
"In some ways the negro is shamefully mistreated — mistreated
through leniency," which permits him as a tenant or employee
to lean upon the whites in a continuous mental siesta and
sponge upon them habitually, instead of requiring him to stand
upon his own moral and economic legs.[2] The same censure
would apply as truly in any preceding generation. The slave
plantation, like other schools, was conditioned by the nature
and habituations of its teachers and pupils. Its instruction was
inevitably slow; and the effect of its discipline was restricted
by the fact that even its aptest pupils had no diploma in prospect which would send them forth to fend for themselves.

❋   ❋   ❋   ❋   ❋

The plantation was a parish, or perhaps a chapel of ease.
Some planters assumed the functions of lay readers when
ordained ministers were not available, or joined the congregation even when Negro preachers preached.[3] Bishop Leonidas
Polk was chief chaplain on his own estate, and is said to have
suffered none of his slaves to be other than Episcopalian;[4]
but the generality of masters gave full freedom as to church
connection.

The legislature of Barbados, when urged by the governor in
1681 to promote the Christianization of slaves on that island,
replied, "their savage brutishness renders them wholly in-

---

[1] J. J. Ampère, *Promenade en Amérique* (Paris, 1855), II, 114, here translated.
[2] Howard Snyder in the *Atlantic Monthly*, CXXVII, 171.
[3] *E.g.*, Rev. I. E. Lowery, *Life on the Old Plantation in Ante-bellum Days* (Columbia,
S. C., 1911), 71, 72. The author was an ex-slave.
[4] Olmsted, *Back Country*, 107 *note*.

capable. Many have endeavoured it without success." [1]
But on the continent such sentiments had small echo; and as
decades passed masters and churches concerned themselves
increasingly in the premises. A black preacher might meet
rebuke and even run a risk of being lynched if he harped too
loudly upon the liberation of the Hebrews from Egyptian
bondage; [2] but a moderate supervision would prevent such
indiscretions. The Sermon on the Mount would be harmless
despite its suggestion of an earthly inheritance for the meek;
the Decalogue was utterly sound; and "servants obey your
masters", "render unto Caesar the things that are Caesar's",
and "well done, thou good and faithful servant" were invaluable texts for homilies. The Methodists and Baptists were
inclined to invite ecstasy from free and slave alike. Episcopa-
lians and Presbyterians, and the Catholics likewise, deprecating
exuberance, dealt rather in quiet precept than in fervid exhortation — with far smaller statistical results. [3]

*   *   *   *   *

The plantation was a pageant and a variety show in alternation. The procession of plowmen at evening, slouched
crosswise on their mules; the dance in the new sugarhouse,
preceded by prayer; the bonfire in the quarter with contests in
clogs, cakewalks and Charlestons whose fascinations were as
yet undiscovered by the great world; the work songs in solo
and refrain, with not too fast a rhythm; the baptizing in the
creek, with lively demonstrations from the "sisters" as they
came dripping out; the torchlight pursuit of 'possum and
'coon, with full-voiced halloo to baying houn' dawg and yelping
cur; the rabbit hunt, the log-rolling, the house-raising, the
husking bee, the quilting party, the wedding, the cock fight,

---

[1] *Calendar of State Papers, Colonial*, 1681–1685, p. 25.
[2] *E.g.*, letter of James Habersham, May 11, 1775, to Robert Kean in London, in the
Georgia Historical Society Collections, VI, 243, 244.
[3] Surveys of religious endeavor among the slaves: Rev. Charles C. Jones, *The Religious
Instruction of the Negroes in the United States* (Savannah, 1842): C. F. Deems, ed.,
Annals of Southern Methodism for 1856 (Nashville [1857]); W. P. Harrison, ed., *The
Gospel among the Slaves* (Nashville. .893).

the crap game, the children's play, all punctuated plantation life — and most of them were highly vocal.[1] A funeral now and then of some prominent slave would bring festive sorrowing, or the death of a beloved master an outburst of emotion.[2]

❋   ❋   ❋   ❋   ❋

The plantation was a matrimonial bureau, something of a harem perhaps, a copious nursery, and a divorce court. John Brickell wrote of colonial North Carolina: "It frequently happens, when these women have no Children by the first Husband, after being a year or two cohabiting together, the Planters oblige them to take a second, third, fourth, fifth, or more Husbands or Bedfellows; a fruitful Woman amongst them being very much valued by the Planters, and a numerous Issue esteemed the greatest Riches in this Country."[3] By running on to five or more husbands for a constantly barren woman Brickell discredits his own statement. Yet it may have had a kernel of truth, and it is quite possible that something of such a policy persisted throughout the generations. These things do not readily get into the records. I have myself heard a stalwart Negro express a humorous regret that he was free, for said he in substance: "If I had lived in slavery times my master would have given me half a dozen wives and taken care of all the children." This may perhaps voice a tradition among slave descendants, and the tradition may in turn derive

---

[1] Doubtless many a plantation was blessed, or cursed as the case might be, with a practical joker such as Jack Baker, who kept himself and his whole neighborhood in Richmond entertained by his talent in mimicry. "Jack's performances furnished rare fun in the dog-days, when business was dull, and his pocket was furnished by the same process." One of his private amusements was to call some other slave in the tone of his master, and vanish before the summons was answered. "His most frequent dupe was a next door neighbor, whose master, a Scotchman, took frequent trips to the country on horseback. During his absence Jack would, before retiring to bed, rap on the gate and call 'Jasper! come and take my horse.' Jasper, aroused from his nap, came, but found neither master nor horse, and well knew who quizzed him. One night the veritable master made the call, some time after Jack had given a false alarm. Jasper was out of patience, and replied in a loud voice, 'D — n you, old fellow, if you call me again I'll come out and thrash you!' After that, poor Jasper was at Jack's mercy, unless he resorted to 'thrashing.'" — DeBow's Review, XXVIII, 197.

[2] Cf. Catherine Bremer, Homes of the New World, I, 374.

[3] John Brickell, The Natural History of North Carolina (Dublin, 1737), 275.

from an actual sanction of polygamy by some of the masters. A planter doubtless described a practice not unique when he said "that he interfered as little as possible with their domestic habits except in matters of police. 'We don't care what they do when their tasks are over — we lose sight of them till next day. Their morals and manners are in their own keeping. The men may have, for instance, as many wives as they please, so long as they do not quarrel about such matters.'" [1] But another was surely no less representative when he instructed his overseer: "Marriages shall be performed in every instance of a nuptial contract, and the parties settled off to themselves without encumbering other houses to give discontent. No slave shall be allowed to cohabit with two or more wives or husbands at the same time; doing so shall subject them to a strict trial and severe punishment." [2]

Life was without doubt monogamous in general; and some of the matings were by order,[3] though the generality were pretty surely spontaneous. This item, written by an overseer to his employer, is typical of many: "Esaw and biner has asked permission to Marry. I think it a good Match. What say you to it?" [4] Here and there a man had what was called in slave circles a "broad wife", a wife belonging to another master and dwelling at a distance. Planters of course preferred their slaves to be mated at home.

In the number of their children the Negro women rivaled the remarkable fecundity of their mistresses. One phenomenal slave mother bore forty-one children, mostly of course as twins;[5] and the records of many others ran well above a dozen each. As a rule, perhaps, babies were even more wel-

[1] Basil Hall, *Travels*, III, 191.

[2] *Southern Agriculturist*, III, 239. These instructions continued: "All my slaves are to be supplied with sufficient land, on which I encourage and even compel them to plant and cultivate a crop, all of which I will, as I have hitherto done, purchase at a fair price from them."

[3] An instance of coercive breeding is reported by Frederick Douglass, in *Narrative* (Boston, 1849), 62. For this item I am indebted to Mr. Theodore Whitfield of Johns Hopkins University.

[4] Phillips and Glunt, eds., *Florida Plantation Records*, 140; see also Olmsted, *Back Country*, 154.

[5] Phillips, *American Negro Slavery*, 298, 299.

come to slave women than to free; for childbearing brought lightened work during pregnancy and suckling, and a lack of ambition conspired with a freedom from economic anxiety to clear the path of maternal impulse.

Concubinage of Negro women to planters and their sons and overseers is evidenced by the census enumeration of mulattoes and by other data.[1]   It was flagrantly prevalent in the Creole section of Louisiana, and was at least sporadic from New England to Texas.   The régime of slavery facilitated concubinage not merely by making black women subject to white men's wills but by promoting intimacy and weakening racial antipathy.   The children, of whatever shade or paternity, were alike the property of the mother's owner and were nourished on the plantation.   Not a few mulattoes, however, were manumitted by their fathers and vested with property.

Slave marriages, not being legal contracts, might be dissolved without recourse to public tribunals.   Only the master's consent was required, and this was doubtless not hard to get.   On one plantation systematic provision was made in the standing regulations: "When sufficient cause can be shewn on either side, a marriage may be annulled; but the offending party must be severely punished.   Where both are in the wrong, both must be punished, and if they insist on separating must have a hundred lashes apiece.   After such a separation, neither can marry again for three years." [2]   If such a system were in general effect in our time it would lessen the volume of divorce in American society.   But it may be presumed that most plantation rules were not so stringent.

❋   ❋   ❋   ❋   ❋

The home of a planter or of a well-to-do townsman was likely to be a "magnificent negro boarding-house", at which and from which an indefinite number of servants and their depend-

---

[1] It is hinted, for example, by the exclamation point in this Virginian letter of 1831: "P. P. Burton has quit his wife, sent her to her father's and gone off with Sandy Burton to Texas and taken a female slave along!"   Manuscript in private possession.

[2] Plantation manual of James H. Hammond.   Manuscript in the Library of Congress.

ents and friends were fed.[1]   In town the tribe might increase to the point of embarrassment.   A Savannah woman wrote: "My only reason for desiring a plantation at times is for my host of little and big people — few to be sure of the latter and quite too many of the former.   The city, to my dear bought experience, is a bad place, though I have nothing to complain of with regard to the conduct of my people." [2]   The domestics were likely to consider themselves entitled to luxurious fare. The wife of a Congressman when visiting her home after two years' absence wrote: "I have been mobbed by my own house servants. . . .   They agreed to come in a body and beg me to stay at home to keep my own house once more. . . .   I asked my cook if she lacked anything on the plantation at the Hermitage.   'Lack anything?' she said, 'I lack everything, what are corn meal, bacon, milk and molasses?   Would that be all you wanted?   Ain't I been living and eating exactly as you all these years?   When I cook for you, didn't I have some of all? Dere now!'   Then she doubled herself up laughing.   They all shouted, 'Missis, we is crazy for you to stay home.'" [3]

Each plantation had a hierarchy.   Not only were the master and his family exalted to a degree beyond the reach of slave aspiration, but among the Negroes themselves there were pronounced gradations of rank, privilege and esteem.   An absent master wrote: "I wish to be remembered to all the servants, distinguishing Andrew as the head man and Katy as the mother of the tribe.   Not forgetting Charlotte as the head of the culinary department nor Marcus as the Tubal Cain of the community, hoping that they will continue to set a good example and that the young ones will walk in their footsteps." [4]

[1] A. P. Peabody, in the *Andover Review*, XVI, 156.

[2] On another occasion this lady had written to a nephew: "I have a great favour to ask you, that you will allow me to send Kate to your plantation until she gets more steady.   She is so much in the streets that I very much fear it will end in trouble." Manuscripts in private possession.

[3] Mary B. Chestnutt, *A Diary from Dixie* (New York, 1925), 22.   But field hands were likely to be much less concerned with their masters' comings and goings.   *Cf.* Olmsted, *Back Country*, p. 286; [Ingraham] *The South-West*, II, 194, 254.

[4] J. P. Carson, *Life of James Louis Pettigru* (Washington, 1920), 431.   In another letter Pettigru conjured his sister: "Do not allow the little nigs to forget that their hands were given them principally for the purpose of pulling weeds." — *Ibid.*, 23.

The foreman, the miller and the smith were men of position and pride. The butler, the maid and the children's nurse were in continuous contact with the white household, enjoying the best opportunity to acquire its manners along with its discarded clothing. The field hands were at the foot of the scale, with a minimum of white contact and privileged only to plod, so to say, as brethren to the ox.

At all times in the South as a whole perhaps half of the slaves were owned or hired in units of twenty or less, which were too small for the full plantation order, and perhaps half of this half were on mere farms or in town employment, rather as "help" than as a distinct laboring force. Many small planters' sons and virtually all the farmers in person worked alongside any field hands they might possess; and indoor tasks were parceled among the women and girls white and black. As to severity of treatment, the travelers were likely to disagree. Schoepf and Stirling thought the farmers' slaves were in the better case, while Russell surmised the contrary.[1] A Georgia physician found himself impelled to plead against over-incitement by small proprietors: "Men who own but few slaves and who share the labors of the field or workshop with them are very liable to deceive themselves by a specious process of reasoning. They say, 'I carry row for row with my negroes, and I put no more upon them than I take upon myself.' But the master who thus reasons is forgetful or ignorant of the great truth that the Negro's powers of endurance are really inferior to his; while in the case of the latter there is wanting those incentives to action that animate and actually *strengthen* the master."[2]

However the case may have been as to relative severity on farms and plantations, there can be no doubt that the farmers' slaves of all sorts were likely to share somewhat intimately such lives as their masters led[3] and to appropriate a consider-

[1] Johann David Schoepf, *Travels in the Confederation*, A. J. Morrison, tr. (Philadelphia, 1911), II, 147; James Stirling, *Letters from the Slave States* (London, 1857), 291; W. H. Russell, *Diary*, 278.

[2] Dr. J. S. Wilson in *DeBow's Review*, XXIX, 113 (July, 1860).

[3] *Cf.* Basil Hall, *Travels*, III, 279.

able part of such culture as they possessed — to be more or less genteel with their gentility or crude with their crudity, to think similar thoughts and speak much the same language. On the other hand, the one instance of wide divergence in dialect between the whites and the Negroes prevailed in the single district in which the scheme of life was that of large plantations from the time when Africans were copiously imported. On the seaboard of South Carolina and Georgia most of the blacks (and they are very black) still speak Gullah, a dialect so distinct that unfamiliar visitors may barely understand it. And dialect, there as elsewhere, is an index to culture in general.

❅   ❅   ❅   ❅   ❅

The life of slaves, whether in large groups or small, was not without grievous episodes. A planter's son wrote to his father upon a discovery of mislaid equipment: "The bridle and martingal which you whipped Amy so much for stealing was by some inattention of Robert's left in Mr. Clark's stable." Again, an overseer, exasperated by the sluggishness of his cook, set her to field work as discipline, only to have her demonstrate by dying that her protestations of illness had been true.

Grievances reinforced ennui to promote slacking, absence without leave, desertion and mutiny. The advertising columns of the newspapers bristled with notices of runaways; and no detailed plantation record which has come to my hand is without mention of them. As an extreme example, here is a summer's account by an overseer, or so much of it as can be deciphered: "August the 20 1844 Randle caught at Mr. Cathram brung home . . . [he had] left on the 12th July 1844 Lem runway on the 25 of July caught on the 2 of August by 1 of Mr Kings negroes Oscar runway on the 27 of August . . . George at tempt to git away I coat him and put a ringe and chane on him under the neck Lem runway on the 21 of August September the 3 Beny Bill Elijah Ellie all gowne together and Carline runway on the 3 stayed out 2 days . . . Joe runway on the 11th September." [1]

[1] Plantation journal of Levin Covington. Manuscript in Mississippi Archives Department.

Certain slaves were persistent absconders, and the chronic discontent of others created special problems for their masters. Thus a citizen in the Shenandoah Valley declined to hire one of his slaves to the proprietors of an iron furnace because "the previous bad character of the fellow in connection with recent declarations of his has left no doubt on my mind but he would make an effort to reach the State of Ohio, and by being placed at your Works it would certainly facilitate his object. Was I to send him I am persuaded that he would render you no services, and it might be the means of losing the fellow entirely." [1] On the other hand, a mistress in the same locality sought an employer for her woman slave because "Ann has become very impudent and should be hired to a strict master who can handle her." [2] But a strict master carried no guarantee of success, as an Alabama news item will show. William Pearce had notified an erring slave that a flogging was to be given him after supper. In due time Pearce called the man, who came from the kitchen with a pretense of submission, "but so soon as he got in striking distance drew an axe which had been concealed, and split in twain the head of his master." [3]

For steady success, indeed, experience taught that the master's authority "should be exercised in a firm but mild manner. He should even to a Negro unite in his deportment the *suaviter in modo* with the *fortiter in re*." This planter continued: "I never saw any degree of courtesy shown to a Negro (that is kept under good subjection) but was returned with usury. Cuffee is hard to outdo in politeness." [4] Another planter accepted the challenge of this task yet more gallantly when urging the value of kindliness and praise: "Give me a high spirited and even a high tempered negro, full of pride, for easy and comfortable management. Your slow sulky negro, although he may have an even temper, is *the devil* to manage." But as to the female of the species: "The negro women are

---

[1] Letter of R. Garland, January 3, 1830, to Messrs. Jordan and Irvine. Manuscript in the McCormick Agricultural Library, Chicago.

[2] Letter of E. Echols, December 20, 1856, to J. D. Davidson. Manuscript as above.

[3] *Daily Messenger* (Montgomery, Ala.), November 13, 1856.

[4] *Farmers' Register*, V, 32.

all harder to manage than the men." [1] A third was almost driven from the planter's career, as he said, "by the great aversion which I have to the manner of cultivating our lands in Virginia by slaves. I feel myself utterly incompetent to the task of managing them properly. I never attempt to punish or to have one punished but I am sensible that I am violating the natural rights of a being who is as much entitled to the enjoyment of liberty as myself." [2] A fourth, less troubled by scruples, was baffled by his problems: "The proper management and discipline of negroes subjects the man of care and feeling to more dilemmas perhaps than any other vocation he could follow. To keep a diary of their conduct, it would be a record nothing short of a series of violations of the laws of God and man. To moralize and induce the slave to assimilate with the master and his interest has been and is the great desideratum aimed at; but I am sorry to say I have long since desponded in the completion of the task." [3] A fifth maintained a strong note of optimism: "The character of the negro is much underrated. It is like the plastic clay which may be moulded into agreeable or disagreeable figures according to the skill of the moulder. The man who storms at and curses his negroes and who tells them they are a parcel of infernal rascals, not to be trusted, will surely make them just what he calls them; and so far from loving such a master, they will hate him. Now if you be not suspicious, and induce them to think by slight trusts that they are not unworthy of some confidence, you will make them honest, useful and affectionate creatures." [4] A sixth, eschewing exalted thought and ignoring profundities, contented himself with being a cheery fellow and relied upon a single prod with a double prong. We may see this Georgian only through the eyes of his slaves. "They say when they cultivated poor lands in Warren County that he used to hurry them by saying 'hurra,

---

[1] *Farmers' Register*, I, 565.

[2] Letter of William Garnett, July 12, 1805, in the *Papers of Thomas Ruffin* (*North Carolina Historical Commission Publications*), I, 80. Garnett persisted as a planter nevertheless, and his later letters do not echo these qualms.

[3] B. McBride, in the *Southern Agriculturist*, III, 175.

[4] *Farmers' Register*, V, 302.

boys, the land is poor — if you don't work hard you'll make nothing.' When he removed to better land on this side the river it was 'hurra, boys, you have got good land to work now, make haste.'" [1]

❋ ❋ ❋ ❋ ❋

By one means or another good will and affection were often evoked. When his crop was beset with grass and the work strenuous, a Mississippian wrote of his corps as being "true as steel." [2] A Georgian after escaping shipwreck on his way to Congress in 1794 wrote: "I have ever since been thinking of an expression of Old Qua's in Savannah a few days before I sailed. The rascal had the impudence to tell me to stay at home & not fret myself about Publick — 'What Publick care for you, Massa? God! ye get drowned bye & bye, Qua tell you so, and what going come of he Family den?'" [3] An Alabama preacher while defending slavery as divinely ordained said of the Negro: "He is of all races the most gentle and kind. The *man*, the most submissive; the *woman*, the most affectionate. What other slaves would love their masters better than themselves?" [4] And a British traveler wrote from his observation of slaves and masters: "There is an hereditary regard and often attachment on both sides, more like that formerly existing between lords and their retainers in the old feudal times of Europe, than anything now to be found in America." [5]

On some estates the whip was as regularly in evidence as the spur on a horseman's heel. [6] That cruelties occurred is never to be denied. Mrs. Stowe exploited them in *Uncle Tom's Cabin* and validated her implications to her own satisfaction in its *Key*. Theodore D. Weld had already assembled a thousand more or less authentic instances of whippings and fetters, of

[1] Letter of Hines Holt, Baldwin County, Ga., April 15, 1824, to Bolling Hall, Alabama. Manuscript in the Alabama Department of Archives.
[2] *Mississippi Historical Society Publications*, X, 354.
[3] T. U. P. Charlton, *Life of James Jackson* (Augusta, 1809, reprint Atlanta, n. d.), 154 of the reprint.
[4] Fred A. Ross, *Slavery Ordained of God* (Philadelphia, 1859), 26.
[5] Sir Charles Lyell, *Second Visit*, 2d ed., I, 352.
[6] *E.g.*, J. W. Monette in [J. H. Ingraham] *The South-West*, II, 286–288.

croppings and brandings, of bloodhound pursuits and the break-up of families.[1] Manuscript discoveries continue to swell the record. Here for example is a letter which lies before me in the slave's own writing:[2]

"Charlottesville, Oct. 8th, 1852.

"Dear Husband   I write you a letter to let you know my distress   my master has sold albert to a trader on Monday court day and myself and other child is for sale also and I want you to let [me] hear from you very soon before next cort if you can I don't know when   I don't want you to wait till Chrismas I want you to tell dr Hamelton and your master if either will buy me they can attend to it know and then I can go afterwards. I don't want a trader to get me   they asked me if I had got any person to buy me and I told them no   they took me to the court houste too   they never put me up   a man buy the name of brady bought albert and is gone I don't know where   they say he lives in Scottesville   my things is in several places some is in staunton and if I should be sold I don't know what will become of them   I don't expect to meet with the luck to get that way till I am quite heartsick   nothing more   I am and ever will be your kind wife   Maria Perkins.

"To Richard Perkins."

We cannot brush away this woman's tears. But it is fair to show the smile of another when writing in mellow retrospect to her ex-master, years after their severance by emancipation:

"Huntington, W. Virginia

"Sunday, June 12, 1881.

"My old boss   i heard that you was still alive and i now take the opportunity to address you a fiew lines   i am well and doing well and i hope you are the same   i am your servant whom you raised from a child up Catherine Miller who married Henry Miller.   i expect you have forgot me but i have not forgot you.   i was glad to hear that you was still alive.   i have wrote home

---

[1] *American Slavery as it is: Testimony of a Thousand Witnesses* (New York, 1839).

[2] Examples of other sorts of hardship may be found in this book, but for endless horrors go to the writings on the West Indies by Thomas Clarkson and his British abolition school.

several times to hear how all the old folks was but i never could find out so i thought i would write you and see if you could tell me. i wish you would send me mine and Mary Janes ages exactly. Mary jane has growed to be such a big girl i don't expect you know her. i would like to see and here you pray once more before I die. i must now come to a close   answer right away and tell me every thing that you think will give me any satisfaction about home sweet home. i hope that you will always remember me in your prayers. please excuse short letter and bad writing. Your old servant Catherine Miller."[1]

❊   ❊   ❊   ❊   ❊

Most of the travelers who sought evidence of asperity in the plantation realm found it as a rule not before their eyes but beyond the horizon. Charles Eliot Norton while at Charleston in 1855 wrote home to Boston: "The slaves do not go about looking unhappy, and are with difficulty, I fancy, persuaded to feel so. Whips and chains, oaths and brutality, are as common, for all that one sees, in the free as the slave states. We have come thus far, and might have gone ten times as far, I dare say, without seeing the first sign of Negro misery or white tyranny."[2]   Andrew P. Peabody wrote of the slaves of his host at Savannah: "They were well lodged and fed, and could have been worked no harder than was necessary for exercise and digestion."[3]   Louis F. Tasistro remarked of the slaves on a plantation at the old battle field below New Orleans: "To say that they are underworked and overfed, and far happier than the labourers of Great Britain would hardly convey a sufficiently clear notion of their actual condition. They put me much more in mind of a community of grown-up children, spoiled by too much kindness, than a body of depend-

---

[1] This letter was addressed to Captain Henry B. Jones, Brownsburg, Va., and was indorsed by him: "Answered 15th June, 1881." For the use of the manuscript I am indebted to the Rev. Henry W. McLaughlin of Brownsburg. For a contrast of sarcasm from another ex-slave see C. G. Woodson, ed., *The Mind of the Negro as reflected in Letters* (Washington, [1926]), 537–539.

[2] *Letters of Charles Eliot Norton* (Boston, 1913), I, 121.

[3] *Andover Review*, XVI, 157.

ants, much less a company of slaves." [1] Frederika Bremer had virtually nothing but praise for the slave quarters which she visited or their savory food which she tasted.[2] Welby, Faux, Lyell, Basil Hall, Marshall Hall, Robert Russell, William Russell, Olmsted [3] and sundry others concur in their surprise at finding slavery unsevere, though some of them kept seeking evidence to the contrary without avail.

The surprise was justified, for tradition in the outer world ran squarely opposite. And the tradition was reasonable. Slavery had been erected as a crass exploitation, and the laws were as stringent as ever. No prophet in early times could have told that kindliness would grow as a flower from a soil so foul, that slaves would come to be cherished not only as property of high value but as loving if lowly friends.[4] But this unexpected change occurred in so many cases as to make benignity somewhat a matter of course. To those habituated it became no longer surprising for a planter to say that no man deserved a Coromantee who would not treat him rather as a friend than as a slave; [5] for another to give his "people" a holiday out of season because "the drouth seems to have afflicted them, and a play day may raise their spirits"; [6] or for a third to give one of his hands an occasional week-end with a dollar or two each time to visit his wife in another county,[7]

[1] *Random Shots and Southern Breezes* (New York, 1842), II, 13.

[2] *Homes of the New World*, I, 293 *et passim*.

[3] Some of these are quoted in Phillips, *American Negro Slavery*, 306–308.

[4] A Virginia woman, talking in 1842 with a visiting preacher from the North, said that her superannuated cook was "as pious a woman, and a lady of as delicate sensibilities as I ever saw; she is one of the very best friends I have in the world." The visitor wrote on his own score: "I am more and more convinced of the injustice we do the slaveholders. Of their feelings toward their negroes I can form a better notion than formerly, by examining my own toward the slaves who wait on my wife and mind my children. It is a feeling most like that we have to near relations." And again as to the slaves: "They are unspeakably superior to our Northern free blacks, retaining a thousand African traits of kindliness and hilarity, from being together in masses. I may say with Abram [Venable, a planter whom he visited], 'I love a nigger, they are better than we.' So they are: grateful, devoted, self-sacrificing for their masters." — John Hall ed., *Forty Years' Familiar Letters of James W. Alexander, D. D.* (New York, 1860), I, 351–353.

[5] Christopher Codrington, in *Calendar of State Papers, Colonial*, 1701, p. 721.

[6] Diary of London Carter, in the *William and Mary College Quarterly*, XIII, 162.

[7] "The Westover Journal of John A. Seldon", in *Smith College Studies*, VI, 289 *et passim*.

and send two others away for some weeks at hot springs for the relief of their rheumatism.[1]

The esteem in epitaphs, whether inscribed in diaries or on stone, was without doubt earned by their subjects and genuinely felt by their composers. One reads: "On the 14th [of May, 1821] Old Bina died, about 12 o'clock, full of days and entitled to the grateful thanks of the whole family. She was a country born slave [*i.e.*, a native of America], and in my wife's family from birth, 75 years. She is now a free woman. Her virtues were numerous, and her vices such as arose from her station in life." [2] A slab in a South Carolina churchyard is engraved: "Sacred to the memory of Bill, a strictly honest and faithful servant of Cleland Belin. Bill was often entrusted with the care of Produce and Merchandize to the value of many thousand dollars, without loss or damage. He died 7th October, 1854, in the 35th year of his age, an approved member of the Black Mingo Baptist Church. Well done, thou good and faithful servant. Enter thou into Joy of thy Lord." [3] And on another Southern stone:

JOHN:
A FAITHFUL SERVANT
AND TRUE FRIEND:
KINDLY, AND CONSIDERATE:
LOYAL, AND AFFECTIONATE:
THE FAMILY HE SERVED
HONOURS HIM IN DEATH:
BUT, IN LIFE, THEY GAVE HIM LOVE:
FOR HE WAS ONE OF THEM [4]

For he was one of them indeed, and his name was well-nigh legion. Ancestral halls were fewer far than ancestral servitors, for a planter's migration would vacate the house but carry the personnel.

[1] *Ibid.*, 308.
[2] Diary of Richard Hugg King. Manuscript in North Carolina Historical Commission, at Raleigh.
[3] William W. Boddie, *History of Williamsburg* (Columbia, S. C., 1925), 333.
[4] *Atlantic Monthly*, CXXXVIII, 175.

On the other hand slaves in large numbers were detached from their masters, whether by sale, by lease to employers or by hire to themselves. The personal equation was often a factor in such transactions. Some slaves were sold as punishment, for effect upon the morale of their fellows. On the other hand some whose sales were impelled by financial stress were commissioned by their masters to find buyers of their own choice; some purchases were prompted by a belief that the new management would prove more congenial and fruitful than the old;[1] and still more transfers were made to unite in ownership couples who desired union in marriage.

In the hiring of slaves likewise the personal equation often bulked large, for the owner's desire for a maximum wage was modified by his concern for assured maintenance of physique and morale, and the lessee on his part wanted assurance from the slave of willing service or of acquiescence at least.[2] The hiring of slaves to the slaves themselves was a grant of industrial freedom at a wage. It was an admission that the slave concerned could produce more in self-direction than when under routine control, a virtual admission that for him slavery had no industrial justification. In many cases it was a probationary period, ended by self-purchase with earnings accumulated above the wages he had currently paid his owner.

Slave hiring and self-hire were more characteristic of town than of country. Indeed urban conditions merely tolerated slavery, never promoted it. And urban slaveholders were not complete masters, for slavery in full form required a segregation to make the master in effect a magistrate. A townsman's human chattels could not be his subjects, for he had no domain for them to inhabit. When a slave ran an errand upon the street he came under the eye of public rather than private authority; and if he were embroiled by chance in altercation with another slave the two masters were likely to find themselves champions of opposing causes in court, or partisans even

---

[1] For a striking example see *Plantation and Frontier*, I, 337, 338.
[2] For a vivid account of a tripartite negotiation see Robert Russell, *North America* (Edinburgh, 1857), 151.

against the constables, with no power in themselves either to make or apply the law.[1]

Town slaves in a sense rubbed elbows with every one, high and low, competed with free labor, white and black, and took tone more or less from all and sundry. The social hierarchy was more elaborate than on the plantations, the scheme of life more complex, and the variety wider in attainment and attitude. The obsequious grandiloquence of a barber contrasted with the caustic fluency of a fishwife. But even the city chain gang was likely to be melodious, for its members were Negroes at one or two removes from the plantation. All in all, the slave régime was a curious blend of force and concession, of arbitrary disposal by the master and self-direction by the slave, of tyranny and benevolence, of antipathy and affection.

[1] *E.g.*, Carson, *Pettigru*, 348; Phillips, *American Negro Slavery*, 414, 415.

CHAPTER XII

SOME VIRGINIA MASTERS

MANY travelers made Southern tours and wrote of what they saw. Basil Hall carried a "camera lucida" by which he made some pre-photographic pictures; and using his mind's eye, which was that of a British naval captain, he found the lot of the slaves in some regards comparable to that of sailors in Her Majesty's service. Bartram, Lyell and Robert Russell went as observers of plants, rocks and weather, but made good notes of human life. Louis Tasistro was an actor on tour, and Tyrone Power likewise; but William Chambers went merely for a "change of air and scene." Paulding, Miss Martineau and Miss Bremer were professional writers, seeking something with which to employ their pens. J. S. C. Abbott was a more or less literary compiler who took ship and train and put forth a book subtitled *Impressions received during a trip to Cuba and the South;* though he might more fittingly have styled it "Impressions retained despite a trip." Philo Tower was an abolitionist who put so much plagiarism and fabrication into his account as to raise a doubt whether he ever left the closet of his New England parsonage. So the list might run much further. Olmsted and William H. Russell are among the few to be classed as expert observers. Solon Robinson, another such, is almost the only one who gave himself to the description of individual plantations; and his accounts have the merit, as compared with Olmsted's, of naming the estates to which they apply. Regrettably his writings remain as yet scattered in the periodicals to which he sent them.[1]

[1] They are now being assembled and edited by Herbert A. Kellar for publication by the Indiana Historical Commission.

As a rule sojourners wrote more illuminatingly than tourists, because more intimately and with some continuity of experience. Philip Fithian, J. H. Ingraham, A. de Puy Van Buren, Emily Burke and Catherine Hopley went as teachers, Nehemiah Adams and T. D. Ozanne as preachers.[1] Solomon Northup went as a Negro kidnaped into slavery, and wrote a vivid account of plantation life from the under side. But ex-slave narratives in general, and those of Charles Ball, Henry Box Brown and Father Henson in particular, were issued with so much abolitionist editing that as a class their authenticity is doubtful.

Many of every ilk who wrote for the press were propagandists of one cause and another, and as such they set their spectacles upon their readers' noses. And travelers' accounts as a body, while indispensable, have essential defects and shortcomings. They are jottings of strangers likely to be most impressed by the unfamiliar, and unable to distinguish what was common in the régime from what was unique in some special case; furthermore they yield mere glimpses here and there from time to time, permitting no steady view of any one's experience or life history. But a present-day student may in a sense make a tour of his own through the South of a century ago, at least a mental journey through the plantation records; and though he may not ask questions at will he may find that planters, overseers and even slaves have more or less unconsciously answered questions of interest and drawn sketches almost as if by interview and request. Some of these records have been printed as they stand, some have been analyzed in detail, some are here used for the first time, and many are no doubt still awaiting discovery. Among those available there is great diversity in form and content. In one case nothing will have survived but a diary of routine, in another financial records only, in a third overseers' reports, in a fourth a miscellany of letters, legal documents and vouchers, often of course mingled with a mass of trivial rubbish. Never do they give singly a view of experience in all phases; but in combination they

[1] Fanny Kemble and sundry others will be discussed elsewhere.

exhibit personalities, operations, problems and adjustments perhaps as well as do the vestiges of past régimes in other parts of the world.

❊   ❊   ❊   ❊   ❊

The Carters, who being lowland Virginians pronounced their name *Kyahta*, may be followed in their scattered plantation records for at least four generations. The chief architect of the family fortune was Robert, born in 1663. His large patrimony was hugely increased by vigorous use of the many devices prevalent among the magnates of the time; and his domineering demeanor in public office gave him the nickname of "King" Carter.[1] By 1700 he was already one of the greatest freeholders in the Northern Neck; and when he made his will in 1726 he designated plantations in groups rather than singly, to be inherited by each of his nine children then living. Upon his death six years later the inventory of his estate made a prodigious catalogue. Along with the furniture of his many-chambered mansion, it embraced a copious library, great stores of cloth, buttons, medicines, nails, tools, groceries, spare sails and miscellaneous impedimenta. In the personnel at his homestead, "Corotoman", there were seventeen indentured white servants (including sailors, tailors and carpenters, a glazier, a bricklayer and a blacksmith) and thirty-three slaves. And on outlying lands in perhaps a dozen counties there were nearly seven hundred slaves, a hundred or so horses, upwards of a thousand cattle, a like number of swine, and some hundreds of sheep. These slaves, with small quotas of livestock, were distributed in half a hundred "quarters" as working groups with a white overseer and a slave foreman at the head of each unit. In size the groups ranged from as few as six slaves to more than thirty.[2] This scheme of operation in small units was maintained in some part by descendants to the third generation, as will shortly appear.

❊   ❊   ❊   ❊   ❊

[1] Memorandum of Governor Nicholson in 1705. — *Virginia Magazine*, VIII, 56.
[2] The will and inventory, the latter in condensed form, are printed in the *Virginia Magazine*, V–VII, *passim*.

"King" Carter's fourth surviving son, Landon of "Sabine Hall", had not only that plantation but also "Mangorike" and "The Forks", which lay near by on the Rappahannock, "Rippon Hall" and "Ring's Neck" on the York, and other tracts in several counties. He married three wives but had only nine children — a modest quota for a Carter. He kept a diary [1] which deals with slaves, crops and overseers, politics and warfare, house parties, barbecues and family quarrels, travel (with a smoke raised to summon a ferry); taverns, one of which was "a very stinking place indeed", a governess for his children, a tutor for his grandchildren, and a free school for his vicinage; apprentices bound to him to be taught the planter's craft; and a parson's unwilling prayer for rain at Carter's own command. In 1776 he noted reminiscently that his father had used no plows and but a single cart, and yet had reaped more abundantly than he himself was now able to do, though he had carts, oxen and plows everywhere.[2] His methods with livestock, however, were primitive. In the spring of 1766, following a very dry year, his cattle were dying of starvation in the woods, his oxen were so badly broken to the draft that only two out of eight in that year's increment were tolerable workers, and famine had reduced his horses to skin and bone; and he was at a loss to prevent a recurrence unless by providing a field of small grain for early grazing. In the next decade, however, he made a water meadow to be irrigated from a millpond. His crops included cereals, tobacco, flax, hemp and cotton — this last reaching a scale of fifty thousand hills in 1776. He fertilized with barnyard manure, though he found its handling to be very troublesome.

His slaves ranked low in his esteem. In 1766 two of them ran away and committed some depredations, whereupon they

[1] For parts of 1766 and 1767 the diary, written in interleaved copies of the *Virginia Almanack*, is preserved in the Clements Library of the University of Michigan. For 1770 and after, copious extracts are printed in the *William and Mary College Quarterly*, XIII–XX, *passim*.

[2] *William and Mary College Quarterly*, XVII, 17, 18. Of his own course he said: "I never used cart or plow in Northumberland till, growing delicate in taste, I would have oysters brought up from thence."

were "outlawed in the several churches two several Sundays."
Apparently the process of outlawry had not been completed
when Simon was caught and Bart came in voluntarily. The
former was let off with a flogging; but Carter wrote of Bart:
"He is the most incorrigible villain alive, I believe, and has
deserved hanging, which I will get done if his mate in roguery
can be tempted to turn evidence against him." But Bart
quickly took French leave, whereupon Carter unbosomed himself at large: "Talbot is a rogue, he was put in charge of
him. . . . John is the most constant churchgoer I have, but
he is a drunkard, a thief and a rogue. They are only honest
through sobriety, and but few of them." At another time he
spoke of "Toney, my only honest slave."

As to work, in May, 1766: "Everything in weeds and all
very backward. People, [*i.e.* his slaves] quite lazy and indifferent, and overseer full as bad as the worst of them." In
late September, 1772: "There is nothing so absurd as the
generality of negroes are. If in the beginning of cutting
tob[acc]o, without watching they will cut all before them, and
now when there is danger of losing tob[acc]o by the frost should
it happen, they will not cut pl[an]ts really ripe because they
may be the thicker, just as if there was time to let it stand
longer. My Jades at the Fork w[ou]ld not cut half that they
might have done yesterday, because they thought it w[ou]ld be
thicker; however I sent them in to-day and made them cut
every good plant." Again, on May Day, 1776: "At ten
o'clock, excessive cold indeed: all my people, tho' well cloathed,
playing at hide & seek. As fast as one drove is carried down
the hill one way, another comes up the other side, w[hi]ch
proves they sham, because they don't want to be seen when they
come in." And of an overseer that summer: "News just come
John Self at Ring's Neck turned a Baptist, . . . and says he
cannot serve God and Mammon, has just been made a Christian
by dipping, and would not continue in my business but to convert my People. This is a strange year about my overseers;
some, horrid, hellish rogues, and others religious villains."

❋   ❋   ❋   ❋   ❋

A second Landon, nephew of the first, may be known from his so-called crop book into which he copied his letters. In 1785 he owned "Cleve" upon which he dwelt in King George County, and four outlying plantations. His crops that year aggregated 188 bushels of wheat, 829 of corn, and nearly 25,000 pounds of tobacco. His overseers were engaged on crop shares, though one of his units was managed by a slave. This planter was not content to follow traditional methods. In 1794 he published an account of his projects for rehabilitating land by the use of cowpeas as a soiling crop. But in 1796, in a letter to George Washington, he described the obstacles he met. A Scotch overseer in his employ at the beginning of his experiments had been skilled in husbandry, but "could not make the slaves exert themselves to modern labor", and furthermore he demanded impossible wages for continuance. Successors to the Scot, in rapid series, showed failings likewise in the control of labor, "and added to that, were unfit for abstract execution." At length: "Harassed thus by frequent disappointment, I resolved to strike out another plan; and choosing out two of the most confidential of my slaves, I fixed them off with a small farm each, under some pecuniary influence. This scheme has operated during one crop, and tho' the full vigour of industry has not been put forth, owing to all around being idle under an indifferent Overseer, yet the venture does not set so much at stake; and a continuance, bound as they are to follow my directions, will serve to exemplify in the effects on the soil." [1]

❋   ❋   ❋   ❋   ❋

A nephew of the first Landon and cousin of the second was Robert Carter of "Nomini Hall", a grandee comparable to his grandfather. His homestead was described by Philip Fithian who served as tutor to his children in 1773–1774. The mansion, with four huge rooms downstairs and a like number above, stood upon a terraced plateau, with a bowling green in front and a "little handsome street" at the rear leading to the kitchen, bakery, dairy and storehouses. The grounds, four acres in

[1] *William and Mary College Quarterly*, XXI, 14. See also XX, 283; XXI, 12, 15, 17.

spread, were marked at the corners by the schoolhouse, laundry, coach house and stable, uniform in size and style. The first of these contained not only a schoolroom but lodgings for the tutor, the master's sons and a clerk, whence they were summoned to meals at the great house by a sixty-pound bell.[1]

Of the household Fithian had much to say in praise. The master, who was a member of the governor's council and one of the wealthiest men in the colony, was courteous and scholarly, musical and ingenious, "and notwithstanding his rank, which in general seems to countenance indulgence to children, both himself and Mʳˢ Carter have a manner of instructing and dealing with children far superior . . . to any I have ever seen in any place or in any family. They keep them in perfect subjection to themselves, and never pass over an occasion of reproof, and I blush for many of my acquaintances [i.e., in New Jersey] when I say that the children are more kind and complaisant to the servants who constantly attend them than we are to our superiors in age and condition."[2]

To Councilor and Mrs. Carter were born eventually seventeen children; and though some of these had not yet seen the light in Fithian's day, the food annually consumed at Nomini Hall amounted already to twenty beeves, twenty-seven thousand pounds of pork, five hundred bushels of wheat and unmeasured corn, along with four hogsheads of rum and three barrels of whiskey, not to reckon the Madeira. For the twenty-eight fireplaces a cart with six oxen hauling four loads a day no more than sufficed for winter needs.[3] To live thus required a copious revenue; yet Fithian and Mrs. Carter, whom he styled "a remarkable economist", agreed that the plantations were earning at a rate so low that the value of the slaves alone if liquidated and lent out would have brought a greater income as interest.

At this period Carter had for the most part withdrawn from public affairs to devote himself to the amenities of life and the

---

[1] J. R. Williams, ed., *Philip Vickers Fithian: Journal and Letters* (Princeton, N. J., 1900), 128–132, 279.
[2] *Ibid.*, 278, 279.   [3] *Ibid.*, 101, 121.

management of his varied business concerns. He had just completed a flour mill on Nomini River with a capacity of twenty-five thousand bushels a year, and was seeking to buy a third of his wheat supply from the James River. Part of his flour product was baked at Nomini Hall into ship's bread, which he was offering in 1774 to sell in schooner loads at prices ranging from 15 shillings per hundredweight for brown biscuit to 33s. 4d. for the best white. At the same time, as part owner of the Baltimore Iron Works, he was shipping pig iron to Liverpool and seeking purchasers for bar iron among the planters and merchants on the James.[1]

In 1773 he sent an order to Liverpool for blanketing, osnaburgs, canvas, linen, bed ticks, sacks, thread, shoe thread, and a gross of coarse hose, along with tools, nails, screws, saddler's tacks, leather, paints and brushes, vials, corks and pill boxes, powder, shot and gun flints, a gross of ale, three gross of glazed pipes, a hundredweight of tallow candles, three reams of writing paper and a box of wafers. But prompted by the stoppage of trade in the first years of the Revolution, he established at "Aries" a factory to make cloth and hosiery of wool, flax and cotton. In 1782 Daniel Sullivan, a weaver, was in charge at a yearly wage of £12 specie, a food allowance and "fifteen pounds of picked cotton." Under him were ten of Carter's slaves and perhaps a dozen white operatives. In 1787 Sullivan, reckoning the wages of seventeen spinners at £17 16s. each per annum and four weavers at £27 10s. estimated the spinning costs at 4d. per pound for brown rolls, 1s. for osnaburg yarn, 2s. for cotton warp for coarse woolen jeans, 1s. 3d. for coarse stocking yarn, etc.; and the weaving costs at 4d. per yard for brown rolls, osnaburgs, jeans and bagging, 6d. for dowlas, and 1s. for his better grade of woolen.

In 1791 the specialized slaves at Nomini Hall comprised eleven carpenters, two joiners, two gardeners, two postilions,

---

[1] Some of Robert Carter's manuscript records are preserved in the Library of Congress, and others in the Virginia Historical Society; but the main bulk is in private possession. From among these last the Massachusetts Historical Society has photostat copies of a letter book, his deed of manumission and sundry slave lists.

a bricklayer, a blacksmith, a miller, a tanner, a shoemaker, a hatter, a sailor, a carter, a butcher, a cook, a waiter and a scullion among the men; and among the women three housemaids, two seamstresses, two spinsters, a dairymaid, a laundress, a nursemaid and a midwife. Shortly before this time there had been a coachman whose veterinary occasions had led him into a wider practice of medicine, to such effect that the Negroes generally preferred his ministrations to those of white practitioners. Perhaps he was not so lavish as they in bloodletting, calomel and cathartics.

The distribution of Carter's slaves of all sorts is given for 1784 and 1791 in the accompanying table. In the interim a notable shifting had occurred from the low country to the distant Shenandoah Valley where six plantations were established. The rapid increase in the gross number of slaves was probably due wholly to a high birth rate; for no less than one hundred and forty-three children were listed in 1791 as being less than seven years old. In both years of the tabulation the mean age among the slaves was about sixteen years.

On most of the plantation units there were a few horses; but Carter's chief reliance for draft animals was upon oxen, which he required to be individualized by numerals in white paint on their sides. In charge of each unit of plantation size was an overseer drawing as pay one ninth of the crop made by his corps; and over the overseers was a steward who made tours of inspection and handled miscellaneous business on his employer's behalf.

This was all very comfortable for Carter; but after passing middle age he became troubled in mind. He shifted his church connection from Anglican to Baptist, then to Swedenborgian, and finally to Roman Catholic,[1] and he developed qualms against slaveholding. To quiet these he devised a plan for the gradual emancipation of all within his possession, and filed in 1791 a deed to this effect with elaborate lists for its application. In each succeeding year those fifteen of his slaves who were

---

[1] Bishop [William] Meade, *Old Churches, Ministers and Families of Virginia* (Philadelphia, 1857), II, 111.

THE SLAVES OF ROBERT CARTER OF NOMINI HALL, AS GROUPED IN 1784 AND 1791

	1784	1791
Westmoreland County:		
Nomini Hall	80	114
Aries	38	42
Old Ordinary	54	44
Taurus	42	21
Gemini	44	14
Forest Quarter	27	21
Cole's Point	38	31
Richmond County:		
Dickerson's Mill	5	
Billingsgate	37	
John Peck's		3
Robert Michel's		3
Cancer	11	9
Prince William County:		
Cancer		23
Loudoun County:		
Leo	34	40
Hired out		8
Frederick County:		
Aquarius		14
Scorpio		26
Capricorn		24
Libra		25
Virgo		29
Sagittarius		18
Total	410	509

nearest age forty-five were to be free, and also such youths and maids as should reach ages twenty-one and eighteen respectively; and all after-born children were to be free in 1809 in the case of girls and 1812 in that of boys. This, he recited in the deed, would not only be consonant with the law but in his opinion it would cause "the least possible inconvenience" to his fellow citizens. Nevertheless in 1796 a citizen of Frederick County wrote to Carter saying that he expressed the views of "a vast majority of the community" in complaining that Carter's freedmen were indolent, thievish and demoralizing to the neighboring slaves, and urging him to remove them and the future increment to some other State, such as Pennsylvania, "where they can do no harm." [1]   Carter himself eventually removed to Baltimore where he died in 1804 at the age of seventy-six.

※   ※   ※   ※   ※

John of "Corotoman", eldest son of "King" Carter, married the daughter and heiress of Colonel Edward Hill, who had built in 1650 a handsome house at "Shirley" on the James.   Their eldest son Charles began residence there in 1771, but finding it small for his family (twenty-three children by two wives), he added a third story by changing the roof to its present mansard form.   In due time Shirley descended through Charles' son Robert to his grandson Hill Carter, who resigned from the United States navy and took charge of it in 1816 at the age of twenty.   He married next year, and in due time begat seventeen children who were born at intervals never exceeding two years.   Three of these babies were stillborn, four died on the day of birth, and two more in early childhood — a rate of mortality not very unusual among the children of even well-to-do folk at the time.

The style of life at Shirley was described by Henry Barnard, a young Yale graduate, after a visit in the spring of 1833. When you wake in the morning, said he, you find that a servant has already built a fire in your bedroom, brushed your shoes and clothing, and stands ready to do your bidding.   At eight o'clock you breakfast with the family at a table bare except for doilies under the plates.   You drink fashionably a cup of coffee and then a cup of tea, and are plied with cold ham "of the real Virginia flavor" and with hot breads in great variety.   You then ride or read at will, for "the Master and Mistress of the House are not expected to entertain visitors till an hour or two before dinner."   About one o'clock guests invited for dinner arrive and amuse themselves in the parlor except when the gentlemen are taken out for a preprandial glass of grog.

[1] Anonymous letter among the Carter papers in the Library of Congress.

Then at three o'clock the host leads a lady to the dining room, followed by the rest of the party in pairs. At one end of the table Mrs. Carter ladles soup, and her husband opposite carves a saddle of mutton. The plates, and the dishes of ham, beef, turkey, ducks, eggs and greens, and the omnipresent sweet potatoes and hominy are handed about by two black boys. Then, after a round of champagne, the upper cloth is removed, and plum pudding, tarts, ice cream and brandied peaches are served as dessert. "When you have eaten this, off goes the second table cloth, and then upon the bare mahogany table is set the figs, raisins and almonds, and before Mr. Carter is set 2 or 3 bottles of wine — Madeira, Port, and a sweet wine for the Ladies — he fills his glass and pushes them on. After the glasses are all filled, the gentlemen pledge their services to the Ladies, and down goes the wine. After the first and second glass the ladies retire, and the gentlemen begin to circulate the bottle pretty briskly. You are at liberty, however, to follow the Ladies as soon as you please, who after music and a little chit chat prepare for their ride home." [1]

When I paid a visit, eighty-three years after Barnard's, the house as of yore faced the placid river, embowered in trees seemingly less ancient than some of the Carter portraits which crowd the walls inside. My errand was the study of records which were graciously put at my service.[2] But the mere bulk of Hill Carter's diary turned me mainly to his book of expenditures and receipts, in which two pages hold a summary for each passing year.

Here are outlays of $27.50 for a "bathing tub" in 1818, when such furniture was quite unusual, of sundry sums for picture cleaning and piano tuning, for season tickets at a Richmond theater, for losses at cards and races (never offset by any credit of winnings), for journeys in the late summer of each year by

[1] *Maryland Historical Magazine*, XIII, 319, 320.

[2] By Mrs. James H. Oliver, born Marion Carter. The diary, in three large volumes, runs from 1816 to 1851, and is supplemented by a thin volume of overseers' journals scrawled in the summers from 1832 to 1845. The financial record extends from 1816 to 1875 when Carter died, but is not systematic after 1861. These writings are now deposited in the Library of Congress.

the master to the mountain springs and by the mistress and her brood to the more accessible Piedmont, for threshing machines, reapers and horse rakes when these inventions were new, for harvest whiskey and harvest hirelings, for the advertisement and recapture of runaway slaves, and for many other significant things.

Though concerned with public affairs, and once a Whig candidate for Congress,[1] Carter was essentially an active and studious planter. When he took charge the estate had been operated for some years by overseers who had depleted the soil. He soon turned three hundred acres of sandy land into pasture and set himself to rehabilitate the remaining four hundred of cleared stiff soil by deep plowing in a rotation of wheat, oats, wheat and clover. This made his initial number of one hundred and six slaves excessive; but instead of pursuing tradition and sending the surplus to distant places of his own, he sold twenty-five in 1818 for $4500, twenty-three in 1821 for a like sum, two singly in later years, and finally six in 1841 for $2126.40.

Meanwhile the maturing of slave children enabled him not only to resume tillage in the pastured tract but to reclaim a tide-swamp of eighty acres for corn culture. Finding that his continued succession of uncultivated crops was fouling his fields with weeds and grass, he changed in 1840 to a five-shift schedule of wheat, corn, wheat, clover meadow and clover pasture. But a brief experience taught that successive years in clover would infest his land with insect grubs to destroy the following grain crops; and he changed in 1842 to corn, wheat, clover fallow, wheat and clover pasture.[2] As a fruit of this the *National Intelligencer* reported his crop of 1843 as eight thousand bushels of wheat from two hundred and seventy acres, and remarked in detail that his reaping of an average of thirty-three bushels from one hundred and sixty acres was "unequaled in Virginia agriculture."[3] This achievement was accomplished not merely

[1] In 1844, at an expense of $330. A fellow Whig who heard him in a campaign speech at this time said: "Mr. Carter injured himself by his passionate manner, which once or twice passed the bounds of discretion."

[2] *Farmers' Register*, I, 105–107; X, 114, 115.

[3] Reprinted in the *Southern Cultivator*, I, 181.

by soiling with clover but by liming and marling and heavy applications of barnyard manure. From his cows he sold surplus butter for many years; and occasionally he sold calves, lambs, pigs, timber, cordwood, anchor stocks, and even ice. Shirley, in short, was operated much as if it lay in Pennsylvania or Ohio. The tobacco staple had been abandoned in the district before Hill Carter was born.

But the labor was done by slaves, perhaps to the proprietor's regret in 1849, when in the height of the harvest the cholera came. The diary runs: June 27, "Harry Tanner [29 years old] was taken sick with cholera one day and died the next." June 28. "Fanny Tanner [39] and her son Fielding [10] died to-day of cholera." June 29. "Sam [39] died to-day of cholera." June 30. "Cholera raging. John Tanner [39], Judy [33] and her baby Peter a year old, died of cholera. Had to abandon the harvest field and give up the wheat." And so it continued for ten more dreadful days till, after a toll of twenty-eight deaths, the contagion ended and the surviving patients began to convalesce.[1] This impairment of the force, which had numbered about fifty laborers, prompted the purchase of three men or boys in 1849 for $1675, three more within the next two years at $775, $800 and $825, and a blacksmith in 1852 at $1481.

Carter's sales of wheat ranged near fifteen hundred bushels in early years. Then, with enlargement of scale and improvements in method and apparatus, the average rose to three thousand bushels in the late 'twenties, four thousand in the 'thirties, and five thousand in the 'forties and 'fifties, to a maximum of 8125 in 1861. His income from the cereals began at $4200 in 1817, fell to $2100 in 1819 when slaves were sold to meet the deficit, then rose to $4100 in 1819, only to be cut in half during the next three years when further slaves were sold. The average rose to about $3500 in the late 'twenties, $6200 in the 'thirties and 'forties, and $12,250 in the 'fifties, with a maximum of $19,361 in the Crimean year 1855.

[1] In this year, as on a previous cholera visitation in 1832, the doctor's bill mounted above $500 as compared with about $100 in normal years.

Carter speculated somewhat in lands, of course, and once in a drove of mules; but his cash receipts from all sources seldom exceeded his expenditures until 1843, when dividends from a legacy and commissions as trustee of an estate supplemented the enlarging Shirley revenues. His accumulated surplus thereafter enabled him to give his four sons seven thousand dollars each as they reached manhood, as well as to build a new barn for twelve hundred dollars and nine new double houses for slaves at five hundred dollars each. The Shirley overseers, at wages generally between two hundred and four hundred dollars, were changed seventeen times during the thirty-five years of the diary.

❊   ❊   ❊   ❊   ❊

A few miles below "Shirley" lies "Westover", one of the most famous estates in Virginia. It was first appropriated by Lord Delaware in 1619, whose family name was West; but it was little developed until 1668 when bought by Captain William Byrd, who made a great fortune in the Indian trade and plantation industry. Westover was inherited in 1704 by the second William Byrd, who built about 1737 the house which has ever since distinguished it. He was a talented author, a leader of fashion, a power in the government, and a capable planter. His son, the third of the name, falling heir in 1744, proved a wastrel, but his widow clung to the homestead until her death. It then passed through several hands until 1829, when it was bought for $18,000 by John A. Selden, who restored the fields and operated the plantation until 1862.

Experimenting in agronomy, Selden put Westover by 1833 upon a four-shift rotation with its distinctive feature a clover fallow which was neither mowed nor grazed but plowed under in August and kept mellow until seeded to wheat in October. This he reckoned to have twice the fertilizing value of barnyard manure. Incidentally, as an advocate of heavy plows, he considered oxen to have little use except for hauling.[1] Two years later, by way of elaborating his argument, he described

---

[1] Letter of Selden to the editor, in the *Farmers' Register*, I, 321–325.

his operations in more detail. Of the twelve hundred acres in the plantation eight hundred were woodland or permanent pasture, while four fields of a hundred acres each gave work for his slave corps and twelve mules. He argued again for heavy plowing and little hoeing, and in support of his contentions he cited his crops of twenty-one and one third bushels of wheat after clover and thirty bushels of corn after wheat, as compared with the common yields of the region which he said were eight bushels of wheat per acre and ten and one half of corn.[1]

Selden was now answered by his neighbor William B. Harrison of "Brandon", who defended the three-shift practice,[2] and by John Tabb of "White Marsh" in Gloucester county, who supported Harrison and also praised the ox.[3] But Selden, far from dropping his fourth shift, added a fifth by fencing another hundred acres. His practice as described at the end of 1839 was to plant each field in clover, wheat, corn, peas, and wheat, thus avoiding a thin crop of wheat which had formerly followed corn. In addition he now had four lots of three or four acres each devoted to grass for three years and to root crops the fourth year: sweet potatoes, turnips, mangel-wurzel and carrots. In breaking clover fallow, he said, a four-horse plow, with a man and boy, would turn the land faster and far better than two two-horse plows. To clinch his general argument, he said his wheat crop of the past summer had averaged twenty-four bushels per acre despite a visitation of chinch bugs.[4]

Selden's later years, and Westover in both its last heyday and its catastrophe, are pictured in his diary.[5] His paternity of fifteen sons and three daughters,[6] and his copious hospitality, with fifty-two persons at a single meal, which he described as

---

[1] *Farmer's Register*, III, 1–8.

[2] *Ibid.*, III, 241–245. The Brandon plantations were described by Edmund Ruffin in 1842. *Ibid.*, X, 274–282.

[3] *Ibid.*, III, 269–270.   [4] *Ibid.*, VIII, 1–5.

[5] J. S. Bassett, ed., "The Westover Journal of John A. Selden, Esqr., 1858–1862" in *Smith College Studies in History*, VI, No. 4. Earlier portions of the diary are known to be extant.

[6] Twelve of his children were living in 1859, and seven sons went into the Confederate army. Eventually six of the sons migrated to Alabama, one to Georgia, and one remained in Virginia. Bassett's notes to the diary as above cited.

"the most magnificent dinner I ever saw", show Selden running true to Tidewater form.   He had two teachers at once instructing his progeny along with two children of friends who, according to the custom of the country, were boarding at Westover for schooling.   He indulged in summer visits to White Sulphur Springs, in a tour to Niagara and another to New Orleans with a body servant, and he bought in 1858 a silver service for $350.   His income was derived in part from a share in a Richmond mercantile house.   The Selden slaves numbered about sixty in 1860.   As a master he was generous with gifts, holidays and privileges, and yet he had occasion for floggings.

Westover affairs were not much disturbed in the first year of the war; but McClellan's landing on the peninsula in the spring of 1862 was ominous.   At the middle of March six of the slaves were requisitioned for work on fortifications at Jamestown; but the redoubts proved futile.   Before the end of the month Selden journeyed into the Piedmont and leased a vacant hotel as a refuge in case of need.   Returning home, he packed his valuables and loaded a boat with provisions in readiness for flight.   Meanwhile, April 8: "My boy Robert gave me insults and ran away, and I shot him in the thigh."   McClellan's approach drove Selden forth on May 6, with two daughters, his best horses, mules and cows and seventeen young slave men and women.   "It was the gloomiest and most heart-rending thing I ever did in my life," he said, "to leave my wife and part of my family behind.   But I did it advisedly, as every friend I had advised me that they should remain.   Never shall I forget my sufferings on the occasion.   Even my negroes that I left behind wept bitterly."   But the slaves' emotions were mixed. Three of those who were carried inland ran away within a month, presumably to reach "the Yankees"; and by autumn a mere remnant of those left at Westover were on hand to greet the returning proprietor.   After the battle of Malvern Hill Westover lay within the lines of McClellan's camp.   When the invaders at length withdrew Selden went home, September 17, to find it home no longer.   "Found the estate entirely ruined, should not have known it" except for the house. Only five slaves remained; "all the rest gone away with the Yankees." On the very next day he wrote: "Sold the Westover estate to Messsrs. Ellet and Drury of Richmond for the sum of fifty thousand dollars cash, fifteen thousand dollars less than I had been offered for it before the war. . . I lost all my crop, 36 negroes, and plantation swept of everything on it except houses. . . . I think my loss cannot be less than 75,000 dollars." So ends the Selden story.[1]

✻   ✻   ✻   ✻   ✻

On the Piedmont course of the James, a day's journey above Richmond, William Bolling kept a diary concerning himself and his three plantations. They were "Pocahontas", "The Island" and his home place "Bolling Hall", each lying within an hour's walk of the others. When the available diary begins in 1827,[2] Bolling was forty-nine years old, and already a grandfather, a vestryman and a local magistrate. He was fond of hunting and not averse to horse races; he bought his whiskey by the barrel and took toddies at the taverns; and when a Frenchman opened a dancing school at Cartersville against the protest of some of the citizens, Bolling sent his daughter to learn her steps. On the other hand he thought it scandalous for some youths of the neighborhood to be gunning for quail on a Sunday. He went occasionally to barbecues; and at Bolling Hall he often dined twenty people or more and lodged them with a little "doubling up." He had orchards and a vineyard, a copious garden with cauliflowers, artichokes, head lettuce and strawberries, and an ice house which never failed of a filling except in 1811 and 1828. Of the former occasion, he wrote reminiscently that typhoid fever was so general and violent among his Negroes that he feared to subject

---

[1] Of operations on "Sandy Point" plantation, which lay below Westover, there is a survey by its overseer in the *Farmers' Register*, IX, 213–216, 343–345, 485–487, 586–589 (1841), at a time when its four units were being consolidated into one. Among its economies this rearrangement was expected to save annually about $750 in the renewals of rail fences.

[2] Manuscript for 1827 and 1828 on deposit with the Virginia Historical Society.

the healthy residue to the exposure of ice-gathering. In the latter case the winter was too warm to furnish an ice crop, and Bolling promptly built a springhouse as a makeshift. Though hospitable, he was by no means undiscriminating, for he held some of his neighbors in low esteem and remarked of a kinsman's visit that it was "entirely without provocation."

Bolling commonly set out about a hundred thousand tobacco plants and seeded some nine hundred acres in wheat; but an advance in the wheat price from ninety cents to $1.90 in the fall of 1828 caused him to add another hundred acres to this crop. His draft animals comprised twenty-six horses and twelve oxen. Sometimes all the force of the three plantations was consolidated, as for shifting the rail fences on the island, for hauling "120 large white-oak logs" for a new "double pen" tobacco house at Bolling Hall,[1] or to complete a belated wheat sowing at Pocahontas. The number and distribution of his slaves are not given, but casualties among them are recorded. A man cut his wrist severely upon a fellow harvester's scythe by trying to seize a rabbit in the wheat field. Another was stunned when thrown by a colt. "Archy Fleming, a valuable honest and well disposed negro, one of my sawyers, died of inflamation of the brain." And again : "Sally, another of our valuable domestic servants, died this morning of what Dr. Vaughan calls Misenteric fever, which makes five likely and useful females within two years that we have lost." He bought several slaves during the time of the diary, and took a woman on hire who was the wife of one of his men. He issued clothing, shoes and blankets to the slaves in October when he replaced oilcloth with carpets on the floors of his home, and clothing again in the spring, when carpets once more gave place to oil-cloth for the "summer establishment."

In the work schedule the seasonal tasks of raising tobacco dovetailed with those of growing wheat, corn and oats, yielding on occasion to such special tasks as the shearing of sheep, the slaughter of hogs, ditch cleaning and road repair. Each of the

[1] On another occasion he moved a smithy, twenty years old, the logs of which were still sound.

two major crops brought some weeks of stress on calendar schedule. In 1827 the wheat harvest was prepared for by the procurement, May 23, of three barrels of whiskey and six of herrings, along with new scythe blades; and an August entry reads: "Worming and suckering tob° with all hands, which at this season of the year is the burden of the planter's song." But some tasks must follow rains which could not be foretold, such as transplanting tobacco seedlings into wet fields or handling the cured crop when its usually brittle leaves had been made pliable by moist air. Either of these might bring overtime work. Thus an entry of April 5, 1828: "Striking Tob° finished about one o'clock this morning. Rain commenced last ev'g, which brought it rapidly in order. I had a supper cooked for my people, sent them whiskey and a lanthorn with candles to the prize house — and thus we have struck our whole crop in the last three days from one season [*i.e.*, rain], which was very favourable." Again on June 29, a Sunday after a rain: "My people all engaged in planting tob°, a thing [Sunday work] I rarely do, but compelled on this occasion by the scarcity of plants not to miss an opportunity so late in the season." Of the following Saturday he wrote: "Gave my people here a holiday in compensation for their work in planting tob° on Sunday last."

As regards overseers, Bolling's experiences were of the normal sort. Here are some of his entries in 1827. On March 15: "stopped my plows both here [at Bolling Hall] and at P[ocahontas] from ploughing where the land is wet, which I find almost impossible to restrain my obstinate overseers from doing." On April 9, following rain: "Immediately after it ceased, Hicks put his people to work, and I had again to stop them." On June 15: "I this day gave notice to Hicks that I should not continue him as manager another year." On July 31: "Bargained with James Brooks to live at Pocahontas next year, to work with my carpenters and to assist me in the management of the plantation, at $250 per annum. August 31: "Went to the Island. Brooks sick with ague and fever. Found him shivering on a pile of straw." December 18: "I took my agricultural tour after dinner, which occasionally I do at an unusual hour, and as is apt in such circumstances to be the case, found neither of my overseers with their people." December 24, Hicks, taking his departure, "has got no business." December 29, resuming work after the holidays: "To re-do several things half done at first, which is the habit with Jones, and to do several jobs neglected by Hicks before his removal from P." And in 1828, July 21 : "Gave notice to Davis Jones, who has lived with me as manager eight years at the conclusion of this, that I should not continue him the next. They all seem to wear out after a while and to require changing. Besides other objections, I had lately discovered that he had been in the practice of selling whiskey to my negroes!" [1]

❋   ❋   ❋   ❋   ❋

Farther inland, close against the Blue Ridge where Tye River takes its rise, dwelt and still dwells the Massie family, whose fortunes were mainly founded by Thomas, a major in the Continental army. This Thomas Massie, who removed from the near-by Buckingham county at the beginning of the nineteenth century and established his seat at "Level Green", was clearly a man of shrewd capacity. Before 1815 he had conquered the lure of tobacco and made his main concern the restoration of his worn lands by diversified husbandry, and the growing and milling of wheat.[2] Incidentally he bought apple trees by the gross for himself and his sons from a nursery on Long Island. He departed from tradition also in firmly resolving to indorse no man's notes and to cherish liquid funds.[3] When he died in 1834 he was possessed of twenty thousand dollars on deposit and fifty thousand dollars' worth of Richmond bank stocks as well as broad acres and many slaves, who ranged in his esteem from high virtue to utter depravity. Long before his death he had given each son a near-by plantation and other

---

[1] At the end of the year Jones removed to a plantation of his own.

[2] His sales of flour at Richmond in six months of 1816–1817 aggregated 1245 barrels and yielded $15,183.

[3] John Randolph was accustomed to describe Virginian estates as having "plenty of serfs, plenty of horses, but not a shilling." — John Hall, ed., *Forty Years' Familiar Letters of James W. Alexander*, I, 356.

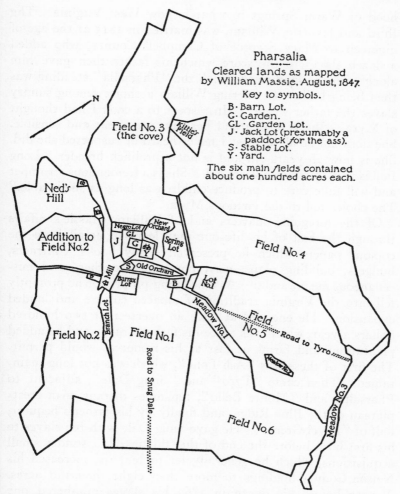

N

Pharsalia
Cleared lands as mapped
by William Massie, August, 1847.
Key to symbols.

B · Barn Lot.
G · Garden.
GL · Garden Lot.
J · Jack Lot (presumably a
paddock for the ass).
S · Stable Lot.
Y · Yard.

The six main fields contained
about one hundred acres each.

Field No. 3
(the cove)

Kittier Field

Ned's Hill

Addition to
Field No. 2

Negro Lot
New Orchard
GL
J G Spring Lot
Y
S Old Orchard
Barrex Lot
B

Lot No.1

Field No. 4

Field No. 5   Road to Tyro

Meadow No.1

Meadow No.2

Mill

Branch Lot

Field No. 2

Field No. 1

Road to Snug Dale

Meadow No. 3

Field No. 6

MAP OF PHARSALIA CLEARED LANDS, 1847

property to the value of some thirty-seven thousand dollars. His eldest, Thomas, was educated as a physician, and thereafter combined medical practice with plantation management in the same county of Nelson. The second son, Henry, discredited himself by dissipation and removed to the neighborhood of Warm Springs in what is now West Virginia. The third and favorite, William, was married in 1815 at the age of nineteen to Mary Steptoe of Campbell County, who added a dozen slaves to the score which his father then gave him along with the land upon which the "Pharsalia" steading was then being built. In offering William a choice among sundry slaves the father wrote: "In respect to a cook I had thought of Myra. She is strong and healthy, very neat and sensible. She does not steal, at least I never heard or suspected she did. She is now 26 years old and is not a prolifick breeder. Long Poll is now thirty-two years old. She is a tremendous strumpet and will take care to produce children as long as she is able." The choice fell to the virtuous Myra.

Of the foregoing matters and of William Massie's affairs through the rest of his life one may learn in detail from the copious papers which he preserved — day books, contracts, budgets, building plans, correspondence, vouchers and miscellaneous memoranda.[1] As a fledgling proprietor he promptly fell into the Virginia tradition of tobacco culture and landed expansion. He engaged at once an overseer at two hundred dollars a year, which was twice his father's rate; and he added plantations and farms as fast as his resources would permit. The first of these was "Ash Pone", which was not long maintained. Then came "Tyro" and "Snug Dale", adjacent to Pharsalia, and "Monte Bello", ten miles distant on a crest-plateau of the Blue Ridge, and finally by his father's bequest, half of "Level Green." He gave Snug Dale with ten slaves to his first-born before the end of the 'thirties; but sundry small acquisitions, which he generally let to tenants, increased his Nelson County holdings to more than eight thousand acres. A year before his death in 1862 his slaves numbered one hundred and thirty-nine, including twenty who by reason of superannuation or other disability were rated as having no value. At all times the slaves were distributed in plantation groups, with twenty to twenty-five field hands as

---

[1] These are now preserved in the library of the University of Texas. Among them are many signed drafts of Massie's own letters.

the Pharsalia corps, a like number at Level Green, forces half as large at Montebello and Tyro, with an overseer, a cook and a scullion as a rule for each gang. In addition there were blacksmiths, wheelwrights, carpenter-coopers, millers' helpers and wagoners, as well as a domestic staff at the homestead.

Massie's tobacco crops in good years were about half a hogshead, or seven hundred and fifty pounds, per field hand, but its grade was always lower than that from "below the James", and its price usually disappointing. Learning in 1828 that a machine had been invented to relieve the heavy labor of "breaking" hemp, and prompted by the protective rate in the tariff of that year, Massie installed apparatus in one of his water mills at a cost of more than a thousand dollars and turned to that staple; but in a few years he reverted to tobacco. In the late 'fifties he expressed an abhorrence of this crop and a resolution to quit its culture, but he never accomplished this resolve. At all times, however, wheat, which he sold as flour, bulked large in his produce, and for a few years a new variety of rye. Furthermore the hams and bacon from two or three hundred hogs each year were cured so well in what a visitor called his Great Western smokehouse that they had a special reputation in the Richmond market; and apples, beeves, butter, liquors and even chestnuts contributed to his money income. Once indeed he proposed to send surplus ice to Lynchburg for sale, but his wagoner brought back a discouraging response. Massie bought clover seed annually for soiling his land; he applied gypsum and guano; he devised a jointed roller to serve on his rocky lands; he built a great cellar to preserve his apples against the months of short supply and advanced prices at Richmond; he made annual budgets to promote frugality on his own part; yet all his efforts were unavailing until the prosperous 'fifties to clear himself of land-buying debts and provide for his marrying children.

Massie was full of the interesting cares of this earth. A fervent Whig and a firm Unionist, he was at one time a member of the legislature and once "high sheriff" of his county, though he farmed out the functions of this office [1] instead of discharging them in person; and he was a promoter of good roads and railroads. Hospitable and cheery, though sometimes choleric; vain enough to dye his prematurely gray hair, and outraged when a new purchase of dye turned it green instead of brown, he was essentially domestic, and particularly resolved that the grim reaper should not keep his hearthside vacant. When his first wife died after a long illness he said "a vile batchelor's life is hell itself to me", and commissioned a friend in Richmond to select "a plain, genteel, respectable, industrious lady" with a view to wedlock if upon their meeting she should prove one "who fully tickles my fancy and whose fancy it may be my good luck to tickle." The result was his marriage to Martha Wiatt, who bore the second and third of his children. After her death he married, again within a twelvemonth, Sarah Clark of Campbell county, whose life at Pharsalia was too brief to yield progeny. The last of the four was Maria Effinger, a sturdy maid of the Shenandoah, who bore ten children and survived her oft-married husband.

In the 'fifties Massie hired a teacher for some of his younger children and took the sons and daughters of sundry friends to board while attending what he styled the Pharsalia Institute. By adopting this pretentious name and procuring printed forms for its reports to parents he added individual touches to the common practice. Meanwhile his eldest son, named for the sage of Monticello, was a source of constant solicitude. Because of the succession of stepmothers at home he had been sent away to school and college and had been given indulgencies which made him an almost incorrigible spendthrift. As a young planter he fell heavily into debt, and again and yet again after his father had rescued him. Though William's thrifty soul was tried, his anger was held in check by a sense of responsibility for the misguidance and by a constant pride in Thomas as "an honorable high-toned gentleman." The two came near a breach when the son married Elizabeth Effinger, ten years his senior; but the sister-in-law who thus became a daughter-in-

[1] This was a frequent practice in Virginia.

law finally won her own place in William's regard, although his corpulence and rheumatism in age had not softened his temper. When seeking once more in 1858 to diminish his debts, Thomas proposed to sell his highly improved homestead in order to retain his slaves. "To know that my little family white and *black*, [is] to be fixed permanently together," he wrote, "would be as near that thing happiness as I ever expect to get. . . . I had rather leave this fine place and go to a much humbler one than to part with my negroes. Elizabeth has raised and taught most of them, and, having no children, like every other woman under like circumstances, has tender feelings toward them." William urged the sale of slaves instead: "Indeed, my son, it seems a blind infatuation that you should be so devoted to that kind of property which must have been greatly instrumental in all your embarrassments. . . . Negroes won't do unless they are made profitable, which yours have not been or you would have made money instead of being ruined. Negroes should be made to live comfortably, not luxuriously and tenderly, be furnished with the necessaries not superfluities of life, made to work on some crop that will pay, and not on buildings and projects; and then they are most generally profitable if the product of their labor is not wasted — but not always."

Another conflict between hard and soft policy appears in a letter from son to father in 1856: "Your conclusions in reference to 'negroes having wives from home' are strong, and I am afraid too true. But it belongs to the 'institution', and all we can do is to make the most of it and modify it when we can. . . . Tho' it impairs his value and is fraught with vexation and annoyance, it, to the slaveholding interest, is a lesser evil than for the whole class to enforce your views — because, 1st. few owners have enough of each sex, unconnected by blood or even otherwise, for them to pair off; 2nd. If they could all get 'wives at home', in a few generations they would be little better than the monkeys of their native land. And in the 3rd. place, or alternative rather, having no wives, even as they stile it, would surely demoralize, mentally and physically, the race; and it (wretched in some respects as it is now) would be con-

sumed by its own vices in the course of a life time or two, or sink
with them the whole land of their habitation."

William Massie seems to have gotten his disapproval of
"broadwives" from his own father, who had written in 1831
when selling him a woman and her child: "Would not Tandy
be the best person to send for her, as he is in grief for the loss of
his wife, and the best way of turning grief (with a negroe) is the
most speedy way of repairing the loss.   And no doubt Jude
would be very glad to exchange my shabby rabbit Sam (who
was her fire maker last winter) for Tandy. . . .   I must request
you to forbid Sam from frequenting your plantation."   In
a divorce of his own initiation in 1836 Massie paid his man
Willis twenty dollars to forsake a broadwife and accept Nancy
at home as a substitute.   In yet another instance, in 1852,
a marriage between two Pharsalia slaves was followed in a fortnight by the groom's detection in theft and the bride's repudi-
ation of him.   Massie proceeded to seek a distant purchaser
for the man in order to safeguard the woman from his impor-
tunities.

Massie bought and sold sundry other slaves, whether on the
ground of matings or on business occasion; but in 1837 he
declined to complete a purchase because, as he said, "entirely
contrary to what I expected, Henry objects to belonging to
me."   Again, in 1852, he took successively a woman and a
young girl from James B. Hargrove, who seems to have been
a dealer at Lovingston, on trial as seamstresses.   The woman
proved in the judgment of Massie and his wife "a neat genteel
servant and very captivating", but anaemic and insufficiently
skilled.   The girl was also rejected, whereupon Hargrove
wrote: "The only regret I have about the matter is produced
through sympathy for her, as she seemed to be so much morti-
fied at having failed to please your wife, so much so that she
wept bitterly, and on being asked why she was crying said she
wanted to go back.   She gives a most flattering description of
your place and people."

More curious was the case of George, afterward surnamed
Jackson, who had been born of Amy in 1810 and bought by

Massie about 1825 at George's urging and under full warrant from the seller. Massie was vaguely aware that James Hopkins, former owner of Amy, had provided by instruments of 1798 and 1802 that all his slaves bent to his son-in-law until they and their children should respectively reach the ages of thirty for females and thirty-four for males, then be hired out for ten years and then be set free. Massie understood this to apply only to slaves born before the death of Hopkins in 1803; but no sooner did George attain forty-four years than he procured an attorney to demand his freedom. Staggered at the assertion that George was entitled to deferred manumission from before his birth, and particularly dismayed that some one (he could not guess who) might be entitled to a decade's wages of an expert wagon-maker, Massie asked counsel from his lawyer, who thought George's claim valid but advised a *pro forma* contest in court as a basis for demanding damages from the seller of nearly thirty years before. George won his suit for freedom and damages in lieu of wages after his forty-fourth birthday; but no one claimed his wages for the preceding decade. Massie's suit against the seller's executor was lost in the county court, gained in the Court of Appeals, and finally compromised. Meanwhile a question arose as to whether George, having been freed, could legally remain in Virginia. Counsel said that he could not unless his manumission be deemed operative from his birth (the law had been changed in the interval), yet advised him nevertheless to stay if he wished, because in case of proceedings the court could be counted upon to give notice which would enable him to depart before a penalty for illegal residence could be imposed. George, in fact, hired himself to Massie for a year at one hundred and fifty dollars and provisions, which was more than some of Massie's white millers and overseers were getting. During the twelve-month George drew pay in cash and sundry goods, including numerous half-gallons of whiskey. At its end his name disappeared from the record. He had been "an invaluable slave"; but perhaps he failed to withstand the temptations of prosperous freedom.

Another George was bought in 1849 from Christopher T. Estis of Lovingston after a correspondence which illuminates an economic phase of slaveholding. Demurring at Estis' price for George at the age of fifty-four, Massie wrote: "If 30 years old he would be cheaper at $1200 than at $400 now. In buying old slaves we could afford a pretty good price if it was certain they would die as soon as past labor; but the possibility, nay probability, of comfortably boarding a superannuated negro 10 to 30 years is appalling. I have now 7 of that kind on my hands, most of whom have been past labor 13 to 18 years." The purchase was made and the apprehension realized; for in a list made by Massie for Confederate tax return George appears, aged sixty-six, valued at zero, and noted as having "diseased ankles."

In 1837 Massie remarked that in his locality no field hand could be worth more than five hundred dollars; and in 1860, contemplating the prices then prevalent, he said, "I look upon it as murder [i.e., financial suicide] to lay out money in negroes to work in Virginia." Yet when his corps fell short he could not resist the pressure. Thus in 1858 he instructed his factors at Richmond to buy him an able-bodied man, which they did at auction, and when reporting it mentioned that while otherwise in superb physique the Negro had a foot swollen by a shackle. This remark threw Massie into dismay for fear of having bought a chronic runaway or possibly a desperado. After a tart correspondence with his factors he learned the name of the former owner, Amos L. Simmons of New Berne, North Carolina, and promptly inquired of him concerning the man's character and record. Simmons replied to the best of his ability, saying, "Jordan is a smart active man but unfortunate for him he is of the Guiney blood and has a desperate temper which he cannot govern." Sundry contretemps in the course of years, Simmons continued, had taught him to handle Jordan with diplomacy; but this year an overseer had been employed who had brought about a crisis. Upon the death of a slave child, this Shepper, instead of having the grave dug on Saturday, waited till Sunday and then summoned Jordan. When

Jordan failed to report, as Simmons narrated with some ambiguity of pronouns and a disregard of punctuation, Shepper "went to his house and found that he had gone to dig the grave he went where he was and when he got there he asked him if he did not send for him   he remarked yes but he did not come and never intended to come for he says you have nothing to do with me   it was your business to have this grave dug yesterday . . . Mr Shepper said to him   Sir you will have to be whiped   whip who   I would rather see you undertake it   you may get me hampered and do it but don't cross my path after you have done it   and lucky for Mr. Shepper he held his pashion." Simmons concluded: "I hated to part with him but I feared my overseer might be induced to kill him and I thought it best to sell him."   In his mention of high temper as an accompaniment of "the Guiney blood" Simmons doubtless alluded unconsciously to the Coromantee strain whose traits we have glimpsed elsewhere.   When Jordan reached Pharsalia the first reaction was favorable.   The lack of subsequent comments upon him implies that he neither met nor made trouble in his new home.

Massie took pride in his own effective discipline, but there were times when its failure cost him dear.   At the end of 1836 he discovered the disappearance of a bushel of wheat and announced that all hands who had been about the barn would be whipped unless the thief were named.   The men laid their heads together and notified Sam that he would be delivered to justice, whereupon Sam set fire to the barn, as he afterward confessed, "thinking thereby", as his master said, "to absorb my mind in a more serious matter and abstract it from the wheat."   Thereby Massie lost the value of some twelve hundred dollars; and Sam assuredly did not save his own skin.

Massie was dolorous at slave deaths and angered by one's flight, but happy that an epidemic of measles in 1858, which claimed sixty-eight patients, took no toll of lives.   In 1855 he sent four slaves to a mineral spring for treatment, and next year he offered to sell the two lads among them to the proprietor of the resort at a bargain price with a view to his completing their cure on speculation. The response was higgling; and the result does not appear.

The slaves were permitted to earn small sums by work on holidays, including Easter Monday, and on Sundays or at night, whether at rates of thirty-seven and one half to fifty cents per day or at job prices for ditching, woodcutting, blacksmithing, cooperage and the like, or by selling produce, including corn and hops. The debits were miscellaneous, with whiskey at seventy-five cents per gallon the most frequent entry; but Jake Cuff applied five dollars to the purchase of "a coat, pantaloons and vest to marry in." Old Peter died with a credit balance on the books, whereupon his account was closed by an entry, April 12, 1848: "To cash in full paid all the heirs of Peter at the distribution of his effects, in presence of Geo. Williams, Thos. J. Massie and others, $9.30." Evidently quite an occasion was made of the episode.

As a reward for his great care with horses, the wagoner Martin was long permitted to haul fractional back-loads from market towns for neighboring planters to his own profit. In 1838 a merchant wrote that Martin had stretched this privilege by draying in the village. In a letter of thanks for this information Massie wrote: "He certainly was for many years the most perfectly faithful slave I ever knew, which caused me to indulge him very much, and that has had (as is generally the case) rather a bad effect. He is notwithstanding the best negro I now own, out of 130. I have owned him 23 years and never lashed him or even spoken harshly to him, and that is something wonderful. . . . He has saved me thousands in horse flesh." In a codicil of 1844 to an early will Massie wrote: "My slave and old waggoner Martin, who was for many years faithful and exceedingly efficient, I desire not to be considered as a part of my disposable estate. It was for a long time my intention, and (except for his increasing fondness for the bottle) I would now direct his emancipation with a provision for his support; but believing as I now do that it would be anything but benevolence to do so, I give him to my wife with a request that she give him light work to do while he is able and keep him comfortable while he lives." To this he added: "My boy Julius (the blacksmith) who I have every reason to consider one of the most respectable men, white or black, in the commonwealth, I recommend to her special attention." Massie's overseers will be considered in another chapter.

❅   ❅   ❅   ❅   ❅

Of George Washington so much has been written [1] that I have not been disposed to thresh the straw of his papers again while such copious harvests from other fields have been coming to my flail. His career was shrewdly logical, but his path to greatness was by no means palpably predestined. When he was fifteen years old, for example, his brother Lawrence procured for him a midshipman's warrant in the British navy; and it may well have been the dissuasion of his uncle, Joseph Ball, which fixed him upon the land as against the sea. Ball wrote from England to George's mother, saying that a sailor's life was a dog's life, preferment in the navy was dependent upon favoring influence, and a transfer to the merchant marine would give little better promise. For, he continued:

"A planter that has Three or four hundred Acres of Land and Three or four Slaves, if he be Industrious, may Live more Comfortably and Leave his family in better Bread than such a master of a ship can; and if the Planter can get ever so little beforehand let him begin to *Chinch*, that is buy Goods for Tobacco and sell them again for Tobacco. (I never knew them men Miss while they went on so). . . . He must not be too hasty to be Rich, but go on Gently and with Patience, as things will naturally go. This Method, without aiming at being a fine Gentleman before his time, will Carry a man more Comfortably and surely through the world than going to sea, unless it be a Great Chance indeed." [2] George improved upon

---

[1] *E.g.*, P. L. Haworth, *George Washington: Farmer* (Indianapolis [1915]).

[2] Letter of Joseph Ball, May 19, 1747, to Mary Washington, in Horace E. Hayden, *Virginia Genealogies*, 77. Washington, however, did not observe one of his uncle's warnings: "neither must he send his Tobacco to England to be sold here, and Goods sent him; if he does he will soon get in the Merchants Debt and never get out again."

his uncle's programme by surveying for Lord Fairfax and marrying the widow Custis; but a planter he was by main predilection from early manhood to death — an enterprising and painstaking husbandman, wedded to "Mount Vernon" not merely as a home but as a plantation. Enlarging the property to dimensions too large for operation as a single unit, he organized it as five "farms", with an overseer in charge of each and a steward supervising the whole. For a time a slave managed one of these units to as good satisfaction as did his white colleagues. This was no great praise upon his master's lips, for Washington cherished a standard of efficiency which was never satisfied. He himself experimented and innovated elaborately, importing asses to breed mules, setting hedges to replace fences, testing seed, fertilizers and rotations, and maintaining correspondence with English and American students of husbandry. While at home he seldom omitted a daily tour of inspection, and while President he corresponded voluminously with his steward upon plantation affairs.

In his later life Washington often expressed a repugnance toward slavery, and in his will he provided for a wholesale manumission. But his gruff tone in speaking to his slaves and his frequent censures of their slackness suggest that in the main he held the Negroes in disdain. This may have been a product of his war-time habituation to the peremptory manner; but certain it is that he showed no tenderness except to a few personal servants. Had he been less of a public servant he would surely have been more of a planter. His resolution to improve methods and equipment and to renovate his land was indomitable; but his long absences, his grand style of living and his impatience of human failings were handicaps not fully overcome. Added to these was the leanness of the hard-packed clay on the Mount Vernon slopes and its proneness to lose its humus by erosion. Lecture his overseers as he might, his crops continued thin, his sheep neglected, his cows dry and his slaves indolent. When Richard Parkinson came as an English farmer with blooded cattle to find a location he examined Mount Vernon, whose fields Washington then desired to let, only to judge them hopeless for his purpose.[1] When Washington resumed residence after his Farewell Address things assumed a better appearance; but his death and his manumissions wrecked the estate. His work, indeed, had a striking lack of sequel. Not only did his mansion and its elaborately ornamented grounds become dilapidated, but by 1833 a visitor describing the denudation of Fairfax County at large said: "Hope and hope only keeps two thirds of the population of this county in it. Like the Jews, they look for something supernatural — they look for that which is not in the stores of time."[2]

In fancy we may join the family groups at Nomini Hall, Shirley, Westover, Bolling Hall, Pharsalia or Mount Vernon, or amble with their masters and chat with their overseers and slaves. But sundry other Virginians whom we should like to visit have in a sense closed their premises against us by leaving no intimate papers to give access. From Delaware, Maryland, Kentucky, Missouri and Arkansas no materials giving vivid portrayal of indentifiable planters or estates have come to my knowledge.

[1] Richard Parkinson, *Tour in America* (London, 1805), I, 50–54. *Cf.* also II, 419.
[2] *Farmers' Register*, I, 553.

CHAPTER XIII

SOUTHEASTERN PLANTATIONS

OF North Carolina plantations clear pictures are not at hand except for some which forsook the distinctive Southern staples. Two of these lay adjoining on Scuppernong Lake in the great "cypress and gum swamp" between Albemarle and Pamlico sounds. To reclaim such land for tillage required bold imagination, large capital and firm perseverance. Josiah Collins, born in Somersetshire in 1735, emigrated from England shortly before his fortieth year, landing at Boston. After a sojourn at Providence he removed to North Carolina, thriving in commerce and ropemaking at Edenton. About 1785 he formed a partnership styled the Lake Company, procured title to a huge tract in the Scuppernong swamp, sent a ship to bring slaves from Africa, made surveys and began drainage and clearing. Eventually he completed his plantation project in essentials, bought out his partners, and at his death bequeathed the property to his son Josiah in trust for his grandchildren. This second Josiah was in possession in 1839 when Edmund Ruffin made a visit to describe the place in the columns of his *Farmers' Register*. From a dam near the lake a canal, twenty feet wide and four feet deep, ran six miles to a sea-level stream, and served the triple purpose of drainage, navigation and power. Fourteen hundred acres of swamp muck had been cleared and drained by a network of ditches, and six hundred of these were in corn with a maximum yield of eight thousand barrels. The rest was mostly in weed fallow. Rice culture had been abandoned as causing excessive illness among the slaves.[1] Three

[1] Work in the wet rice fields doubtless brought more sickness in this latitude than in the warmer clime farther south.

large granaries stood upon the canal bank near the gristmills and sawmills; and from a power-driven shelling machine in one of them the corn was mechanically lifted to the fourth floor and poured through spouts into barges which carried it down the canal to ships bound for the Charleston and Savannah markets.

The homestead, "Somerset Place", fronted the lake, with the slave quarter and a slave chapel near by. On a Sunday morning of Ruffin's visit a lay reader in the Collins family conducted the Episcopal service; and in the evening the Bishop of North Carolina came to deliver an address, after which the local clergyman administered the sacrament to the bishop, the white household and some thirty of the slaves.[1]

Reached from Somerset Place by the road along the leveed front of the lake, lay the neighboring plantation of Ebenezer Pettigrew, somewhat smaller in scale and less elaborate in apparatus. Like many other planters, Pettigrew permitted his slaves to raise little crops of their own and kept accounts with them. His purpose was explicitly the maintenance of morale. For example, he noted in 1817: "Settled with Tom, George, Cromwell and Lewis for their ditching the nine feet ditch. The settlement is nothing more or less than presents for their good behaviour while working in it." On various occasions he debited slave accounts for theft or breakage, or confiscated their credits for running away or other "outrageous conduct."[2]

*　　　　*　　　　*　　　　*　　　　*

Though of Southern birth, Henry K. Burgwyn and his brother Thomas were living at the North when they inherited an estate on the Roanoke River near Halifax with a hundred or so slaves. Disrelishing slavery, they took possession with a purpose of manumitting the Negroes when a suitable plan could be framed; and with a view to substituting white labor they imported

[1] Edmund Ruffin in the *Farmers' Register*, VII, 698–703, 724–732; G. P. Collins in the *Southern History Association Publications*, VI, 24, 25.
[2] Rosser H. Taylor, *Slaveholding in North Carolina* (Chapel Hill, 1926), 84, 85.

about a hundred Irishmen. This experiment brought a loss of some two thousand dollars and appears to have reconciled the brothers to the retention of their slaves.[1] Meanwhile they turned from cotton to wheat and set themselves to improve their lands. They drained their broad bottom fields elaborately; they procured the most effective plows and ran them ten inches deep instead of the mere three inches customary thereabout; they applied varied fertilizers copiously, and they prospered and bought more lands right and left. On their two plantations, "Thornburg" and "Occonachee Wigwam", they were living in "tall style" when an agent selling McCormick reapers paid them a call in 1854; but their elegance of life did not relax their energy. While some Southerners baffled this salesman by saying "If we use these labor saving machines we shan't have anything for our niggers to do", the Burgwyns made additional purchases to bring their total to about fifteen reaping machines. Not all of these were expected to be used at any time in the harvest of their seventeen hundred acres of wheat, but it was expedient to have a reserve against breakdowns.[2]

In the next year, as told by a traveling reporter, Henry Burgwyn alone had nine hundred acres in wheat, four hundred and fifty in corn and five hundred in clover, not to speak of minor crops. His wheat yielded twenty-three thousand bushels, and brought $2.25 per bushel when sold at Petersburg. For 1856 his cast of clover was nine hundred acres, part of it intended as meadow, part as pasture, and part as fallow to be turned under for soiling. The numerous horses, mules and cattle were well kept; and as to the Negroes the sojourning Yankee said after a week's observation that the master "provides so well for the animal happiness of the slave that it

---

[1] Henry, indeed, became a warm supporter of the Southern system, as evidenced by his *Considerations relative to a Southern Confederacy* (Raleigh, 1860). This anonymous pamphlet is rightly attributed to H. K. Burgwyn on the catalogue cards of the Library of Congress, though the name is wrongly spelled "Berguin."

[2] Letters of A. D. Hager to Cyrus H. McCormick, May 9 and 15, June 7, 14 and 15, 1854. Manuscripts in the McCormick Agricultural Library, Chicago. For these items and many others I am indebted to Mr. Herbert A. Kellar.

necessitates one to continually summon up his principle to resist falling in with it and heartily approving the whole system." [1]

＊　　　＊　　　＊　　　＊　　　＊

For the lower South our examples are closer to the traditional stereotype, except that the three which here follow, comprising two plantations in each instance, were estates of absent proprietors. Charles Manigault, however, was as a rule resident during the warmer months of each year.

The Manigaults and Heywards, intricately intermarried, had a status in lowland South Carolina comparable to that of the Carters in Virginia. The founder of their fortunes was Gabriel Manigault, son of a Huguenot immigrant, who prospered through commerce, marriage, rice growing and public office until at his death in 1781 he was reputed to be the richest man in the commonwealth. His plantation, "Silk Hope" on Cooper River, fell to his grandson Gabriel Manigault, who had two hundred and ten slaves thereon in 1790; but afterward it was conveyed by him to his brother-in-law, Nathaniel Heyward, to be one of the fourteen estates on which when he died in 1851 he had two thousand and eighty-seven slaves. A daughter of Heyward who had married Charles Manigault now inherited Silk Hope; but her husband was already operating two plantations, "Gowrie" and "East Hermitage" on Argyle Island in the Savannah River; and thither he carried the century-old plantation bell from Silk Hope as a symbol of residence by the head of the Manigault family. On Gowrie was the home of the master, on East Hermitage the overseer's house; on one was a great brick threshing house, on the other a large pounding mill to hull the crop and polish it for market; on each was a group of slave cabins with forty or fifty inmates. Under Charles Manigault and his son Louis these adjoining units were operated as one.[2]

[1] R. Norris Copeland in the *New England Farmer*, VIII, 173, 174 (April, 1856).

[2] The Manigault manuscripts are in private possession. Some of them are printed in U. B. Phillips, ed., *Plantation and Frontier Documents*, I, 122–126, 134–149, 337, 338; II, 32, 33, 94.

The value of the property, including the slaves, was well above a hundred thousand dollars. From the four or five hundred acres of heavy red land in rice the potential crop was perhaps thirty-five thousand bushels in the husk, which might bring nearly as many dollars after milling, whereas expenses were not expected to exceed five thousand dollars. In actual experience net revenues fell far short of such a reckoning. In 1852 and 1854 cholera killed many of the best slaves, and in the same years freshets broke the banks and greatly diminished the crops. In other years hurricanes, floods, mismanagement or market conditions generally held the crop within half of the potential volume and the net income below ten thousand dollars. In 1856, furthermore, $11,850 was expended for nineteen slaves to fill the gaps made by cholera, and $2200 for a tract of pine land, a dozen miles distant, to serve as a place of summer sojourn for slave children and a refuge for the whole corps in time of epidemic.

Manigault made a point of issuing durable clothing to the Negroes and building them substantial houses on brick foundations higher than flood could reach. His instructions laid emphasis upon safeguarding health and the speedy sending of any injured slave to a hospital at Savannah; and the payment of fifty-one dollars in 1858 for surgical attention to Hector's eye suggests that practice comported with preaching. To promote good order, outside matings were forbidden and Sunday was fixed upon for the weekly issue of rations as a deterrent from roamings on that day. The slaves ranged in esteem from good to bad, with the largest category indifferent. Jack Savage, the head carpenter, surnamed from a previous owner, was a capable craftsman, but lazy and so surly that Louis Manigault had some fear of an attack by him; Old Betsy was thought to have poisoned a group of slave children in her care at the summer camp; Young Fortune was at length sold as an incorrigible runaway, and some others played truant on occasion. But in general the master said, "my Negroes have the reputation of being orderly and well disposed"; and the mill crew in particular was efficient and reliable to a degree which prompted him to tell his overseer to leave the machinery to their skill.

The dread of malaria made the master an absentee from each May to November, and left the overseer in full charge. When the death of the competent Stephen F. Clark vacated this post at the end of 1855, Leonard Venters, twenty-four years old, was chosen from a crowd of applicants on the strength of his testimonials; and though his first year's crop was impaired by mistakes in flowing and draining the fields, he was retained on the maxim, "never change an overseer if you can help it." The next year's crop was better; but upon Manigault's return from the summer's absence he learned as to Venters that, "elated by a strong and very false religious feeling, he began to injure the plantation a vast deal, placing himself on a par with the Negroes by even joining in with them in their prayer meetings, breaking down long established discipline which in every case is so difficult to maintain, favouring and siding in any difficulty with the people against the drivers, besides causing numerous grievances." Venters was discharged, leaving a mulatto son among the slaves as a memento. The next incumbent was William N. Bryan, employed at eight hundred dollars and provisions as compared with three hundred for Venters. After a summer in Europe Manigault found that Bryan had enjoyed a long vacation at the pine-land camp, to the gross neglect of the plantation. He was of course discharged, and the master was in sole command until April, 1859, when he engaged his own distant cousin, William Capers, Jr., at one thousand dollars and food for his family of six children. Capers had his troubles with the weather and with runaways, but he was retained in high esteem until his death in 1864. His repute for skill in the handling of slaves came in part from his procuring a faithful new foreman at a bargain price. Learning that this man, who had been in authority under him on another estate, was now for sale as a drunkard, he persuaded Manigault to make the purchase; and within two months he reported John's complete recovery from the demoralization which he attributed wholly to bad management. On one occasion Capers reported the loss of a slave by suicide during his absence. Ralph, the driver, had been about to punish London, when the latter ran into the river. Ralph then parleyed from the bank, saying if London would come ashore he should not be whipped until the overseer's return. London replied that he would drown himself instead, and promptly did so. Capers found the corpse floating in slack water, but by way of deterring other slaves from such a course he ordered it not to be touched until the tide should take it away.

Louis Manigault, when recording the issue of summer clothing in 1861, noted it as being "the first year of the sovereignty and independence of the Confederate States of America — Praise God for same!" Twelve months afterward he summarized his first year of experience in "the unrighteous and diabolical war now raging." Quiet had prevailed upon the island until November when Federal forces captured Port Royal, not far away. Thereupon panic spread among the whites about Savannah, and murmurings among the slaves. Capers found a store of powder and shot in Ishmael's cabin; and at his advice the master determined to send to Silk Hope ten men who were suspected of intention to join the "Yankees." Seven of these went willingly, the others attempted to escape, were caught and handcuffed. The presence among these of Hector, his young master's favorite boathand and often in times past his constant companion, caused Louis to say: "This war has taught us the perfect impossibility of placing the least confidence in any Negro. In too numerous instances those we have esteemed the most have been the first to desert us." In February thirteen more prime slaves were sent to Silk Hope, and arrangements were made for complete evacuation of Gowrie and East Hermitage at short notice.

In the summer of 1862 a number of slaves on the Savannah died of a new disease. "They would suddenly swell in every part of the body, and in five or six days the case would invariably prove fatal." This was attributed to the use of rice as a sole food. Negroes had killed the plantation hogs; the cows had been sold to escape a similar fate; corn, bacon and molasses were not to be had in the market; fishhooks likewise could not be bought; and the leaden weights from the nets had been run into bullets. So the fish "which abound in Savannah River and which in times of peace are caught in large numbers by the Negroes were now allowed to remain in their native element."

The quietude of the vicinity brought a fuller scale of operations in 1863 by the return of most of the slaves who had been sent to Silk Hope; but disaster fell on Christmas Eve of 1864 when a rapid advance by Sherman's forces drove the master and overseer in headlong flight and brought the burning of the major plantation buildings. After the war operations were undertaken afresh, with an ill success which we shall not here narrate.

❋   ❋   ❋   ❋   ❋

The plantation known as "Butler's Island" on the Altamaha River is unique in that all the known records concerning it have long been in print and, thanks mainly to Fanny Kemble, the reports of its tone are sharply conflicting. Major Pierce Butler, born in Ireland in 1744, came to America in command of British troops; but before the Revolution he married a rice-plantation heiress and resigned his commission. From his home on Ashley River he went to the Federal Convention and to the United States Senate, where he was a "flaming" champion of Southern interests. Meanwhile he shifted his industrial operations prosperously to the Georgia coast, built a handsome home on St. Simon's Island and finally a great house in Philadelphia where he died in 1822. Always proud of a noble descent, this adaptable, magniloquent Irishman engaged and held the affection of his family and friends and the devotion of slaves. His daughter had married a Philadelphia physician, and her two sons, Pierce and John, inherited jointly the grandfather's estate and changed their surname from Mease to Butler. The elder of these, a young lawyer, musician and man-about-town when Fanny Kemble took the theater-going public by storm, was infatuated to such degree that he followed her on tour and persuaded her in 1834 to marry him.

The family revenues had been drawn mainly from "Butler's Island", a rice plantation great enough to require four clusters of slave cabins. This property was long in charge of R. King and his son of the same initial. The elder King, as related by the younger, assumed control in 1802, finding the slaves demoralized by reason of rapid alternation among the preceding overseers. Definite rules were now promulgated, and "a few forcible examples made, after a regular trial. . . . But the grand point was to suppress the brutality and licentiousness practiced by the principal men on it — say the drivers and tradesmen." In the younger King's régime, "no driver in the field is allowed to inflict punishment until after a regular trial. When I pass sentence myself, various modes of punishment are adopted, the lash least of all", but rather confinement in stocks, labor when the well-behaved were at leisure, and most commonly a mere deprivation of town leave. The slaves were encouraged to work for their own profit in free time. "Surely if industrious for themselves they will be so for their masters; and no Negro with a well stocked poultry house, a small crop advancing, a canoe partly finished or a few tubs unsold, all of which he calculates soon to enjoy, will ever run away. In ten years I have lost by absconding forty-seven days out of nearly six hundred Negroes." By careful observance of equity in assigning tasks and by rewards of half-time on Saturdays, he said, brisk and willing performance was procured. "All these things are not to be slipped into at once; it has been the work of nearly twenty-seven years, and I find many things yet to correct." To save labor and assure adequacy, two cooked meals per day were issued to all slaves, and in summer an extra meal to the children. In consequence, "there is not a *dirt-eater* among them — an incurable propensity produced from a morbid state of the stomach, arising from the want of a proper quantity of wholesome food and at a proper time." In conclusion: "It is a great point in having the principal drivers men that can support their dignity; a condescension to familiarity should be prohibited. Young Negroes are put to work early, twelve to fourteen years old; four, five or six rated a hand. It keeps them out of mischief, and . . . they acquire habits of perseverance and industry." [1] After another decade of service King departed to become a planter in Alabama, and this caused Pierce Mease Butler to go with his wife and babies and their white nurse for a winter on the Altamaha properties.

In her English girlhood Fanny Kemble had acquired an abiding horror of Negro slavery which her marriage did not diminish; and resolving to keep a journal of her observations and experiences in the régime, she registered her drastic repugnance in advance: "Assuredly I *am* going prejudiced against slavery, for I am an Englishwoman, in whom the absence of such a prejudice would be disgraceful. Nevertheless I go prepared to find many mitigations in the practice to the general injustice and cruelty of the system." [2] The resulting book is a monotonous view of the seamy side, and an exhibit of the critic's own mental processes. On Butler's Island the overseer's house in which the sojourners dwelt was crude and cramped, the servants unkempt and ill-smelling, the slave cabins and hospitals unclean, and all things unpleasing. The filth and stench in British and European peasant hovels, she granted, was as great; but in the case of the Negroes she said "slavery is answerable for all the evils . . . from lying, thieving and adultery to dirty houses, ragged clothes and foul smells." [3] Again, their food and bedding were deficient and their work excessive, though in other connections it was noted that many of the workers were in perfect physique; many of them ended their tasks by the middle of the afternoon; they sold on their own account large quantities of Spanish moss, the best of materials for mattresses; and their ducks and chickens swarmed under the orange trees in the quarters and added to the filth in the cabins.

[1] Letter of R. King, Jr., to William Washington, September 13, 1828, in the *Southern Agriculturist*, I, 523–527 (Charleston, December, 1828).

[2] Frances Anne Kemble, *Journal of a Residence on a Georgia Plantation* in 1838–1839. (New York, 1863), 15.

[3] *Ibid.*, 24.

The head foreman, like several other slaves, was judged upright, intelligent, neat and self-respecting, "with a courteousness of demeanor far removed from servility." Was his a case of alleviation? No, it "exhibits a strong instance of the intolerable and wicked injustice of the system under which he lives. Having advanced thus far toward improvement in spite of all bars it puts to progress," he is forbidden further improvement.

This visiting lady, who when addressed as "Missis" begged the Negroes "For God's sake do not call me that", on occasion "addressed the girls most solemnly, showing them that they were wasting in idle riot the time in which they might be rendering their abode decent." She also addressed to her husband, who "seemed positively degraded in my eyes as he stood enforcing upon these women the necessity of their fulfilling their appointed tasks", so many protests that he finally forbade the further conveyance of complaints by her.[1] Such recitals as these crowd out of the journal most of what might be expected in description of the plantation and its working. It does appear, however, that the overseer had trouble in distinguishing sickness from shamming, that a steam engine drove the thresher, that plows were being introduced at this time to diminish the labor of hoeing, that the slaves were permitted to attend church and market in Darien, and that they made brave if barbaric display of finery on Sundays.

The sojourners next went to St. Simon's Island, where lay a sea-island cotton plantation which in Major Butler's time had yielded riches from a high-priced staple.[2] But now the crop had ceased to pay, and the old mansions thereabout were mostly in ruin. The sturdiest of the slaves had been removed to the rice fields; the remnant, "owing, I suppose, to the influence of the resident lady proprietors of the various plantations and the propensity to imitate them in their black dependents, . . . all seem to me to be much tidier, cleaner,

---

[1] Frances Kemble, *Journal*, 170.

[2] His cotton was of a grade that brought maximum prices in the 1790's. — Thomas Spalding, in J. A. Turner, *The Cotton Planters' Manual* (New York, 1857), 285.

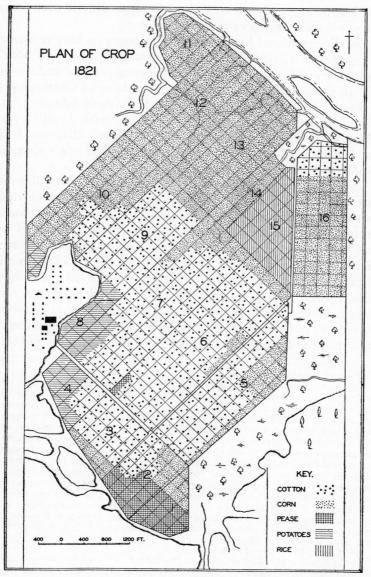

PLAN OF CROP
1821

KEY.

COTTON

CORN

PEASE

POTATOES

RICE

400   0   400   800   1200 FT.

MAP OF HOPETON ON THE ALTAMAHA

and less fantastically dressed than those on the rice plantation where no such influences reach them." [1]

The diarist visited James Hamilton Couper on his rice estate, "Hopeton",[2] and commended this "worthy, canny old Scot" for his home-keeping and thrifty amelioration of land and slaves, though she did not speak with the enthusiasm of Charles Lyell or Frederika Bremer. And as regards Butler's Island it was hardly to be expected that she would see with Lyell's eyes: "The Negro houses were neat and whitewashed, all floored with wood, each with an apartment called the hall, two sleeping rooms, and a loft for the children." [3]

The stress between Pierce M. Butler and Frances Kemble was ended by divorce in 1849, the children staying with their father who continued to dwell in Philadelphia. His finances became strained, and the panic of 1857 forced the sale of his half of the plantation slaves. These were carried to the race course at Savannah and sold in family groups in 1857, in one of the greatest slave auctions on record. The total of 429 men, women and children brought $303,850.[4] Butler gave each of them a dollar in farewell; but his concern with the plantations proved not to be ended. Receiving reports at the beginning of 1866 that the former slaves, including some whom he had sold

---

[1] Frances Kemble, *Journal*, 180.

[2] Since this book went to press a crop record of Hopeton, extending from 1820 to 1831, has become available in the library of the University of North Carolina. This includes annual maps, of which a specimen is reproduced herein. The plantation, including Carr's Island which lay alongside in the Altamaha River, comprised about eleven thousand acres and was valued in 1826 at $80,412 when its three hundred and thirty slaves were appraised at $99,000. The record shows notable rotation and experimentation. Corn, sweet potatoes and cowpeas, all for home consumption, were shifted from field to field. Until 1825 the main market crop was cotton, some of it specified as "New Orleans" or short-staple. For the next three years rice exceeded cotton in acreage, and then cotton was completely replaced by sugar cane. But the sugar experiment presumably did not long persist. As an enterprise remote from Hopeton, Couper established a mill at Natchez in 1833 to extract oil from cotton seed and maintained it for a number of years. For these data, as well as for the map, I am indebted to Dr. Guion S. Johnston and to Professor J. G. de Roulhac Hamilton of the University of North Carolina.

[3] Sir Charles Lyell, *Second Visit*, 2d ed., I, 333.

[4] *What became of the slaves on a Georgia Plantation? Great auction sale of slaves at Savannah, Georgia, March 2d and 3d, 1859. A Sequel to Mrs. Kemble's Journal* (n. p., 1863). This is a reprint from the New York *Tribune.*

away, were willing to work for their old master but were menaced with starvation, he made his way to the plantation in
company with his daughter Frances. The daughter's journal [1]
is the record of a practical woman, with little doctrine but much
kindliness, meeting grave problems with earnest resolution.

Welcoming "Old Maussa" with vociferations of joy and
loyalty, the Negroes readily accepted his plan of cropping
and sharing half-and-half. An agent of the Freedmen's
Bureau, suggesting a doubt of Butler's good faith, said to one
of them : "Why, Bram, how can you care so much for your master — he sold you a few years ago?" "Yes, sir," replied the
old man, "he sold me and I was very unhappy, but he came
to me and said, 'Bram, I am in great trouble; I have no money
and I have to sell some of the people, but I know where you
are all going to, and will buy you back as soon as I can.' . . .
And now that we are free, I came back to my old home and my
old master, and stay here till I die." [2]

But of course the Negroes "remained the same demonstra-
tive and noisy childish people they had always been", readier of
lip service than of labor. Field work was inconstant, regardless of the needs of the crop. The employer had no authority;
and the "captains", who replaced the foremen or drivers of old,
could merely tally the presence or absence of the members of
their squads. As to special tasks, the young mistress wrote:
"I generally found that if I wanted a thing done I first had to
tell the Negroes to do it, then show them how, and finally do it
myself. Their way of managing not to do it was very ingenious,
for they were perfectly good-tempered, and received my orders
with 'Dat's so, missus; just as missus says,' and then somehow or other left the thing undone." [3] A scanty crop was
reaped and a new one cast when Butler died and Frances was
left in sole charge until 1871 when she married an English
clergyman who at times lent a hand.

At each year's end when accounts had been cast, credit

---

[1] Frances Butler Leigh, *Ten Years on a Georgia Plantation since the War* (London,
1883).
[2] *Ibid.,* 34.   [3] *Ibid.,* 57.

balances paid to the Negroes, and debit balances carried over, there was tedious palaver about contracts for a new season; and agreements once made were hard to maintain.   In April, 1868: "I have had a good deal of trouble this last week with my people — not serious but desperately wearisome.   They are the most extraordinary creatures, and the mixture of leniency and severity which it is requisite to exercise in order to manage them is beyond belief.   Each thing is explained satisfactorily to them and they go to work.   Suddenly some one, usually the most stupid, starts an idea that perhaps by-and-by they may be expected to do a little more work, or be deprived of some privilege; upon which the whole field gets in the most excited state; they put down their hoes and come up to the house for another explanation, which lasts till the same thing happens again." [1]   By the end of that year the Negroes were getting quite out of hand despite the services of the mistress as school-teacher, physician and preacher; and she slept with a pistol by her bed.   "Poor people! it seems impossible to arouse them to any good ambition, their idea and desire being — not to work." [2]   Their numbers in the district, furthermore, were decreasing from destitution and death. A neighboring planter procured a corps of Chinese coolies; and Butler's Island imported a group of English farm laborers, only to find them drunken shirkers in contrast with the Irish ditching gangs which continued to come each winter.   But at length a change of system with the Negroes from crop sharing to wage labor diminished the occasions for misunderstanding; they gradually recovered "their senses and 'their manners'"; and the production of rice began to approach its old-time dimensions.

When ending her own story, Mrs. Leigh quoted from two letters which she found among the family papers.   They were from R. King, Jr., to his employer in 1827 and 1828.   In the first he wrote: "I killed twenty-eight head of beef for the people's Christmas dinner.   I can do more with them this way than if all the hides of the cattle were made into lashes."   In

---

[1] Frances Butler Leigh, *Ten Years*, 113.   [2] *Ibid.*, 147.

the second: "You justly observe that if punishment is in one hand, reward should be in the other. . . . We save many tons of rice by giving one to each driver; it makes them active and watchful." [1] With never a mention of her name nor an allusion to her book, and perhaps with no direct intention, the daughter thus refutes her mother's argument and poses experience against theory as to Negro quality, white responsibility, Pierce M. Butler's character and the régime on Butler's Island.

*   *   *   *   *

Another seaboard family of note was that descended from Noble Jones, a gentleman colonist who came to Georgia with Oglethorpe and established a seat at "Wormsloe" on an inlet near Savannah. The name of the estate suggests the concern with silk which prevailed when the colony was founded. But these fruitful worms would not thrive thereabout; and the land failing to produce anything else of much worth, except possibly indigo, the plantation became at length a mere country home of people whose income came from urban property or distant fields. Through public office, discreet marriages, sound investments and good management the family held high place among the gentry until George Noble Jones, with whom we are chiefly concerned, came to man's estate. After gaining experience through the management of an inland Georgia cotton plantation which his mother and aunts had inherited, he married in 1840 the widow of William B. Nuttall and thereby came into control of two cotton plantations in "middle Florida."

While a province of Spain and a territory of the United States the so-called Land of Flowers was generally avoided by immigrants because of the great sandiness of the soil. But in 1827 the territorial governor, paying a visit in Virginia, sang the praises of the district about Tallahassee. A citizen of Richmond wrote: "Our heads have been turned by a scheme to make a fortune in the purchase of Florida lands. Governor Duval has lately been at my house, and he represents the

[1] Frances Butler Leigh, *Ten Years*, 233, 234.

country as a perfect Canaan, flowing with milk and honey, and so healthy that the aged who have become settlers there have reacquired the vigor of health and youth." [1] It was probably in response to this that John, the father of William B. Nuttall, made a purchase of several thousand acres near Tallahassee and in 1828 sent the son from Virginia with fifty-two slaves to establish a plantation which was named "El Destino." Upon John's death William acquired the property, and by marriage with Mary Savage of Savannah doubled its corps of slaves. But by plunging heavily in land and bank-stock speculation he left a virtually bankrupt estate at his death in 1836. The widow continued the operation of El Destino, and now inheriting about eighty slaves from an uncle, she bought for their employment a second tract, called "Chemonie", six miles away. Her marriage to Jones put him in charge for the rest of a long life.

George Noble Jones maintained the traditions of his house and its manner of life. He loved good food, wine and sport, smooth adjustments, and cool summers, whether in Rhode Island or Switzerland. Somewhat studious as a proprietor, with a project indeed of building a factory on El Destino so as to sell his cotton as cloth instead of as lint, Jones attended well to business, requiring his overseers to keep detailed work journals and to send him fortnightly transcripts with accompanying letters. [2] He was thus an absentee owner, paying winter visits to his plantations until the reverses brought by the Civil War caused him to take residence for some years on El Destino. Upon these visits he doubtless experienced at the hands of his overseers and their wives what a Savannah friend described as "the peculiar horror of country life, that of keeping company all day, with the onus of talking thrown upon me."

[1] Letter of James E. Heath, October 13, 1827, to William Massie. Manuscript at the University of Texas.

[2] Copiously printed in U. B. Phillips and J. D. Glunt, eds., *Florida Plantation Records from the papers of George Noble Jones* (St. Louis, 1927, Publications of the Missouri Historical Society). For additional discussion and documents concerning El Destino and Chemonie see the *Florida Historical Quarterly*, 1929.

Jones' Georgia plantation attained in the 'fifties a scale of twenty-five plows and an output of three hundred bales of cotton; and its overseer, who was a veteran in that employ, was paid seven hundred dollars a year. The Florida units were somewhat smaller and their overseers were on wages of four hundred or five hundred dollars. El Destino was the larger of the two, but for Chemonie the records are fuller. In 1855, for example, its eighty-five slaves all told furnished eighteen plow hands including some women, eighteen hoe hands rating as fifteen able-bodied, and in addition a carpenter, a stock tender, a cook for the overseer, another for the gang, a scullion, and an old man who mainly raked leaves for fertilizer. The cast of crops was three hundred and eighty acres in cotton, three hundred and sixty in corn and cowpeas intermingled, one hundred and fifty-five in oats, and small tracts in sweet potatoes, peanuts, rice, and sugar cane for sirup. The large ratio of grain acreage indicates a low expectation of grain yield per acre. The cotton product of one hundred and twenty-eight bales, averaging somewhat less than five hundred pounds each, was perhaps not more than half of what perfect seasons might have brought as a maximum, often dreamed of but seldom attained. Enough pork was killed and cured on each plantation commonly to supply its personnel throughout the year; and part of the supply of cloth and all the baskets, mule collars and plow lines were made on the place. Mules, implements, bagging, rope, most of the cloth and any salt pork needed were bought from distant sources.

The overseers' journals are filled with the record of routine, more or less comprehensive according to the capacities and inclinations of their semi-literate writers. Some include notes of floggings, others omit such. The letters are concerned with the state of the crops and livestock, the health of the slaves, and any special occurrences. In the middle 'fifties the overseer on Chemonie was John Evans who though he begot two mulatto children before he took a wife, was trustworthy, sagacious and steady-going. He did not spare the lash when slaves fought among themselves or injured their mules, or indeed when they fell short in industry or cleanliness; but he was not a niggard with provisions, praise or small indulgencies. In consequence he had no crises, though at one time he expressed a fear that Jacob might attempt his life. An instance of his capacity is afforded by the case of Diana, who proved intractable on El Destino and was shifted to Chemonie. Evans promptly reported that she was among the fastest of his cotton pickers, gave no trouble, and would be welcome as a permanent member of his corps. An example of his indulgence was the sanction of a divorce: "Lafayette Renty asked for Leaf [*i.e.*, leave] to Marry Lear I also gave them Leaf. Rose, Rentys other wife, ses that she dont want to Live with Renty on the account of his having so Many Children, and they weare always Quarling so I Let them sepperate. Lear ses she is willing to Help Renty take care of his children." [1] In 1856, after five years of service, Evans had a mild quarrel with Jones and set himself up as an independent farmer with a few slaves of his own; but before the end of the decade he was again in charge of Chemonie.

On El Destino in 1854 D. N. Moxley became overseer upon the departure of an easy-going predecessor. The newcomer erred on the side of stringency. After some of his women had fainted while picking cotton on a specially hot August day he seems to have moderated his requirements for a while, but increased the stint when cool weather came. In early October he whipped four women for deficit of pickings, whereupon they ran off to Tallahassee in search of a protector. They went to Tom Blackledge, father of one of the group, and he enlisted the sympathy of his employer, Doctor Davis, who wrote to Jones in complaint. But the local jailer, learning of the fugitives, took them into custody and returned them to the plantation, after collecting his legal fees. Meanwhile a fifth girl, Venus, was caught by Moxley on the road, and was caught again when she broke away. Thereupon Aberdeen, her brother, advanced upon Moxley with an ax, but was seized by Prince, the foreman, and put into the plantation prison. This crisis was more than Moxley wanted to handle alone. He might

[1] *Florida Plantation Records*, 63.

have delivered Aberdeen to a public officer for trial on a charge of having committed a capital offense. Instead he summoned Evans from Chemonie, to witness the flogging of Aberdeen and to investigate the situation. Evans duly reported to Jones that the women's backs gave no evidence of excessive whipping, and he advised the retention of Moxley with a warning against future severity. After an investigation of his own Jones thanked Davis for his interest in the welfare of the Negroes concerned, but adopted Evans' advice in regard to the plantation.[1]

In the following July Moxley described a different tone of affairs: "You could not find grass anuff in the cotton crop to fill a cart bodey and as for the people I dont want eney better to mang [*i.e.*, manage] than they have bin. I want to give them a diner one day this weak for their good work and good behaver." [2] The crisis had cleared the air except as regards Tom Blackledge, whom Jones had ordered to keep away from the plantation because of a suspicion that he had prompted the women to run away. In the spring of 1856 this ban was lifted. Moxley protested, but Jones replied that feelings of humanity forbade him longer to exclude Tom, whose record for twenty years had been good, from access to his wife, "an old family servant, decent, well behaved woman", and his daughters who were "good negroes." The letter concluded: "Your authority has been firmly established, and I see no reasonable objection to Tom's visiting his family, provided he conducts himself with respect to you and conforms to the rules of the plantation." [3]

On the Jones estate in Jefferson County, Georgia, a similar stampede was narrowly averted. The overseer reported in August, 1858: "The Hands or a part of them are not doing so well. It seames that they are doing all they can to get up a riot with the Driver, and they are taulking of takeing the woods. I have seen some of the head ones and taulked to them, Phillip and big Abram. I have not settled the fuss they had, but will have to before I leave, and I am fearful from what I hear

[1] *Florida Plantation Records*, 107–125.   [2] *Ibid.*, 137.   [3] *Ibid.*, 151–153.

from them some of them will leave, though I will taulk to them well beforehand." A fortnight later he was able to write: "The riot I wrote you about with the Negroes I have settled by a promise from them that they would do so no more. They all seam satisfy and are doing well at this time." [1] Regrettably he fails to say what concession was made by the management in the solution of the crisis.

Some of Jones' slaves reared sheep as well as poultry of their own; all were privileged to cultivate patches on private account; and from some source they procured funds for the purchase of whiskey at Christmas. The work schedule of course was as constant as the weather permitted, except for three days at Christmas, a "lay-by" holiday in midsummer, and an occasional half or whole of a Saturday for clothes-washing, rest, or work upon the slaves' own crops. Virtually no work, of course, was done at night or on Sundays.

There were no epidemics recorded, but numerous cases of fever, most of which were presumably malarial; and among numerous other grounds of incapacitation an instance of persistent "dirt eating" by a Negro boy. A special cause of illness was reported by the mill manager in May, 1852: "There was forty one 41 of your Negroes Baptised Last Sunday in the Canall above the Bridge by James Page. It was the largest Negroe meeting I ever saw — Davy and Polly and all the young set. . . . N.B. . . . Filis Wallis was Baptised, and hur and Winter is down sick but not dangerous." [2]

Jones bought or sold hardly any slaves until 1860 when he reorganized his plantation affairs. He then sold to or through Joseph Bryan, a slave dealer at Savannah, fifty-three of the Chemonie corps, including three superannuates rated as having no value, for $47,750 less a deduction of $3550 for expenses and commissions. He filled the vacancy by dividing El Destino's overgrown corps; and he applied the proceeds to the purchase of his sister's interest in the Georgia plantation. The sandy loam of middle Florida was by this time so seriously

[1] Manuscripts in the Georgia Historical Society.
[2] *Florida Plantation Records*, 31.

depleted that many of its planters were moving to the west; [1] and Jones appears to have been prompted by short crops to reduce the scale of his operations in the district.

The war time is mainly blank in the Jones records. As to later experiences they are vivid again, but without reflecting light upon *ante-bellum* life. Suffice it here to say that Chemonie and El Destino gradually decayed until the twentieth century when the boll weevil made them virtually derelict. Urban investments, on the other hand, kept the proprietors within the ranks of the well-to-do. It is doubtful that these Florida plantations under absentee control were highly profitable at any time.

[1] "During the past two or three years there has been going on quite an important emigration of planters from Florida to the Mississippi Valley and Texas. . . . They say the delightful climate of Florida does not compensate the planter for the loss he suffers in consequence of the inferiority of the Florida soil as compared with that of the western river bottoms for the production of the great Southern staples. . . . Those who have tried the experiment for a year or two have all been greatly benefitted pecuniarily; and it seems probable that most of the heavy planters in Middle and West Florida will before long be drawn away from that country." — *Daily Crescent* (New Orleans), January 25, 1860.

CHAPTER XIV

PLANTERS OF THE SOUTHWEST

STATE boundaries were of little concern in the search for wealth. A senator from Georgia forsook his constituents — though not his office till the term expired — to join an Alabama stampede. This was Charles Tait, who, born in Virginia, had married and moved to Maryland when his father migrated to northeastern Georgia. Afterward he settled in the same Georgia county of Elbert, entered law and politics, became a circuit judge, and served from 1809 to 1819 as a senator in Congress. When his father died in 1816, leaving a parcel of Negroes, the senator and his son, James Asbury, who was now married and possessed of slaves, resolved upon a joint removal to a place of brighter prospect.

That winter James made a land-looking tour to the lower course of the Alabama River; and a year afterward with a few slaves he made a clearing and built some cabins in what is now Wilcox County.[1] His father, staying to set the main corps upon its journey, was embarrassed by the exorbitant prices demanded by his neighbors for the "broadwives" and children of two of his Negro men. But Hercules, forty-five years old, consented to leave his wife on an understanding that he was to revisit her within two years. In consequence Charles Tait wrote of the Negroes: "The manner they have acted and promise to act in leaving all cheerfully to go with us, I think, entitles them to much consideration. They deserve to be treated well; not only with justice but with tenderness. Too much cannot be done for Hercules. His noble and disinterested example has mainly effected this temper and disposition among our

[1] The Tait papers, comprising letters and a book of plantation jottings, are on deposit in the Alabama Department of Archives at Montgomery. For facilitation of their use I am indebted to Miss Ann Tait of Camden, Ala.

people." From the other end of the line came the news in due time that the cavalcade reached its destination "safe and in high spirits, as they were heard some time before they were seen." The father went to his duties at Washington, and in a letter thence described his ideal of a location which he hoped ere this the son had procured at the public land sales: "It unites fertility, salubrity and navigation," and as minor advantages has "a never failing spring at the foot of a hillock on the summit of which a mansion-house can be built in due time", an extensive range in the rear where cattle and hogs may grow and fatten without the aid of the corn crib, and on either flank an expanse of good land "where will settle an extensive body of good neighbors, and . . . we can have a post office convenient to us." The tract purchased proved somewhat malarious, however, and for a time the proprietors contemplated shifting their establishment from the river lands to the interior "pine barrens." But, perhaps because the slaves were expected to become immune, this sacrifice of transportation facilities and fertility for the sake of health was not made.

Shortly the Taits wanted to enlarge their force of slaves by purchase in a low market. After some inquiry Charles, who had now gone to Alabama, advised James to travel to Virginia with the money on his person, make his purchases and carry them home. A friendly slave trader had offered his companionship and aid in negotiation, and the father thought this opportunity should be embraced. The plan was not executed, for in 1821 inquiries were being made in the Mobile market without avail. But by the next spring at least one purchase had been made, which proved unsatisfactory. James wrote to his father: "The fellow you bought of Tutt is fitified or subject to convulsions. If he is comatible I would make him take the Negro back or sue him for the money." [1]

[1] A mere lack of toes where a slave had been bought on a presumption of completeness in his members might give rise to a lawsuit. An Alabama planter wrote to a Tennessee Dealer:

"Oakland, 20 Sepr., 1818

"Sir,

"I am sorry that I knew you so ill. I traded with you as an honest man; and you have practiced on me a base and monstrous imposition. It was night when I got

While Charles Tait was on a journey to Philadelphia one of his correspondents was a slave, Harford by name, who appears to have written an excellent hand. His letter, with omissions partly caused by a mouse's gnawing of the manuscript, reads as follows:

"Mobile, Nov. 6, 1826

"My dear Master

"Your kind favor to me through Mr. Caulborne has been duly recᵈ and I now hasten to answer the same and inform you how your affairs are going here. I left the plantation the 31ˢᵗ ultimo at which time they were coming on very well with the crop. Eighty Bales had then been packed, and they think they will have eighty more. I think the cotton is much cleaner than it was last year (ample room). The corn crop is very good, and I think they will have plenty for the next year. . . . I am sorry to have to inform you that nine of the children have died at the plantation, mostly with the Hooping Cough. . . . There will be five births at the plantation, and among the number Nancy is to give birth to one, after a suspension of fourteen years. . . . Times have been so hard that I have made but little for myself, but I am in hopes that I shall now do better. . . . I have another son named after myself . . . the respects of you affec. Sᵛᵗ unto D[eath] in hopes ever to merit your esteem

"Your most dutiful servant
"Harford."

Regrettably nothing more of Harford is to be found. His tale of children's deaths was one to distress any master.

home yesterday. This morning my overseer came to inform me that the negroes I bought of you had arrived, *and that the fellow had no toes to his feet.* I was satisfied of the fact by personal inspection; and then it was that I learnt the anecdote of the cotton so cunningly stuffed in front for show. To say that I have any longer any respect for you would be saying a falsehood. An honest man could never be guilty of such an act. The means of redress, however, are in my hands and I know how to use them. Much as I abhor lawsuits, I shall hold myself bound to expose you before a jury of your country unless you come down speedily, take back your negroes, and repay me my money. . . .

"I am, Sir,
"J. W. Walker."

Addressed to Chapley R. Wellborne, Fayetteville, Tenn. Manuscript in Alabama Department of Archives.

Charles Tait wrote to James two months afterward: "Our loss of little negroes has been great the past year, but I hope it will not happen again. Let us feed, clothe and house them well, and I do not fear but they will increase rapidly. With the stock we have there is a good prospect for the next generation."

Expansion of scale brought a separation of establishments.[1] Charles, who became a Federal judge with an Alabama circuit, set up two plantations, "Weldon" and "Springfield", and James eventually acquired four units. Each employed overseers, among whom J. B. Grace, in charge of Springfield and himself a slaveholder, has left the clearest view of his concerns. In August, 1834, he wrote to his employer: "The helth of ower negrowes is impruvin, thow thar is 8 field hands not abel to worke yet." In September: "I am agiting out coten just as [well as] I cold expect. Ower hans seemes as they cant git helthy." And in October: "I have had 5 hands dowen with the chill and fever all this week." 'In this letter and another of December he mentions a slave man bought by him, husband of one of his women, and discusses the problem of their employment. He might bring them and their children to swell the force on Springfield; but some of Tait's Negroes might get a notion that Grace's were better treated, so it would perhaps be better to hire them to some person elsewhere if the Negroes would consent to it.

In the spring of 1835 Charles Tait bought three young girls from some northward source, whereupon James advised him: "You are apprised, I suppose, that negroes from the north have to be favored the first year. Like Kentucky mules they have to be moderately worked, carefully treated, etc." Charles in turn wrote in the same tenor to Grace, who replied: "You

---

[1] It also brought a temporary embarrassment. James wrote in the fall of 1822: "I expect the alarming debt in Claiborne and Mobile together, and what with the pork and the cattle, will more than absorb the last year's crop [which as yet remained unsold]. These hairbreadth escapes are rather appalling to a man of my cloth. I do not know how it is with you. For my part I feel disposed to return to the good old first principles, of economy, keep clear of embarrassments, use the same means to preserve your property as to get it."

nede not be one esy about the new handes worken to hard
becase ower work is lite and they git out of task by 10 and 11
oclock in A.M." James Tait approved the purchase particularly because it was of young girls; but Grace had a special
reason for wishing they were older. His remarks in these
premises are perhaps the most vivid extant in regard to slave
matings: "I wish the three girls you purchest had been all
grown. They wold then bin a wife a pese for Harise & King &
Nathan. Harris has Jane for a wife and Nathan has Edy.
But King & Nathan had sum difuculty hoo wold have Edy.
I promist King that I wold in dever to git you to bey a nother
woman sow he might have a wife at home. He is envious that
you wold git a nuther woman, as he has quit his wife that he
had at Netoles, thinking that he wold git Edy for a wife. I
am willing to take Vilet at the same price you give for her and
pay you the expence in bringing her from Mobile, or eny other
expence you were at. As she is too young for eney of your men
a wife and you hav small girls enough for your young boys,
and then you can by a woman in her place for King a wife."

The lack of romantic atmosphere in this proposal was not
likely to diminish the strength of its appeal, for Charles Tait
himself, tiring of widowhood and casting about in his mind for
a fitting mate, who he said must be a childless gentlewoman
not less than forty-five years old, had proposed by letter in
1822 to a Georgia widow whom he had not seen for twenty
years. She accepted, and met him at Mobile where they were
married.

The death of Charles in the fall of 1835 doubtless accounts
in the main for the trebling of his son's slaves between 1832
and 1837, though James' own women were prolific, their children were cherished, and he continued to purchase parcels until
the end of his available record. In 1837, when his landholdings
aggregated some four thousand acres, the statistics as shown
on page 279 are available for his four industrial units.

The weight of the bales is not given; but if the crop as picked
yielded no more than one fourth of its weight in lint, they were
of about five hundred pounds each; and the crop at the current

| | SLAVES | | PLOW HORSES AND MULES | ACRES IN COTTON | SEED COTTON PRODUCED (POUNDS) | COTTON BALES MARKETED | CORN REQUIRED (BUSHELS) |
	Over 10 Years	Under 10 Years					
Old Place . . .	55	36	16	320	370,000	191	3000
Lower Place . .	27	3	7	180	262,000	134	1200
Over River Place	50	23	14	260	345,000	178	2500
Dry Fork [1] . .	8	9					800
	140	71	37	760	977,000	503	7500

prices must have brought some thirty-five thousand dollars. Whether included in the tabulation or additional thereto, there were produced some fifteen tons of seed cotton [2] from the slaves' own patches, returning more than a thousand dollars for apportionment among them.

The corn crop was cast each year with a view to home needs only, at an expectation of twenty bushels per acre. In 1832, when the slaves numbered seventy-two, the prospective need of corn was analyzed as follows in Tait's book of plantation jottings:

785 for bread, at a peck of meal per week for each slave over ten years and half as much for young children, plus the needs of the planter's family and the overseer
200 for stock hogs, at fifty ears per day
200 for fattening hogs, fifty in number
375 for ten plow horses during five months
120 for four gin horses during four months
200 for the hogs and the horses at Dry Fork
1880 as the total estimate

In hoeing the cotton crop James Tait used the task system, with fifty rows "an acre in length" as the standard stint in the spring season when the work required some care. After the middle or end of June, when the stalks were sturdy, the task was doubled unless the fields were foul. Children were set

---

[1] "Dry Fork" may have been the grist and sawmill which Tait operated, though the name seems inappropriate.

[2] Seed cotton is the crop as it comes from the field, *i.e.*, before the lint and seed have been separated by ginning.

to work at the age of ten, each child for his first year to help its mother perform a single stint. As the years advanced the requirement increased, but no full task was assigned until the teens were ended. Child-bearing women had their stints reduced, and men and women alike after passing their fiftieth years. On May 30, 1838, Tait noted that two thirds of his hoe hands had finished their tasks by eleven o'clock in the morning. The fact that he made this jotting implies that the occurrence was quite unusual, as of course it must have been.

During the whole season of cultivation the hoes and plows were plied with such constancy as the weather might permit. The first working of the crop of 1837 on the "Over River Place", for example, required fourteen days of plowing with twelve horses, and eleven days of hoeing; and the second cultivation only awaited the completion of the first. One year, doubtless because of the stimulation of the grass by frequent rains, his cotton fields were hoed six times. The ending of work on the growing crop left a few short weeks for general jobs, and perhaps a bit of holiday, before the harvest began, which in its early portion was esteemed a "sickly season", requiring special precautions for health. The Negroes then, Tait said, must never leave their quarters before sunrise so long as the cotton foliage remained green; and when their work lay on the farther side of a field a path must be cleared "so that the dew on the cotton will not get on them till they get to their work." The picking squads, furthermore, must come back to the quarters at noon: "To straighten up and walk to the houses and back again is a great relief to them."

When the picking was completed there came once more a few weeks for jobs out of crop. In Tait's winter program of 1836–1837, mules were to be broken and horse pens made in the swamp, timber cut and put through the mill, a flatboat built, new grounds cleared and fenced, two cotton houses erected, and all such cabins as had stood for three years in one place moved to new spots. In explanation of this last Tait remarked: "Negroes' houses ought to be moved regularly once in two or three years — I mean cabins. The filth accumulates under the floor so much in two years as to cause disease." To this filth, indeed, he attributed the prevalence of diphtheria — "putrid sore throat" he called it — which had brought one winter the deaths of four Negro children.

In 1839 Tait planned to replace his cabins with brick barracks. The one designed for his "Old Place" was to be three hundred feet long, eighteen feet wide in the clear, with walls eight feet high. Partitions were to be built at fifteen-foot intervals, and a fireplace provided for each room. He negotiated with one McPhaii to superintend the making and do the laying of the one hundred and thirty thousand brick required, for a lump sum of five hundred dollars; but the available record is silent as to performance. It may be that the collapse of the cotton market at the close of that year prevented the accomplishment.

As regards clothing, Tait in the late 'thirties had a standing order with R. G. Hazard of Peace Dale, Rhode Island, for four bales of yard-wide cotton homespun or osnaburgs, to contain twenty-five hundred yards, at a price of about seventeen and and a half cents per yard; and from other sources he procured annually some eight hundred yards of twilled woolens at about thirty-two cents. His own seamstresses made this into clothing, to supply each man with two shirts and two pair of cotton breeches every spring and a woolen jacket and a pair of woolen breeches in the fall. Each woman was issued two chemises and two cotton frocks in the fall, and a woolen jacket every other year. Women were notably less expensive to clothe than men in that régime! Annual issues of shoes also are mentioned in the records. The silence concerning hats and children's clothes is not an evidence that these were lacking.

James Tait seems to have changed his overseers nearly every year. One in 1837 was particularly annoying. Among his offenses were a failure to tan leather, though he pretended to have done it; neglecting a fire in the field and permitting a fence to burn; neglecting livestock and slaves, with consequent deaths of two horses, a mule, a steer, a slave woman and a boy:

letting the Negroes get fence rails from a neighbor's woods and otherwise embroiling Tait with adjacent planters; and "making my negro men run away by interfering with their wives, or on account of the women." These experiences prompted him to jot maxims, never to talk to an overseer about his neighbors, and with special emphasis: "A legacy to my children. — Never employ an overseer who will equalize himself with the negro women. Besides the morality of it, there are evils too numerous to be now mentioned."

Hiring a slave carpenter at two dollars a day for nearly a year, Tait had built himself a permanent home in 1834–1835 at a cost of twenty-six hundred dollars, and expended twenty-two hundred dollars for a piano and other furniture. The house was of a pattern standard in that country, with a hall running from front to rear on each floor, flanked by two rooms on either side, a two-story veranda in front and a one-story porch at the rear. As to sash and blinds he deliberated between ordering these from Boston or having the carpenter 'Kiah and his helper 'Lijah make them on the spot; but he fails to say which alternative he chose. In that homestead Tait spent his remaining years, and from it he sent a son or two to the University of Alabama; but after the end of the 'thirties his pen grew negligent in his book of jottings — and except for his one outburst against an overseer he confided to paper, from first to last, few of his joys or sorrows.

❊   ❊   ❊   ❊   ❊

Another migrant from Georgia was Benjamin Fitzpatrick, who in Alabama married a daughter of Governor Elmore and for some years practiced law at Montgomery. In 1829 he removed to "Oak Grove", a dozen miles up the Coosa River, where he spent the rest of his life except while serving as governor and senator. In February, 1860, a traveling correspondent visited his plantation,[1] which then had some four hundred acres of rich land in cultivation. Behind the mansion, which commanded a broad valley view from its verandas, were the

[1] His report is in the New York *Herald*, March 8, 1860.

dairy, the smokehouse containing thirty thousand pounds of pork, the barn, corn cribs and wagon sheds, and, somewhat removed, a group of Negro cabins. On a stream bank stood a grist and sawmill, and in another part of the tract a second slave quarter and the overseer's house. In the senator's absence a son was in principal charge. The reporter visited the home quarter in the evening when the Negroes were clustered about blazing pitch-pine fires. Mary, the nurse and "doctoress", boasted that she had not lost an adult patient in two years; and the longevity of superannuates, one of whom had done no work for twenty-five years, suggests that Mary's care or some other factor was effective in some cases beyond the point of economic advantage. Betsey, the mother of sixteen children, still had vanity enough to make "a display of crinoline that would have satisfied the most fastidious Broadway belle."

March, a mulatto field hand, had earned thirty dollars from his cotton patch the last year, and "throwed most of it away" in the purchase of a watch. A sage of seventeen years, he was disinclined to matrimony. "These women must dress, you see, and after using up their pile they fall back upon ours, which keeps us poor all the time. No, sir; I'll never get married." Jack the miller made one or two hundred dollars a year by milling on his own time, and Adam the carpenter one hundred and fifty dollars from a peach and apple nursery which was his fad, and a like amount from his cotton patch. He owned an ox and cart, and had one thousand dollars on loan to neighboring planters for which he held their interest-bearing notes. Dennis the deacon and Austin the blacksmith gave tales of their own achievements and ambitions, while all were disposed to praise the talents of Bill the fiddler.

In the preceding year thirty-one bales of cotton had gone to market from the slaves' own patches, grading higher and bringing better prices than the master's crop. The proceeds, the young master said, were most commonly drawn in silver and buried in the woods for safe keeping; but some of the slaves were learning the virtues of savings banks. The overseer was asked whether he could get as much work from Negroes as might be expected from white people. "Yes, sir," he replied, "I could if I was to watch them close. You see negroes are naturally lazy and require pushing. Some of them, though, never require talking to, and will do a fair day's work whether you are watching them or not." As to the females of the species, "Some of them work better than the men. I have got three women here that I will back against any three men in the country for ploughing, I don't care whar you bring them from." Truancy was rare and always followed shortly by voluntary return. Some among the slaves had never felt a lash in their lives. Except for the reminiscent remarks thus reported, we have no continuing view of this group's experience.

❈   ❈   ❈   ❈   ❈

The affairs of another Easterner moved west may be gathered from his daughter's book [1] which if rose-tinted is evidently veracious in all important matters. A scion of John Daubigné, a Huguenot whose listed descendants exceeded six thousand within two centuries, Thomas Smith Dabney was cousin to most of the Virginia notables of his day. After schooling in New Jersey and at William and Mary College, he dwelt in seeming permanence as a wealthy planter at "Elmington" fronting the Chesapeake, until 1835 when he caught the western contagion. Now, in his thirty-eighth year, he had buried his first wife and her children, and had married a girl of sixteen who was to bear him sixteen living children and never to be without a babe in arms for thirty years.

After journeying to Mississippi and buying a group of adjacent farms in Hinds County, Dabney returned to lead forth his family and slaves and a group of kinsfolk who resolved to settle near his new home. On the eve of the trek his Virginia neighbors, including John Tyler, Mann Page and many others, gave his party a public dinner at Gloucester Courthouse at which many Godspeed sentiments were drunk and duly reported through the *Richmond Enquirer*. Dabney had notified his slaves that he would buy or sell at their preference to prevent

[1] Susan Dabney Smedes, *Memorials of a Southern Planter* (Baltimore, 1887).

the separation of families; but none asked to be sold, and several abandoned their broadwives or husbands whose masters refused to sell them. The journey, routed through East Tennessee and carefully managed, was made without mishap, and the new plantation, christened "Burleigh", was prosperously settled. Its four thousand acres of hill and dale were of good soil, particularly the "newgrounds" which were cleared year by year. In one banner season he made six hundred bales of cotton on as many acres. To wagon such a crop forty miles for shipment at Grand Gulf was itself no small task. The back haul was light, for he cast his grain crops and bred hogs, cattle and sheep on a scale to assure full food supplies for his family and his two hundred slaves.

Though he long dwelt in a makeshift house, Dabney's manner of life was always elegant and punctilious. Never an early riser, "he maintained that it did not so much matter when a man got up as what he did after he was up." His dress was of broadcloth with plated buttons and doubtless of ruffled shirts; and his children had tutors and his sons attended college in Virginia. One of these went to Harvard for later study, with a special gift of a thousand dollars with which to buy books. At Burleigh dinner was a ceremonious meal for which every one was expected to be ready and at hand five minutes before the second bell was rung. There were summer sojourns at Pass Christian on the Gulf coast, and summer visits with eight or ten in the party to relatives in Virginia. In the autumn Dabney would lead a group of companions to camp in the prairies of Scott County, in central Mississippi, where one year they killed more than a hundred deer; and in winter he would travel to New Orleans to sell his cotton, play whist and talk Whig politics at the Boston Club,[1] and buy finery for his wife and daughters. Some plain folk among his neighbors found this grandee to be objectionably patronizing; but to his slaves he seems to have been ideal as a master, and his wife as a mistress. Preferring rewards to punishments, his continued prosperity proved his benign discipline effective. In the course

[1] So named not from the city of Boston but from a game of cards.

of his life he sold no slaves except four offenders, one of whom had tried to kill the overseer.   Among the few whom he bought was Alcey, a cook who had belonged to his mother.   Leaving her husband in Virginia till negotiations for his purchase could be completed, Alcey found herself such a belle at Burleigh that she soon said: "Tell Marster not to bother 'bout sendin' for him.   He lazy an' puny an' no 'count."

Dabney survived the war's cataclysm by two decades, to die in poverty but not in depression, far from his beloved Burleigh; but we shall not follow further his devoted daughter's tale except to quote with her a last expression.   "I could never forget that I was born a gentleman."

❋   ❋   ❋   ❋   ❋

A contemporary of Dabney in Hinds County, offering many contrasts to that mellow patrician, was Martin W. Philips, energetic and irascible, impatient of genteel inhibitions, loquacious of tongue and pen, eager to test innovations, and greedy for fame as a promoter of betterments.   Philips put himself copiously on record by contributing perhaps a hundred articles to a dozen farm journals and by writing a diary which has found its way into print.[1]   He journeyed much to attend fairs and conventions, whether agricultural, Democratic, or Baptist; and his home, "Log Hall", was a favorite place of call for such traveling correspondents as R. L. Allen and Solon Robinson.

Born in 1806 at Columbia, South Carolina, and reared through a frail youth by a strict father, Philips took a degree in medicine; but, "forced from want of patients to quit the pill-tile and give up the spatula", he turned to farming and moved to Mississippi in company with his father-in-law.   A purchase of slaves on credit enabled him to attain a considerable scale until the panic of 1839 brought a visit of the sheriff and a reduction of working force to ten hands.   For some years thereafter an overseer was a luxury beyond his means; but his

[1] *Mississippi Historical Society Publications*, X, 305–481.   The diary extends from 1840 to 1863.

brother Zachariah assumed most of the management and left Martin partially free to continue his indefatigable inquiries, experiments and scribblings. He calculated the distance his best plowman walked in a day while skimming the cotton furrows, and found it to be twenty-one miles. He reckoned the expense of spreading forest leaves on a corn field, appraising a day's work at forty cents per hand and twenty-five cents per mule, and concluded that it must increase the yield by three bushels per acre for two years if the cost of the work were to be recouped. He counted the cotton seed in a pound; he tested them as feed for pigs, with disaster, and as fertilizer, with marked benefit. He bought blooded pigs, and weighed them periodically. He bought blooded cattle and sheep also, and the latest types of plows, cultivators and feed cutters. He had hoes made specially of steel in place of iron, and required them to be kept sharp by filing. He tested every strain of cotton in the market as to growth and yield, ease of picking, and the ginning ratio of lint to seed; and he advertised approved strains of seed for sale. He studied his soils and in some degree rotated his crops; he set hedges of osage oranges, wild peaches and Cherokee roses; he dug drains and built levees in his lowlands; he devised hopeful methods for producing a hundred and fifty bushels of corn per acre; he set large orchards of many varieties of apples and peaches, budding, grafting and topping the trees; and he tried virtually every sort of grain, grass, melon and garden vegetable he could find in seedsmen's lists or procure from correspondents or the patent office. He sought to compare the merits of seldom as against frequent cultivation of the growing cotton, and the relative economy of speed as against care in the picking of the crop. His conclusion here was that striving for quantity instead of quality in picking was the more profitable, because the market's discount on trashy bales did not offset the differential in the volume harvested. He confided all these things to the public prints or to his diary. "I am not orthodox," he wrote, "nor do I hope there is a solitary man simple enough to follow me. My object is to ferret out the best plan, not caring whether science or tom-foolery gives the principles." [1]   And again : "I cannot accumulate property, nor do I have that sort of a desire : I see so many things I want, that I spend my dollars before I get them to jingle." [2]

The name "Log Hall", which Philips did all he could to celebrate, was itself an advertisement of his heterodoxy, for most dwellers in log houses were not inclined to publish the fact.   The structure, well built of hewn timbers, had a central chimney affording a fireplace to each of its four rooms, and therefore was without the usual hallway.   Flanked by a guest house, it stood embowered by primeval trees which afforded nesting places for mocking birds, doves and orioles.   From the porch the flower garden was in view, bordered with box, studded with roses and cape jessamines, and brilliant with many sorts of annuals and perennials.   To the rear, beyond the detached kitchen, was a vegetable garden ample for the slaves as well as the master, yielding cabbages by the thousand, asparagus, tomatoes, berries, and many other things which Philips listed but we need not.   Separately clustered were the overseer's house, the Negro cabins, and a cook house for the service of the gang, with a copious barn, the stables and a hog house conveniently near.   He made a point of having his mule troughs never empty ; and in answer to a correspondent he wrote on a June day : "I have no 'poor starved niggers.'   So far from it, I guess they dine on as nice bacon, cabbage heads, beans and Irish potatoes as any other man white or black." [3]

In the summer of 1854, when his corps had for some years been supplemented by a number of slaves belonging to his son-in-law, he described his scale and method of operation in a letter to the New York *Tribune:* [4]   "We now have in this estate 1168 Acres of land ; on the place 66 negroes, twenty work horses or mules, five yoke of choice oxen.   We plant 270 or 280 acres in cotton, and 125 in corn.   We send to the field thirty-four negroes, old and young, rating them at thirty hands ; have one carpenter ; a woman who cooks for the above,

---

[1] *American Agriculturist*, VI, 317.
[2] *Cultivator*, n. s., V, 255.   [3] *American Agriculturist*, V, 286.
[4] Reprinted in F. L. Olmsted, *Seaboard Slave States*, 697–699.

with all children in charge." The overseer, he continued, owned and fed his own maidservant; and nine slaves, including seamstresses and two delicate children, were fed in the master's kitchen. For the remaining fifty-six the plantation cook was furnished twenty-two to twenty-four pounds of fat bacon daily, and unlimited meal, vegetables and buttermilk. No cooking was permitted in the slaves' own cabins. "We do not permit negroes to stir out before day, nor to get wet if possible, nor do any night work save feeding horses and shelling corn. . . . We give a day or a half-day's holiday occasionally during the summer, two to four days at Christmas, and a dance when the young ones desire it." Whippings were very seldom: "Although very hard work this year, owing to so much rain, no grown negro has required more than calling his name and telling him to hurry." His low ratio of corn land to cotton, as compared with that customary in more easterly regions, was due to his high yield of forty bushels per acre. Cowpeas were always planted between his corn rows, and in addition there were fields or patches of oats, millet, sweet potatoes, peanuts, rice and melons.

Philips's own slaves did not multiply. Within thirty years he lost "five grown negroes and no telling the number of young ones." Of nineteen children borne by his woman Amy, for example, nearly all died in infancy. The adults were often ill,[1] though he sometimes judged one to be "more lazy and mad than sick." He suspended the pulling of fodder and the threshing of oats when the work proved injurious; he built cisterns as a source of more healthful water than springs; but slaves, and blooded livestock likewise, died despite his care and to his keen distress. One man only stands out as having never lost a day's work except from a case of measles until a mule's kick laid him upon his deathbed. Thereupon an epitaph was inscribed in the diary: "Peyton is no more: aged 42. Though he was a bad man in many respects, yet he was a most excellent field hand. . . . I wish we could hope for his eternal

---

[1] "If I could keep my negroes as straight by night as by day," he said in 1846, "I never would fear disease." *Southern Cultivator*, IV, 127.

state." When recording another death, that of a slave boy, Philips said he was "a remarkable child of his age, a pet of us all. I feel as if I had lost some dear relative."

The slaves were permitted to raise cotton in patches assigned them, and were paid for splitting shingles and doing other jobs in their free time. On the other hand their liberty was restrained in a measure on Sundays by a requirement that they attend preaching. This rule was a grievance to an overseer, Champion by name, who said it was "a sin to make negroes attend, and against his conscience." A predecessor, Elisha Nail, begat a mulatto son on the plantation, who was born after his father's departure but named for him nevertheless. A successor, Samuel Simms, rode off in a rage after ten days of service because some new-coming Negroes were lodged in an unused part of his house. In general the overseers, whose wages ranged from two to five hundred dollars, seldom served for more than a year, except one Gordon who was adjudged by Philips in 1861 to be the best he had ever had. Of a slave who was tried as a foreman Philips wrote: "Jerome is totally unfit to direct. It will not do to trust him." And he remarked at large, "negroes . . . are a don't care sort of fellows." Some, however, took thought enough to run away, and one was a persistent absconder. As to punishments there are no entries; but the lack of record is not an evidence that none were applied.

The diary ended in 1863 when Philips became a refugee from the Federal invasion. He lived a quarter-century longer, but was not afterward a planter. At last report Log Hall still stands, though its appearance no longer suggests the name, for like many another hewn-log dwelling it has been weatherboarded without and plastered within, to the concealment of its original walls.

*   *   *   *   *

For the source of the next family whose plantation records are fruitful [1] we turn to an unusual quarter. William Palfrey

---

[1] The Palfrey papers are in private possession. For access to them I am indebted to the generosity of Mr. William G. Palfrey and to the good offices of Mr. Worthington C. Ford.

SCHERTZ RESIDENCE

PARLANGE

OAK GROVE

Louisiana Houses of Informal Types

was a Boston merchant, not merely trading locally but using the sea lanes to sell goods, including slaves on occasion, in Virginia, Carolina and the West Indies, and proving a chatty visitor when accompanying his cargoes. On the James River he learned backgammon from a jovial tavern keeper, and undertook without success to give a Quaker as many thee's as he got. On the Ferguson estate near Charleston in 1774 he chided his host for holding so many men in bondage, and got in reply nothing, he said, but "hackneyed arguments", which is a surprising phrase in these premises at such an early time. When lost at sea in 1780 he left a widow, a son John and a daughter Susanna, who lived in straightened circumstances until the widow married a wealthy Bostonian as a second husband. John Palfrey, born in 1768, went out in 1789 as clerk to a merchant in Demarara, which may be found upon the map of South America in the present Guiana. There he shared in diverse affairs, thence he ordered ruffled shirts and lottery tickets to be bought in Boston, and thence he went home in 1792, only to return at once to Demarara as a merchant with William Loring of Boston as a partner. He bought a slave or two and was about to shift from commerce to plantation business when disturbances in Europe spoiled the sugar prospect and sent him back to Boston. He now married Mary Gorham, made sundry voyages as a supercargo, plied a shipchandler's trade in partnership with Gamaliel Bradford, and went bankrupt.

Upon the purchase of Louisiana by the United States he removed to New Orleans as a ship-chandler, only to meet bankruptcy again. Next he undertook the management of a sugar plantation on the "German Coast" of the Mississippi, belonging to his wife's brother-in-law, George Phillips. When Phillips was dispossessed by bankruptcy in 1809, the establishment was taken over by Palfrey, with James Johnson of New Orleans as partner and under heavy mortgage. The corps of slaves had come partly from Maryland, partly from Africa. Its thirty-two men were badly proportioned to the twelve women and five children; and this may have contributed to the troublous experience encountered. In the expense-book payments to slaves for night and Sunday work were no more frequent than outlays for the recapture of runaways. The goings and comings of these are usually noted in detail, but under date of October 25, 1807, is an entry: "American Hercules runs away and is brought back so frequently or returns 'of his own accord', that I don't deem it necessary to note it." American Hercules, so styled in distinction from an African of the same name, continued a problem until the following June, when he hanged himself. There were difficulties with other chronic runaways, a violent contretemps with an overseer crazed by drink, — and a bankruptcy dispossessing Palfrey and Johnson in 1810.

Whatever his traits as a master, Palfrey thus far had qualities which bound friends to him through fair times and foul. He now made a land-looking journey to the Bayou Teche district, and, aided by a loan from his stepfather and credit from a slave-dealing firm at New Orleans, he bought a new parcel of slaves and a tract of wild land on Bayou l'Albaye, not far from the present St. Martinsville, with a view to producing cotton. But his latest bankruptcy and the death of his wife had broken his spirit. He named his new place "Forlorn Hope", and upon it spent the rest of his life in almost uninterrupted seclusion. Thither came, one after another, four sons whom he had left at Boston for schooling, and thence after a time he sent them successively as articled clerks to merchants at New Orleans. Of these sons Edward died of yellow fever in 1816; George was wounded in a duel in 1824 and recovered only to fall victim to the yellow scourge; while Henry William and William Taylor outlived their father, and their many letters to him supplement the Forlorn Hope journals as well as narrating their own careers.

The journal of 1811 records the arrival of John Palfrey at Forlorn Hope on April 6 and the prompt beginning of work by his corps. The twenty-three slaves, mostly in family groups, were in good ratio as to age and sex, but some of them shortly proved not well disposed. Amos and Harry ran away on

May 11, but were brought back in a few days. On July 24 these twain made off again and stayed out for some weeks before being restored through Opelousas jail. Amos now stayed at home with a shackle on his leg; but Harry, though presumably shackled, seldom let a month pass until the next summer without a flight, finding, however, no long reprieve nor much comfort. After a five days' truancy in April, for example, he was caught "in the neighborhood of the cabins, in pursuit of provisions, nearly famished. By his account he has eaten but once since he ran away." Amos meanwhile had had his leg iron removed by a blacksmith, but Harry continued to wear his until September. The work record shows offenders being disciplined by Sunday work, and there is suggestion also that the lash was not withheld.

Crude buildings had been quickly raised and the prairie sod readily broken by oxen after softening rains. A fairly full crop was cast the first year, and the yield was such as to keep the corps picking cotton from September to February. Three women picked as steadily as the weather permitted, gathering at the maximum about a hundred pounds each per day. Several boys and girls were as regular at lesser weights. The slave men joined the squad when not at other tasks; and two sons of the master, Henry and Edward, lent their help on occasion, turning in weights near the maximum. Lacking a gin of his own, Palfrey could not send his crop to market until a neighbor had ginned it in the course of the summer of 1812. By that time the outbreak of war with Great Britain had reduced the price to distressing levels, at which Palfrey's pressure of debt forced him to sell. Meanwhile the crop of 1812 had been cast — fifty acres in cotton, and other acreages not specified. The season proved capricious and the cotton yield was light, though the corn fields gave a surplus for sale. The next year, 1813, was one of adversity. A great flood in June and July killed much of the cotton, and upon receding left a plague of malaria so unsparing that the cooking of meals must have been suspended had not ague among the women come upon them on different schedules. Palfrey himself was among

those severely invalided.   Happily there was no toll of deaths;
but the doctor's bill and other expenses could be met only
by the sale of a slave man for five hundred and twenty-five
dollars.

The war's dislocation of trade now prompted Palfrey to
forsake tillage for the time and shift his force down Bayou
Teche to boil salt and profit from the famine price thereof.
But no sooner had he built his works and overcome the difficulties of a novice than the return of peace broke the salt
market.   The price of cotton went skyward, to thirty cents or
more; but Palfrey had let Forlorn Hope and could not regain
possession till the end of 1815.   His bad luck was becoming
proverbial among his sons.

When planting was begun again in 1816 the diary was not
resumed except in skeleton form.   For a dozen years he persisted with cotton.   He built a gin in 1822 and procured new
seed from Tennessee of a strain permitting harvest to begin in
early August instead of mid-September.   He shipped two crops
to Liverpool, hoping for better prices than were offered at New
Orleans.   But his devices were of little avail.   To explain
his inability to pay his long-standing debt, he wrote his stepfather that his best exertions had never brought more than
a frugal subsistence.   The rot in his cotton fields and the
low prices of the staple "particularly when the crop was by
any means tolerable", had been his chief handicaps.

In truth, the moist climate of the Teche region made it
poorly suited to cotton; and Palfrey, learning this from painful
experience, now began a shift to sugar, which was completed
in 1829 by the building of a mill to work up this product.   The
new staple brought fairly steady if modest prosperity.   Of
course it gave no surcease from "this everlasting hunting for
overseers",[1] but added instead a new task of getting a specialist
in sugar-boiling for each harvest.   It brought, indeed, a frantic
but unavailing search in 1833 for hands on hire to help in the

---

[1] He changed overseers eight times in fifteen years.   Their wages were usually
$200 or $250 a year.   Incidentally Palfrey employed an Indian as huntsman in 1817,
at $6 per month.

harvest of a specially heavy crop. But it permitted the old man to clear himself of debt before his death.

Meanwhile, whether engaged in cotton or sugar, the Palfrey slaves had multiplied. Some of his women bore children almost as regularly as two-year intervals passed. As compared with sixty-eight births, there were twelve deaths of babies before they were named, three deaths in later infancy, and five among adults. The net result was that by natural increase the corps of twenty-three in 1811 was more than trebled when Palfrey died in 1843. This is the more remarkable in that Forlorn Hope had never known a mistress. It plainly tells that Palfrey had learned to be a much more considerate and effective master than the record of his runaways indicates for his first Louisiana decade.

At the end of the Forlorn Hope journal William T. Palfrey penciled the following:

"January 1, 1845.

"The Plantation having been sold to Mr. A. J. Magill, possession was this day given by its former to its present owners.

"It has remained in possession of the same individual during a period of thirty-two, and the same family thirty-four years — an uncommon thing in this country.

"Its history has presented many vicissitudes. It was commenced 'from the stump', the settler in very straitened circumstances, owing a large debt. He succeeded, however, in paying up honestly all he owed, leaving a considerable estate to his heirs, and what they value more, an honest name behind him.

"The writer, one of his sons, is now one year older than was his ancestor when he came to settle on this place, has remained with him or near him since the year 1818, attended him in his last sickness, saw him laid in his peaceful grave, has settled his estate as executor under his will, and now takes leave of his 'patriarchal acres', his memory crowded with the recollections of many pleasing as well as affecting scenes he has passed through and with the hope that during that period he has not been unmindful of his filial duties toward one who was not only his father but his friend."

SEVEN OAKS   BELLE GROVE

WOODLAWN

Louisiana Mansions

The writer was by this time a substantial planter on his own score. At the close of a mercantile apprenticeship he had gone to sea for several voyages; but having drawn a large prize in a lottery, he converted it into slaves and for some years joined his fortunes with his father's on Forlorn Hope. He then became sheriff of St. Martin's parish, and later a banker and local judge at Franklin on the lower Teche. Meanwhile he married into a planting family, and in partnership with his brothers-in-law he bought a plantation near Franklin and proved himself a capable manager. His corps was swelled by the employment of one Jacobs as overseer who brought six slaves of his own. Jacobs proved not only a good farmer but something of a physician as well; and by dint of experience his employer acquired some skill in handling malaria and combating the yellow fever which decimated his district in 1839. He had already studied cholera during the epidemic of 1832, and had learned from a physician's error that an ague-stricken patient should not be bled.

This planter was often hampered by illness in his corps and his family, by hurricanes and excessive rain. His low latitude, however, gave his sugar cane a long growing season; and sometimes a wholly frostless year-end brought the luxury of leisured harvesting in a fully ripened crop. His scale, thrice as large as his father's, was such as occasionally to yield three hundred hogsheads of sugar. He was expert, steady-going and never unprosperous, and his liking for plantation life caused his lines to lie in pleasant places.

His brother Henry followed a different scheme of life. While yet a youth a kinsman at New Orleans wrote of him: "I think he is a little disposed to be *creolized*, but I gave him such lectures about his balls, plays, etc., as I believe restrained him a great deal. He is certainly very industrious and money making, and will make it where other boys would starve, but I tell him he is sometimes rather too much of a *Yankee* in his bargains, which will be got over, no doubt, when he sees a little more of the world." In 1817 he was part owner[1] of a hydraulic com-

---

[1] His partnerships were of kaleidoscopic succession.

press to reduce the size of cotton bales for export, together with a few slaves for its operation. This seasonal business brought a problem of idle summers. In 1818 he left town for a while, only to write upon return: "I found all my hands had been playing their pranks during my absence. Two were runaway, one sick, another complaining of all kinds of diseases, another drunk, and only one at work." And shortly afterward, to his father again: "If you can procure me a good overseer who is accustomed to the management of negroes and is capable of taking charge of six of the greatest scoundrels here, I will thank you to do it." When the next summer approached he sent some of them to his father's plantation "to have respite from drunkenness, sickness and laziness." One was a mulatto, Scott, "who can do any two men's work at any trade or job, or indeed (to be candid) at any rascality." In further description: "Scott is about 24 years old, a first rate cooper, a good blacksmith, bricklayer, cartman and oarsman, . . . speaks English, French and Spanish, . . . will steal, but seldom gets drunk." A second, Jack by name, was described as a capable workman and no runaway, but addicted to theft and drink. These two were to be sold if practicable. Concerning a third: "As Friday is the most harmless and best disposed fool in the country, I will keep him, as he answers very well to haul cotton." Scott was not sold on the Teche, but returned to the compress and commended himself so well that his master wrote in 1825: "Scott has become the most valuable fellow in our employ, and holds out extremely well 21 and 22 hours out of the 24, and has reformed astonishingly." But in 1827 he disappeared from the record after stealing two bales of cotton and escaping from custody before punishment.

Yellow fever in 1822 gave Henry so many patients to attend that he said "another month's practice would make me a tolerable quack doctor"; but four years later he lost four slaves by smallpox. In the fall of 1827 he described his pressure of occupation: "The fact is, with three c[otton] press establishments, two rope walks, improvements making, produce selling and shipping, negroes to nurse, flog, etc., etc., etc., etc., it is no easy matter to run off."

Henry Palfrey was ever inclined to over-expansion. He began to be embarrassed by debt in 1829, and after suffering losses to a total of one hundred and twenty thousand dollars, went bankrupt in 1833. He then shifted to the factorage business and prospered more or less until the stringency which began in 1837 and became the more intense as half a decade passed made him bankrupt again in 1842, without recourse. In the last year of his father's life Henry's wife was taking boarders, and he was too nearly penniless to pay Forlorn Hope a visit. In years later than the time of these letters he seems to have gotten upon his financial feet once more, aided without doubt by his father's bequest.

The eldest son of John Palfrey, John Gorham by name, who has not hitherto been mentioned, did not go to Louisiana except upon seldom visits. Precocity in youth had marked him for the ministry, and he spent his life in Boston and Cambridge. Upon becoming editor of the *North American Review* he borrowed a large sum from his father, whose sin of slaveholding receives no mention in his letters. Upon John's death, however, John Gorham went to the plantation, took his share of the inheritance in slaves, carried them home for manumission, and shortly became prominent among anti-slavery politicians — a Whig like the rest of his family, though with a sharp difference now upon the Negro question. But this is taking us beyond the scope of John Palfrey's papers.

❊   ❊   ❊   ❊   ❊

The shift made by Palfrey from cotton to sugar was duplicated at a later period on the one Texan estate for which detailed record is available. This is the "Peach Point" plantation of James F. Perry, which lay where prairie bordered forest on the tidal stretch of the Brazos River.[1] Perry, who had married a sister of Stephen F. Austin, left Missouri for

[1] The record has been analyzed, and part of it printed, by Abigail Curlee in the *Southwestern Historical Quarterly*, XXVI, 79-127.

Texas at Austin's instance, and after a land-looking tour settled Peach Point at the end of 1832. The first years, in which the chief tasks were clearing, construction and the cultivation of food crops, were marked by malaria among the dozen or two slaves who had been brought from Missouri; and the middle of the decade was disturbed by the war for Texan independence. By 1838 the plantation was in full swing with the cotton staple, its fifteen hands reaping one hundred and twenty-seven bales of about five hundred and fifty pounds average weight. The rich land sent up cotton stalks higher than a man's head, and some of the Negroes were adept enough to pick four hundred pounds of the staple on their best days; but worms and wet weather kept the crop in most years far below expectations. The yield in 1846, for example, was but forty-six hundred and sixty pounds of lint; and in 1849 after Joseph Hext had been hired in the rapid succession of overseers, at twenty dollars per month with a bonus of five dollars more if one hundred and ten bales were made and sold at seven cents a pound, the crop was a mere thirty-nine bales.

Sugar cane was grown in the late 'forties, along with tobacco, on an experimental scale. Then seed cane was bought by the acre as it stood in a neighbor's field, and a mill was built. That the new staple proved better than the old is suggested by the net proceeds of $6781.13 from sugar and molasses in 1855 after deducting $2579.63 for hired labor and other expenses. Whether in the cotton or sugar régime, there were incidental sales of surplus corn and potatoes, poultry and eggs, butter, tallow, pork and lard, hard soap and pecans. Some of these sales, and of cotton also, were for the account of slaves, each man among whom had an acre assigned for his own use. In addition the slaves were paid a dollar a day for Sunday work when sugar-making required it.

The tone of the household may be gathered from the remarks of Rutherford B. Hayes, who formed a college-mate friendship with Guy M. Bryan, a stepson of Perry, and paid a joyous visit to the plantation in 1849. Of Bryan, Hayes wrote: "He is a real gentleman, holds his honor dear, respects the wishes and feelings of others, is a warm and constant friend"; of Perry, "a sensible matter-of-fact sort of man, full of jokes and laughter"; and of his wife, "an excellent motherly sort of woman, whose happiness consists in making others happy." [1] The functions of the mistress were most impressive to the visitor:

"Mrs. Perry, for example, instead of having the care of one family, is the nurse, physician and spiritual adviser of a whole settlement of careless slaves. She feels it her duty to see to their comfort when sick or hurt, and among so many there is always some little brat with a scalded foot or a hand half cut off, and 'Missus' must always see to it or there is sure to be a whining time of it in the whole camp. Besides, to have anything done requires all time. It may be I am mistaken, but I don't think Job was ever 'tried' by a gang of genuine 'Sambos'!" [2]

The friendship of Hayes and Bryan persisted through years of separation and political divergence, to be revived after the war of the 'sixties in a correspondence which enlightened the policy of Hayes while President.[3] As to "Peach Point", it maintained a hospitable roof until about the end of the century when the competition of more favored regions brought abandonment.[4] With the whole expanse of Texas to choose from, Perry hit upon one of the few districts which are now decadent.

* * * * *

From northward of the cotton belt the western cases available through the hazard of circumstance are of unusual sorts. William Hugg King, born in North Carolina in 1767, a graduate of Princeton, a Federalist politician and whiskey gauger, was "converted" at a camp meeting about the turn of the century and applied for admission into the Presbyterian clergy. When told that two years of study would be required for this, he

[1] C. R. Williams, *Life and Letters of R. B. Hayes* (Boston, 1914), I, 47, 248.

[2] *Ibid.*, I, 255.

[3] "The Bryan-Hayes correspondence" in the *Southwestern Historical Quarterly*, XXV, XXVI, *passim*.

[4] Abner J. Strobel, *The Old Plantations and their Owners of Brazoria County, Texas* (Houston, 1926), 7.

procured Methodist ordination and afterward shifted to the Presbyterian ministry. About the beginning of 1819 he removed to East Tennessee, where he functioned whether *seriatim* or simultaneously as a preacher, a planter, a miller, a lumberman, a boat builder and a schoolmaster. When the extant portion of his diary began, [1] in the spring of 1819, he was paying for his plantation by instalments and completing a sawmill and a grist mill on a creek near its junction with the Tennessee River below Knoxville. But within a twelvemonth he lost nine slave women and girls by death, several of his men ran away,[2] part of his own family was prostrated by fever, he began to suffer from a diseased leg, low water kept his mills idle, and he found "money extremely scarce, my own difficulties great." Next year he hired some white men at ten dollars a month to help with his crops (corn, wheat, oats, and a little tobacco, flax and cotton) and to saw lumber and build flatboats. The largest of these, seventy-three by eighteen feet over all, said then to be the largest ever seen on the upper course of the Tennessee, he sold for a hundred and fifty dollars. In 1821 he moralized: "Edwin Osborn, Edwin Sharpe and Sandy Osborn all gone to poverty, disgrace and contempt with intemperance. These young men all once had fair prospects, good professions, respectable family connections, and well established in life. But idleness and spirits, bad examples from parents, has blasted all for time and Eternity. Merciful Heaven, keep and preserve me and mine!" But his own treading of the strait path did not bring prosperity or happiness: "My trials great, mills doing no good, and domestic affairs going crooked. . . . The heaviest trials of my life, may they be sanctified." Next year he sold a slave or two and undertook a school at the Blount County Iron Works; and in 1823, hoping to satisfy his creditors, he advertised his plantation for sale. With this the diary drew to a close.

[1] The manuscript diary and a typescript of an autobiography (mainly filled with religious philosophizing) are in the North Carolina Historical Commission, at Raleigh.

[2] *E.g.*, "I had to chastise Jack, I thought from a sense of duty. On the morning following he ran away."

Seven miles west of Nashville dwelt in 1846 Mark R. Cockrill, whom Solon Robinson [1] found to be fluent, hospitable, and "smart as a steel trap." Within the preceding decade he had consolidated twelve farms and put their fifteen hundred acres of rough limestone hills into bluegrass and fifty acres of low ground into corn. He was maintaining two thousand fine sheep, forty Durham cattle, and sixty mares and jennies to breed mules; but he kept no hogs because they would eat lambs. By virtue of the master's untiring vigilance the flocks and herds and crops were tended by four field hands, with occasional aid from women servants. "Mr. Cockrill thinks it folly," Robinson reported, "to keep a large capital in Tennessee invested in 'woolly heads' when 'woolly backs' afford so much better returns of interest." Cockrill also owned a cotton plantation in Mississippi on which he had one hundred and thirty-five slaves; but he was seeking to sell that establishment because at current prices cotton could not compare in profit with wool. But Cockrill's vigor and shrewdness might well have prospered an enterprise of any sort, while inconstant dabblers of Hugg King's type could expect riches only in another world.

This concludes our tour of the plantation belt, made mainly under escort of the planters themselves. We might have tarried to see the routine day by day, but in the twentieth century three long chapters are doubtless enough. The diversity shown may be surprising; but it would surely be greater if more cases were available. Neither planters nor slaves, nor overseers as we shall see, were cast in one mold — traditions, romances, diatribes and imaginative histories to the contrary notwithstanding. Plantation life and industry had in last analysis as many facets as there were periods, places and persons involved. The régime nevertheless had a unity palpable always; and the essence of this lay not so much in the nature of the crops as in the matter-of-course habituation of all the personnel to responsible and responsive adjustments between masters and men of the two races.

[1] *American Agriculturist*, V, 211–213.

CHAPTER XV

OVERSEERS

On a farm, as in a handicraft shop, the proprietor works alongside any helpers he may have, he gives them direction as needed and inspects their work from the corner of his eye as he plies his own tools. If the establishment expands it will at some stage reach a scale where its owner can no longer combine manual work with supervision but for the sake of efficient management must bend his whole energy to planning, control and marketing. At this point where full differentiation of administration from labor occurs, the shop becomes a factory, the farm changes into a plantation, whatever the number of its operatives may be. Upon still further enlargement the proprietor may find that supervision is needed in several quarters more or less constantly and often simultaneously. Since he cannot be in two places at once he will need assistance in the control. This may perhaps be rendered by a working foreman, or it may require a superintendent's full time. Eventually the enterprise may grow so great as to evoke a whole hierarchy of administration. In factory parlance this will consist of a general manager, superintendents and foremen. In *ante-bellum* rural nomenclature it would comprise perhaps a steward in charge of a group of plantations, an overseer on each physical unit of operation, and a slave foreman, or "driver", at the head of each gang whether of plowmen, hoe hands, carters, ditchers or the like. Meanwhile the growth of scale might swell the proprietor's income to such volume that he could afford to sojourn or even dwell permanently at a distance; or ill health might incapacitate him, or his death convey the property to a woman or minor children unfitted for control in the field. In a few cases great plantations were converted from individual into corporate ownership; and in rare instances a college or a church inherited a plantation and its corps of slaves. For example Washington College, now known as Washington and Lee University, received such a bequest from John Robinson in 1826 and, as required by the will, kept it in operation for a number of years.[1] Overseers therefore were in fairly copious demand, with functions varying with the vigor and location of their employers, the tenor of their instructions, and manifold other factors in the human and physical equation.

The first overseer in English America, in a sense, was the governor of Virginia under the London Company; and the captains of the "particular plantations" were next in succession. As soon as private estates in any colony attained a plantation scale, overseers here and there became a matter of course. The extent of the practice was described, with some exaggeration, by a French sojourner on the Chesapeake in 1686: "It is a country so good and fertile that when a man has fifty acres of land, two men servants and a maid and some cattle, neither he nor his wife have ever anything to do except to make visits to their neighbours. The greater number of them do not even take the trouble to watch their slaves at work, for there is no house so ill provided which has not an overseer, as they call him who usually is an indenture man recently enfranchised. To him they give (say) two servants in charge. The overseer feeds, directs and himself works with these servants. He receives a third of the tobacco and grain or whatever else they put in the ground, and so the master has nothing to do except take his share of the crop." [2]

The system by which the overseer added his own labor to that of the gang and drew as recompense just the share which his muscular exertions produced, was praised in its day; [3] but by the beginning of the nineteenth century depletion of soils

---

[1] Manuscript records in private possession. For mention of a slaveholding congregation see J. D. Paxton, *Letters on Slavery* (Lexington, Ky., 1833), 11.

[2] [Fairfax Harrison, ed.] *A Frenchman in Virginia* ([Richmond] 1923), 97–99.

[3] Hugh Jones, *Present State of Virginia* (1724), Sabin's reprint, 36, 37.

brought intelligent proprietors to subordinate immediate returns to ultimate advantage by adopting methods of rehabilitation. In addition the rise of slave prices intensified the occasion for conserving their lives, health and contentment. The old system of overseers on shares was abandoned with one accord as crudely exploitive,[1] and they were engaged on fixed wages instead.[2] Further, the opening of the West increased poor men's potential opportunity through migration and forced concessions from Eastern employers. This was doubtless responsible for a distinctive feature in the Virginia régime according to which planters must give notice as early as June as to whether an overseer was to be retained for another year.[3]

Many overseers in addition became relieved of the obligation to work manually with their gangs. A contributory reason for this may have been such experiences as that of a South Carolinian whose overseer, he reported, "worked harder than any man I ever saw", but whose industry proved rather a vice than a virtue; for "he would do *all* and leave the negroes to do virtually nothing; and as they would of course take advantage of this, what he did was more than counterbalanced by what they did not." [4]

❋   ❋   ❋   ❋   ❋

On the rice coast from early times, by reason of the climate and the superior advantage of large units for the control of water, overseers had relatively good wages and exemption from manual duties. What might occur was exemplified by Thomas Ferguson,[5] born in 1726 as the son of a ferryman on Cooper River. Laboring first as a sawyer with two slave helpers, he became successively a plantation overseer, a steward

[1] It was trenchantly condemned by John Taylor of Caroline in his *Arator* (Georgetown, D. C., 1813), 76–78.
[2] *Farmers' Register*, IV, 1. Occasionally a contract provided for a supplementary bonus under certain conditions.
[3] A Virginian complained of this in 1836 as a great abuse (*Farmers' Register*, III, 713–715), but it was not remedied.
[4] U. B. Phillips, *American Negro Slavery*, 282.
[5] Ferguson's career is sketched in Harriette K. Leiding, *Historic Homes of South Carolina* (Philadelphia, 1921), 54–56.

and a planter. In 1774 he was a son-in-law of Christopher Gadsden and the possessor of nine plantations near Ashley River. First and last "Colonel" Ferguson married five times, always prosperously, begot some twenty-seven children, and bequeathed property to each of the survivors somewhat in proportion to what their respective mothers had brought him. A similar opportunity is suggested by an advertisement at Charleston in 1821: "Wanted, a manager to superintend several rice plantations on the Santee River. As the business is extensive, a proportionate salary will be made, and one or two young men of his own selection employed under him. A healthful summer residence on the seashore is provided for himself and family." [1]

In Virginia on a blithe May day of 1810 young Andrew Reid of Lexington was traveling by stage to Richmond to become a member of the Governor's Council. In Goochland County he espied and hailed his friends Nancy and Polly Rodgers in a gig bound in the same direction. The stage obligingly stopped, as did the gig; and the girls, introducing their mounted escort as Richard Sampson, said they were going to their uncle's wedding at "Tuckahoe." Reid wrote to his brother: "The meeting between us was joyful indeed and contributed much to the pleasure of my journey, for I exchanged my seat in the stage for Miss Nancy's in the gig, and Polly and myself drove on most merrily indeed for ten or twelve miles. I suspect that Miss Polly and Mr. Sampson are about to be married. He is a remarkably clever young man, of handsome fortune, and a most extraordinary manager. He is now employed in the management of Mr. Wickham's estates, for which he gets a salary of upwards of $1500 per annum." [2]

We next encounter Sampson more prosily through the pen of Edmund Ruffin, who visited him as a notable planter in 1837, when he and his Polly may have become grandparents. Sampson, as Ruffin relates, had begun his career between plow handles on his father's farm. Upon coming of age he procured the management of a James River estate and retained that

---

[1] *Southern Patriot*, January 9, 1821.   [2] Manuscript in private possession.

yielding a low grade of tobacco and scanty grain, could hardly afford better wages even when, as in some cases, the overseers worked with the gangs. The net result was that Massie conducted unwillingly a training school for novices who would surely seek better jobs if they proved worthy and would be discharged if they did not.

On "Pharsalia", Massie's home plantation, the first incumbent of note was Reuben Cash, to whom his employer's general indictment would not apply. When he died in 1837 after ten years of service, Massie wrote an obituary in his record book dispraising his "expensive, unreasonable, illdisposed and exceedingly piratical wife", but saying of the man himself: "Cash if differently raised and well educated would have made an exceedingly clever man. His mind was of the first order, and he was really a gentleman in his manners and feelings. I never communicated a wish to him while in my business that it did not seem to give him pleasure to execute. I hope and believe that he has gone to a better world."

Cash was followed by William Harvie who served four years at wages advancing to two hundred and thirty-five dollars. Then, in the midst of hard times, Massie found a cheaper man in William Bonds, who had previously served him as distiller, harvest hand and carpenter, according to season. Bonds began at a yearly wage of one hundred and twenty-five dollars and advanced to one hundred and forty dollars plus a bonus of twenty-five dollars if the crops met no adversity; but in 1851 he was given notice of discontinuance with the comment: "He has exhibited some very valuable qualities, and except for his being so extremely slovenly and withal such a fool, he would yet suit me pretty well." To succeed him James Fulcher was shifted at one hundred and ten dollars from lesser duties on "Tyro." He proved courteous and accommodating "but in the general management of my stock, and in fact all other business, he is entirely incompetent. . . . He also causes my hands to leave their work and go into my pastures for horses for his children to ride. His children are very decent, but this thing won't do." After a year of Fulcher came for a like space

James P. Hambleton and Doctor Thomas Smoot, who presumably had failed in a former profession only to fail again in this. Finally Bartlett Thompson, who owned a family of slaves, entered a service in 1855 which lasted to 1863 at wages advancing from one hundred and fifty dollars to one hundred and seventy-five dollars by 1859, when Massie remarked "they are high enough, God knows."

At "Level Green", the second of Massie's principal plantations, James Giles was in charge from 1836 to the end of the decade at a wage of £40.[1] To succeed him Leroy Mitchell was shifted from "Snug Dale" when Massie gave that unit to his son. Mitchell drew two hundred dollars a year until, after fifteen years of service, he was given notice in 1846. "I am melancholy at the thought of parting with you," Massie wrote; but the low return from the tobacco crops impelled a reduction of costs. Next came Nelson Monroe, who advanced from one hundred and twenty dollars to one hundred and forty dollars, plus ten dollars bonus by 1850. Although Massie rated him in most regards the best he had ever known, he dropped him after five years because he failed to send sick Negroes to the hospital at Pharsalia; he flew into passion if a slave mentioned Massie as his superior; he took slave children without leave to wait on his wife: "Fourth and worst of all, he is under the influence of a heartless black wench (Beck) who can and does at her pleasure cause him to tie up any of my negroes and whale them unmercifully. Independently of the above, he is too savage and cruel in his infliction of stripes, and too brutal in taking every rag off the women, young and old when he chastises them." At the same time Massie answered an inquiry from a distant planter saying that Monroe's planning was fine, his execution prompt and his work always beforehand. "He don't work himself, but has more work done than any man I ever had. . . . But, my Dear Sir, to use the vulgar phrase of a vulgar crew, 'he is hell upon a negro!' " Finally came William Hambleton, who began at one hundred and

---

[1] In Virginia reckoning this amounted to $133.33. During 1839 three minor sons of Giles were employed as field hands by Massie, and likewise a son of his successor in 1843.

twenty dollars in 1851, advanced to one hundred and seventy-five dollars in 1859, and continued until 1867 or afterward in the employ of Massie's widow.

On "Tyro", where less than a dozen slaves were working, the overseers' wages never exceeded one hundred and twenty dollars until 1860, nor did the service of any last longer than five years. "Montebello" was of the same scale; but, perhaps because it lay ten miles from the master's home, its management was less interrupted. Reuben Bernet was in charge for six years ending in 1841, when he left "with all his worldly goods and with his wages [of $120] paid in full. He is, I believe, as honest as is common, but not good for much." William Ramsey followed for a single term; and then John P. Hambleton began a service which ran for two decades until the record's end.

Inquiries for overseers came to Massie from other planters near and far, even from one who had moved from Virginia to Louisiana. To his brother Henry he sent in 1832 Peachy Cash, who made an excellent impression of muscular strength, knowledge of crops and understanding of Negro character. But next spring several of the slaves combined in assault upon Cash, and fled in sequel. The proprietor wrote in April: "My desperado, George, was tried on the 18th ultimo and was let off with fifty lashes and burning in the hand. Cash was permitted to inflict the lash. I had him instantly recommitted to jail, and shook him off my hands early next day for almost nothing ($340) to a negro trader, one Roberts. He is thus destined to the Mississippi country. . . . Gib (George's companion in crime) I have not heard of, but keep him advertised. I hope yet to get him, if only to inflict well merited punishment. Cash is going on very quietly with the small stock of hands left. They will no doubt well earn their support." William Massie was thereafter very cautious as to testimonials. He preferred to have no share of responsibility in any disaster which might occur; and in any case good managers within his acquaintance were none too numerous for his own wants.

✻   ✻   ✻   ✻   ✻

Just over the Blue Ridge dwelt Massie's friend Samuel McDowell Reid, clerk of Rockbridge County, the windows of whose home in Lexington gave a clear view of his plantation, "Mulberry Hill." On this there dwelt a score or more of slaves, and in the 'forties a working overseer at a wage of some ten dollars a month. At the end of the 'fifties and for some years afterward a man was in charge who tells his own tale in the letters he wrote during his employer's absences from home.[1] This was L. P. Wallace, himself the son of a considerable slave-holder, sagacious, loyal, and qualified all round, even if not always a perfect speller.

In the winter of 1859–1860 an epidemic of smallpox in Lexington prompted Wallace to order all hands to report for vaccination and to keep away from town. Willis the blacksmith, "miffed" at being included in the home-staying order, refused to be vaccinated; and Wallace left the discipline of that dignitary to be handled upon the master's return. Among lesser folk, John and Jim were given "decent dressings" and in further punishment for drunkenness John, who had previously had some lighter employment, was put into the regular gang. The truants were thereby quite sobered. They "now walk up to the mark, and I have not had occasion to say one word to either of them about work or anything else. They come and feed the stock every Sunday regular which was not done before." And of John in particular, "he is as good a hand on the plantation as there is in the country, strong and quick." The manifold affairs of the plantation were in good order, though several slaves were sick and Wallace was himself made ill for some days by the dust of the clover-seed threshing. The hog-killing yielded fourteen thousand pounds, the tobacco in process of stripping promised twenty thousand pounds, the eight fattened beeves, weighing eleven thousand, were sold on the hoof for four hundred and forty dollars. In March, when the master's absence was about to end, the tobacco plant beds were "burned" and seeded; timber was cut for fence rails, charcoal and lime burning; the ditches were cleaned and the water

[1] Manuscripts in private possession.

turned upon the meadow; plowing was in good progress; and the wheat was looking "tolerable well."

In a letter of the following February Wallace remarked of politics: "As for voting for a Democrat, that is out of my line of business. If we could get rid of the Democrats and Tobacco worms it would be a great benefit to the country certain, for they have caused moore troble to the cuntry than any other beings I know of, for they are never satisfyed and never will be as long as ther is one left."

In the war time Wallace's crop routine and experience were much as before except for tobacco's discontinuance; but the trend of his concerns was of course considerably changed. In January of 1862 Little Dave took to the woods, but drew sustenance from the plantation by robbing the corncrib and killing hogs. Before the end of the next month Dave sent word that he was ready to return but he would keep out of the overseer's reach until some member of his master's family came to witness the flogging he was bound to receive. Military needs were now exigent, and Wallace wrote that he would probably "have to gow and show the Yankees the road home before they are checked. I shall hold to the militia, for if they run it will be no more than will be expected of us." In March he was called into active service as a militiaman, and he improvised arrangements for the conduct of the plantation during his absence. In May, when he was at home again, the enemy's approach caused him to send away the recalcitrant Dave and to put the rest of the slaves and the livestock into readiness for flight into central Virginia. But Stonewall Jackson soon removed the menace, and for the rest of the year the routine was little disturbed.

In January of 1863 the Confederacy drafted four of Reid's slaves for work at Richmond. Wallace sent them forth with new hats, clothes and blankets, extra shoes, and a food supply upon which they were to draw in case the government rations fell short. Next month he sent more meal and bacon to these Negroes, for fear they might be sickened by a change to a diet of beef and wheaten bread. Upon learning that one of the four had been sent to a hospital, he urged Reid to procure his

removal to the care of a physician more competent and attentive than an army surgeon was likely to be. In September,
when a second draft of slaves was in progress for labor on
fortifications, he advised that those nearest the upper limit of
age be sent, because "old negroes can take better care of themselves than young ones"; and he doubtless would have added
if he had expressed his whole thought, that old slaves would be
the lesser loss if they died or otherwise failed to return. Clearly
Wallace considered the war a nuisance, for it disturbed his
business at Mulberry Hill.

❋   ❋   ❋   ❋   ❋

James K. Polk fell heir to a plantation, called "Pleasant
Grove", in western Tennessee; but his absorption in law
practice at Columbia, near the middle of the State, and in his
functions as congressman, governor and president made him
lean heavily upon others for its management. His overseer
was required to make monthly reports; [1] and his brother-in-
law, Doctor Silas Caldwell, who had an estate in the next
county, made occasional visits of inspection.

Near the end of 1833 a preceding overseer yielded his troublous place, at a wage of three hundred and fifty dollars, to
Ephraim Beanland, who shortly wrote : "Your negroes has . . .
bin let run at so loce reined that I must be verry cloce with
them." [2] The occasion was the flight of Jack and Ben in sequel
to punishment. Ben made his way to Columbia to seek protection. He said that Jack had not only been whipped severely
but brine had been poured upon his raw back at intervals in the
flogging; his own whipping had not been so drastic, but he
dreaded a worse in case of return, and said in short that he
could not live under Beanland. Jack, on the other hand,
aware that his past record of misdeeds would bar him from
sympathetic hearing, set a course for parts unknown. Some-

---

[1] Many of these are printed, with excellent elucidation, in J. S. Bassett, *The Southern
Plantation Overseer as Revealed in his Letters* (Northampton, Mass., 1925).

[2] *Ibid.*, 54. His meaning was, your Negroes have been driven with so loose a rein
that I must tauten the control.

where about the Mississippi he was encountered by two white men who chained him and thievishly set forth in a rowboat to sell him somewhere down stream. But one Hughes, in search of another fugitive, came upon this party and clapped all three into jail on suspicion. After hearing Jack's tale he sent news of the capture, along with a bill of one hundred and forty dollars for services and expenses. Reports and advice went to Polk at Washington from his brothers-in-law who thought the slaves' complaints well grounded, and from Beanland who said that unless the fugitives were sent back to him for discipline his authority over the rest of the corps would be wrecked. This plea prevailed; but on the plantation an argument ensued in which Jack broke a stick over Beanland's head, and Beanland subdued him by stabbing.[1] Jack was afterward sold as incorrigible.

"Pleasant Grove" proving of little profit, Polk bethought him "to make more money or to lose more" by a venture in the newly-ceded Choctaw lands to the southward. He sold Pleasant Grove in 1834, took the infirm slaves to the homestead at Columbia, bought others to enlarge the able-bodied corps, and in partnership with Doctor Caldwell undertook a plantation on a tract of eight hundred and eighty acres in Yalobusha County, Mississippi, for which they paid ten dollars an acre. Beanland was commissioned to buy the broadwives of Polk's men, but the owner of Caesar's wife refused to sell because she refused to migrate; so Beanland reported: "I tell Seaser that she dose not care anythinge for him and he sayes that is a fact." Caldwell and Beanland in January of 1835 led the trek of twenty-eight slaves, together with mules and cattle, a drove of hogs and a wagon load of equipment. Arriving after a week of travel, the corps built in eighteen days a house for the overseer and his newly wedded wife, four Negro cabins, a smoke house and a kitchen. Caldwell procured cotton seed locally, sent a wagon to Memphis for tools, ordered pork from Cincinnati, directed Beanland to plant his full need of corn and such cotton as he could. He then went home, leaving the overseer

[1] Bassett, *The Southern Plantation Overseer*, 67.

"much pleased with his situation, and the Negroes only tolerably well satisfied."

The first year of the new project was disappointing. Three of the men ran away and their capture involved expense; another was killed when thrown by a mule; Beanland suffered from malaria; and the cotton crop yielded barely twenty bales. At the year's end Beanland was discharged and went to a farm in Tennessee, where he prospered sufficiently to acquire three slaves in five years. On the Yalobusha meanwhile Polk acquired Caldwell's interest in the enterprise.

The successor of Beanland, erring in the opposite direction, demoralized the slaves by indulgence, and gave place after a year to George W. Bratton, who gradually restored control and eventually praised the corps for good conduct. His efficient service was ended by death in 1839, and John I. Garner harvested the crop of one hundred and thirty-six bales which Bratton had brought to prosperous fruitage. Garner's crop of 1840 was likewise good; but during the year several Negro babies died, and in the fall three men ran to Tennessee to complain of his harshness. This led to his replacement by Isaac H. Dismukes, who held the job four years. Like his predecessors, Dismukes was hampered by the flight of slaves to seek a champion in some kindly member of the Polk family. Following the same course as Beanland, he wrote of his general problem and of the runaway Gilbert in particular: "do not sell him if you wish to brake them from running away for they had reather bea sould twise than to bea whip once . . . I beleave that they believe that tennessee is a place of parridise and the all want to gow back to tennessee so stop them by ironing tham and send them back agan and they will soon stop cumming to tennessee." [1] After his first year Dismukes had no trouble of note with the Negroes, and his crops were steadily good. Having nothing else to say, he wrote at the conclusion of one of his letters to his employer, who was soon to become President: "when this you sea remember mea though many miles between us bea." On another occasion he invited Polk unavailingly to

[1] Bassett, *The Southern Plantation Overseer*, 159.

share with him in the purchase of a barrel of whiskey. At length when some neighbors reported that he was excessively convivial by habit, he was notified of discontinuance.

John A. Mears, at wages of five hundred dollars and later five hundred and fifty, took charge in 1845 and continued through the remaining fourteen years of the record — throughout his employer's term in the White House and in the employ of the widow after Polk's death. His many terse letters tell of drought and flood, of crop conditions and equipment needs, of sick slaves and truants, of births and deaths (particularly from an epidemic of whooping cough), of yields in cotton, corn and pork, and of cotton shipments, two of which were lost by the burning of steamboats. Some new features appear in the sale of the slaves' own crops of cotton, yielding two hundred dollars or more for distribution; in an expression of doubt by the overseer that whipping was a sure cure for truancy; and in an assertion of willingness that a persistent runaway should be sold. Mears' output of cotton averaged about one hundred and fifty bales; but ironically his best prospect, in 1852, was heavily diminished by the sickness of his corps and his inability to get recruits to save a large part of the crop from ruin in the fields.

As to the slaves there would be little record of shining virtues had not two of them sung their own praises. Mariah sent a message to her mistress in 1841 "that she is worth at least $30 more than when she left Tennessee. She can spool, warp and *weave*, and with a little more practice thinks she will make a first rate weaver." [1] And the next year Harry the blacksmith wrote for himself: "I would wish to be remembered to all of my people old mistrs esphhirly   Tell the old Lady Harry is hir servent untill dath   I would be gld to see Hir one mor   I Expect to come out a cristmust to see you . . . Dear master I have Eleven children   I have been faitheful over the anvill Block Evr cen 1811 and is still old Harry." At this time he was hired to a village employer at wages rising from three hundred and fifty to four hundred and fifty dollars a year

[1] Bassett, *The Southern Plantation Overseer*, 157.

— as much as Polk was paying for an overseer. Petitioning without success for the privilege of hiring his own time, he was afterward shifted to a shop at home where in 1851 he booked $487.76 in outside patronage as well as meeting the demands of the plantation.[1]

❋　　❋　　❋　　❋　　❋

An overseer in South Carolina, writing anonymously in 1836 after long experience,[2] said that his early employers had given him no instructions but merely told him where he was to live. But a new patron, whom he had now served for fifteen years, had instructed him promptly and explicitly. "Among an hundred other things, he impressed upon my mind that I was to be his representative; to regulate his slaves in their moral and general conduct; to sustain my employer's reputation among merchants for the quality of his productions; and to make his plantation a pattern of regularity and order to the neighborhood around. . . . Most of my duties he had committed to writing." Thereafter this overseer discussed problems freely with his employer, his driver, and any other persons available. In result he developed policies and rules of his own. The driver was encouraged to "maintain a pride of character" before the Negroes under him; and any needed precepts or scoldings were given him in private. If slaves brought tales against him a trial was held and if the evidence proved false the accuser was punished; but in one case where the fault was flagrant he gave the driver a public flogging, reduced him to ranks and appointed a successor in his stead. When a slave has been punished, he continued with wisdom, the fact should be dismissed, "and his spirits should not be broken down by continually reminding him of his past misconduct." Praise and flattery are often more effective than chastisement, he remarked; and with a generous gesture: "If I have been successful as an overseer I attribute it all to the advice of my employer."

A parallel instance, in which the names and details may be

[1] Bassett, *The Southern Plantation Overseer*, 161–163.
[2] *Farmers' Register*, IV, 114–116.

specified, occurred on "Retreat", a plantation in Jefferson County, Georgia, belonging to the Telfairs of Savannah and serving as their summer home. In a body of written instructions Alexander Telfair prescribed that the overseer was not to have a driver, but was to set the tasks in person and require of every hand "a reasonable day's work, well done." Pork and meal were to be issued on the standard schedule, with fresh beef as a variation in July, August and September; and turnips and peas were to be grown plentifully. The slaves were permitted to plant anything for themselves except cotton; and were to be given "tickets" permitting them to pass and repass to sell their produce or visit friends. There was to be no night meeting or preaching except on Saturday night and Sunday morning. "If there is any fighting on the Plantation, whip all engaged in it — for no matter what the cause may have been, all are in the wrong"; but no slave is to have more than fifty lashes, however great the crime. "Elsey is the Doctoress of the plantation," to give place to a physician when she finds a case beyond her cure. She is also permitted to serve as midwife "to black and white in the neighborhood who send for her." The over-- seer was to keep a regular journal, recording the names of the sick, the state of the weather, the progress of work, births, deaths and all other occurrences of importance; and with the journal before him he was to write and send to Telfair a full report on the last day of each month.[1]

Under Telfair and his daughters after him Elisha Cain conducted the work on Retreat for a quarter-century ending with 1850. He had his troubles with occasional truants, with a woman who kept her house mates in terror, and with sickness, including as a new thing "the venereal disease" which Telfair's butler had spread upon the plantation and which baffled Cain's art and Elsey's.[2] But thanks partly to the stimulating effect

[1] Telfair's instructions are printed in *Plantation and Frontier*, I, 126–129. This particular draft was made for another of his plantations, but its equivalent without doubt applied to "Retreat." The overseer's letters, used below, are in the same work, I, 314, 330–336; II, 39, 85.

[2] In a jotting upon this report Telfair said that it was his practice to have all his domestics examined each summer before leaving Savannah.

of private "patches", in which the slaves were allowed after 1837 to include nankeen cotton [1] among their crops, Cain could report of the Negroes in general that they wrought well when in health, "and some of them appear to have a kind of pride in making a good crop" for the plantation.

As the years passed Cain took the initiative in various matters. In 1836 he attributed his fine crop to the Petit Gulf cotton seed which had been procured at his instance. He now proposed a change in another department, for experience and inquiry showed him that cotton yarn for the weaving could be bought from a factory at much less than it was costing in the labor of able-bodied spinsters. The four women he named were probably shifted to field work as he proposed. But another innovation brought him a mild rebuke. The working corps having increased by 1840 to some ninety hands and the cotton crop to three or four hundred bales, the tillage often required the division of the force into several squads, working far apart. To diminish idling, quarreling and abuse of mules during his absence from any gang, he appointed John to be foreman with the duty of reporting derelictions but without authority to whip. Jacob when reported by John ran off to escape the lash, and made his way with a plausible tale to his mistress, who sent him back with a letter of protection and remonstrance. In reply Cain wrote that he would obey Miss Telfair's order "altho I feel that it will be at the expense of justice and an injury in the future government of these negroes." On the general issue he continued: "You mention in your letter that you do not wish your negroes to be treated with severity. I have ever thought my fault on the side of lenity; if they were treated as severe as many are, I should not be their overseer on any consideration." That Cain continued prosperously in charge for another decade gives evidence that solutions were found for this and all other difficulties.

❋   ❋   ❋   ❋   ❋

[1] The nankeen variety had for this purpose the virtue of a brownish color so distinctive that no slave might filch the white staple from the master's field to swell the volume of his own crop.

Sundry other planters wrote elaborate instructions, and some put them into print for private use or public edification. With one accord they laid main emphasis upon the provisioning, sanitation and general upkeep of the slaves and the steady maintenance of system in routine; and most of them urged the promotion of religion and morality as well as of morale. As to crops, they generally ordered a full acreage in foodstuffs and then such cast in the staple as the corps could handle. They asked of the overseer as constant attendance as possible with the gangs in the fields by day and at the stables night and morning; and they deprecated severity and forbade indecency in the infliction of punishment.[1]

One of these included among his rules: "Having connection with any of my female servants will most certainly be visited with a dismissal from my employment, and no excuse can or will be taken." Another proprietor, not in this group of grandees but a frontier Mississippian in 1808, who surely had no written rules, related in a letter to his nephew and niece in North Carolina: "I turned away my overseer this morning about Harriot and my house girl, for they both say they are big to him. I think if they are I shall pay them for their gallantry. I caut him and my gals abed together last night."[2]

Many homilies were addressed to overseers through the public prints; but a South Carolinian summed the essentials when he advertised for two who must be "capable, sober and not passionate."[3] The need of zeal and perseverance went without saying, though it was often elaborated.[4] These qualities were obtained not more often than was to be expected. William Byrd wrote in irony of an employee who "hates to have

---

[1] Several sets of rules are analyzed in U. B. Phillips, *American Negro Slavery*, 261–279. In the group is included James H. Hammond's "plantation manual" (manuscript in the Library of Congress). Hammond's rules, without his name and with the omission of his paragraphs concerning homeopathy and whiskey, were printed in the *Carolina Planter* and reprinted in the *Farmers' Register*, VIII, 230–231.

[2] Manuscript in private possession. For a copy I am indebted to Professor A. O. Craven.

[3] *South Carolina Gazette*, January 6, 1787.

[4] *E.g.*, James C. Luskey in the *Biennial Report of the State Agricultural Bureau of Tennessee, to the Legislature of 1855–1856*, pp. 325–327.

his sweet temper ruffled, and will rather suffer matters to go a little wrong sometimes than give his righteous spirit any uneasiness." In the same community a century afterward an overseer virtually confessed his own incapacity: "Your negroes are all well but . . . I had to correct sevrl of them. I have more to incounter with them than I can well do." And of his successor a neighbor wrote: "I regret very much to hear that your overseer (Herndon) has again been drunk. . . . I would respectfully advise that you, without letting Herndon know anything about it, immediately set about employing another person." [1] With more vigor an Alabamian wrote in a similar case: "I assure you I would give such a man $150 dollars to quit any time & give a good overseer $500 rather than have him on a place of mine." [2] Violence of temper, on the other hand, would not only qualify one for membership in Massie's "cowhide fraternity", but sometimes brought a contretemps in which either the tyrant or his victim or both lost their lives.

Some plantation rules declared explicitly the right of any slave to convey a grievance to the master; and in our notes of Polk and Telfair experience we have seen slaves making secret way for a hundred miles to the seat of authority. On other occasions the masters did the traveling, and at full speed. Thus did one Simpson, a merchant of New Orleans, hasten in 1812 when an overseer's mismanagement caused seven slaves to flee from his plantation. [3] Thus doubtless did N. C. Flournoy take the road in Georgia in 1837 upon learning that six of his men had vanished overnight. "There was a part of them had no cause for leaving, only they thought if they would all go it would injure me moore." [4] The overseer continued, "They want more whipping and no protecter," but it is not likely that

[1] Manuscripts in private possession.
[2] *Plantation and Frontier Documents*, I, 326.
[3] Manuscript in private possession.
[4] Phillips, *American Negro Slavery*, 303. A lack of rarity in such occurrences is indicated by a grand jury presentment in New Granada, a small West India island, complaining that among twenty-seven slaves who had quit "Mirabeau", a plantation of Alexander Douglas, and had returned to duty after several weeks in the woods, not one had been punished. This, said the jurors, "we conceive may have a very bad effect on that estate as well as on the island in general. . . . And as a proof of

the master concurred in such a formula. Again, while Judge Thomas Ruffin was holding court at Raleigh in 1851, as he related : "A misunderstanding arose between my Overseer and some of my negroes, and *Eight* of them went off early in March. During that month I returned home and thereupon six of them came in, or had done so." [1] Slaves thus by concerted stampede might enter upon a strike; and utilizing other Negroes of the neighborhood as a channel of communication, might negotiate after a fashion as to the terms upon which they would resume work.

Of Ruffin's earlier overseers we have glimpses in letters from his son. In January, 1831, after a change of personnel : "Your overseer . . . is at the barn before day each morning, and every night; and of course the horses look much better than they did under Mr. Moore's administration. . . . Adcock and the negroes agree pretty well; he has had recourse to the rod on three or four occasions, but they have peaceably submitted to it and appear to respect and fear him." In the next month : "The best Painter could not depict . . . a face more indicative of grief and despair than is his when one engages with him in conversation upon the weather and the state of the farm." Of a successor after two years : "He seems industrious, but I should say quite as little of a *manager* as poor Adcock. He ought to be severe at the start, for his father's negroes have no respect for him, and yours will, I presume, have the same feeling towards him unless he makes them fear him at the beginning." By the summer of 1834 this incumbent or a successor was determined that, even at the cost of beauty in the planter's premises, his crop should not lack labor. Young Ruffin wrote again : "I never knew so *pushing* a man. Mama complains grievously of her garden. . . . She says it is a 'wilderness of

such a precedent, we are informed that 16 negroes belonging to Mrs. Hooke have within the last week absented themselves, perhaps expecting upon their return to be treated with the same ill-timed and impolitic lenity with which those of Mirabeau have been treated." — *St. George's Chronicle and New Granada Gazette*, September 17, 1790.

[1] J. G. de R. Hamilton, ed., *The Papers of Thomas Ruffin* (Raleigh, N. C., 1918), II, 328.

weeds', and declares that she will never again be cheated of the labour of her gardener by an overseer." [1] Clearly no man might please all parties, unless he had more tact than the generality could muster.

Another Ruffin had a more profitable experience than his cousin Thomas, for he ascribed much of his own agricultural knowledge (and he was editor of the *Southern Planter*) to his practice of daily conference with overseers: "Though uneducated, often bigoted, and averse to change because instinct teaches them that when they leave the beaten track of practice they have no compass to guide them through the wilds of theory, yet they have commonly an amount of shrewd sense, and a happy knack of raising [*i.e.*, removing] difficulties that often baffle the more cultivated employer and saves him many a fall from a freshly mounted hobby." [2]

❊   ❊   ❊   ❊   ❊

Of course, like the rest of mankind, overseers were "very much given to stretching their prerogatives in matters pertaining to their own inclinations, but very strict constructionists" on other occasion.[3] M. W. Philips voiced a plaint that the generality of these folk, seeking reputations merely by making large crops in the staple, were scornful of all other concerns: "I have heard an overseer say he 'would oversee for no man who would not give up control of his hands.' A pretty spot of work this. Am I to give up the management of my own affairs to any man, that he may make a character? Brethren of the South, we must change our policy. Overseers are not interested in raising children, or meat, in improving land . . . or animals. Many of them do not care whether property has depreciated or improved, so they have made a crop to boast of." [4] One of the craft met this challenge with defiance: "I would now say . . . to my brother Overseers that I would advise them never to agree to oversee for a man who wants you to 'go by direc-

---

[1] *The Papers of Thomas Ruffin*, II, 22, 25, 69, 119.
[2] F. G. Ruffin in the *Southern Planter*, XVI, 50 (Richmond, February, 1856).
[3] John B. Lamar in *Plantation and Frontier Documents*, I, 181.
[4] *American Cotton Planter*, I, 377 (December, 1853).

tions'; for I assure you, that man is mistaken; he only wants a driver; and you will be more troubled by him than forty negroes." [1]

To this "A Plain Old Farmer" had replied two decades in advance: "If you lose oversight of your overseer, he will lose sight of your business — strict employers make attentive overseers. An overseer neglected is one soon ejected. If the master is much at home, the overseer is but seldom abroad — if one is a man of pleasure, the other will be a man of leisure." And as to drivers: "When an overseer puts a black man in his place, he gives a lesson to his employer. If 'Uncle Tom' is to manage, let Uncle Tom have the honor, and his master save the wages." [2] Numerous planters found by experience, indeed, that foremen were what they wanted. Anthony Robinson, Jr., of Henrico County, Virginia, was fortunate in such a solution. When a committee for the award of certain prizes visited his "beautiful and highly improved farm" in his absence, they were shown about by "his faithful servant and foreman Charles, whose attachment to his master, zeal in his service, and honest pride were manifested in a manner exceedingly gratifying to the committee." [3]

But the shortage of sable paragons, and in some cases the requirements of the law, upheld the demand for overseers. The supply was various, as we have seen. One was of such humble walk that his wife must needs cook and wash for the slaves until, to her great rejoicing, he got a better job. Another was the prospective heir to a fine estate, seeking apprenticeship to an expert planter. Young or old, wise or foolish, ambitious or plodding, dour or debonair, harsh or indulgent, they were alike only in their weather-beaten complexions and their habituation to the control of Negro slaves as a daily routine.

[1] G. B. Harmon, Cedartown, Ga., *ibid.*, II, 214 (July, 1854).
[2] *Farmers' Register*, III, 495.
[3] *Ibid.*, IX, 649. *Cf.* also *American Agriculturist*, IV, 319.

CHAPTER XVI

HOMESTEADS

As the nests of birds follow the pattern of their kind, so to a degree do the houses of men. Englishmen in founding Jamestown built huts of wattle and thatch like those of cotters at home;[1] and when their palisading against Indians gave the thought that upright posts might form walls for houses they used this awkward device. It remained, so far as we may gather, for New Sweden to transfer from forested Scandinavia to the limitless woodlands of America the notion of cribbed logs for housebuilding. When this device was once introduced the back country was committed to the log cabin as its basic type. For temporary or even semi-permanent purposes this construction had convincing merits. On every steading the material was immediately at hand as waste in clearing fields for crops; and the same ax which felled the trees could notch the logs to make the house corners firm as the walls were built up. A frow to rive clapboards for the roof, a saw to cut apertures for door, windows and fireplace, and a hammer to drive a few nails completed the necessary tools.[2] A shack or cabin of round poles could be built almost in a twinkling, a chimney of smaller cribwork soon added; and a daubing to fill the crevices all round and cover the fireplace walls thickly with clay would leave only the batten door and window shutters to be made and hung on wooden or leather hinges. Here then was a house of a single room, which might be duplicated with variations for stabling and storage or for added lodging whether for the proprietor's family or for slaves.

[1] Fiske Kimball, *Domestic Architecture in the American Colonies and Early Republic* (New York, 1922), 4. This is an excellent study of the general theme.

[2] A maul and wedges to split floor puncheons could be made on the spot.

Expansion of the cabin proper followed a standard pattern, in the cotton belt at least.[1]   On the same front with the first crib a second was built at a distance of ten or fifteen feet, a continuous roof was laid over the two cribs and the intervening passage, and all three spaces were floored on the same level, when they were floored at all.   This made a "double cabin", with a sheltered but uninclosed space in the middle.   Such a house would stand for years if the sills, on blocks or stones, were clear of the ground; but the bark and sapwood invited boring insects, and the round surfaces easily lost their daubing. A house of hewn logs was desirable as a replacement.

The construction of this was a heavier task.   From the thick trunks of trees timbers eight or ten inches square and eighteen or twenty feet long were hewn with adze or broadax, and their ends notched for mortice.   These were laid in the usual cribwork, but with more care to make the walls plumb and the joints true. The crevices were filled with boards or flat stones and mortar; and chimneys were built of stone or brick.[2]   The hewn log house was likely to follow the same floor plan in the first instance as the double log cabin, but from this it might be expanded in several directions.   A lean-to or perhaps a separate crib might be built at the farther end or at the rear of either or both rooms, or a second story be raised upon the cribs of the first.   In further improvement the passage might be inclosed to constitute a hall, and porches added in front and rear to compensate for the loss of out-of-door sitting space.   Such a house, if its roof and its daubing were kept intact, would resist rot indefinitely.   As an evidence of esteem for its solid worth, I have recently seen in Ontario a log house mounted upon rollers, being moved to a new location.

When sawmills were set up here and there, and planking became available, many a house of hewn logs was given an

---

[1] Basil Hall, *Travels*, III, 271; [anon.] *The Old Pine Farm: or the Southern Side* (Nashville, 1860), 20.

[2] Contract specifications for a hewn-log house in 1761 are printed in Lyman Chalkley, *Chronicles of the Scotch-Irish Settlement in Virginia* (Rosslyn, Va., 1912), I, 494.   Details for rebuilding one in Texas in 1827 are given in the *American Historical Association Report* for 1919, II, 1682.

outer dress of weatherboards and perhaps an inner surface of plaster. But younger houses of frame construction, or even of brick, perpetuated the plan and contour of the old. The community was habituated to a hallway running from front to rear on one or two floors, and chimneys at the gable ends. The influence was in some cases extraordinary. A brick house built by one of my great-grandfathers has, upstairs and down identically, a hall from front to rear and another from side to side, separating each of the four chambers from every other. In planning it he must have thought that four separate cribs covered by one roof offered the best floor plan available.

❋   ❋   ❋   ❋   ❋

On tidewater from Maryland to Louisiana the trends were various, for ships brought fashions as well as men and books, and no proprietor need be wholly his own architect. For the first century on the Chesapeake fortunes were small and houses were plain. The dormered English cottage of a story and a half with low ceilings was perhaps the most common type.[1] But with the rise of large fortunes in the middle third of the eighteenth century, elegance began to be sought in architecture, as in costume, horseflesh and equipage. Sons returning from school in England, and even a few professional architects,[2] brought praise and plans and elevations of manor houses. The "great hall" had its vogue, forming the stem of an E, or the bar of an H as at "Stratford" and "Tuckahoe", but the convenience of a parlor which was not a thoroughfare and a

---

[1] Cf. A. G. Bein, "A Day in Williamsburg", in the *American Architect*, XCV, 209–216. In the neighborhood of Norfolk a Dutch style prevailed. — W. S. Forrest, *Historical and Descriptive Sketches of Norfolk and Vicinity* (Philadelphia, 1853), 58.

[2] At Charleston: "Ezra Waite, Civil Architect, House-builder in general and Carver, from London, Has finished the Architecture, conducted the execution thereof, viz.: in the joiner way, all tabernacle frames (but that in the dining room excepted), and carved all the said work in the four principal rooms, and also calculated, adjusted, and draw'd at large for to work by, the Ionick entablature, and carved the same in front and round the eaves, of Miles Brewton, Esquire's House on White-Point for Mr. Muncrieff." He has had twenty-seven years of experience on the houses of noblemen and gentlemen in England, and invites patronage. — Advertisement in the *South Carolina Gazette and Country Journal*, August 22, 1769, reprinted in Harriette K. Leiding, *Historic Houses of South Carolina* (Philadelphia, 1921), 5.

dining room which might be shut off between meals turned the main preference to rectangular houses, which might be lengthened gracefully, as at "Westover", "Homewood" and "Montpelier", with one-story flanking structures.[1]   Meanwhile the ceiling grew higher, in response to the climatic need of cool spaces.   The "English brick" of which tidewater houses were built were more commonly of English type than of English manufacture.   Some brick doubtless crossed the ocean as ballast, but the volume was little nearer the latter-day repute than was the furniture which came in the *Mayflower*.

The dwellings in colonial times might show classic touches in their details; but adornment in the form of Doric, Ionic or Corinthian porticoes and colonnades came after the Revolution, mainly as a fruit of Thomas Jefferson's enthusiasm.[2] He designed in person the Virginia State Capitol, the University of Virginia,[3] his own Monticello, and numerous classic porches to decorate the homes of his friends already standing.   The fashion spread till few dwellings were thought to be full-style without pillars and pediment or entablature.   Columns plain or fluted, round or square, every formal house must have; and the nearer a home resembled a temple the better.[4]   Marble was ideal but unattainable, and the native stones were not readily dressed.   Stuccoed brick was used where workmanship was competent, but wood, painted white, was the chief recourse.   The columns must rise to the height of the eaves, and the more massive the better.   "Arlington" with its immense pillars was designed specifically for effect when viewed from the distant city of Washington.   In Athens and La-Grange, Georgia, Huntsville, Greensboro, Tuscaloosa and Florence, Alabama, and sundry other towns, nearly every

---

[1] *Cf.* H. W. Desmond and H. Croly, *Stately Homes in America* (New York, 1903).

[2] Fiske Kimball, "Thomas Jefferson as an Architect: Monticello and Shadwell", in the *Architectural Quarterly of Harvard University*, II, No. 4.

[3] "The impression of Jefferson's whole plan is of grave intellectual beauty, boldness, style, aristocratic statement, masculine sentiment." — Stark Young in the *New Republic*, LI, 101.

[4] The classic vogue also swept over the North in the 1830's, but the fashion there shifted by mid-century to the Gothic, with no cottage complete without a cupola. — A. J. Downing, *Rural Essays* (New York, 1853), 206.

house of any pretension acquired a colonnade across the front, if not along the sides as well. The results were sometimes graceful, sometimes awkward. The country houses were not far behind those in town, though colonnettes — or posts, in plain language — continued to support many a porch roof.

Most of the plantation homes were at all times more commodious than elegant; and many had not even a rambling spaciousness.[1] Almost universally the kitchen stood well apart, that its odors, its music and its clatter be not too near. In many cases also the dining room was semidetached, standing across a porch from the main body of the house. A Federal officer in the Wilderness campaign said of the Virginia steadings: "They have a queer way of building on one thing after another, the great point being to have a separate shed or outhouse for every purpose, and then a lot more sheds and outhouses for the negroes. You will find a carpenter's shop, tool room, coach-shed, pig-house, stable, and out-kitchen, two or three barns, and half a dozen negro huts, besides the main house where the family lives."[2] The "village aspect" of the typical steading was noted by travelers early and late; and it persists in many cases to the present day.

✻   ✻   ✻   ✻   ✻

A wise planter when settling in a new location was likely to defer the construction of a permanent house until more needful things had been accomplished. An English lady remarked in 1775 of a homestead in the lowlands of North Carolina: "There is a show of plenty at Hunthill beyond anything I ever saw. . . . I assure you they keep a good house, tho' it is little better than one of his negro huts, and it appeared droll enough to eat out of China and be served in

[1] For example, along the highway from Tuskegee to Montgomery and thence to Greensboro, Alabama, there is a striking succession of old one-story houses containing four or six rooms behind their stereotyped porches. This is in a zone of gently rolling red land, noted for its lasting fertility; and its people were prosperous from cotton on a plantation scale. — A. J. Pickett, "The Red Lands of Alabama", in the *Southern Cultivator*, V, 10 (January, 1847).

[2] G. R. Agassiz, ed., *Meade's Headquarters, 1863–1865: Letters of Col. Theodore Lyman* (Boston, 1922), 115, 116.

plate in such a parlour.   He has however an excellent library
with fine globes, . . . and tho' the house is no house, yet the
master and the furniture make you ample amends." [1]   Scenes of
this general sort shifted in due time to Mississippi, where Solon
Robinson described them in 1845,[2] and to Texas, where young
Rutherford Hayes found "city refinement and amusements in
a log cabin on the banks of the Brazos, where only yesterday
the steam whistle of the steamboat was mistaken for a
panther." [3]

Not all were stanch enough to resist the makeshift influence
of crude surroundings.   Many indeed fell into ways of easy-
going comfort and retained them after new housing had made
slack arrangements incongruous.   A rambler in the Natchez
district wrote in the 'thirties: "A huge colonnaded structure
. . . struck our eyes with an imposing effect.   It was the abode
of one of the wealthiest planters of this state. . . .   The
grounds about this edifice were neglected, horses were grazing
around the piazzas, over which were strewed saddles, whips, horse
blankets and the motley paraphernalia with which planters love
to lumber their galleries.   On nearly every piazza in Mississippi may be found a wash-stand, bowl, pitcher, towel and
water-bucket, for general accommodation. . . .   Here they
wash, lounge, often sleep, and take their meals."

At another homestead: "The planter was sitting upon the
gallery, divested of coat, vest and shoes, with his feet on the
railing, playing in high glee with a little dark-eyed boy and
two young negroes who were chasing each other under the
bridge formed by his extended limbs.   Three or four noble
dogs . . . were crouching like leopards around his chair. . . .
A hammock . . . contained a youth of fourteen . . . whose
aide de camp in the shape of a strapping negress stood by the
hammock, waving over the sleeper a long plume of the gorgeous
feathers of the pea-fowl."   On this porch also, whether hung
upon antlers or tossed upon the floor, were hats, coats and

[1] Evangeline W. Andrews, ed., *Journal of a Lady of Quality* (New Haven, 1922), 185.
[2] *The Cultivator*, n. s., II, 271, 272, 365.
[3] C. R. Williams, ed., *Diary and Letters of Rutherford B. Hayes*, I, 257.

harness, guns and shot-pouches, brogans and slippers, along with a broken "cotton slate" to tally the picking of the crop.[1] Even in Virginia neatness was far from universal. An English governess jotted on a lowland plantation in 1860: "A want of finish, and untidiness about the yard and buildings, rather surprised me amid signs of wealth and abundant labour, for in every direction negroes were to be seen, not only men and women working in the fields, but children whose business appeared to consist in waiting on the elder ones, otherwise in doing nothing."[2] And again in the Piedmont: "With every requisite at hand, and able workmen among the negroes, it seemed astonishing that people should be so regardless of comfort as to countenance shabby fences, leaky apartments, and a thousand other minor miseries. . . . Much of this is to be traced to negro inefficiency always, and in the present instance to the impracticability of the lady in chief of Milbank, who, rather than exert herself to walk about the house and supervise her servants, permitted an unlimited degree of disorder and dustiness, if nothing worse."[3] A house might be highly formal in design, and its inmates quite otherwise. A swarm of children anywhere tended to put things topsy-turvy, and a swarm of slave domestics would not keep the house or the grounds shipshape unless master or mistress, mammy or major-domo, one or all, were stanch devotees of order.

Many, nevertheless, achieved not only neatness but beauty, and some a considerable splendor. In a lawn of ten acres at "Rose Hill" near Port Tobacco, Gustavus R. Brown had a box-bordered garden, "the most extensive and artistic to be found in Maryland", having "assembled a rare and most valuable collection of roses and other flowering plants from all parts of the world." It was equipped for irrigation, and there was a large hothouse for winter service.[4] At the home of Abram Venable in the Virginia Piedmont, south of the James, a visitor in the spring of 1842 counted sixty-six beds of tulips with about

[1] [J. H. Ingraham] *The South-West*, II, 97-100.
[2] [Catharine C. Hopley] *Life in the South*, I, 43.   [3] *Ibid.*, I, 228.
[4] H. E. Hayden, *Virginia Genealogies*, 173. Brown died in 1804.

a gross of blossoms in each.[1] These, like the famous Magnolia Gardens and the Middleton Place near Charleston, were special instances; but many more could be found on a comparable scale, such as the Ferrell estate near LaGrange, Georgia. Esthetics and elegance conspired with a long growing season to promote floral indulgence. I have a boyhood remembrance that beauty in time of drought cost heavy labor at the well; but it was gratifying to say that I could name half a hundred varieties among my mother's roses.

Trees were an easier means of beautification, for when once planted they would mostly take care of themselves. Live oaks, so named from their evergreen habit, were given preference wherever they would thrive. Magnolias, crêpe myrtles and Pride of India, cedars and Lombardy poplars were also favorites, whether for shading a yard or lining a drive. Native giants of the forest also were cherished in home groves, except for chestnut trees, whose fallen burrs would not be pleasant for the bare feet of romping children.

From a remarkably detailed map of 1780[2] we may gather that the road from Savannah toward Augusta ran parallel to the river, but far enough away to avoid the mud of the low grounds where the rice crops throve. Unless a wayfarer took one of the frequent lanes leading off to the right, he would see no human structures except at long intervals a church, a mill or a tavern; he would hear little but the plod of his horse's hoofs in the heavy sand or the sighing of the wind in the pines. A stranger would be likely to surmise falsely that wilderness lay upon every side. So, also, if one journeyed from Yorktown to Richmond, from Gloucester Point to Fredericksburg, from Charleston to Columbia, from Natchez to Vicksburg, the steadings would as a rule be screened by the forest; or if by chance the road ran past open fields, the homes in their groves would stand at some distance removed.[3]

❋   ❋   ❋   ❋   ❋

[1] John Hall, ed., *Forty Years' Familiar Letters of James W. Alexander*, I, 356.
[2] Archibald Campbell, *Sketch of the Northern Frontiers of Georgia, engraved by Will M. Faden*, 1780, partly reproduced herein.
[3] [Paulding] *Letters from the South*, I, 100; [Ingraham] *The South-West*, II, 112.

Whether at the roadside or at the farther end of its "avenue", a visitor encountering a gate would do well to halloo the house and await the coming of some inmate, or the hounds were likely to demonstrate a hostile alertness. Inside the inclosure, with the dogs quieted and greetings exchanged, life resumed its normal sway with minimum diversion by reason of the guest's presence, for Southern visits were of hours' if not of days' duration. The hens cackled, with cocks ejaculating indorsement, the guineas quadracked, the martens chattered in their suspended gourds, and a mocker imitated every bird that came to mind and added improvisations of his own. A cowbell tinkled in the distance. Conversation rose and fell on the piazza as palmetto fans stirred the quiet air of midsummer noon.

The strokes of a tall clock in the hall were of little more concern than the silent shadow on the sundial outdoors. It was twelve o'clock until it was one, and one until it was two. Dinner was ready when the cook gave word for the bell to be rung. Through the hall and across the back porch to the dining room went the adults, and thither the children thronged after a hasty scrubbing, unless they were crowded out and scheduled for a "second table." Above the viands a negro girl waved a long brush languidly to keep the flies at a distance. All the meats and vegetables, and there were likely to be several of each, were on the table from the first, according to "country style." Ham was almost as constant as the cloth; sweet potatoes, except in the summer months before the new crop came in; rice, or perhaps either grits or lye hominy as alternatives, the year round. Hot biscuit and cornbread came from the kitchen often enough to keep supplies always capable of melting butter. The master of the house, though perhaps not loquacious before, would press upon each person a second helping of string beans or fried chicken, as if his aim in life were to produce a surfeit. The dessert might be a deep, rich, peach pie or a blackberry dumpling, with syllabub as a frothy companion.

After dinner came a stroll to the orchards, the melon patch, the fish pond and perhaps the brandy still beside a rill where crushed peaches were fermenting in open vats. In mid-afternoon old and young were summoned to attack an array of watermelons, cooled in the springhouse, half a sugary sphere to each participant. At dusk, whatever its hour, came a more moderate supper. Then the children were made to wash their feet for bed; and erelong older folk turned in, to be sung to sleep by the katydids and the mocking birds, while in the distance a hound on his haunches persistently bayed the moon.

Here again I find myself recording mainly my own recollections from a barefoot age, confirmed by later observations and the reading of earlier narratives. It may be particularized that a great-uncle whose home I visited for part of every vacation dwelt in a story-and-a-half house of hewn logs which before my day had been surfaced with weatherboards. The chairs were mostly homemade, unvarnished, from the fine-grained white oak, and bottomed with woven splits of the same tough, pliable wood. Feather ticks remained from times when corded bedsteads, lacking springs, needed something softer than a mattress to make them pleasant. The round dining table had above it, as a device for diminishing the need of attendance, a disk which might be revolved to bring to hand any dish desired. The old man, busy out of doors by day, would read at night in his bedroom, holding his newspaper with his left hand and in his right a solid-wicked sperm lamp without chimney or shade. There were clear-flamed kerosene lamps in the parlor, but he continued in the custom of his younger years. His wife, sturdier in physique, was even busier than he, depending less upon servants than upon herself.

The front yard was crowded with zinnias, dahlias, hollyhocks and rambling roses; the backyard, shaded and sandy, was vocal with the joys and sorrows of white and black children. These grounds were fenced with whitewashed pickets, and the kitchen garden high-paled with riven white-oak strips, weathered gray. The orchards, the pasture and the cornfields were bounded by zigzag rail fences, for the merits and economy of barbed wire had yet to be demonstrated in that neighborhood. With daily mails and free delivery far in future, a small boy twice a week rode a gray mare to the crossroads post office. From time to time a wagon would carry corn to be ground at a creek-side mill, and perhaps continue on to a village with watermelons for sale at five or ten cents apiece or peaches at fifty cents a bushel, or chickens, eggs or butter at corresponding prices. Farm products were cheap in the 'eighties and 'nineties.

On Sundays when the circuit rider was due, the household would attend Asbury Chapel, and a specially copious dinner be made ready at home against the "coming by" of a crowd of guests. On some week day of early summer the whole Methodist population of the vicinage would assemble at the church for an "all day singing with dinner on the ground", the hymns interspersed with labor in clearing underbrush from the grove and weeds from the graveyard.[1] These customs had held on from preceding generations, along with the murmur of "studying aloud" in the schoolhouse, whose session still avoided the months in which the children were needed to pick cotton.

At all hours negro men with hat in hand, or women with arms akimbo, would come from field or cabin to the planter's house for instruction or equipment, medicine or advice, or the redress of some grievance. The blacks in my day were free tenants or wage laborers; but the planters and their wives were by no means emancipated in full from the manifold responsibilities of "slavery times."

[1] I sometimes attended the Flat Rock and Warm Springs camp meetings in Heard and Meriwether counties, but our county of Troup was not primitive enough to maintain one of these.

CHAPTER XVII

THE PLAIN PEOPLE

THE census of 1860 reported 46,274 heads of families as holding twenty or more slaves each. Assuming five persons on an average to constitute a family, and twenty slaves of all ages to be roughly a minimum for the plantation method, it appears that the planter class numbered less than a quarter of a million souls in the fifteen commonwealths. Thrice as many heads of families held from five to nineteen slaves and ranked perhaps as a middle class of large farmers and comfortable townsmen. Five times as many more owned or hired from one to four slaves each to help in their farms or shops or serve in their kitchens. This leaves nearly six of the eight million whites out of proprietary touch with the four million slaves.[1]

The non-slaveholders and the small slaveholders were scattered everywhere, but in widely varying proportions. In the cotton counties of the Mississippi delta they were not to be found except as overseers and perhaps woodcutters to supply the steamboats with fuel.[2] In the mountains, in some parts of the pine barrens, and on the borders north and west, they comprised nearly all the population. Everywhere else they dwelt as neighbors of the planters and of well-to-do townsmen.

[1] Through the full span of the Federal census from 1790 to 1860 the ratio of whites to slaves in the South as a whole kept steadily at about two to one. The southern free colored population increased somewhat more rapidly, and in 1860 numbered about a quarter of a million. It should not be forgotten that an appreciable number of these are included in the count of slaveholders.

[2] Tyrone Power jotted on a winter voyage up the Mississippi in 1835 (*Impressions of America*, Philadelphia, 1836, II, 118): "We frequently drew alongside the forest for a supply of wood, which the proprietors keep ready prepared in piles for the use of boats, being paid for it by the cord. . . . I always landed at these places; and above Baton Rouge, where the French population is less general, I commonly found the labouring woodcutters to be North-country men, or from the western part of Michigan. They informed me that they can clear fifty dollars a month for the seven months they can work in this region, and that four or five seasons are sufficient to enable a saving man to buy a farm in the West."

Their standards of comfort and propriety, their manners and morals, varied with the vicinage, with health and wealth, with education and opportunity, and with individual proclivities and predilections. Joseph E. Brown, war-time governor of Georgia, emerged from a mountain farm with a yoke of oxen as pay for schooling; John Letcher, his contemporary as governor of Virginia, began adult life as a carpenter; C. G. Memminger, Confederate Secretary of the Treasury, was an orphanage boy; and Andrew Johnson a tailor's apprentice, illiterate until a wife took him in hand. These and their fellow millions cannot be lumped as "poor whites" and dismissed with a phrase whether it be "ancestrally degenerate", "oppressed by the slave system", or "debilitated by the climate." Sweeping statements are likely to be as false as they are facile.

The plain folk did not make records comparable to those of the planters. The letters they wrote were few, and their significant, explicit items fewer still. From a family parcel preserved from 1860 by one of the Georgia Smiths the following passages are taken. A sister to her brother: "I take my pen in hand to drop you a few lines I received your letter requesting me to begeting off with myself I can tell you I was about to be off with myself but the neighbors all cryede out A way with such an I dia as that for it wold disgrace the whole family and be my ruin the preachers also cryede out A way with it so I thought it best not to go if you knew as much as me you would not want me to go" But she fails to tell us what reprehensible thing she had done. To the same brother from another sister who had moved with her husband to farm in the "fresh country" of Butler County, Alabama:[1] "I am very well pleased with the country and people as much so as any settlement I was ever in fo the time I have been hear I have a pig but no cow or chickens or dog." But a month of teaching school, "a very unpleasant occupation", jaundiced her view: "I do not know where we will go to yet but we will not be apt to stay in butler I think it is a very good country for farming but ther is no society nor no nothing elce her the people is

[1] They were bound for Texas, but stopped for a crop to finance their farther trek.

more like hogs and dogs than they are like folks . . . I will try to stay heare this year without saying much." We may doubt that she succeeded in holding her tongue. A brother who stayed on the old homestead was in better humor: "As it respects marrying that is clear out of the question at present. I am easy on that point — and if I don't make a rise some way I expect to be easy perhaps forever — if I can make a good strike in honorable business I can make also a good one in marrying — though I never expect to marry for fortune yet I wont object to a little boot if it comes in the way — I loves all the little gals but I cant love a big gal as I wonto." [1]

Migrant farmers, who had no female kin at call to fill domestic vacancies, must needs have wives. A native of the Shenandoah wrote home from Illinois where he had lost a wife and six of ten children: "Now this is the 20th of November 1849 and I can tell you som more about me a gitting married   a week or two after Christmas is the time sot for the time . . . it may Posibel Be Broke off yet if the partys dos not tak good care for nare a one will give a way to the other to a gree for she is tolerabel Partickler and that makes me so two for I think she wants to git married   But does not let on and that is the way with me and she thinks that I am verry anxious to marry and so nare a one can git along with one a nother   She knows that I cant git a long without marrien and that is the [way] with her   But I could bet you that I will not wait for her enny more   I will look out for a nother   I have waited two months for her now   She may fool herself yet or I may." [2]

❁   ❁   ❁   ❁   ❁

[1] A neighbor of George Washington was more mercenary: "I could [have] been able to [have] Satisfied all my old Arrears some months AGoe by marrying [an] old widow woman in this County, She has Large soms [o']' cash by her and Prittey good Es^t — she is as thick as she is high — And gits drunk at Least three or foure [times] a weak — which is Disagreable to me — has Viliant Sperrit when Drunk — its been [a] Great Dispute in my mind what to Doe, — I beleave I shu'd Run all Resks — if my Last wife had been [an] Even temper'd woman, but her Sperrit has Given me such [a] Shock — that I am afraid to Run the Resk Again, when I see the object before my Eys [it] is Disagreable." — S. M. Hamilton, ed., *Letters to Washington*, IV, 66.

[2] Manuscript in private possession, a neat philological specimen. Never a one in full English, ne'er a one in colloquial speech as well as in poetry, "nare a one" is rare. "Nary a one" is the present-day backwoods expression, its users unconscious that the *y* of *nary* is the former *a*. "Not nary a one" is the final phase in the degradation.

In the mountain coves luxuries were never known, and leisure was mere loafing. Gradations ranged only from homespun comfort to habituated eking of the barest livelihood. With a wool hat, a cotton or tow shirt, and jeans breeches upheld by a single "gallus", a man was fully clad, though he might use coat and shoes against winter's chill. The cotton shifts and poke bonnets of the women, and their shapeless linsey-woolsey gowns, varied not with the fashions of Paris or Philadelphia. The great world of men and books was kept alien by remoteness and illiteracy. "We uns"[1] lived our own clannish lives between the steep walls of the cove[2] except when a feud called for a foray up over in back or a sheriff took an offender against lowland law to a lowland jail. The mountains denied ambition; the mountaineers acquiesced with a sturdy, self-respecting simplicity. A tourist remarked in 1816: "There is a striking air of conscious independence about them. . . . At first it seems a little unpleasant, but reflection soon reconciles us to this proud badge of liberty." And of a stalwart young farmer-hunter, he "talked with a degree of manliness, intelligence and decorum that would have astonished people who measure the fineness of a man's intellect by the texture of his coat."[3]

Not long afterward a Shenandoah lawyer had an errand beyond the rim: "Arrived at Huntersville, the seat of justice of Pocahontas county — a place as much out of the world as Crim Tartary." The so-called town, he said, comprised two clapboard-covered log houses, inferior to his own slave cabins. "One of these wretched hovels is the residence of John Bradshaw, the other is called the Loom-house, for the people are

---

[1] "You all," commonly compressed into "y'all", is a standard expression in the lower South to distinguish the plural from the singular of the second-person pronoun; but "we all" is rare. Among the mountaineers "you uns" is a fairly general equivalent of "you all." "We uns" doubtless originated by analogy among those who failed to note that "we", unlike "you", permits no confusion of plural with singular. Horace Kephart, *Our Southern Highlanders*, each edition better than the last, is an intimate and elaborate study of life, including dialect, in the North Carolina mountains of our own time. A century has brought little change.

[2] On taking a short cut over a ridge, Kephart quotes a native saying: "Goin' up, you can might' nigh stand up straight and bite the ground; goin' down, a man wants hobnails in the seat of his pants."

[3] [J. K. Paulding] *Letters from the South* (New York, 1817), I, 198, 200.

self-sustaining.   They spin and weave.   The big wheel and the little wheel are birring in every hut and throwing off the woolen and linen yard to be worked up for family purposes. . . .   In Bradshaw's dwelling there is a large fireplace which occupies one entire side, the gable end.   The chimney is enormous and so short that the room is filled with light which enters this way. It is an ingenious contrivance for letting all the warmth escape through the chimney, whilst most of the smoke is driven back into the chamber. . . .   Pocahontas is a fine grazing county, and the support of the people is mainly derived from their flocks of cattle, horses and sheep, which they drive over the mountains to market.   There is little money among them except after these excursions, but they have little need of it — every want is supplied by the happy country they possess, and of which they are as fond as the Swiss of their mountains." [1]

A young Englishman in search of livelihood and adventure sojourned in the Virginia mountains before moving on to the Kansas border and thence to the Texas plains.   A mountain steading at which he dwelt comprised a two-story cabin of eighteen by twenty feet, a detached kitchen, a spring house, a stable and a cow house, all of logs.   In the dwelling the first floor was the bedroom of the proprietor and his wife, serving also as a living room for all.   As bedtime approached the daughters, the sons, and any guests climbed the ladder in separate groups with a lighted pine splinter to the dormitory above; and at the first streak of day the girls made exit, leaving the men and boys to dress in masculine unrestraint.   Ablutions were made on the porch, where, lacking a bowl, each person in turn dipped water from the cedar bucket with a calabash and poured it over another's hands.   Supper and breakfast comprised identically bacon and eggs, cornbread and coffee.   At dinner there were vegeta-

---

[1] J. H. Peyton to his wife, September 1, 1823.   [J. L. Peyton] *Memoir of John Howe Peyton* (Staunton, Va., 1894), 48, 49.   In another district, not so good for grazing, hogs were the chief reliance.   In 1828 a settler who had hoped to pay a debt from the sale of corn explained to his creditor that although the crop was good it had no sale, for "thar is a grat whit oak mast her that ever was known in this part . . . the hogs must take the mast, for tis so plenty her [It] is hard times for money." — Manuscript in private possession.

bles in season from a "truck patch", the cultivation of which fell within the women's province.[1] The standard of this family's comfort was perhaps higher than the average. The land, except for small stream-side pockets, was niggard and steep, and game was meager. In fact, thin as the population was, the coves received and retained more people than they could support except in stark poverty.[2]

Kinsmen to the mountaineers but more varied in their fortunes were the people of the great valley chain stretching from the Shenandoah to northeastern Alabama. Broad fields of lasting fertility gave substantial revenues to many, from wheat and whiskey and a bit of tobacco where freighting was not too dear, from livestock otherwise. But market relations were too slender to serve as more than a subsidiary recourse. Households must in the main make their own furniture as well as their bread; work must be steady, and living somewhat plain. A sprinkling of slaves gave sluggish assistance to their owners, and a few establishments grew to plantation scale; but as a rule the people dwelt and wrought much as did those of inland Pennsylvania whence these had come. The houses of the better sort were snug, their stone fences strong, their pastures lush, their horses brawny, their Valley pike smooth, and their whiskey not too free. At the same time poverty as dire as that amid the mountains could be found with little seeking, for the Valley was not an Eden. The distinguishing feature of the régime was merely that most of the well-to-do had no cult of urbanity, of nicety in speech or fashion in dress, of distinction in house or equipage, of competitive expenditure or conspicuous waste. In short, they were plain men and women, not ladies and gentlemen.

❊   ❊   ❊   ❊   ❊

As in the mountains and the Valley, so in the Piedmont and the plains, poverty was in some cases personal, in some cases

[1] R. H. Williams, *With the Border Ruffians* (London, 1908), 13–28.

[2] These conditions in the Blue Ridge and the Alleghenies were repeated in the Ozarks. — C. O. Sauer, *The Geography of the Ozark Highland of Missouri* (*Geographic Society of Chicago Bulletin*, no. 7).

regional. The developments in Georgia will serve to show the divergencies. The lands within the present limits of the State were distributed in the first instance almost uniformly in small plots — by the trustees as part of their charity, by the royal province and the early commonwealth on headrights, and by the State from 1803 to 1833 in successive lotteries in which every head of a family had a chance to draw a farm tract without price. The public distribution was thus on a steadily equalitarian basis. But no sooner was the trustees' prohibition upon slave labor repealed than the rice lands began to be engrossed into plantation units; and the cotton belt was destined to similar if not such thorough change. In each interior district as a rule the first influx was of small farmers, all of them to grow cotton for sale at an equal price, pound for pound and grade for grade. But some chanced upon rich lands, others upon poor; some were near navigation, others were far; some were expert, vigorous, frugal and far-sighted, others were slack, spendthrift or merely perhaps unlucky. Profits from efficiency and good fortune enabled some to buy slaves and then to buy neighboring lands and attain eventually the scale and rank of planters. For their added lands they paid prices acceptable to those who heard the loud call of the West; but they could force no man to sell who was not so minded. A legion of Naboths held their vineyards, several farmers to every planter, throughout the best cotton zone, each producing cotton in sturdy competition with his neighbor great or small.

In the upper half of the Piedmont, though the climate was adapted to cotton, ruggedness of contour diminished the size of available fields, and distance from navigable streams enhanced the cost of marketing. The opportunity to expand farms into plantations was therefore not so great as in the middle region, and the slaves in the gross were fewer than the whites. In most of the southern quarter of the commonwealth, on the other hand, a plantation development was restricted not by remoteness but by the leanness of the lands. The growing season was very long and the rainfall copious, but the sandy soil had not enough plant food to support any vigorous growth except the forest of pines and the tough wire grass on its floor. Turpentine and perhaps lumber would yield livelihood, but agriculture was penury. Thus Georgia was broadly banded: a strip of sea-island cotton and rice plantations on the coast, with a dense negro population; the pine barrens with sparse whites and very few slaves; the main cotton belt spreading southwestward across the State, with mingled farms and plantations and the negroes more numerous than the whites; the upper Piedmont with farmers predominating; and the mountains with of course no plantations and virtually no slaves. This belting, with its lines curving variously, was characteristic of the South at large.

With land initially gratis, in Georgia at least, and its price always restrained by the absorption of capital in the purchase of slaves, no monopoly of locations can explain the differentiation of individual fortunes as between planters and farmers. It was rather the variance of talent, resolution, health and mere luck. The divergencies, furthermore, were not sharply between rich and poor but of continuous gradation from millionaires to paupers; and the classes were by no means constant in personnel. Many a planter was stripped by bankruptcy; many another bequeathed two or three dozen slaves in equal distribution among a dozen children; many a breadwinner was taken by pneumonia or crippled by a falling log or killed in a duel, to the lasting destitution of his family; on the other hand, many a son of humble parents took the tide which led to fortune. Nevertheless inherited wealth generally brought continued comfort; and inherited poverty was hard to conquer, particularly if accompanied by illness and enervation. Herein lay the contrast between two classes often but erroneously confused, the "poor whites" and the yeomen. A healthy child was likely to make a vigorous man, but to suffer a chronic malady was to drag a ball and chain.

In striking contrast with the robust immune blacks, travelers noted repeatedly the sallow skins, the languid manner and the frequent fevers among the white dwellers in swampy places.[1]   A contemporary student said that their indolence was not innate but came from "the want of health, which produces an apathy or aversion to work, and frequently a relaxation or want of natural excitement in the powers of life, which seek artificial stimulant." [2]   He was awkwardly trying to say that some chronic invalids develop unwholesome habits in attempts to solace their morbid cravings.   Alcoholism was an easy consequence if the means were at command.   But poverty might impel such practices as the sucking of rosin or the "eating" of clay by sticking bits of it against the roof of the mouth and swallowing the muddy saliva.[3]   In that generation "malaria", embracing sundry remittent and intermittent fevers, was the standard explanation.   But later discoveries have added hook-worm as the major cause of the typical anemic debility.[4] Infestations by this parasite might have been relieved quite readily by medicine or prevented by the mere wearing of shoes; but its existence unsuspected, no prevention or cure was applied. The victims, "lank, lean, angular and bony, with . . . a natural stupidity or dullness of intellect that almost surpasses belief ",[5] "the most degraded race of human beings claiming an Anglo-Saxon origin that can be found on the face of the earth ",[6] suffered the contumely of their contemporaries who might better have given sympathy if they could not afford relief.

These wretchedly genuine "po' white trash", scorned even

---

[1] *E.g.*, Henry Ker, *Travels* (Elizabethtown, N. J., 1816), 352; Tyrone Power, *Impressions* (London, 1836), II, 96; J. S. Buckingham, *Slave States* (London, 1842), 113. Negroes had a general immunity to malaria if they dwelt continually in malarious districts.   From hookworm it may be that they suffered as much as the whites.

[2] [Zephaniah Kingsley] *A Treatise on the Patriarchal System of Society* (4th ed., n. p. 1834), 5.

[3] Cases of clay eating in authentic records are most numerous among negroes, merely because masters procured for their slaves far more medical inspection than poor whites procured for themselves; but probably the vicious practice was as common among the whites.   Thomas Roughly, *Jamaica Planters' Guide* (London, 1823), 118; *Southern Medical Reports* (New Orleans, 1849), I, 190, quoted in V. A. Moody, *Slavery on Louisiana Sugar Plantations*, 83 *note*; P. H. Buck, "The Poor Whites of the Antebellum South", in the *American Historical Review*, XXXI, 44, citing various travelers.

[4] George Dock and C. C. Bass, *The Hookworm Disease* (St. Louis, 1910).

[5] Daniel R. Hundley, *Social Relations in our Southern States* (New York, 1860), 264.

[6] Frances A. Kemble, *Journal*, 146.

by the slaves, could not embrace opportunities. Any crops they might plant were likely to die of neglect, any jobs they procured were apt to be lost by default, any lands to be taken for debt. They commonly fell to drifting as tenants or squatters in wilderness clearings [1] unless they chanced upon barren lands where they might cluster in communities of their own squalid kind. These listless, uncouth, shambling refugees from the world of competition were never enumerated, but there is cogent reason to believe that they comprised only a small portion of the non-slaveholding population.[2]

*   *   *   *   *

Of course mere poverty was not an index of languor, nor was plain fare or scant furniture an evidence of shiftlessness. A migrant to Missouri wrote home to Virginia in 1860 reporting his house rent at two dollars and fifty cents per month and listing his domestic equipment as two chairs, a trundle bedstead and bedding, an oven, a teakettle, a coffeepot, four knives, four forks, a bucket, a set of cups and saucers, "3 wings to fan the fire — no table — no plates. We eat off a goods box." His emphasis: "The inventory above is no hoax, but strictly true," and his explanation: "We have commenced on a very saving plan, having in mind our former experience in a similar undertaking" [3] show that he and his wife were not habituated to such furnishings nor disposed to abide them as a permanence.

A traveler in southeastern Mississippi stopped for the night at a lonely farm where the provender for his horse was a trough of sweet potatoes and a rack filled with their dried vines. At supper a roast fowl was stuffed with sweet potatoes, a hash of wild turkey had them intermixed, flanking platters offered sweet potatoes baked and fried, others were in the biscuit and the pie, and a decoction of parched sweet potatoes was drunk instead of coffee. After a glass of potato beer the guest went to

---

[1] Achille Murat, *America and the Americans* (New York, 1849), 43-45. This is a translation of Murat, *Esquisse des États-Unis* (Paris, 1832).

[2] G. W. Dyer, *Democracy in the South before the Civil War* (Nashville, [1905]), argues this with good effect.

[3] Manuscript in private possession.

bed. Next morning he had a sore throat, which his hostess relieved with a hot potato poultice and a dose of potato-vine tea.[1] Discounting this for humorous exaggeration, we still may not doubt that sweet potatoes were a main resource. My own memory vouches for the proneness of people with bounteous crops to make the most of them by serving sweet potatoes three times a day, not from poverty but merely from thrift.

The wide reliance upon cornbread had the same basis. A traveler benighted in the "Choctaw purchase" of central Mississippi found shelter with a pioneer household. The husband soon arrived bearing venison as the fruit of his hunting. The wife "took from a keg about a half gallon of meal, sifted it, poured boiling water on it, threw in a little salt, made it up into small pones, wrapping each very carefully in the inner shucks of corn, fresh from the ear, scraped away the embers from one corner of the ample fireplace, laid them down and covered them over deeply with hot ashes and embers." Shortly these "ash cakes" and broiled venison, served on the lid of an old pine chest, made an excellent supper.[2]

Philip Ludwell when traveling in southeastern Virginia in 1710 wrote of a frontier hostess: "She is a very civil woman and shews nothing of ruggedness or Immodesty in her carriage, yett she will carry a gunn in the woods and kill deer, turkeys, &c, shoot doun wild cattle, catch and tye hoggs, knock down beeves with an ax and perform the most manfull Exercises as well as most men in those parts."[3] Later in that century an Englishman found as the keeper of a tavern in the North Carolina lowlands "the largest and strongest woman, perhaps, in the world. She was six feet two inches and a half in height, well

---

[1] J. F. H. Claiborne in the Natchez *Free Trader and Daily Gazette*, December 21, 1841, reprinted in the *Mississippi Historical Society Publications*, IX, 533.

[2] James R. Creecy, *Scenes in the South* (Philadelphia, 1860), 90. The simple ingredients of the ash cake will produce a hoecake if spread thin on a hoe or other iron sheet and turned over while cooking in the open air. For pone the composition is the same, but the cooking is in an oven. All of these when well made of white cornmeal are toothsome. But this is a matter of taste and habituation. An Englishman in Virginia found hoecake "extremely harsh and unpleasant."—J. F. D. Smyth, *Tour* (London, 1784), I, 48.

[3] *Virginia Magazine*, V, 10.

built in proportion, strong, robust, and muscular as a man of the same stature. She possessed a boldness and spirit inferior to no man; and there was no bully, bruiser, wrestler or any other person that excelled in athletic power and agility, for fifty miles around, that she had not complimented with a fair and complete drubbing. . . . I submitted to some small imposition in her charge, rather than enter the lists with her in dispute and run the risque of experiencing her prowess." [1]   In the same region a Confederate officer noted of an old woman with whom he was lodged: "She has some rather masculine characteristics, one of which is a propensity to enforce her rights with a cudgel whenever it is necessary. She swears a little when she is angry, and would not be called refined or fashionable by the least fastidious, but she can boast a better heart and more charity than many a lady who has a good education and greater opportunities for doing good." [2]   These Amazons were acquainted with poverty but strangers to lassitude.

*   *   *   *   *

An official of the royal province of Georgia, impressed by the great number of uncouth "crackers" coming from upland Virginia and the Carolinas, expressed a fear that they might overrun even the rice plantations and spread a general disorder.[3] A woman from New England dwelling in the Georgia Piedmont reported to her father in 1787: "There are a few, and a very few, Worthy good people in the Country near us, but the people in general are the most prophane, blasphemous set of people I ever heard of. They make it a steady practice (if they have money) to come to town, . . . and sometimes when any public business is done, which is often, fourteen or sixteen hundred, . . . and perhaps not one in fifty but what we call fighting drunk. . . .   They have spent in our cellar for liquor

---

[1] J. F. D. Smyth, *Tour*, I, 111.
[2] *William and Mary College Quarterly*, XXV, 79.
[3] Anthony Stokes, *A View of the Constitution of the British Colonies* (London, 1783), 140. This is an early use of "cracker" to designate a backwoodsman. Tar Heel in North Carolina, hill billy, red neck, and wool hat in the Gulf region, Hoosier in Indiana, and jayhawker in Kansas are partial equivalents.

in one day Thirty Pounds Stg., and not a drop carried 1 rod from the store, but sit on a log and swallow it as quick as possible." [1]   These writers were describing a part of what was in their time the wild west. It was tamed with considerable speed, as every other frontier has been.

The county of Wilkes, where as above reported the liquor went so quickly down men's throats, had been organized in 1779; and on August 25 of that year, the first court held session at the residence of Jacob McLendon. The grand jury that day in-dicted James Mobley for "High Treason vs. the State, Horse-stealing, Hogg Stealing and other misdemeanors." On arraign-ment Mobley pleaded not guilty, and "Put Himself on God and his Country for Trial." Next day a petit jury heard the evi-dence, received a charge from the bench, and retired. "On return of the Petit Jury they brought in their Verdict Not Guilty, and so say they all." The court, however, ordered that Mobley be kept in custody; and two days afterward, on motion of the State's attorney supported by new evidence, the case was reheard, the jury returned a verdict of guilty, and the prisoner, along with eight others convicted in the interim, was condemned to death by hanging.[2]   No maxim prevailed that a person be not put in jeopardy twice for the same offense; and the law had no delays.

But the courts were not the sole or the strongest agency in bringing order from chaos. Economic and social forces were operating automatically. Such "crackers" as prospered were bent upon safe enjoyment of their good fortune, and those who procured slaves were specially concerned with security. Leav-ens of respectability and of gentility in the middle and higher levels were working to lessen the crudeness and conquer the rudeness of the mass. Fisticuffs, gougings and shooting affrays persisted for some decades among the lower orders, and stab-bings were not unknown among men of some pretension; but

[1] Mrs. David Hillhouse to Elisha Porter, Washington, Ga., January 26, 1787, in [Marion Boggs, ed.] *The Alexander Letters* (Savannah, 1910), 17. The proportion of drunkenness was doubtless exaggerated.

[2] The records of this session were printed in the *News-Reporter* (Washington, Ga.), August 25, 1922.

sobriety, decency, quietude and in some cases fine serenity were not long in coming. They were hastened by women's influence and the concern of parents for the wholesome upbringing of children.

A youth at Stockbridge, Connecticut, wrote on a July day of 1851 to a former schoolmate in Virginia: "With us industry on the part of the farmer and pleasure on the part of the aristocracy seem at present to take up the whole time, thought and conversation. . . . As usual at this season our country is filled with city boarders, who seem to have nothing to do but to ride from place to place through the country. I often think when in the field at work as they pass, if I was only rich how I too could ride about and see the operatives well employed." [1] This tells us what romantic tradition denies but common sense affirms, that leisured elegance was by no means confined to the South in that generation, and that the poor are more desirous to be like the rich than to reform them. But whatever flights his fancy might follow, this young citizen did not try to train his plow-team to prance, nor spend an hour at his dinner because that was done in high society. His life was apart from dreams, and so those of Southern farmers and their sons. Meals were a matter of food to be dispatched, not of elegance and repartee. Men of dainty palates might sip their wines or their juleps; a son of the soil took his whiskey straight, with a shiver and a smack, disdaining water to check the scorch in his gullet. The planter might have a siesta on a couch; the farmer could snatch a few winks with his trunk and head resting on a chair turned over to give a sloping surface. The gentry chatted on their ample piazzas; the rustics used the wayside, each sitting on one heel and resting an arm on the other knee. Wet ground was thus no bar to long conversation.

A Northern immigrant in Mississippi described a characteristic scene at Natchez: "Seated in a circle around their bread and cheese were half a dozen as rough, rude, honest-looking countrymen from the back part of the state as you could find in the nursery of New-England's yeomanry. They are small

[1] Manuscript in private possession.

farmers — own a few negroes — cultivate a small tract of land and raise a few bales of cotton which they bring to market themselves. Their carts are drawn up around them forming a barricade to their camp, for here, as is customary among them, instead of putting up at taverns they have encamped since their arrival. Between them and their carts are their negroes, who assume a 'cheek by jowl' familiarity with their masters, while jokes . . . pass from one group to the other, with perfect good will and a mutual contempt for the nicer distinctions of color." [1] An Englishman crossing Georgia remarked "that in proportion as the distance from the coast increased, the conditions of the negroes are materially improved. We saw them working in the same field with white men ; and I more than once saw a black man seated in the same room with a free person — a thing never dreamt of elsewhere." [2] If he had entered a cabin at mealtime he might have seen whites and blacks eating at the same table.

"As we view it, respectability is one thing and gentility or fashion is quite another. It is respectable to labor — to acquire an honest livelihood by one's own industry — all the world over; but where, we should like to know, is it considered genteel or fashionable?" [3] This is from an Alabaman who wrote in 1860 the best appraisal yet made of the Southern middle class and yeomanry. He grants to each worthy man a consciousness of character and a pride of performance whether exalted or obscure, a blacksmith at his anvil, a farmer at his plow, with a slave helper or without. He contends that these plain people of the South were in all essentials like those of the North, provincial in speech and outlook, jealous of authority, resentful of superior pretenses, matter-of-fact in daily life, self-respecting and substantial. Accumulating records tend to confirm his analysis.

[1] [J. H. Ingraham] *The South-West* (New York, 1835), II, 26.
[2] Basil Hall, *Travels* (Edinburgh, 1829), III, 279.
[3] D. R. Hundley, *Social Relations in Our Southern States*, 121.

CHAPTER XVIII

THE GENTRY

FRANCIS TAYLOR of Orange County, neighbor and cousin of James Madison and uncle of Zachary Taylor, found a squire's life in Piedmont Virginia so full of pleasures that he had no time for great affairs. Except that he kept a diary [1] he was much like a thousand others. As a justice of the peace he sat sometimes for the trial of petty offenders, though not willingly, we may suspect, if the session conflicted with a squirrel barbecue, an oyster supper or a cock fight. His record has occasional notes of his crops and slaves, but more often of his vegetables and fruits, the brandy his peaches made, the lemons he bought for punch, and the hunts of wolves, foxes, rabbits, raccoons, quail, snipe and wild pigeons. Though he generally slept at home, [2] he was not often there by day unless there were guests to keep him. Taylor was without question a "Tuckahoe",[3] hedonistic, epicurean, eager for play along the road of life, whatever its end might be. Another was Thomas Massie, who took it ill that his plantation lay in a stoic neighborhood of "Cohees": "If I could waive the sense of self respect that

[1] Manuscript in the Virginia State Library, one small volume for each year from 1786 to 1799, except for 1793, which is missing. Taylor was in his fortieth year when the extant diary began.

[2] His house was built in 1786 at a cost of £107; the detached kitchen was of logs, the interstices "crammed with clay." On May 6, 1799, there were visitors with a special but characteristic purpose: "Mrs. Porter, Mrs. Wood and daughter came here before noon. Mrs. Wood looked at my house, said she intends to build, and wants a plan."

[3] J. K. Paulding noted while in the Shenandoah about 1815: "The people of whom I am now writing call those east of the mountain *Tuckahoes*, and their country Old Virginia. They themselves are the *Cohees*, and their country New Virginia." (*Letters from the South*, I, 112.) He set forth at some length the contrasting cults of elegance by the one and plainness by the other. The name Tuckahoe was derived somehow from the Indian designation of an edible swamp root; Cohee may have come from the archaic phrase "Quo' he" (quoth he).

requires reciprocity in visiting, I should still feel difficulty in going to the houses of those whose time is so engrossed as to make it unpleasant to give up any of it. In truth, social intercourse in this part of the country is actually forbidden by the habits of the people." [1]

On the other hand a Cohee youth when serving in 1844 as a tutor on the Chesapeake shore found himself endlessly torn between pleasure and ambition. Books were plenty, but the time to read them never came. After a succession of dances and visits without special occasion, a Tabb of "White Marsh" returned with a medical degree from the University of Pennsylvania and married. On Monday his father gave a great entertainment, with fireworks at eleven, supper at midnight and dancing until two. Champagne flowed in its proverbial manner, and "everything gave evidence of wealth and fashion. Party will succeed party for sometime to come. On Wednesday night at Ancon Plains (Mrs. Roy's), on Friday at Mr. Patterson Smith's, on Monday next at Waverley (Capt. Tabb's) and on Tuesday at Warner Hall — all evening parties. . . . I shall have to take part in the festivities . . . and to say truth I enter into it with great readiness. But such gayety is far removed from the studious habits I would like to cultivate . . . and that is one reason why I cannot return to Glo'ster. Dulce est dispere in loco — but here there is but one time for pleasure and that is all the time." [2]

A few years before this time Edmund Ruffin had made a journey to the same county of Gloucester, to study the soil and husbandry; but his purpose was defeated in part, he said, "by the urgent claims made on my time by the hospitable attentions of gentlemen to whom before I was personally unknown and whose kind invitations and attentions there was no resisting. The hospitality of Gloucester . . . is carried to an injurious and blameable extent. . . . That so many of the land-holders are still rich, or in easy circumstances, is only to be accounted

---

[1] Thomas Massie to his brother William, February 9, 1838. Manuscript at the University of Texas. The writer's home lay in a cove of the Blue Ridge.

[2] Diary of James B. Dorman. Manuscript in private possession.

for by the general fertility of the land which they have to cultivate. . . . The Gloucester people welcome the coming, and feast the staying, but do not 'speed the parting guest.' "[1]

As an advocate of industrial reform Ruffin lamented the cult of hospitality even more than the neglect of lime in agriculture: The main cause of lowland adversity, said he, "is that which is our great boast and pride at home, and the continued theme of praise abroad — 'the hospitality of old Virginia.' . . . Such effects are certainly not produced merely by the meat and liquor consumed by friends and visiters; but it is our custom to give up to all visiters not only the best entertainment but also the time, the employments and the habits of the host — and this not only for friends and visiters whose company is pleasing and desirable but for every individual of the despicable race of loungers and spongers which our custom of universal hospitality has created."[2] Patricians by reason of these habits, he said again, were prone to decay while frugal plebeians in the same neighborhood would prosper.[3]

Bankruptcies indeed were numerous, but of course by no means universal. The grace of life, the grandiloquence of gesture which tended to spread with the plantation system throughout the South had as a fairly constant companion a

[1] *Farmers' Register*, VI, 188.

[2] *Ibid.*, II, 96. In another district, which we have glimpsed before, heyday and decline were described in "Recollections of Chotank", by "E. S." in the *Southern Literary Messenger*, I, 43, 44 (1834): "Can I ever forget the happy days and nights there spent: the ardent fox hunt with whoop and halloo and winding horn: And . . . the old family bowl of mint julep, with its tuft of green peering above the inspiring liquid — an emerald isle in a sea of amber — the dewy drops, cool and sparkling, standing out upon its sides — all, all balmy and inviting? And then, the morning over and the noon passed, the business of the day accomplished, the social board is spread, loaded with flesh and fowl and the products of the garden and the orchard. . . . But Chotank, like many other parts of the Old Dominion, is not now in its 'high and palmy state.' Some fifteen or twenty years ago it obtained that celebrity which makes it famous now. The ancient seats of generous hospitality are still there, but their former possessors, so free of heart, so liberal, and blessed withal with the means of being free and liberal, where are they? 'And echo alone answers where are they.' Their sons can only hope to keep alive the old spirit by the exercise of more prudence and economy than their fathers possessed."

[3] *Ibid.*, IV, 527. The shrinkage of estates is exemplified in Wilson M. Cary, *Sally Cary* (New York, 1916), 46, 47, *note*, and the *Virginia Magazine*, XII, 436.

common-sense inhibition against genteel extravagance as well as against riotous living.

George Alsop had said of early Maryland in comparison with England and Europe: "Neither hath Youth his swing or range in such a profuse and unbridled liberty as in other Countries; for from an ancient Custom at the primitive seating of the place, the Son works as well as the Servant, (an excellent cure for untam'd Youth) so that before they eat their bread they are commonly taught how to earn it," so that when property comes into their possession "they manage it with such a serious, grave and watching care as if they had been Masters of Families, trained up in that domestick and governing power from their Cradles."[1] A Texan settler, having learned from experience the costliness of the grand manner, advised his sister as to the rearing of her sons: "Place your boys in some situation, severally as they arrive at a proper age, whereby they may gain a correct knowledge of some kind of business. . . . They are now young, and you have time to mark out the path they are to pursue, either to plenty and ease or to wretchedness and want. . . . We can profit by the errors of our father without casting any undutiful reflections on his memory. It is time to throw away *vain foolish pride*. I have banished it from me intirely. I confess I once possessed a large share, as is natural for Youths in the situation I then thought myself. They all aught to be raised merchants. It is no shame or dishonor to bind them untill they are of an age to act and think for themselves."[2]

❋   ❋   ❋   ❋   ❋

Here was a problem inescapable by gentlefolk everywhere — how to give their children a sense of ease without encouraging habits of sloth and self-indulgence. Skillful technique in industry, commerce or statecraft comes of persistent application, of work not play, of thought not impulse. Lessons will

[1] George Alsop, *A Character of the Province of Mary-Land* (London, 1666), 23.
[2] J. E. B. Austin to Emily M. Perry, November 10, 1825. *American Historical Association Report* for 1919, II, 1232, 1233.

aid greatly, but practice alone makes perfect; spontaneity is of high value, but endurance and self-control are indispensable. A North Carolina teacher spoke of the difficulty with plantation youth; but his remarks, with a substitution of automobiles for horses and of city diversions for rural, describe the dilemma of well-to-do parents in our day: "These young persons have never felt the pressure of want and the necessity of exertion. While at home they have been accustomed to pass their time in ease and amusement, and when they leave that home for school or college the change must be irksome. The confinement of a schoolroom, the demand of close application to uninteresting studies, the stern obligation of performing a regular task, and the privations of a boarding house must go hard with a boy after being accustomed to ramble about his father's plantation, with dogs at his heels and a gun or fishing-rod on his shoulder until he is tired, and then to return to the house, open his mother's pantry, and there fish with more success among jars of sweetmeats and jellies. . . . Would he consider it a very serious misfortune if for inattention to his books or some youthful prank he should be sent home to the scene of his former amusements? . . . He may a little dread the first interview; but he knows that after a good scolding, his time will pass as pleasantly as before." [1]

John Rutledge gave sage counsel in 1769 to his brother Edward, studying law in England: "The very first thing you should be thoroughly acquainted with is the writing of short-hand, which you will find an infinite advantage. . . . By no means fall into the too common practice of not attending a place of worship. . . . If you stick to French and converse generally in that language you may soon be master of it. Whatever study you attempt, make yourself completely master of it; nothing makes a person so ridiculous as to pretend to things he does not understand. I know nothing more entertaining and more likely to give you a graceful manner of speak-

---

[1] William Hooper, *Lecture on the Imperfections of Our Primary Schools* (Newbern, N. C., 1832), 8. An intimate account of life and problems at the University of Georgia is given by E. M. Coulter, *College Life in the Old South* (New York, 1928).

ing than seeing a good play well acted. Garrick is inimitable,
mark him well and you will profit by him. You must not
neglect the classics. Get a good private tutor who will point
out their beauties. . . . Read the apothegms of Bacon, English history, and the enclosed list of law books; and when I say
read, I don't mean run cursorily through them as you would
a newspaper, but read carefully and deliberately and tran-
scribe what you find useful in it. . . . One word in regard to
your deportment. Let your dress be plain always, in the city
and elsewhere, except when it is necessary that it should be
otherwise, and your behaviour rather grave." [1] Joseph Allston, who like Edward Rutledge became a governor of South
Carolina, seems to have carried no such burden of precepts:
"Introduced from my infancy into the society of men, while
yet a boy I was accustomed to think and act like a man. On
every occasion however important, I was left to decide for
myself; I do not recollect a single instance where I was controlled even by advice; for it was my father's invariable maxim
that the best way of strengthening the judgment was to suffer
it to be constantly exercised." [2] To put old heads on young
shoulders, a constant effort of elders and an essential in the
maintenance of civilization, led now to one device, now to
another, to inculcate maxims of one's own experience or to
hasten maturity by throwing the youth upon his own resources.
Each worked well in some cases and ill in others. The hazard
of circumstance and the quality of the human clay were more
decisive than the choice of method.

Planters were pathetically eager to procure good tutors, that
parental influence be not removed. An instructor described his
reception by the Drayton household in the South Carolina lowlands: "The affability and tenderness of this charming family
in the bosom of the woods will ever be cherished in my breast.
. . . My wants were always anticipated. The family Library
was transported without entreaty into my chamber . . . and
once, having lamented that my stock of segars was nearly

[1] Quoted in Mrs. T. P. O'Connor, *My Beloved South* (New York, 1914), 140.
[2] Joseph Allston to Theodosia Burr, quoted in the *Atlantic Monthly*, CXXXV, 664.

exhausted, a negro was dispatched seventy miles to *Charleston* for a supply of the best *Spanish*." [1]   Fearing to continue in the Carolina climate because it had proved fatal to many Englishmen, he went to Virginia where on the banks of Bull Run a new employer "congratulated himself upon the acquisition of a man of letters in his family. . . .   The following day every farmer came from the neighbourhood to the house, who had any children to send to my Academy, for such they did me the honor to term the log-hut in which I was to teach.   Each man brought his son or his daughter, and rejoiced that the day was arrived when their little ones could light their tapers at the torch of knowledge! . . .   No price was too great for the services I was to render their children; and they all expressed an eagerness to exchange perishable coin for lasting knowledge." [2]

When an employer's need was ended, he would recommend the tutor to a friend as the most valuable service he could render.   Thus a Georgian wrote to a kinsman in Alabama: "Mr. Blanchard is still with me pursuing his studies, but not on wages.   He appears willing and even desirous to go on to Alabama and teach for some time longer. . . .   He is a man of very few words, but deeply skilled in all the sciences taught in the colleges, and an agreeably quiet inmate of a family.   He is himself the greatest student I ever knew.   If you employ him you had better restrain his studies while engaged in teaching — say work so many hours in the day for you, and the balance for himself." [3]   In default of tutors, some parents undertook the burden.   A traveler visited a planter near the Potomac, "and when I was introduced to him it was in a place at a distance from the house, in the garden, which he called his office.   He was instructing his children. . . .   He told me he had been so troubled to get his children educated, that at last he had found more satisfaction in doing it himself than pursuing any other method.   He told me his eldest son was at Annapolis

---

[1] John Davis, *Travels* (London, 1803), 84, 85.
[2] *Ibid.*, 362.   *Cf.* [Catherine Hopley] *Life in the South*, I, 48.
[3] Hines Holt to Bolling Hall, August 15, 1822.   Manuscript in the Alabama Department of Archives.

college, and when he came home in the holidays his manners were such that he was disagreeable to him; and as for the boys he had at home, he had an intention of sending them to England." [1]

What a gentleman wanted in a daughter was usually what he had found in his wife. A Virginian on request gave counsel: "The control of the temper is of the first importance to the elevated standing of every woman. Learn to be cheerful, sociable and agreeable. . . . Half the difficulties and disappointments and vexations we meet with in the world had as well be the subject of our amusement as our tears." [2] Such injunctions were not invariably followed, as Chiswell Dabney discovered when on a Sunday in his Lynchburg home a "slumbering volcano bursted, . . . Mrs. Dabney throwing candlesticks at him and declaring eternal vengeance upon him — he doing nothing or saying nothing but evading the missiles thrown at him. On Monday morning he left the house and never returned." [3] The shrew was not an extinct species even in Virginia.

* * * * *

Plantation life was in itself something of an education. Of horsemanship in Virginia: "The boys are centaurs, and I wonder daily at the coolness with which Mrs. C., a very cautious mother, sees her son, 9 years old, galloping like the wind through the woods and over fences and ditches on a colt or a mule or anything that has legs." [4] And in another quarter: "The Mississippian sits his horse gracefully, yet not, as the riding-master would say, scientifically. He never seems to think of himself or the position of his limbs. They

---

[1] Richard Parkinson, *Tour in America* (London, 1805), II, 474. In the first half of the nineteenth century fairly substantial beginnings were made with public schools; but the sparseness of population and the spirit of individualism hampered their growth. On the other hand colleges North and South were patronized by the planters to a notable degree.

[2] J. H. Peyton to his daughter Susan, in the *Memoir of Peyton*, 132.

[3] S. M. Cobbs to William Massie, Lynchburg, Va., February 18, 1857. Manuscript at the University of Texas.

[4] John Hall, ed., *Forty Years' Familiar Letters of James W. Alexander*, I, 353.

yield, as does his whole body, pliantly and naturally to the motions of the animal beneath him, with which his own harmonize so perfectly and with such flexibility that there seems to be but one principle actuating both. . . . He seldom goes out of a pace. If he is in haste, he only paces the faster. Of every variety of gaited animals which I have ever seen, the Mississippian pacer is the most desirable." [1]   A knowledge of the performance and the lineage of the good horses within his ken was part of every gentleman's equipment.[2] Dog lore and woodcraft, crop knowledge and politics came from experience, conversation and study.

Thomas Jefferson wrote resoundingly: "The whole commerce between master and slave is a perpetual exercise of the most boisterous passions, the most unremitting despotism on the one part, and degrading submissions on the other. Our children see this and learn to imitate it. . . . The parent storms, the child looks on, catches the lineaments of wrath, . . . and thus nursed, educated and daily exercised in tyranny, cannot but be stamped by it with odious peculiarities." [3] John Taylor replied: "To me it seems that slaves are too far below, and too much in the power of the master, to inspire furious passions; that such are nearly as rare and disgraceful towards slaves as towards horses; that slaves are more frequently the objects of benevolence than of rage; that children from their nature are inclined to soothe and hardly ever suffered to tyrannize over them; that they open instead of shut the sluices of benevolence in tender minds; and that fewer good public or private characters have been raised in countries enslaved by

---

[1] [J. H. Ingraham] *The South-West*, II, 79. In the eastern South the gallop, or the more moderate canter, was known as "the planter's pace"; but with many the singlefoot was the favorite gait. To ride at the trot was to confess that the mount had had no schooling. Fondness for the gallop caused it to be used considerably even in harness, when wagoning.

[2] Of a Virginia congressman an acquaintance wrote: "I knew John Roane Jr. well. He died at 'Uppowoc' in King William, his patrimony, in 1838, aged 72. He was a living encyclopedia of Virginia pedigrees for men and horses." *William and Mary College Quarterly*, XVIII, 270. On the improvement of breed from "quarter horses" to thoroughbreds see [Fairfax Harrison] "The Equine F. F. Vs.", in the *Virginia Magazine*, XXXV, 329–370.

[3] *Notes on the State of Virginia*, query 18.

some faction or particular interest than in the those where personal slavery existed." [1] An anonymous writer in 1827 clinched the argument: "The high sense of personal dignity with which the habit of authority and command inspires him [the slaveholder] makes him courteous in his manners, liberal in his sentiments, generous in his actions. But, with his disdain of all that is coarse and little and mean, there often mingle the failings of a too sensitive pride, jealousy of all superiority, impatience of contradiction, quick and violent resentment. His liability to these vices is so obvious that it is often an especial purpose of early instruction to guard against them; and thus is formed in happy natures such a habit of self-command and virtuous discipline as to make them remarkable for their mildness and moderation." [2] The planters, of the better sort at least, were engaged in the humane discipline of themselves as well as of their slaves; and as regards the planters' children, the Negro nurses and other domestics were auxiliaries in that discipline.

A fair product was Joseph Bryan of "Nonchalance" near Savannah, upon whose death even John Randolph's pen was moved to eulogy: "Educated in Europe, . . . he was utterly free from taint of foreign manner. He lived and died a Georgian. . . . He possessed wonderful activity and strength of body, united to undaunted resolution, but he was not more terrible as an enemy than as a friend he was above all price. His mind was of the first order, and stored with various and desultory reading. His honor unsullied. Quick in his resentments but easily appeased when injured, and equally ready to acknowledge an error when wrong, provided the appeal was made to his sense of justice, for he knew not fear. He was brave even to rashness, and his generosity bordered on profusion." [3] Nonchalance was a fitting name for his home, though upon one occasion the quality failed him. He wrote to Randolph in 1800: "I paid my addresses to an accomplished young woman, of both family and fortune, in Carolina —

[1] *Arator*, no. 14.   [2] *American Quarterly Review*, II, 251, 252.
[3] H. E. Hayden, *Virginia Genealogies*, 213.

quarrelled with my father and mother because I would not relinquish the pursuit — followed her with every prospect of the desired success for eighteen months — went to her abode last Christmas, with the comfortable idea of marrying her on the commencement of the new year — and was discarded by her parents because mine would not consent to the match. . . . I was in a hell of a taking for two or three days. But I found that keeping myself employed made it work off to a miracle." [1] After five years he found better success in Maryland. To Randolph again : "Jack ! what have I done to induce the good God to favor me so highly ? . . . I, having sought among the beauties of the earth, have found and obtained the loveliest and best, which I am willing to prove against all comers on foot or on horseback, in the tented field with sword and spear, or on the roaring ocean at the cannon's mouth." [2]

Bryan's challenge to all and sundry led to no combat on land or sea. But among his fellows in the tradition of high spirit "affairs of honor" were grievously frequent. Yet the punctiliousness which sometimes bore sinister fruit in dueling produced more often a gallant recognition of responsibilities and a frank readiness to make amends.[3]

Social ease, often heightened into "winning kindness and cordiality", came not only from precept but from an accustomed expectation of meeting these qualities in others. The physical plan of life promoted this, as Wade Hampton said in 1805 to a

[1] H. A. Garland, *Life of John Randolph of Roanoke* (New York, 1851), I, 177, 178.
[2] *Ibid.*, I, 212.
[3] The occasions for duels were often trivial. *Cf.* J. P. Carson, *Life of Pettigru*, 300. But good humor might solve a crisis. A Virginian visiting Charleston in 1791 gave an example : " I found Capt. *Robertson* under Preparation for a Duel with Capt. *Sweetman*, an *English* Gentleman and Merchant. — I acted as a Mediator betwixt them, and happily terminated the Dispute to their mutual Satisfaction by decreeing that they both possessed indubitable Courage. . . . That Capt. *Sweetman* had been too *precipitate* and Capt. *Robertson* too *hasty:* — that they therefore make their reciprocal Concessions, and be at Peace; and that neither might infringe the Punctilios of military Etiquette, they should stand 10 Yards asunder, then advance to the Centre, make their Concessions at the same Instant, *protruding their dextral Hands until they came into Contaction, as an Indication and Declaration* of a *Continuation of Pacification:* that they should then repair to the Hotel and take a *Compotation of a late Importation from the* Madeira *Plantation in Corroboration of the* aforesaid *Pacification.*" — John Pope, *Tour* (Richmond, 1792, reprint New York, 1888), p. 86 of the reprint.

tutor from Connecticut: "He wishes to be two or three miles at least from any neighbors. He utterly disapproves of the custom of farmers in Connecticut who for the sake of society cluster together in villages and hamlets. . . . He thinks the tendency of these village settlements is to make people more contracted, less hospitable and less friendly." [1] Seclusion was valued not only for the sake of serenity but as heightening the welcome and grace of social contacts on occasion.

The long possession of leisure and a modicum of luxury developed a taste for the novel and the beautiful which any true gentry is prone to indulge not merely by buying and perhaps making books and pictures but by travel and by the cultivation of well-ordered life. The need of summer sojourns in cooler climes made Southerners in some degree the discoverers of the charms of Newport, Narragansett Pier and Saratoga, as well as of the Virginia springs and the Carolina Blue Ridge. The Hot Springs, the Warm, the Sweet, the Red Sulphur and the Greenbrier White Sulphur one or all became health resorts within the eighteenth century; and fashion erelong followed those who went for the cure. [2]

By reason of its "exclusiveness", simplicity and excellence of management [3] the White Sulphur was the most esteemed of all as a rendezvous of the gentry; and for long it was a meeting ground for politicians from every quarter of the South. In

---

[1] Diary of Edward Hooker, in the *American Historical Association Report* for 1896, I, 850.

[2] That gambling and other vices were not limited in either direction by Mason and Dixon's Line is elaborately but unconsciously shown in *The Life and Adventures of Robert Bailey, written by Himself* (Richmond, Va., 1822).

[3] "There is a sort of major-domo here who regulates every department; his word is law, and his fiat immoveable. . . . No one is allowed accommodation at these springs who is not known, and generally speaking, only those families who travel in their private carriages." — Captain Frederick Marryatt, *Diary in America* (London, 1839), II, 173. "Mr. Caldwell, the proprietor, is a polite old gentleman, who was never intended for an innkeeper, as his white hair and small cue carefully tied with a black ribbon would convince any one at a glance. He distinguishes those persons whom he considers deserving of his attention by asking them to take wine sometimes at his house; and very good wine he has." But toddy and juleps were "greatly preferred to any other drinks of the kind." — James L. Pettigru to Susan P. King, White Sulphur, September 21, 1845. J. P. Carson, *Life of Pettigru*, 250, 251. The criterion of exclusiveness was not financial. In 1825 the charge for boarding and lodging a guest or a horse was eight dollars per week, and for a servant half as much.

mid-century summers the accommodations for seven hundred guests in the single hotel and its detached cabins [1] were seldom adequate to the demand; and people on a waiting list would quarter themselves at minor resorts in the vicinity. DeBow lamented in 1859 that railroad facilities were bringing a less desirable element: "We are glad to say, however, that much of the olden times still lingers here, the propriety of demeanor, polish of manner, courtesy and cleverness which seem inseparable from Southern Society." [2]

The "olden times" lingered at White Sulphur and on the plantations. Lusty manhood withered with age and found place under new slabs in the family burying-grounds. Young mothers, with old mammies to help them, led their children in the way they should go, and fathers took striplings in hand that they might be men in turn. Courtships calm or tumultuous led to marriages with or without settlements to secure the bride's property to her and her children. Generations went and generations came, new households in old houses, old burdens on young shoulders, fresh voices to speak old phrases: "The ways of industry are constant and regular"; "order and system must be the aim of everyone"; "the care of negroes is the first thing to be recommended"; "no man should attempt to manage negroes who is not perfectly firm and fearless and in entire control of his temper." These rules of great planters for their overseers were also maxims for themselves and their sons. They served for two centuries, and most of them are not yet outworn.

The olden times had prevailed but a hundred years in the Virginia Piedmont, and half as long in most of the cotton belt; but that was ample to hallow them in the minds of those who had found them congenial. The scheme of life had imperfections which all but the blind could see. But its face was on the whole so gracious that modifications might easily be lamented, and projects of revolution regarded with a shudder.

---

[1] Numerous resorts are pictured in [D. H. Strother] *Virginia Illustrated* (New York, 1871).

[2] *DeBow's Review*, XXVII, 368. The word "cleverness" is here used in the Southern colloquial sense of obliging disposition.

INDEX